RISKING THEIR LIVES

RISKING THEIR LIVES

NEW ZEALAND ABORTION STORIES
1900–1939

MARGARET SPARROW

VICTORIA UNIVERSITY PRESS

VICTORIA UNIVERSITY PRESS
Victoria University of Wellington
PO Box 600 Wellington
vup.victoria.ac.nz

Copyright © Margaret Sparrow 2017
First published 2017

This book is copyright. Apart from any fair
dealing for the purpose of private study, research, criticism
or review, as permitted under the Copyright Act, no part
may be reproduced by any process without the
permission of the publishers

A catalogue record for this book is available from
the National Library of New Zealand.

Printed by YourBooks, Wellington

CONTENTS

Acknowledgements	7
Introduction	9
1. Setting the Scene	11
2. The McMillan Report	41
3. Medical Matters: Mainly Sepsis	61
4. Contraception: Mainly Barriers	85
5. A Flawed Law	128
6. Doctors	171
7. Chemists	202
8. Nurses	238
9. All Sorts	277
10. DIY Abortion	309
11. Some Observations	340
Notes	351
Further Reading	366
Index	368

ACKNOWLEDGEMENTS

I am grateful to the staff of Archives New Zealand for access to the coroners' reports, to researcher Rachel Brown, who volunteered the coroners' reports she had accessed for her MA history study on maternal deaths from 1890,* and to the librarians at the Wellington Medical and Health Sciences Library (University of Otago, Wellington) and the Wellington Central Library. Papers Past is a wonderful digital resource at the National Library of New Zealand, from which I obtained a great deal of useful information and illustrations for this book.

I am grateful for the support of ALRANZ (Abortion Law Reform Association of New Zealand). President Terry Bellamak and author Alison McCulloch read the first draft and suggested revisions. Lynn McKenzie provided valuable comments, and my granddaughter Noemi Roche gave feedback from a youthful perspective.

Without the support of Fergus Barrowman of Victoria University Press this contentious topic would remain hidden. My sincere thanks to Fergus and his team. For making these bleak stories more readable I am especially indebted to Kyleigh Hodgson for her editorial expertise.

---

* Rachel Brown, 'Private Tragedies Made Public: A Study of Maternal Mortality in New Zealand, 1890–1915', unpublished manuscript (Wellington: Victoria University of Wellington, undated).

INTRODUCTION

This book is another in the series recording the history of abortion in New Zealand and examines the early years of the 20th century, from 1900 to 1939.

Abortion Then and Now: New Zealand Abortion Stories from 1940 to 1980 focused on personal stories from women who had had abortions, augmented by accounts from others involved – doctors, nurses, police and some activists – at a time when most abortions were illegal and clandestine, and the emphasis was on punishing serious offenders.

That changed in the 1970s. Feminists protested. Intense public controversy raged. The government appointed a Royal Commission, which in 1977 was responsible for significant law changes. Alison McCulloch documented these turbulent politics in her book *Fighting to Choose: The Abortion Rights Struggle in New Zealand*.

Rough on Women: Abortion in 19th-Century New Zealand took a step backward in time to examine the experiences of colonial women. The first New Zealand statute on abortion, in 1866, was an exact replica of the harsh 1861 English law, which decreed a maximum penalty of life imprisonment.

In the early years of the 20th century, abortion came to be recognised not just as a crime but also as a major public health problem. Because of the embarrassingly large number of deaths from septic abortion, the Government in 1936 appointed a Committee of Inquiry to investigate the issues.

Much has already been written about the 1930s and I am particularly indebted to contemporary authors Barbara Brookes, Philippa Mein Smith, Lesley Smith, Joanne Richdale, Andrée Lévesque and Sandra Coney, and past authors Mary Findlay and Drs Doris Gordon and Francis Bennett. (Their works, along with the other books in this series, are listed at the back of this book for those who would like to read further on the topic.) Less is known of abortion in the first two decades of the 20th century, and I have salvaged many untold stories from the coroner's reports and newspaper reports of that time. Is this history worthwhile reclaiming? I wondered about this until an event in October 2015, when I listened with some misgivings to a memorial oration eulogising Dr Doris Gordon, a notable woman from this era who vigorously opposed abortion.

Had people really forgotten how women risked their lives in the early years of the 20th century? I decided a reminder was definitely needed. I pulled an old manuscript out of the filing cabinet, put aside because readers said the effect of too many sad stories along similar lines was counter-productive. After some judicious pruning, the narrative is still grim, but I make no apology for that. This is an honest retelling of our past, primarily letting the stories speak for themselves.

Margaret Sparrow
Wellington
June 2016

1. SETTING THE SCENE

The four decades from 1900 to 1939 were challenging in many ways: two wars (the Boer War and World War I) and the beginning of a third (World War II), a major influenza pandemic, two powerful earthquakes (Murchison in 1929 and Napier in 1931) and a severe economic depression.

At the turn of the century New Zealand had been a British colony for a mere six decades, but had made some significant achievements in that time. Such achievements included the stabilisation of relations between Māori and Pākehā following the New Zealand Wars (1845–1872), functioning political and legal systems based on the Westminster model, the growth of transport and communication networks, and a viable meat, wool and dairy industry supplying the British market. New Zealand was internationally regarded as a country that valued social progress: it had near-universal primary education from 1887, and was the first country in the world to introduce a means-tested pension for the deserving elderly, in November 1898. And in September 1893, women had gained the right to vote, another world first for a self-governing nation.

Significant though these changes were, it took many years before there was any substantial change in the status of women. Yes, women entered the workforce, but usually only in the years after leaving school and before getting married and raising a family. Employment for women was largely domestic, as servants in private homes or boarding houses, or in small factories making garments or processing foods, although the number of women in the professions, such as teaching and nursing, gradually increased as women sought a more emancipated lifestyle with fewer children.

Sexual immorality was a topic of great public interest. Premarital and extramarital relationships, unplanned pregnancies, illegitimate children, contraception and abortion were all publicly condemned. An editorial under the heading 'A Social Cancer' in *The Press* of 23 March 1900 remonstrated about a report from the Charitable Aid Board that over £1,000 a year was now being paid for the support of illegitimate children.[1] A case was cited in which a woman had gone to the Samaritan Home to be delivered of her ninth illegitimate child. This resulted in condemnation both in the press and from the pulpit. The Reverend Canon Harper, preaching in the Christchurch Cathedral, appealed to the men of the community to 'set a high value on a life of chastity and restraint'.

The public interest in morality was not confined to Christchurch. Under the heading 'The Wellington Press and Public Morals', the *Evening Post* of 12 November 1900 reported on remarks made by Justice Edwards to the grand jury regarding a letter he had received from a 'body of ladies' recommending that publication of the details of a charge of abortion should be prohibited and that cases should be held behind closed doors. The learned judge admonished the ladies for writing to him, pointing out that all communications to a judge must be in open court. Nevertheless, he went on to express his opinion and said that he was not aware that he had any power whatever to prohibit the publication of abortion proceedings or to hear cases behind closed doors; nor if he had any power would he be inclined to exercise it without the very gravest reasons. He agreed with the ladies that it was entirely undesirable that the details of a case should be published, but it would be still more undesirable to allow anyone to be tried secretly and not under the eyes of the public. He was not persuaded of the need for a prohibition on publication and complimented the Wellington newspapers for their discretion in reporting cases.

In 1905 *NZ Truth* commenced publication as the first national weekly tabloid newspaper, modelled on its Sydney predecessor. Given the newspaper's reputation for fearless, irreverent, vulgar and salacious journalism, its readership expected a generous component of sexual topics, and divorce proceedings were a steady source of scandal. A hard line was taken on abortion. An editorial in *NZ Truth* of 19 January 1907, titled 'Sin, Seduction and Sorrow: Accommodating Medical Men', expostulated:

> Private enquiries made as a result of disclosures during the hearing of a recent affiliation case at Christchurch disclose that there are numerous doctors in the city who are always

ready, for a substantial consideration, to operate on girls whose amours have been too passionate, with results of a dreadful and dispiriting character. And some of these obliging doctors are only too willing to take the attendant risks which these delicate operations involve. The charge is anything from £15 upwards, and if the erring man can't put up all the bunce [money] at once they are satisfied to take instalments. The inquiries go to show that a large and thriving business is done in this illegal way, and that procuring abortion is a most profitable side-line indeed.

Of course there is a good deal of a gamble about sexual immorality, especially if the man doesn't intend to splice [marry] the girl, but very often the aid of the doctor, or the seller of steel pills and other atrocities is invoked, and things are unpleasant if anything goes wrong. There is a great deal of thrilling human interest about a doctor's consulting room, and not the least pathetic is the couple who go along wearing an air of sorrow and state their tale in a lachrymose manner. Whether he is inclined to operate or not they induce him to adopt nefarious means to overcome the difficulty, and the blossom of true love is not allowed to bud.

It matters not to the medico the history of the cause; he meets the girl who has been seduced, the giddy girl who doesn't at all mind being seduced and the girl, who, after some frilly function, with quickened pulse, and fair form all a-quiver gives way to the intoxication of the hour, and falls. And the cause thereof, who foots the bill afterwards, is the green young fellow who must get assistance from his parents, or the practised lover, or the severely respectable citizen who is trusted by severely respectable parents to trot out their severely respectable daughters, and whose subsequent interview with a severely respectable doctor means the handing over of a severely respectable sum. And the sawbones [doctor] doesn't find it a weariness of the flesh to hold out his paw for it, either. Some girls are alleged to have been operated on three times in as many years, which shows that they have no morals and darned little sense.

That preventives are largely sold in Christchurch is, of course, well known, but it appears instruments are also. One firm's name was mentioned in this connection in an affiliation case, but whether the victim of man's wiles was to use it on herself, or get someone else to do so, wasn't stated. However it would appear that the pill and phial brethren do a lot of risky illegal business, and that if femininity is in trouble there is no insuperable difficulty placed in the way of her getting out of it.

All this isn't very pleasant reading for the prudish person, but even the censorious prudish person, the head and front of social convention, doesn't possess all the cardinal virtues, and is just as likely to trip over the Satanic hot-wire laid across the path of virtue as anyone else – especially when the right person happens along to sin with. Meanwhile cradles are at a discount.

The Christchurch affiliation case referred to was that of Sarah Boulton, who sought an order for maintenance of her illegitimate child from George White, 26, tram driver. He denied paternity and there was insufficient evidence to award maintenance, usually set at 7/6- (seven shillings and sixpence; about $60 in today's currency) per week. He was subsequently accused of lying, but managed to survive two Supreme Court trials for perjury when the juries could not agree. At that point Justice Chapman ordered a stay of proceedings. This humiliating ordeal would act as a deterrent to other women seeking maintenance for their children. Law changes in 1910 brought some improvement for those seeking maintenance.

Another editorial in *NZ Truth* on 18 May 1907 reflected a populist view of population issues. The headlines railed: 'About These Babies. Why Kill Any of Them? Let 'Em All Come'. The thrust of the article was a racist concern at the decline in numbers of the 'white race' and the threat from 'coloured races'. The solution was to breed. The following were condemned: married women who used contraception, all women who resorted to abortion, abortionists and those who covered for them (such as alleged nurses), doctors who performed or condoned abortions, advertisers of contraceptives and abortifacients, chemists supplying any form of preventive or corrective, and baby killers. A suitable punishment for convicted abortionists was hanging or imprisonment for life. These attitudes intensified over the next two decades, culminating in the debate surrounding abortion in the 1930s.

౸

The focus of this book is to tell personal stories, and what follows is a timeline of significant events that impacted on women's lives, family life and relationships, just sufficient to put these stories into historical perspective.

1899 In October the Boer War broke out in South Africa, and New Zealand was the first colony to volunteer a contingent of mounted rifles. Further contingents were deployed between 1899 and 1902, mainly volunteers and a few professional soldiers. A number of New Zealand nurses served in South Africa during the war, although they were not part of an official New Zealand nursing contingent. Some nurses served with British organisations. Many paid their own way or were sponsored by local patriotic groups.

ANOTHER INJUSTICE TO NEGLECTED MAIDENHOOD
Sweet Fifty: 'Now this is what I call too bad – sending another thousand marriageable men away. How does Mr Seddon think we girls are going to get husbands? Presently only the scrubbers will be left.'

('Boer war, Government sends troops', *Observer*, 15 March 1902)

1901 Queen Victoria died after reigning for 63 years. She was succeeded by Edward VII (1901–1910), George V (1910–1936), Edward VIII (January–December 1936) and George VI (1936–1952). Allegiance to the Crown was undisputed and patriotic.

1905 Rugby football was the national sport. The original All Blacks toured for the first time beyond Australia, to Britain, France and the USA. They played 35 matches and were defeated only once, by Wales. The All Blacks' triumphant Northern Hemisphere tour in 1924–1925 confirmed rugby's status as the national game. Its importance is highlighted in a report of a parliamentary debate in 1937, in which Hon. William Perry pointed to the dangers of a declining birth rate. From the figures presented in the book *Gentlemen of the Jury*,[2] he calculated that 17 abortions were occurring in New Zealand every day, or one every 90 minutes. He emphasised the loss of this human potential by appealing to the aspirations of New Zealand men, stating that during the forthcoming encounter between the All Blacks and the Springboks, an event lasting 80 minutes, 'one child, perhaps a potential All Black, will have been wilfully destroyed in the womb of its mother'.[3]

1907 On 26 September the colony became a Dominion, implying a sense of identity although ties with Britain remained strong.

1908 Early feminists in New Zealand would have been aware of the struggles of their sisters in England to gain the vote. The largest ever mass gathering of suffragettes, known as Women's Sunday, was held in Hyde Park on Sunday 21 June 1908. Later, on 4 June 1913, Emily Davison died from injuries sustained when she fell in front of the King's horse at the Epsom Derby. In the face of intense opposition to women's rights in general, abortion rights were not on the agenda, neither in England nor in New Zealand.

A MAN'S A MAN FOR A' THAT
On behalf of the central Society of the Woman's Suffrage League in London, Lady Frances Balfour and Mrs Henry Fawcett presented an address to Mr Seddon acknowledging his services in the cause of woman suffrage. King Dick: 'Intelligent interest in politics? Oh dear, yes. Why, it takes quite a time for the ladies of New Zealand to look through the photos of candidates and to decide which is the best looking man for their support.'

('Women's Suffrage', *Free Lance*, 16 August 1902)

1910 The Destitute Persons Act 1910 enabled women to seek maintenance orders against the fathers of their children at least until the age of 16. Accessing this could be a humiliating experience.

1911 The population of New Zealand reached one million, and for the first time the urban population exceeded the rural population. There were just over 800 registered medical practitioners serving the population, much fewer than modern workforce figures.

1914 The League of Nations endorsed the Declaration of the Rights of the Child and urged governments to improve child welfare, maternal working conditions and income support programmes.

From August 1914 to November 1918 World War I dominated life for New Zealanders at home and abroad. The focus was predominantly on patriotism and men's issues. When Britain declared war against Austria-Hungary and Germany, New Zealand offered an Expeditionary Force (NZEF) under the command of Major-General Sir Alexander Godley. Stationed at first near Cairo in Egypt, together with Australian troops, the ANZACs suffered huge losses at Gallipoli in 1915 and on the Western Front in France and Belgium in 1916. The loss of a generation of young men had a significant impact on New Zealand society. Over 60 per cent of New Zealand men aged between 19 and 45 years served overseas with the NZEF – no fewer than 100,000 men out of a total population of just over a million. The official number of war dead is about 18,000. It is estimated that each of those 18,000 dead soldiers held a close relationship to about half a dozen people – mothers, fathers, siblings, wives, girlfriends, children, grandparents, lifelong friends – so about a tenth of the population suffered an intimate loss.[4] A further 42,000 non-fatal casualties brought the total casualty figure to some 60,000. Thousands of non-fatal casualties made full recoveries, but thousands more did not. Some veterans were scarred for life, either physically, mentally or both, placing an immense strain on their families.

During World War I, sexual health pioneer Ettie Rout campaigned to prevent the venereal diseases syphilis and gonorrhea, estimated to affect some 15 to 20 per cent of New Zealand soldiers. She recognised the far-reaching consequences of venereal disease on relationships and families, although the women of New Zealand did not appreciate her efforts.⁵

1918 In the wake of World War I, when the movement of large numbers of troops by sea and rail greatly facilitated the spread of infection, troops returning to New Zealand brought a particularly lethal strain of influenza virus from Europe, the 'Spanish flu'. This was New Zealand's worst infectious disease disaster, reaching epidemic proportions from late October, peaking in late November and over by early December. The pandemic killed more than 50 million people worldwide, and 8,500 in New Zealand. Many deaths were due to secondary infection causing pneumonia. Unlike other countries, where male and female deaths were about equal, New Zealand death rates for males were double those for females in the worst-affected age groups. The Māori death rate of 42.3 per 1,000 people was at least seven times that of the European population, and this is probably an underestimate, given incomplete Māori death registrations. Nationwide, 135 children were bereaved of both parents, while 6,415 children lost one parent.

In Britain, Marie Stopes's book *Married Love* was an overnight success. The message that a man should take responsibility for giving his wife sexual pleasure was sensational. Stopes took issue with the common notion of sex as something men wanted or needed, and women put up with; a kind of penalty that relegated marriage to a transaction rather than a loving commitment. The book was banned in some countries but not in New Zealand, at least initially.

1919 New Zealand was bitterly divided as it voted in the referendum on prohibition. On one side were the women's temperance groups and the Protestant churches determined to stamp out drunken behavior, and on the other side, for the status quo, were the liquor trade, the Catholic Church and returned soldiers. The status quo prevailed as the prohibition lobby failed to gain the required 60 per cent majority.

Although the 1920s were overshadowed at either end by World War I and the Great Depression, many cultural changes took place during this decade. Road and rail transport, along with the introduction of radio, improved communication. Silent films were a popular form of entertainment, as were the 'talkies' when they arrived in 1929. Music and dancing reflected overseas trends, and jazz and band music were all the rage. In 1928 the Charleston was the dance craze. The emancipation of women was obvious in their use of makeup, shortened hair styles and raised hems.

1925 The New Zealand Child Welfare Act 1925 established child welfare as a branch of the Education Department, which became responsible for orphaned, destitute, neglected and 'out of control' children. Foster care and adoption replaced institutional care, and Children's Courts were established.
1926 The Family Allowance was introduced for married mothers in low-income families with three or more children.
1929 In October the Great Depression was triggered when the New York stock market crashed. The economic and social effects spread rapidly around the Western world. New Zealand was vulnerable because it depended on Britain buying its agricultural exports, wool, meat, butter and cheese. As export earnings plummeted, farmers stopped spending, with drastic effects. The result of the Depression was mass unemployment in New Zealand. Job and wage cuts left people desperate and, despite some work relief schemes, families and charities struggled to cope. In 1932, the unemployed rioted, demanding better help from the government. This set the scene for a change in government, and in 1935 Labour swept to power, ushering in the comprehensive reforms of the welfare state.

ଓଃ

Between 1900 and 1939 the New Zealand government had nine changes in leadership. None gave priority to women's issues.

Richard Seddon (1845–1906)
Liberal Premier, May 1893–June 1906

'King Dick' dominated politics for 13 years, the longest tenure of any leader. He was the pronatalist father of six daughters and three sons, and was alarmed at the declining fertility rate in New Zealand. In 1901 he introduced a Sale of Preventives Prohibition Bill into Parliament, but it was defeated. He opposed the enfranchisement of women but took credit for it happening during

'Mr Seddon at the home of his childhood.' Seddon visiting his birthplace in Lancashire, St Helens, the name he gave to St Helens maternity hospitals.
(*Otago Witness*, 17 September 1902)

'Opening of St Helens Maternity Home, Dunedin: group including the Premier, at the entrance to the building.' To Seddon's left is Dr Emily Siedeberg, who features later in this book.
(*Otago Witness*, 11 October 1905)

his term of office. He supported sending troops to the Boer War. In 1905 he opened the first state maternity hospital in Wellington, named St Helens after Seddon's birthplace in Lancashire, England. This served as a 'lying in' hospital for the wives of the working class (but not single mothers) and as a training school for midwives. Other St Helens hospitals followed in Dunedin (1905), Auckland (1906) and Christchurch (1907). In 1905 a state housing scheme was introduced under his watch. He died while in office.

Richard John Seddon. This photograph was probably taken in 1897 when he was attending a colonial conference in London. (Lafayette Ltd Photographers. Original prints from ATL Photograph Section loose print sequence. Ref: PAColl-3861-30-01. Alexander Turnbull Library, Wellington, New Zealand)

William Hall-Jones (1851–1936)
Liberal Prime Minister, June–August 1906

This was an interim appointment until Sir Joseph Ward returned from Europe. Nineteenth-century premiers became twentieth-century prime ministers, and this title has endured.

Sir Joseph Ward (1856–1930)
Liberal Prime Minister, August 1906–March 1912 and December 1928–May 1930

Ward led two governments 16 years apart. He came from an Irish Catholic background and fathered five children. During his first period of leadership, in 1909 the Department of Public Health took over the control of hospitals, and in 1911 a pension for widows was introduced; prior to that widowed mothers with dependent children had to rely on charity, other family members or their own meager earnings (no wonder some became abortionists). During World War I he was Leader of the Opposition, and he became Deputy Leader and Minister of Finance when the Liberal Party formed a coalition with the ruling Reform Party. Ward resigned at the age of 74, due to poor health.

Thomas Mackenzie (1854–1930)
Liberal Prime Minister, March–July 1912

After governing for 21 years, the Liberals were defeated by the New Zealand Political Reform League (the Reform Party) in 1912. From 1912 to 1920, including the difficult war years, Mackenzie was High Commissioner in London.

William Massey (1851–1925)
Reform Prime Minister, July 1912–May 1925

'Farmer Bill' formed a coalition with the Liberal Party during World War I and spent long periods in London serving on the Imperial War Cabinet. Massey and Ward were both opposed to Ettie Rout's campaign for prophylaxis to protect the troops from venereal disease. Massey signed the Treaty of Versailles, the peace agreement at the end of the war. In 1919 he kept his promise to introduce the Women's Parliamentary Rights Extension Bill, giving women the right to stand for the House of Representatives and to be appointed to the Legislative Council (upper house). In 1919 three pioneers did so, each as an Independent Liberal candidate: Aileen Cooke in Thames, Rosetta Baume in Parnell and lawyer Ellen Melville in Grey Lynn. None were successful despite a number of attempts, and there were no female members of Parliament until 1933.

Sir Francis Henry Dillon Bell (1851–1936)
Reform Prime Minister, 10–30 May 1925

Bell was the first New Zealand-born Prime Minister, who spent only 16 days in office in May 1925. He had been acting Prime Minister when Massey was overseas, so when Massey died he was appointed Prime Minister, but he opted for lesser roles in government. He was a lawyer and was elected three times as Mayor of Wellington in the 1890s.

Gordon Coates (1878–1943)
Reform Prime Minister, May 1925–December 1928

Dubbed the 'Jazz Premier', he epitomised the double standards of the day. In his early days he fathered children to at least two Māori women prior to a conventional marriage that produced five daughters.[6] He earned a Military Cross and Bar in World War I. In 1926 the government introduced a means-tested family allowance of two shillings per week for families with more than two children.

George Forbes (1869–1947)
United Prime Minister, May 1930–December 1935

A member of the United Party (a remnant of the Liberal Party), Forbes succeeded Sir Joseph Ward on his resignation due to ailing health. During the difficult years of the Depression he formed a coalition with the Reform Party. Under his watch, in 1933 Elizabeth McCombs became the first woman elected to Parliament when she won the Lyttelton seat for Labour, succeeding her deceased husband.

Michael Joseph Savage (1872–1940)
Labour Prime Minister, December 1935–March 1940

Savage was the first Labour Prime Minister and one of the most popular; a bachelor raised and buried as a Catholic but throughout his life a rationalist. Taking advantage of the recovering economy, his party introduced comprehensive social welfare with the promise of 'Security and Prosperity for All'. In 1936 the government introduced a means-tested pension for deserted wives. Because of concerns about maternal mortality the government appointed a

Committee to Inquire into the Various Aspects of the Problem of Abortion in New Zealand, its deliberations popularly referred to as the McMillan Report. This is discussed in more detail in the next chapter.[7]

Michael Joseph Savage. (Original photographic prints and postcards from file print collection, Box 1. Ref: PAColl-5471-055. Alexander Turnbull Library, Wellington, New Zealand)

The following stories from the war years and the Depression years illustrate how these events impacted on the lives of women. Doctors serving overseas created a shortage of medical practitioners within New Zealand and more women doctors filled roles previously secured by men. Ellen's story is just one example of how this shortage affected medical practice, possibly making the difference between life and death.

Ellen's story[8]
Deceased 30 July 1915, aged 33 years

Ellen Aston was married to Charles, a bootmaker in Christchurch. They had been married for only 16 months and had a six-month-old baby boy when she found herself pregnant again. Ellen had not been able to breastfeed her infant son and he had spent nine weeks in St Helens Hospital. She was afraid of another pregnancy so soon after the first, so when she miscarried she said she was glad it had come away. Whether she miscarried naturally or not will never be known, but her sudden death raised suspicions.

The coroner's verdict simply stated she 'did die from septicaemia following an abortion'. Dr Pairman, who conducted the post-mortem, criticised the care provided and felt she should have received earlier medical attention.

In fact, her husband Charles experienced great difficulty finding a doctor. Ellen's doctor, Dr Brownlee, was not at home when Charles rang, so he left an urgent message. When Dr Brownlee received the message at 10.45 pm he refused to come as he was physically exhausted, having been up for two or three nights, and he thought the callout was probably 'just an ordinary case of miscarriage'. He asked Charles who his own doctor was and he replied 'Dr Irving'. He was serving overseas at the front, but Dr Guthrie was looking after his practice. Charles got Dr Guthrie to come, but by the time he arrived at 11.30 pm it was too late. Ellen was already dead.

༄

War had a disruptive effect on relationships and the outcome was sometimes messy for all concerned.

Trial of Mrs Phillipa Scott, 1917[9]

Mrs Scott of Wordsworth Street, Christchurch, was separated from her husband and lived with Mr Wilson as his housekeeper. She had a reputation as an abortionist, and police described her as a 'bad woman'. In August 1916, police charged her with unlawful use of instruments on Mrs Ivy Cusack.

Ivy, whose soldier husband was at the front, had an affair with another man and, much to her embarrassment, became pregnant. With the support of her mother she went to Mrs Scott's home for an abortion. Due to complications Ivy stayed there for three weeks and her young child came and stayed with her. Mrs Scott charged her £5 but nothing extra for board and lodging.

The operation was unsuccessful and Ivy delivered a child in December 1916. Ivy made no formal complaint but someone else did, and the police interviewed her in January 1917. At Mrs Scott's trial in the Christchurch Supreme Court the procedures were described in detail and the instruments found on her premises were exhibited. The jury brought in a verdict of guilty and Justice Denniston sentenced her to five years' imprisonment. The newspaper headline was both triumphant and disparaging – 'An Abortion Harpy Convicted'.

൙

Some capitalised on the war for their own benefit. Peter Dewar practised in Auckland, calling himself a 'health specialist' although he had no qualifications. He advertised in the newspapers and used the war theme in this advertisement for ladies' complaints (menstrual regulation):

> WAR WAR – Ladies, thousands of Victories by using Orange Lily. Mr Dewar, Health specialist, 5 and 6 Strand Arcade. Phone 4108[10]

Dewar apparently did not perform surgical abortions but referred women to an abortionist, Mrs Rush. A young war widow, Mrs Elsie McFarland, and another woman, Miss Amelia Snell, sought his help, and because of this Dewar ended up in court.

Trial of Peter McFarlane Dewar and Mrs Mary Rush (alias Haslett), 1918[11]

Mr Dewar, 69, and Mrs Rush, 37, were charged with performing an illegal operation on Mrs Elsie McFarland on or about 27 November 1917. Elsie, widowed three years before, became pregnant to a soldier and went to see Dewar at his business in the Strand Arcade. She paid five shillings for an examination and when she asked if he could 'fix her up' he gave her the address of 141 Grey Street and told her to ask for the lady of the house. Elsie did so and Mrs Rush asked her to purchase a catheter and a bottle of Lysol. The following day the operation took place at the home of Elsie's brother and sister-in-law, where Elsie was staying. Subsequently Elsie visited Mrs Rush several times, and on 8 December, accompanied by her sister-in-law, she paid the balance of the fee of £5 5d. She paid in instalments from her widow's pension, received from Melbourne.

When conducting a search of Mrs Rush's home, police found a letter from another woman, Miss Amelia Snell, who was willing to testify. She gave a similar story of visiting Mrs Rush for an operation on the advice of Dewar. In the Magistrate's Court, Dewar and Mrs Rush pleaded not guilty and were committed for separate trials in the Auckland Supreme Court.

Mrs Phillipa Scott (*NZ Truth*, 20 January 1917) and Peter McFarlane Dewar (*NZ Truth*, 9 February 1918).

Dewar's case was heard first, with Justice Cooper presiding. Dewar's defence lawyer argued that the only evidence against Dewar was that of the two accomplices. The jury deliberated for nearly three hours and returned a verdict of not guilty. When the foreman made the announcement, His Honour looked astonished, then, turning to Dewar, said, 'You are discharged, consider yourself a very lucky man.' Then he admonished the jury: 'Gentlemen, retire to the body of the court. I hope you have pure consciences, but that is purely for your concern.'

In Mrs Rush's case, the jury returned after a retirement of only seven minutes with a verdict of guilty, and Justice Stringer passed a sentence of five years' imprisonment. Considering this harsh sentence, Dewar was indeed lucky.

In the Dunedin Supreme Court, Justice Sim was more sympathetic when he presided over two cases appearing in the same session – a woman struggling with her family while her soldier husband was overseas, and a man who would serve his country better overseas than in prison.

Sentencing of Mrs Ethel Eadie and Mrs Jane Hughes, 1917[12]

Mrs Eadie and Mrs Hughes were close personal friends, and police charged both with procuring abortion on or about 13 December 1916. In the Dunedin Magistrate's Court both pleaded guilty and made written confessions. The magistrate cleared the court and directed that no evidence be published. Sentencing took place in the Supreme Court.

Mrs Eadie, 33, had four young children aged four to eight years and was described as a particularly good mother. Her husband had been away for two or three years in Manila and she had struggled to bring up her children alone.

Mrs Hughes, 53, was the mother of 16-year-old Victoria, who confided in her mother when she became pregnant. Her mother in turn confided in her friend. Mrs Eadie confessed that in a weak moment she did what she did only because Victoria was suicidal. For her help Mrs Hughes gave her £5.

When Victoria became ill after the miscarriage her mother immediately called for a doctor. She recovered but charges resulted. Mr Hanlon defended Mrs Eadie and made a strong plea for leniency. Justice Sim said although Mrs Hughes had not participated in the operation she had persuaded her friend to do so. He would be justified in sentencing them to imprisonment but the term would be a short one, namely six months on each of the charges (procuring and using an instrument), the sentences to be served concurrently.

Sentencing of John Blake and John Kean, 1917[13]

These two men were charged with obtaining a noxious drug to procure abortion on Mr Blake's 16-year-old daughter, Violet. The drugs were obtained from Mrs Towler in the Dunedin Arcade. Both men pleaded guilty and were sentenced in the Supreme Court.

John Blake, 76, cared for his two daughters and a son after his wife left him for another man some 12 years before. One of the girls married and the other, Violet, went to spend a holiday with her sister and got into trouble. The suspected culprit was the brother-in-law. The father, not surprisingly under the circumstances, was distraught.

John Kean was described as a clean-living man, happily married. He had enlisted for the war and was to have joined the 26th Reinforcements. It was Mr Blake's tears that induced him to get the drugs.

Both lawyers, Mr Hanlon for Blake and Mr Scurr for Kean, argued strongly and successfully for probation. His Honour said that had Blake been a younger man it would have been his duty to sentence him to a term of imprisonment but he had lived a blameless life and because no harm had resulted from the use of the drugs, a lesser penalty was justified.

Having dealt leniently with Blake, he said he would deal with Kean likewise. Also in Kean's favour was the fact that he had volunteered to fight for his country. He ordered both of the accused to come up for sentence any time during the next three years and to reimburse the country for the cost of the prosecution, which amounted to £8 7d each.

ଔ

The far-reaching psychological effects of the war are inherent in the difficulties faced by two returned soldiers and their families.

Trials of Hugh Richard Hollis, 1918 and 1921[14]

In August 1918, Hollis was charged in the Takaka Magistrate's Court with having stolen one soldier's pay book, one soldier's discharge, one pension certificate and £12, the property of Robert Allan. Hollis, himself a returned soldier, pleaded guilty and was committed to the Wellington Supreme Court for sentencing.

The defence outlined mitigating factors. Hollis was married with three children. He served at Gallipoli for three weeks and was then discharged as unfit. He suffered from epileptic fits. He received a pension of £5 per month from the government, and was not always able to work, owing to his health. His brother-in-law, a farmer, was now willing to employ him, and he thought he could borrow the money from him to make restitution. He had burned the stolen papers the next day, fearing discovery.

Justice Hosking said it was a mean sort of theft but as this was a first offence he granted Hollis probation for a period of two years, restitution of the stolen money to be made within a week.

Three years later Hollis was found guilty in the Nelson Supreme Court for using a certain instrument on his wife Ruth with intent to procure miscarriage. He was sentenced by Justice Hosking to one year's imprisonment with hard labour. Ruth was also charged and found not guilty of permitting the use of a certain instrument.

Trials of Richard Pahoro Edmonds, George Arthur Kelly and William Michael Wilkinson, 1924[15]

Police charged Edmonds and Kelly jointly in the Dunedin Magistrate's Court with unlawfully using an instrument with intent to procure the miscarriage of a young woman, 19, employed in a hotel. The alleged abortion took place on 28 November 1923. Police also charged Wilkinson, a chemist, with supplying pills and noxious items to procure miscarriage. The outcomes were very different for each defendant: Edmonds, the boyfriend, received a light sentence; Kelly, the abortionist, received a severe sentence; and Wilkinson, the chemist, was discharged.

Kelly, 33, was at one time a medical student whose career was interrupted when he was called up to serve in the military in 1917. He was in one of the first drafts to leave New Zealand. His war experience had unsettled him and on his return he did not resume a legitimate medical career. He was married with three children and earned a precarious living. Short of money, he was tempted into crime through his association with Wilkinson, an unregistered chemist with premises in the Dunedin Arcade.

Edmonds, 21, a porter at the railway station, lived with his widowed mother and had known his girlfriend for about seven months. When she became pregnant Edmonds bought her two boxes of pills at Wilkinson's but she said she did not take these. In November Edmonds arranged for her to go to Wilkinson's and ask for 'Dr Casey'. She went and was told that 'Dr Casey' was not in but to return later. When she did she saw the 'doctor', subsequently identified as Kelly.

Kelly told her to meet him next day at the public library and to bring £20 to cover the cost of the operation. She and Edmonds met him as arranged but they had not been able to raise the money and he would do nothing until the fee was paid. They returned with the money to the library on 28 November. Kelly then allegedly carried out the operation in an unoccupied house.

Edmond's girlfriend became unwell and was admitted to hospital, where doctors operated on her for pelvic infection. She was finally discharged on 29 January. While in hospital she was interviewed by detectives, and Kelly and Edmonds both implored her to deny the statements she had made.

The men were committed for trial in the Dunedin Supreme Court presided over by Justice Reed. At the first trial the jury could not agree and the judge ordered a retrial. This time Wilkinson was found not guilty but Edmonds and Kelly were found guilty. Edmonds was sentenced to three months' gaol with hard labour. The judge said the leniency was due to his youth, his circumstances and the fact that he did not contradict the young woman.

In sentencing Kelly, the judge said,

> It is quite clear that you were mixed up with another man (the chemist, Wilkinson) and that you were establishing a business of procuring abortion in this city. Apart altogether from the morality of the practice, practitioners like yourself who procure abortion on a woman, practically put that woman's life in danger, as it is impossible to conduct an operation of that kind and observe the surgical cleanliness necessary to carry out the operation successfully. You took on the practice simply for the sake of making money for which you risked human lives. Experience shows that imprisonment does not stop abortionists and that they resume their practice when they come out. I intend to impose a sentence of imprisonment, followed by a term of reformative detention. During the latter term you might arrange to start some honest class of business when you come out. You will be sentenced to three years' imprisonment with hard labour, to be followed by a term of three years' reformative detention.

CR

Worse than these war stories is one concerning baby farming. In 1923, more than a quarter of a century after the hanging of the notorious Minnie Dean in 1895, baby farming surfaced as a lingering problem with the sensational case that became known as the Newland baby farm murders.[16]

Trial of Daniel Richard Cooper and Martha Elizabeth Cooper, 1923

Daniel Cooper, builder, land agent, travelling salesman (of medical books), health specialist and abortionist, led a crooked life behind a religious façade as a Seventh Day Adventist. His first unhappy marriage ended in July 1917 with the death of his wife in suspicious circumstances when she was eight months pregnant with their third child. In January 1918, he married Martha Stewart. There were no children of this marriage, but as a result of a sexual liaison between Cooper and Beatrice Beadle, a young woman who joined their household, two babies were born in 1920 and 1921. Cooper arranged for the 'adoption' of both babies and they were never seen again. Martha apparently condoned the relationship between Cooper and Beatrice because her own health impaired marital relations.

Daniel, 41, and Martha, 29, established themselves as health specialists with offices in Lambton Quay in downtown Wellington. They offered a variety of remedies – ointments, face creams and hair restorers – and specialised in products for women. The police, however, suspected that the health business was a front for Daniel's illegal abortion activities and kept him under surveillance. The Coopers also cared for women who did not want to undergo abortion, sometimes offering rental accommodation on their Newlands property. When the babies were born, mothers were led to believe they would be adopted out. The fee for this service was £50, usually extracted from the putative father. However, placements were not easy and, as it transpired, the babies were instead killed and illegally disposed of.

On 30 December 1922, Daniel was arrested and charged with procuring abortion. Two days later, as a result of further investigations and the discovery of a female infant body buried on their Newlands property, he and Martha were taken into custody. This launched an extensive unearthing of criminal activity – two more infant bodies buried on the Newlands property, and a further ten abortions allegedly performed by Daniel over the previous 12 months.

The abortion charges against Daniel were heard in the Magistrate's Court between 31 January and 2 February 1923, and he was committed for trial in the Wellington Supreme Court. However, the abortion trial never eventuated, as the murder charges took precedence. The Supreme Court trial commenced

Setting the Scene • 33

"FOUL DEEDS WILL RISE"
COOPERS TRIED FOR MURDER
THE MASSACRE OF THE INNOCENTS
OUT--HERODING HEROD

MARTHA ELIZABETH COOPER

"Murder will out—that see we day by day." Never in the history of criminal investigation in New Zealand has there been a case to equal in dramatic incident and human interest that of the notorious Coopers, Daniel Richard and Martha Elizabeth, husband and wife, whose trial on a joint charge of murder of a newly-born infant, with other charges pending, commenced in the Wellington Supreme Court on Monday. Of the private life of the "polygamist" Cooper and of his accused wife, and of dark doings at Newlands in the house of death, well back from the road and concealed by trees, among which three dead bodies were buried, the public heard much in preliminary hearings. An intense interest was aroused and at 9 o'clock in the morning a queue formed outside the Court waiting for the commencement of the trial at 10.30 a.m. When the doors were opened to the public the ladies' gallery filled and the body of the Court was crowded to the doors. A police guard had to be placed at the outer door to prevent blockages in the passageways through which it would have otherwise been impossible for officials to have moved. Among the exhibits to be produced in the trial are two tiny skeletons, the mortal remains of infants which the Crown declares went into Cooper's tender care for adoption. The charges are being taken separately. The first to be dealt with is that referring to the child of Margaret Mary McLeod. Whether it will ever come to a hearing of the others will probably be decided by the verdict in this.

DANIEL RICHARD COOPER

'FOUL DEEDS WILL RISE'. Baby farming at Newlands, Wellington. Daniel Cooper was found guilty and sentenced by Justice Chapman to hang; Martha Cooper was found not guilty.
(*NZ Truth*, 19 May 1923)

Martha and Daniel Cooper in court. (*NZ Truth*, 13 January 1923)

on 14 May with Justice Chapman presiding. Crowds queued up to hear the gruesome evidence.

Daniel faced four charges of murder and Martha three. The charges were to be dealt with separately, with the outcome of the first determining whether the others would proceed. The first case concerned Mary McLeod, who gave birth on 12 October while staying in a cottage on the Newlands farm. The Coopers cared for Mary and her baby for eight days, then told her a Palmerston North couple had come to collect the baby. The police found no adoption records, no corroboration of the adopting couple and no evidence the child was alive. However, none of the three exhumed bodies corresponded with the lost infant – the only weakness in the case. Mary's partner, William Welsh, paid Daniel £50 for 'costs'.

Beatrice Beadle and a third woman, Lily Lister, also gave evidence of their babies being 'adopted'. The trial lasted a week and received enormous publicity. At the conclusion, the jury deliberated for one and a half hours before returning their verdict – Daniel guilty, Martha not guilty. His Honour assumed the black cap and sentenced Daniel to death, saying that he had never known such a cruel, heartless murder. The defence appeal failed and Daniel Cooper was hanged at the Terrace Gaol on 16 June 1923.

ଓଃ

The Depression years were rough for both men and women. Mary Findlay, née Wilkinson (1915–1974), was employed on a farm as an 18-year-old home helper at Lake Hayes, eight miles from Queenstown.[17] The year was 1933 and times were desperate. In her biography, Mary describes in detail the self-abortion of May, 46, the farm manager's wife. May was three and a half months pregnant.

> I didn't think it would go so far. I tried all the usual things, Epsom salts, hot baths, jumping off chairs, quinine and ergot. Nothing worked. Then I got desperate and used a knitting needle. Desperate situations need desperate remedies. I hated doing it because I love babies but Stan's nearly 60 and he'll find it hard to get another job like this. We may have to go anyhow but if I had a young baby we'd certainly have to leave. The conditions of our job here are for a married couple with no children.

Stan was Catholic and May did not tell him about the abortion.

Their only daughter Gwen had died a year before. May had a strong constitution and came to no harm, and this was probably the case for most women attempting self-abortion. Less fortunate was the impoverished and fertile Ada Legge, and there were many like her.

Ada's story[18]
Deceased 1 July 1930, aged 32 years

Ada was married to Athol Legge, a plumber, and they lived in Richmond, Christchurch. They had a family of five, ranging in age from nine months to 15 years. Ada thought she was pregnant again and consulted Dr Cotter. He said he did not think she was pregnant and wrote a referral letter to the superintendent of the local hospital requesting admission because of menstrual problems and repair of a bad tear she had sustained during childbirth. She had not had time to arrange for childcare to follow up this non-urgent admission to hospital.

On Saturday 28 June, she was bleeding heavily and complained of feeling unwell. On Sunday Athol sent for Dr Cotter, and he called in on Monday morning leaving a prescription. When Athol returned home on Monday evening, Ada was experiencing severe abdominal pains and he sent again for the doctor. Dr Cotter thought she was suffering from a bladder infection and gave her an injection. He still did not suspect a pregnancy or miscarriage. She had a terrible night and at 8 am Athol sent again for the doctor, but by the time he arrived at 8.15 am, Ada was dead.

At the post-mortem, Christchurch pathologist Dr Thomson found signs of a recent miscarriage, which caused septicaemia and widespread gas gangrene affecting multiple internal organs. A rupture of the spleen had caused internal haemorrhage. The cause of the miscarriage was not disclosed but in the opinion of the doctors it would almost certainly have been induced. Police made enquiries, to no avail. The coroner said one thing was certain – there was not the slightest reproach against the husband. Small comfort for a man left with a family of five.

଍

The onset of World War II was an event which created a division between the early and latter years of the 20th century. In the following story the war is there in the background.

Joan's story[19]
Deceased 31 October 1939, aged 18 years

Joan Sims lived in Onehunga with her parents. Her father was a retired gardener. Joan was a machinist employed by the Slimform Girdle Company, in High Street, Auckland. On 28 October, she got up at 6 am to do the washing, which was her usual chore on a Saturday morning. She had breakfast as usual but about 10 am came in looking very pale and tired, saying, 'I'm all in, Dad!' Her father suggested she lie down, and she remained on the sofa all day, retiring to bed at 7 pm. On Sunday she again rested on the sofa, but in the afternoon she complained of stomach pains and her father called in Dr Noakes. He thought it was not serious but said he would call again, which he did. The next day he prescribed some medicine. On Tuesday afternoon Joan became very restless and Dr Noakes sent her to the hospital in an ambulance.

On arrival, the house-surgeon, Dr Lusk, found the uterus enlarged to the size of a five-month pregnancy. Joan was practically moribund with a very weak pulse and signs of advanced generalised peritonitis. She told Dr Lusk someone, not a doctor, had inserted a catheter and injected Dettol solution into her uterus about 10 days previously, and that she had passed the fetus a few days later. This accorded with her father's evidence that on Friday 20 October Joan said she was going to see her married sister and would stay there the night. Then she told her father she would go and stay for the weekend with her best friend Mary Peterson, 19, who was a workmate at Slimform. This turned out to be untrue. Her father wondered if she had lied to cover up a visit to an abortionist, as it was the only time she was away from home.

Dr Lusk obtained instructions from his superiors to insert an intravenous drip and prepare for a life-saving stab drainage of the peritoneum. However, Joan's condition worsened and she died at 10.30 pm, five hours after admission.

Dr Gilmour, pathologist at Auckland Hospital, conducted the post-mortem, which confirmed the clinical finding of peritonitis. There was still some necrotic placental tissue within the uterus. There were no obvious signs of injury. The coroner, acting alone, found in accordance with the medical evidence that 'death was due to general peritonitis following a septic abortion'. The police investigated and at the inquest two boyfriends, Harold Grimmer, 39, hotel porter, and Leonard Quedley, 21, motor driver, both gave evidence.

Joan and her friend Mary often went to the pictures together and Joan told her about her two boyfriends, Harold and Len. From their workroom at Slimform, Joan used to watch Harold cleaning the windows at the hotel opposite, but she still kept in touch with her old boyfriend Len.

Len's version of events was that he first got to know Joan when she was 16 years old and working for the Yates seed firm in Auckland. He started going out with her and courted her for about 18 months. During that time they had sexual intercourse on several occasions, commencing about six months after the relationship started. After that he said he became tired of her and stopped taking her out. He then resumed taking her out about once a fortnight and continued to have intercourse with her, always using a sheath. (This is the only reference to any method of contraception in any of the coroner's reports.)

Len turned 21 on 15 August and received a present from Joan through the post. The following night he went to thank her for the present and took her out in his car. While sitting in the car he commented that she was getting pretty fat and asked her if she was in the family way. After a while she told him she was pregnant to Harold despite the fact that Harold had told her he was incapable of getting her pregnant.

Joan told Len that Harold wanted to marry her but she did not want to marry him. She also said that he had promised to take her to a doctor to 'get fixed up' but he kept putting it off. Joan asked Len if he knew of anyone who would 'fix her up' and he told her he thought there was a man named Crawshaw, a chemist in Symonds Street, Auckland, who had a home where she could go to be 'fixed up'. After that she used to write to Len regularly, and the letters were exhibited at the inquest. Len said he did not reply to the letters.

> *Letter 1. Undated. Not posted. Found in unstamped envelope.*
>
> Dear Len,
>
> I am afraid my boy friend is just another dirty rotten Aussie. I don't think he ever had any intention of doing anything to help me. I was a fool to trust him from the beginning and believe anything he said but it's too late to think about that now. He did two dirty rotten things on Saturday which convinces me he's all gas and wind.
>
> He has joined up (for the war) and will be called up

any time now and that will be his excuse for not doing anything. I haven't any right to ask you to do this for me but would you go and see that Chemist who you said might do it and ask how much he charges and how long I'd have to stay at his place and when he'd be able to do it. It is my last resort and I know you won't let me down. I will be grateful to you all my life and will never forget how straight and swell you are. That is not a lot of Bull either, I really mean it.

There is a lot more my boy friend has said but I will tell you that on Wednesday night. I think that is all I have to say just now so until Wednesday night I will say Cheerio. Joan.

Letter 2. Undated in envelope stamped 29 August 1939.

Dear Len,

I have not been to the Doctor yet as he was too busy but I will be going next Friday if everything goes well. Will you come out and see me on Wednesday night if you can please. I will close now. So cheerio for the present. Joan

Letter 3. Dated 4 September 1939

Dear Len,

Here I am again. I have not been to the Doctor yet but I saw my boy friend today and he was going to see the Doctor at 5.30 pm tonight. I think I will know definitely tomorrow when I'm going to see him so I will write again tomorrow night and let you know.

I think everything is going to turn out alright. Isn't the war terrible. I'd like to go and put a bomb under old Hitler. Well I think that's all just now. Hoping I'll see you soon. I am yours truly, Joan
P.S. I'm sorry but I've written this all back to front.

Letter 4. Undated.

Dear Len,

Once again I have to tell you that I have not been to the Doctor yet. He says now that I will have to stay Saturday, Sunday and Monday, at his place wherever it is.

I suppose that it is better that it is done properly than half done. That is all just now so until Wednesday night I hope, I'll say cheerio, Joan.

Letter 5. Undated.

Dear Len, I am going to the doctor tomorrow night after work. I suppose you haven't any benzine to come out and see me so perhaps you could write me a little note just to let me know that you're still alive and kicking.

You'll have to buy a nice little push bike to ride until the war is over.

Well I guess this is all for now so until I see you or hear from you I'll say cheerio. Joan.

P.S. If you are coming out tomorrow night come about 8 o'clock.

Letter 6. Undated but in envelope stamped 19 September 1939.

Dear Len,

I have not been to the doctor yet. Every time my boy friend went to see him he would put the price up a little bit more until he wanted to charge £35. I am going to a woman in Dominion Road. I hope to be going on Thursday night if all goes well. I think that's all for now so until Wednesday night I'll say cheerio. Joan.

Letter 7. Undated. Not posted.

Dear Len,

Just a little note to let you know I am alright. I hope you don't mind me writing but I thought I would like you to know.

My boy friend was absolutely marvelous. He came to see me every spare minute he had and he was the happiest man in the world when it was all over. I could never let him down now on any account. I did a very foolish thing about three weeks ago which made him lose his job but he still stuck to me. Well I had better not bore you any more with my troubles so I'll say, Cheerio, Joan.

Harold's version of events was quite restrained. At the time of the inquest he had changed jobs and was now a barman-porter at the Masonic Hotel in Devonport. In evidence he stated that he got to know Joan when he was working at the hotel opposite her workplace. They went out together and had intercourse on several occasions without using preventatives. He said he did not think he was responsible for the pregnancy because he was impotent. Joan told him about Len but he did not know his other name and had never met him. Harold was not Australian but had been to Australia and was nicknamed 'Aussie' by some of the staff at the hotel. In September, a few days after war was declared, he enlisted. He denied any involvement in Joan's abortion. No charges were laid.

ଔ

Joan's story, and the others in this chapter, illustrate the disruptive effect of war and poverty on relationships and family life. Desperate women, faced with an unplanned pregnancy in a condemning society, sought remedies from unscrupulous practitioners. Doctors were constrained by the law, interpreted conservatively by judges. Public opinion as reflected in the newspapers of the day reinforced the stigma surrounding abortion. Politicians paid scant attention to the needs of women.

2. THE McMILLAN REPORT

The 1936 Inquiry into Abortion came about because New Zealand maternal mortality statistics compared unfavourably with those of other developed countries. In 1920 the rate of 6.48 maternal deaths per 1,000 live births was shockingly high. More than one third of these deaths were from puerperal sepsis or childbirth fever contracted at the time of birth, often due to unsterile equipment or infection transferred via birth attendants. At that time, most New Zealand mothers had their babies at home or in small unlicensed one-bed nursing homes.

The infection could be localised to the uterus (endometritis), or it could spread to involve the Fallopian tubes (salpingitis) or the pelvic or abdominal cavity (peritonitis). More widespread infection via the bloodstream (septicaemia or blood poisoning) could affect all other organs. Peritonitis and septicaemia were often fatal in the pre-antibiotic era. Widespread infection and the production of toxins could cause multiple organ failure, septic shock and death. Another cause of maternal deaths was toxaemia. Most maternal deaths from toxaemia were due to eclampsia, associated with high blood pressure and fluid retention, leading to convulsions and coma. The solution was better antenatal care and improved treatment.

Some doctors were dissatisfied with the management of maternal welfare by the Health Department and in 1927 the New Zealand Obstetrical Society was formed, with Dr Doris Gordon as the Honorary Secretary and her husband Dr Bill Gordon as the Honorary Treasurer. Later in 1932 the name was changed to the New Zealand Obstetrical and Gynaecological Society (O&G Society). The aim was to improve maternity services in New Zealand through education and collegial support, but the O&G Society also challenged the bureaucracy of the Health

Department. One particular issue was to refute the allegation that forceps-wielding doctors contributed to the increase in sepsis.

Between 1920 and 1936 more mothers had their babies in hospital, and this coincided with better infection control through strict antiseptic techniques. From 1927 onwards, statistics separated the total maternal mortality (abortion deaths included) and genuine maternal mortality (abortion deaths excluded). With better control of puerperal infections and toxaemia the increased proportion of maternal deaths from septic abortion became alarming. Over the period 1927 to 1935, maternal mortality from all causes other than septic abortion dropped. The sharp rise in septic abortion began in 1929 and reached its height (42 deaths) in 1934. During the five-year period 1931–1935, 176 women died from sepsis following abortion, and in the same period there were 70 deaths from puerperal sepsis.[1] Abortion had become riskier than childbirth.

Early in March 1936 the O&G Society discussed the setting up of a Royal Commission by the government to investigate abortion deaths. The Director-General of Health, Dr Watt, who was also a member of the O&G Society, formulated a proposal to the Minister of Health, Peter Fraser, in June 1936 and a Special Committee of Inquiry (not a Royal Commission) was appointed on 4 August 1936 to report to Parliament on the incidence of septic abortion, the underlying causes of its occurrence, the best means of combating and preventing its occurrence and any other appropriate recommendations and observations.

The chairman of the committee was a member of Parliament, Dr D. G. McMillan (1904–1951). Three other doctor members were Dr Sylvia Chapman, Medical Superintendent of St Helens Hospital, Wellington; Dr T. F. Corkill, President of the O&G Society; and Dr T. L. Paget, Director of Maternal Welfare for the Department of Health. One lay person, Mrs Janet Fraser, wife of Peter Fraser, was appointed for her background in social welfare and membership of the Wellington Hospital Board.

The McMillan Report attributed the high rate of septic abortion to illegal interference by unskilled abortionists. The assumption was that illegal abortions caused sepsis, natural miscarriages did not. This was largely true, although some doctors, including the O&G Society, believed that autologous infection (i.e. infection from within the woman's own body) was also significant. Women habitually douched for personal hygiene and used vaginal preparations for contraception and this interference with the normal protective bacteria inhabiting the vagina may have increased the risk of sepsis. It is possible that the infecting organisms may have been more virulent at that time. Sepsis is discussed again in the next chapter on medical issues.

Dr David Gervan McMillan, medical practitioner, MP for Dunedin West and chairman of the 1936 Committee of Inquiry into Abortion. (*The Press*, 28 September 1934)

It was often impossible to determine whether an abortion was natural or induced. The terms miscarriage or spontaneous abortion were often used for a natural event and the term abortion for one that was induced, but these terms are interchangeable. It was sometimes impossible for medical professionals to distinguish between the two. The following story is most likely about a natural miscarriage.

Myrtle's story[2]
Deceased 20 June 1934, aged 26 years

Myrtle Wilson was married to Allan, a lorry driver of Hastings. They had been married for seven years and had two children, aged six and three. Apart from treatment for goitre three years before her death and a recent bout of gallstones, Myrtle kept good health, although in the weeks before her death she did complain of a general feeling of being unwell. At that time she was more concerned about her two children, who needed medical attention from the district nurse and doctor for measles and pneumonia.

At times Allan's job kept him away from home but he usually managed to come home for the weekends. When he arrived home on Saturday 9 June he remembered Myrtle was having her menstrual period, as expected. Her mother also confirmed Myrtle's menstrual history. Mother and daughter were very close, visiting each other nearly every day. Myrtle often had difficult periods, requiring bed rest for a few hours. On Sunday 10 June she felt cold and shivery and went to bed. When Allan left on Monday morning Myrtle said she felt better.

On Tuesday Myrtle stayed in bed and her mother came to help out. Allan asked his mother-in-law to call Dr Kitchen and on Wednesday the doctor arranged for Myrtle's admission to Napier Hospital. Allan visited her on Sunday 17 June when she appeared quite well. When he received the news at work on Wednesday 20 June that Myrtle was dead, he was devastated. He had not spoken to the hospital doctors and was disbelieving when his brother informed him two days later that Myrtle had died from septicaemia following an abortion.

Dr Foley, medical superintendent of Napier Hospital, who conducted the post-mortem, found signs of a recent pregnancy with some tissue still adherent to the walls of the uterus. Because of her menstrual history, Dr Foley took the precaution of sending Myrtle's uterus for examination by Wellington pathologist Dr Lynch. His report confirmed either a natural miscarriage or an abortion, with sepsis affecting the wall of the uterus. The pregnancy was about four months' gestation. Unusually, women may bleed at the time of their expected menstruation during pregnancy. The post-mortem gave no clues as to the cause of the miscarriage or abortion.

Allan was incredulous. He said at the inquest:

> I had no reason to believe that my wife was pregnant at any time during the few months prior to her death. I am of the opinion that had she known she was pregnant my wife would have told me of it. I have known my wife since childhood and since our marriage she has not been in the habit of keeping anything secret from me. We were happily married and as far as these matters were concerned, she always discussed them with me. My wife was not conversant with any person except myself regarding our

home life and had she known she was pregnant I would have been the first person she would have mentioned it to. I believe that if she was in that condition, she could not have been aware of it. If it is a fact that my wife had a miscarriage, I am unable to account for it. As far as I know, the only medicine my wife took prior to her going into hospital was some 'Aspro' tablets which she took for headaches. There was no other medicine in our house except some medicine prescribed for the children.

The noncommittal coroner's report found that 'death was due to septicaemia due to general sepsis'.

The distinction between natural and induced was often more problematic.

Isabella's story[3]
Deceased 26 April 1904, aged 36 years

Isabella Simpson lived in Christchurch. She was unusual in that she was a woman of independent means and had recently sold her Colombo Street fruit shop. For the past two months she had boarded with Mrs Mitchell, occupying herself with sewing or needlework. About a fortnight before she died she became unwell but to anyone who asked she said she had a severe cold. Mrs Mitchell thought she should see a doctor but Isabella refused.

A few days before her boarder died, Mrs Mitchell was concerned enough to send for Isabella's father. He insisted she see a doctor but she died before being seen. All those who had seen her in her last few days denied knowing anything about a pregnancy, let alone a miscarriage. She was regarded as a respectable woman and Mrs Mitchell did not know of any male companions.

The post-mortem by Dr Syme revealed the classic signs of septicaemia. In his opinion abortion had taken place about ten days before at about nine weeks' gestation. There were no signs of injury and he could not say whether the miscarriage was natural or illegally induced. At the coroner's inquest, the jury of six men confirmed Isabella 'died from blood poisoning as a result of a miscarriage but whether such miscarriage was illegally produced or not there was no evidence to show'.

Public pressure was an important factor in establishing the 1936 Committee of Inquiry, and most influential was the well-publicised death of Miss Mora May MacKenzie in April of that year. In dealing with this tragedy, the coroner's deep frustration resonated with the government, the medical profession and the general public.

Mora's story[4]
Deceased 11 April 1936, aged 29 years

Mora MacKenzie lived with her sister Clare in North East Valley, Dunedin. They were both single and worked as typists. Mora enjoyed good health and hardly missed a day's work. Their father had died six years before and their mother three years before. Sometime in March, when Mora became aware of a possible pregnancy, she consulted Dr Moody, who had been her doctor for some years. He said he was unable to help her obtain an abortion and in hindsight he wondered whether she might have sought out an illegal option.

Uncharacteristically, she became ill and stayed in bed. Clare could not look after her sister during the day because of work, so Mora arranged to stay with a friend, Irene, who lived in Anderson's Bay. She planned to go there for a week to convalesce. Mora had befriended one of her employers, Mr Alexander McKinnon, a departmental manager at Wright Stephenson's, and she later named him, a married man, as the one responsible for her pregnancy, although he adamantly denied this. On 20 March, in the evening, McKinnon took Mora in his car to stay with her friend Irene. McKinnon also asked Dr Borrie to call and see Mora. The doctor found her miscarrying and he recommended she be transferred to the Chalet private hospital for care. Here, Dr Borrie performed a curette, emptying the uterus of a two-month pregnancy. Mora remained in the Chalet until Tuesday 24 March, when she took a taxi back to her friend Irene's place at Anderson's Bay. No-one had kept her sister informed and she was unaware of Mora's admission to the Chalet. Dr Borrie supervised her care in the Chalet and at Anderson's Bay.

On Friday 27 March, her friend Irene expected visitors, so Mora returned home by tram. Clare was concerned about the state of her sister's health. On Sunday 29 March, Mora's condition worsened and Clare asked Dr Moody to call, not realising Dr Borrie had cared for her over the preceding nine days. Dr Moody admitted her to Braemar private hospital and recommended a blood transfusion. Dr Moody later learned Mora had been receiving treatment from Dr Borrie, and on Thursday 2 April Dr Moody was so concerned about Mora's condition he consulted Dr Borrie. They decided to carry out a second curetting but did not obtain very much material as the uterus was empty. On 5 April, when Mora began to develop rigors, Dr Moody thought she should be transferred to the public hospital, where it would be easier to have another blood transfusion.

When admitted to the hospital at 4 am Mora received a blood transfusion, but although seriously ill she was not officially put on the 'seriously ill' list. When questioned by the house surgeon who admitted her, she told him she had had an operation about two weeks before, carried out by Mrs Clark, a well-known Dunedin abortionist. Clare was surprised to learn her sister had had a miscarriage. Mora was unhappy about the treatment and conditions in the public hospital and against medical advice discharged herself and returned to Braemar.

On Thursday 9 April she had what was termed an 'abdominal crisis', experiencing acute pain and fever with signs of developing peritonitis. On Friday, on the advice of the doctors, she made her will but refused to make any statement for the police concerning any illegal interference. On Easter Saturday, 11 April, she died, and Dr Moody said he would provide the death certificate, citing firstly general peritonitis, secondly septic abortion and thirdly pelvic peritonitis as the cause of death.

Mora was buried at 10.30 am on Monday 13 April; at the time of burial, Dr Moody had not actually written the death certificate, which was dated 14 April. The police were notified of her death on 13 April and referred the matter to the coroner, Mr J. R. Bartholomew S.M. He ordered that the body be exhumed for a post-mortem, and on 24 April this was carried out by Dr D'Ath, pathologist, Dunedin Hospital.

The findings were unusual and interesting from a medical perspective. In Dr D'Ath's opinion, Mora had had a miscarriage (either natural or induced) and infection had spread to the pelvis and beyond. The two curettings had removed any continuing source of infection and the reproductive tract was now clear of infection. However, infection had lodged in the spleen, and three abscesses had unusually formed in that organ. One had burst, releasing pus into the abdominal cavity, and this was presumed to have caused the abdominal crisis.

With this information, the coroner reported that 'the cause of death was generalised peritonitis due to the rupture of an abscess of the spleen which condition resulted from criminal abortion performed by some person unknown'. At the inquest, the burial of the body without a death certificate was viewed by the coroner as a serious breach of the law, whereas Dr Moody said it was customary to post a death certificate to the undertaker following a telephone conversation.

J. R. Bartholomew, Senior Magistrate, Dunedin.
(*NZ Truth*, 26 April 1924)

Dr Moody's failure to report a suspected illegal operation to the police was condemned by the coroner. Defending his actions, Dr Moody said he was relying on the direction from the British Medical Association of 27 January 1915, and also a ruling of the Director-General of Health for the guidance of the medical profession given to the New Zealand Obstetrical Society and published in the *New Zealand Medical Journal* on 29 October 1932:

> The Department is advised that a doctor is under no legal obligation to inform the police as to the cause of death of a person which has been due to an illegal operation. He is, of course under an obligation to insert in the certificate of death which he furnishes under the Births and Deaths Registration Act 1924, the cause of death, both primary and secondary. In that certificate, when death was the consequence of an illegal operation, he should insert the nature of the operation as the primary cause of death. He need not of course, describe it as an illegal operation, but he would describe the type of operation and the reason why such operation was the primary cause of death, e.g., owing to incompetence or ignorance, if that be the case.

'This,' said Mr Bartholomew, 'invites a cloak to be cast over a serious criminal offence in respect of which a charge of murder may lie. It is no part of a doctor's duty to act as a detective, but it is equally certain that it is no part of his duty to act as a screen for the professional abortionist. In my opinion it is altogether wrong and irregular for a death certificate to be given.'[5]

No charges were laid, but even as the Committee of Inquiry was being held, changes were made to the Births and Deaths Registration Act, section 12:

> On the death of any person who has been attended during his last illness by a registered medical practitioner, that practitioner shall forthwith sign and deliver to the Registrar of the district in which the death occurred a certificate, on the printed form to be supplied for that purpose by the Registrar-General, stating to the best of his knowledge and belief the causes of death, both primary and secondary, the duration of the last illness of the deceased, the date on which he last saw the deceased alive, and such other particulars as may be required by the Registrar-General, and the particulars stated therein shall be entered in the register together with the name of the certifying medical practitioner.

The medical practitioner shall at the same time sign and deliver to the undertaker or other person having charge of the burial a notice on the printed form to be supplied for that purpose by the Registrar-General to the effect that he has furnished a certificate under the last preceding subsection to the Registrar.

In any case where, in the opinion of the medical practitioner, the death has occurred under any circumstances of suspicion, the practitioner shall forthwith report the case to the Coroner.

Every medical practitioner required to give a certificate and a notice as aforesaid, or to report to the Coroner as provided by the last preceding subsection, who refuses or neglects to do so is liable to a fine not exceeding five pounds.

Although the Health Act 1920 provided for the notification of septic abortion as a public health matter, medical professionals did not always report cases, and practice varied from one hospital to another. Police sometimes became involved through the notification process. While doctors may or may not have been aware of their duty to report a septic abortion, some still regarded this as a breach of patient confidentiality, as in the following story from 1927.

Martha's story[6]
Deceased 7 July 1927, aged 33 years

Mrs Martha Toohey of Greymouth had been widowed for about two and a half years. For six months she had been employed as a housekeeper for a plumber, Mr George McGirr, caring for George and his father, brother and sister. Martha and George had known each other for ten years but they came to a parting of the ways and Martha left about the middle of May. She was pregnant and her understanding was that George still intended to marry her.

She had a good friend, Mrs Jessie Roberts, who also lived in Greymouth, the two having known each other since their schooldays. On Saturday 7 June, they both went to Christchurch and stayed at a boarding house. According to Jessie she was to be a witness at Martha's wedding in Christchurch but Martha received a telegram from George saying he could not come. Jilted, they returned to Greymouth. Two days later, on Wednesday 11 June, the two women made a second trip together to Christchurch.

Martha's whereabouts between 12 and 21 June are unknown, and Jessie refused to divulge any details. According to evidence given at the inquest, Martha told one of the nurses she had visited a woman and paid £20 for an abortion.

After returning to Greymouth, Martha became seriously ill and Dr McBrearty made a house-call. She told him she had been 'fixed up' in Christchurch on Friday but declined to provide any more details. Dr McBrearty telephoned Dr Moore, Medical Superintendent, Grey River Hospital, and arranged for her admission. On Monday 23 June, Dr Moore performed an operation and a small amount of foul-smelling placental debris was removed and the interior of the uterus irrigated. Her condition improved until 27 June, when she developed pneumonia. About 3 July she developed symptoms suggesting abdominal complications, and on the morning of 7 July she collapsed.

At the time of the collapse Dr Moore realised she was in extremis and communicated with the police at about 11 am. When the police visited her she was too ill to answer questions. She corroborated the statement she first made to Dr Moore that she had been 'fixed up' in Christchurch but refused to incriminate anybody. Treatment was unavailing and Martha died at 4.45 pm. The two doctors jointly carried out the post-mortem and found widespread peritonitis and severe inflammation. The kidneys, liver and spleen all showed signs of sepsis. The lungs were congested. There was no evidence of injury.

The coroner asked Dr Moore why he had not communicated with the police earlier, and he explained that would be betraying the patient's confidence. In Dr Moore's opinion, current thinking was that sepsis after a miscarriage could come as much from within the patient as from without. If the woman had recovered, he would not have advised the police. The coroner, acting alone, found 'death was due to toxaemia following an illegal operation performed in Christchurch between 12–21 June 1927 but there was no evidence before the Court to prove who performed the operation'.

ಬ

The Committee of Inquiry heard evidence from the New Zealand Branch of the British Medical Association, obstetricians and gynaecologists, nurses, many women's organisations, the police, the churches and other groups. Much has been written about the inquiry, so only a summary is provided here.

Incidence of abortion

The committee distinguished three types of abortion: spontaneous, therapeutic and criminal. It was not possible to assess the incidence of abortion with accuracy, but some indication of the frequency could be obtained from the statistics of various hospitals. Abortion deaths were often hidden behind other diagnoses, such as pneumonia or unspecified peritonitis.

On the basis of the statistics, the committee estimated that the total abortion rate was about 20 per 100 pregnancies and, of these, six to seven were spontaneous abortions. The incidence of criminal abortion was therefore at least 13 per 100 pregnancies, and this could be regarded as a conservative estimate. One estimate for the year ending March 1936 was about 6,000 abortions, of which nearly two-thirds, or 4,000, were criminally or self-induced.

Underlying causes of abortion

According to the committee, the main causes of abortion were economic and domestic hardship, changes in social and moral outlook, pregnancy among the unmarried and, in a small proportion of cases, fears of childbirth. Ignorance of effective methods of contraception was another factor, but the committee did not make any recommendations regarding this, despite a number of submissions speaking of the need for improvements. Advertising contraceptives and abortifacients was deplored, as was the widespread use of contraception in the unmarried. However, women's groups called for more information on reliable methods of birth control.

Possible remedial measures

Paramount among the remedies proposed to reduce the abortion rate among married women was the relief of economic stress, es-pecially for the wives of the unemployed or precariously employed, and farmers' wives. Financial and domestic help was recommended. The committee expressed confidence in New Zealand's obstetrical services and supported the St Helens Hospitals' policy of not admitting single women, despite criticism of this discrimination.

With regard to controlling abortion among the unmarried, the committee found the main cause to be 'looseness of the moral standard', and the remedy was careful education of the young in matters of sex. The committee considered that contraceptives should be severely restricted and their sale by mail order made illegal. The committee also recommended that supply of contraceptives to young persons be made unlawful.

Two lines of action were recommended:
1. To direct knowledge of birth control 'through more responsible channels' (i.e., doctors).
2. 'To appeal to the womanhood of New Zealand in so far as selfish and unworthy motives have entered into our family life, to consider the grave physical and moral dangers, not to speak of the dangers of race suicide which are involved.'

Medico-legal aspects

The committee opposed any change to the law on abortion and believed the law allowed therapeutic abortion when the mother's life was seriously endangered. This was more an endorsement of current clinical practice than reliance on specific legislation. Any widening of the law was seen as unnecessary. Abortion for social and economic reasons was utterly opposed.

The failure of juries to convict was referred back to the government without any recommendation from the committee. With regard to the duties of doctors, the committee approved the adoption of guidelines from the Royal College of Physicians.

The committee concluded: 'Although State aid and legal prohibitions may do something to remove causes and to deter crime, the ultimate issue rests with the attitude and action of the people themselves.'

The most liberal submission advocating legalised abortion came from Mrs R. D. Baker, representing a group of women who felt it was their right to decide how many children they should have. They noted that no method of contraception was fully dependable, and advocated more research into contraceptive methods. The group submitted that abortion at the hands of a doctor should be made legal and readily available.

The McMillan Report was made public on 10 April 1937, and received wide publicity. Under the headline 'New Zealand's Unborn Citizens', the *Dominion* newspaper in Wellington carried a summary of the findings and opined that the government and the country had been well served by the committee.[7] The editor of the Christchurch *Press* was less complimentary.[8] He was disappointed that important issues had been sidestepped, and was especially critical of the vague recommendations regarding the teaching of contraceptive advice. The most critical and radical appraisal came from a letter writer in the feminist magazine *Tomorrow*:[9]

> The committee estimated that some 6,000 abortions occur every year in New Zealand; that deaths are almost entirely confined to illegally and self-procured abortions, and that pregnancy among the unmarried is of great importance in a consideration of the causes of this problem.
>
> These were some of the most important findings, but prejudice prevented members of the committee from emphasising that the vast majority of girls don't die; or from stating, what I believe is true, that abortions can be performed quite simply without permanently bad after effects. So much then for prejudiced findings . . .
>
> When it is believed that at least 6,000 females yearly undergo abortions, and that those operations legally performed are not dangerous, then surely the logical and unprejudiced thing to do is to make abortion legal, for it is indisputable that neither the danger nor the illegality of the illegal operation deters a girl . . .
>
> To conclude . . . it is in the interests of national health, present and future, that the safe procuring of an abortion be legally placed within the means of every girl desiring it.

Some women's groups were disappointed that the recommendations regarding contraception were so restrictive. The principal reasons for opposing contraception were that access would be harmful to young people and more contraception would aggravate the declining population. A 1936 pamphlet by A. E. Mander, *To Alarm New Zealand*, warned about the dire consequences of the population decline. The directive to 'populate or perish' was a theme widely supported. A more political motive was that supporting contraception would alienate Roman Catholic voters.

It was not generally appreciated that marital fertility had been declining since the 1870s, and this trend continued in the 20th century.[10] Between 1901 and 1921, the fertility rate among married women aged 15–44 years declined from 243.8 to 180.7 births per thousand. The rate declined further, to 161.5 births per thousand in 1926, and by 1936 it had declined to its lowest level yet recorded of 131.3 births per thousand. This was in part due to the emancipation of women and the use of contraception and abortion. But it was also due to demographic changes in the proportion of females, their age at marriage and the spacing of births.

The McMillan Report • 55

Dr Doris Clifton Gordon. (Ref: 1/2-127025-F.
Alexander Turnbull Library, Wellington, New Zealand)

Very soon after the release of the McMillan Report, Dr Doris Gordon and Dr Francis Bennett published their book *Gentlemen of the Jury*,[11] which provided more ammunition for those opposed to contraception and abortion. Dr Bennett later distanced himself from the publication, saying that he was coerced into joint authorship and describing the collaboration as hopeless and the book as 'very bad'.[12] To summarise its contents: the birth rate was falling, immorality among the unmarried was prevalent due to the emancipation of women, and the death rate from septic abortion among the married was rising. Contraception prevented women from fulfilling their role as mothers. Doctors should approve abortions and sterilisations only in cases of genuine medical need. The Protestant churches should take a lead from the Roman Catholic Church. Juries must convict abortionists. The solution was threefold: firstly, educate the public about the facts; secondly, make motherhood more attractive; and thirdly, tighten up the legal framework.

Dr Gordon did not just write the book. She campaigned at meetings throughout the country and wrote articles expounding her views. In an article for the *New Zealand Nursing Journal*,[13] she said:

> It is significant that whereas 20 years ago it was rare for a woman to request an abortion and if she did so she would sneak into the surgery with the demeanour of a thief. Women now walk in frequently, unblushingly, and tell you they have come to arrange for an abortion just as calmly as if they were ordering a tube of toothpaste.

This was reiterated in *Gentlemen of the Jury*. Both the McMillan Report and *Gentlemen of the Jury* were referred to in a 1937 trial.

Trial of Mrs Agnes Burns and Mrs Gertrude Grace Taylor, 1937[14]

These two Christchurch women had known each other for about 15 years and operated a joint abortion business, with Mrs Burns taking cases into her home and Mrs Taylor operating with a catheter. Mrs Burns, known to be fond of alcohol, received about £3 for her part in the business.

At their trial, two clients testified as principal witnesses. A young woman, 21, from the West Coast, said Mrs Taylor operated upon her in Mrs Burns's home in 1936 and again in March 1937 when she found herself pregnant once more to the same man. On both occasions the fee was £12. The other young woman, 21, from Christchurch, said her boyfriend paid £8, although £10 was requested. Mrs Taylor performed two operations upon her as the first was not successful. She was admitted to hospital on 9 April 1937, at which time the police became involved.

At the first Christchurch Supreme Court trial in October 1937, presided over by Justice Northcroft, the defence lawyer warned of the danger in accepting the uncorroborated evidence of accomplice witnesses: 'The men involved, if they had been called, would also have given evidence as accomplices but they had not even been asked to face the humiliation of coming to court. The evidence of the two young women might have been at the price of their immunity from facing charges.'

The jury was out from 4.20 pm until 8.20 pm. Mrs Burns was found guilty and sentenced to six months' imprisonment. Court staff escorted her sobbing from the dock. His Honour took into account the jury's recommendation for mercy on account of her age and physical condition; however, he believed these were not isolated cases; the women were performing abortions systematically and as a business. The jury was unable to agree on the verdict for Mrs Taylor, the operator, and she was committed for retrial. The defence pointed out discrepancies in the evidence of both witnesses and their difficulty identifying Mrs Taylor.

At the retrial the following week, presided over again by Justice Northcroft, Mrs Taylor was defended by Mr Hardie Boys of Wellington. In his address to the jury, Hardie Boys said not a small part of the campaign against abortion had been directed against juries and the jury system:

> A book had been published which by its title was directed at juries. It was said that in abortion cases juries did not convict and unless they did 'this and that would happen.' The view appeared to be that the accused had only to be put in the dock and it was the duty of the jury to convict. But the jury was not in Court on a heresy hunt or as a social welfare committee, and unless the evidence proved the accused to be guilty a verdict of guilty should not be returned.

His Honour, in summing up, said the jury must not be influenced in making a decision by outside interest and agitation about abortion, or by the opinion of the presiding judge or counsel on either side. It was indeed true that the public was anxiously interested in abortion, and it was proper for those interested in social questions to address themselves earnestly to the problem of abortion, but that was not the duty of the jury, who were to decide the case on the evidence.

After analysing the evidence His Honour said that the subject of abortion was an uneasy one for many people and its prevalence was in danger of seducing juries from their duty. He reminded the jury that if there was any danger to the jury system it was not from outside but from the juries themselves, who were bound on oath to decide the case on the evidence. The jury was out for only 45 minutes and returned a verdict of not guilty. It seems unfair that Mrs Taylor, the abortionist, was acquitted while Mrs Burns, the accomplice, was jailed.

Portrait of Joseph Bernard Dawson, Professor of Obstetrics and Gynaecology at Dunedin Medical School. (Raine, William Hall, 1892–1955. Original photographic prints and postcards from file print collection, Box 11. Ref: PAColl-6304-41. Alexander Turnbull Library, Wellington, New Zealand)

Many doctors were involved in the setting up of the 1937 Inquiry into Abortion, and many participated in the inquiry. Professor J. B. Dawson, the inaugural Professor of Obstetrics and Gynaecology at the Dunedin Medical School, presented figures from Dunedin Hospital. Between 1932 and 1936 there had been 640 admissions for abortion. He estimated the frequency of abortion to be one abortion for every three births; nationwide this suggested a total of 7,623 abortions annually. This figure, however, included spontaneous abortions, which occur in about 25 per cent of all pregnancies. Dr Sophia Ruth De La Mare, a representative of the Hamilton Branch of the National Council of Women (NCW), was the only doctor who presented liberal views on abortion to the McMillan Inquiry. She submitted that, in the absence of completely reliable contraception, abortion was necessary as a means of controlling fertility. Dr De La Mare suggested that a woman who had borne two children should be able to have an abortion under the best surgical conditions as this was no more detrimental to a woman's health than bearing an unwanted child. The Dunedin Branch of NCW objected to this viewpoint as unrepresentative of NCW.[15]

Apart from bringing into the open the extent of abortion and the tragedy of deaths from abortion, one positive outcome of the McMillan Report was the setting up by the Minister of Health of another committee to inquire into maternity services throughout the Dominion. Dr McMillan again chaired this committee, and other members of the Inquiry into Abortion were also retained – Dr Sylvia Chapman, Mrs Janet Fraser, Dr Corkill and Dr Paget. Additional appointments were Mrs Amy Hutchinson and Mrs Agnes Kent-Johnson.[16] The report of this second inquiry led to the Social Security Act 1938, which introduced a Maternity Benefit scheme entitling every mother to have a doctor attend her throughout her pregnancy, delivery and after care. The benefit allowed women to give birth in a hospital and stay there for 14 days free of charge. An alternative, less utilised, option was a home birth with free domiciliary nursing care for 14 days.

Imagine what it was like for many women in 1936. The country was emerging from a deep economic depression. Many husbands were out of work. Childbirth was perceived as a hazardous experience due to perinatal sepsis. Another extra mouth to feed was well beyond the budget. The low birth rate meant that in the absence of reliable contraception couples practised restraint, fearful of another pregnancy. For a single woman facing an unplanned pregnancy the options were extremely limited and recourse to abortion was a frequent outcome. The tragic death of Miss Mora MacKenzie made the country stop and take stock. But looked at from the perspective of the 21st century, the McMillan Report that resulted was moralistic and conservative. Regarding abortion primarily as a moral problem was ultimately unhelpful for women.

3. MEDICAL MATTERS: MAINLY SEPSIS

Sepsis was the most feared complication of pregnancy and it took far too long (about 100 years) for birth attendants to adopt preventive practices. As early as 1773 **Dr Charles White** (1728–1813),[1] obstetrician and cofounder of the Manchester Royal Infirmary, advocated absolute cleanliness, including handwashing in the lying-in chamber and also the isolation of infected patients with puerperal (childbirth) fever. By adopting these precautions he reduced mortality considerably. He expounded his views in the first edition of a textbook, *The Management of Pregnant and Lying-in Women* (1773).

Serious epidemics of puerperal fever occurred in Aberdeen between 1789 and 1792. **Dr Alexander Gordon** (1752–1799)[2] cared for 77 patients with the disease, 25 of whom died, usually around the fifth day after birth. In 1795 he published his experience in *A Treatise on the Epidemic Puerperal Fever of Aberdeen*. He maintained that puerperal fever was contagious in nature, and recommended that nurses and doctors 'ought carefully to wash themselves and to get their apparel properly fumigated before it be put on again.' In doing so he challenged the prevailing theory that the infection was caused by 'bad air' (miasma).

On the other side of the Atlantic, **Dr Oliver Wendell Holmes** (1809–1894),[3] Dean of Harvard Medical School, published an essay in 1843 on the contagiousness of puerperal fever, based on his armchair observations of White, Gordon and others. He concluded from his study of the literature that 'The disease known as Puerperal Fever is so far contagious as to be frequently carried from patient to patient by physicians and nurses.'

Dr Ignaz Semmelweis (1818–1865),[4] a Hungarian obstetrician working at the Vienna General Hospital in 1847 noticed the dramatically high incidence of death from puerperal fever among women who delivered at the hospital attended by doctors and medical students, whereas births attended by midwives were relatively safe. He realised the doctors had usually come directly from autopsies. Asserting (as had White, Gordon and Holmes) that puerperal fever was a contagious disease, Semmelweis made staff wash their hands with chlorinated lime water before examining pregnant women, and thereby reduced maternal mortality from 18.27 per cent to 1.27 per cent.[5] In doing so he offended other doctors, the medical establishment rejected his theories, and the hostility and ridicule gradually drove him to a nervous breakdown. He died two weeks after being committed to a mental hospital. Ironically, the cause of death was infection by the same pathogen he had protected new mothers against for most of his professional life.

Joseph Lister (1827–1912)[6] worked as a surgeon at Glasgow Royal Infirmary. When he became chairman of the Surgery Department it was normal for about 50 per cent of patients with amputations to die of sepsis. Lister saw the connection between Semmelweis's observations and the deaths in his own hospital. Studying first animals, then humans, he examined the effects of disinfecting skin and instruments with carbolic acid. By doing so, Lister drastically reduced post-amputation mortality. Unlike Semmelweis, Lister managed to persuade his colleagues of the reasonableness of his antiseptic method. In 1867 he published his landmark paper 'On the Antiseptic Principle of the Practice of Surgery', advocating the use of carbolic acid (phenol) to cleanse wounds.[7]

Professor Louis Pasteur (1822–1895)[8] conducted more formal experiments on the relationship between germs and disease between 1860 and 1864. Some 50 years after Semmelweis's work, at a lecture on 13 March 1879, Pasteur announced that *Streptococcus pyogenes* was the main organism responsible for puerperal fever and recommended using boric acid to kill the germs before and after confinement. German microbiologist **Robert Koch** (1843–1910)[9] further advanced the science of bacteriology. He finally laid to rest the idea that 'bad air' caused disease, by proving that specific organisms caused specific infections.

In 1900 a bubonic plague pandemic caused a scare. Although it spread throughout the world, only one case occurred in New Zealand. **Dr James Mason** (1864–1924),[10] an experienced bacteriologist, took advantage of the scare to make far-reaching changes to the health system. Born in Scotland, he immigrated to New Zealand in 1895. He was one of the few doctors in New Zealand trained in public health. In 1898 he instigated the first state laboratory for bacteriological testing, and he was also responsible for the Public Health Act 1900, which established one of the world's first national departments of public health. He established District Health Offices in Auckland, Napier, Wellington, Nelson, Christchurch and Dunedin. Dr Mason was instrumental in the passage of the Tohunga Suppression Act 1907, aimed at Māori healers, a blunt and rather ineffectual law that failed to distinguish between safe and unsafe practices. The Act was repealed in 1962, but in the intervening years Māori lost much cultural knowledge. He also advocated for the Quackery Prevention Act 1908.

Dr James Malcolm Mason creating a photomicrograph image.
(Duncan, Miriam D, fl 1977: Photographs relating to life and work of Dr James Malcolm Mason. Ref: PAColl-0022-002. Alexander Turnbull Library, Wellington, New Zealand)

In 1913, after the death of a patient in St Helens Hospital, Auckland, the government appointed a Commission of Inquiry.[11] Mrs Laura Chamberlain gave birth on 11 August 1912, suffered a rupture of the perineum and died on 9 September 1912 from puerperal septicaemia. The Commission made wide-ranging recommendations for improved care.

'THE SKELETON IN THE CUPBOARD – ITS ONLY SAFE REFUGE. Judge Cooper: Hands off! This is the one haven where secrets are safe and sacred from your sacriligious investigations.' Following the death of a woman in 1912 the Government appointed a Commission of Inquiry into the administration of St Helens Hospital, Auckland. Justice Cooper ruled in the Supreme Court that the contents of privileged documents need not be divulged. (*Observer*, 29 March 1913)

Although doctors in New Zealand began adopting antiseptic principles at the turn of the century, when compared with other countries (as previously mentioned in Chapter 2), New Zealand had a high rate of maternal mortality in pregnancy and childbirth. The Board of Health established a committee to investigate the problem.[12]

The Maternal Mortality report, presented to Parliament in October 1921, confirmed that puerperal septicaemia was the principal cause of maternal deaths, and the committee regarded it as largely preventable through infection control. More controversially, it laid blame on other factors such as diminished resistance, the virulence of organisms (not proven), unsuitable housing, and instrumental deliveries (which angered the doctors). Because of the combative personalities of those involved in the Health Department (Dr Truby King, Dr Henry Jellett) and the Obstetrical and Gynaelogical Society (Dr Doris Gordon), reforms were protracted.[13]

Puerperal sepsis remained a concern, and the public was justifiably alarmed when there were three deaths and one non-fatal case of septicaemia between July and November 1923 in the upper-class Kelvin Private Maternity Hospital in Remuera, Auckland. The government appointed a commission to investigate these and other deaths in Auckland hospitals, and the report found that five of the six women investigated died of sepsis.[14] Kelvin Hospital closed in July 1924.

ଓ୫

As already mentioned in Chapter 2, improvements in hospital care, greater attention to sterility, better antenatal care and a significant reduction in the other causes of maternal mortality highlighted the problem of deaths from abortion. Most deaths were due to illegal interference by the woman herself or another, but not all, as in the case of Violet.

Violet's story[15]
Deceased 3 November 1930, aged 25 years

Violet Bernard was married for six years to Herbert, a fireman and engine driver for the New Zealand Government Railway Department. They had two daughters, aged five and two years, and lived in Te Kuiti.

On Saturday 1 November the family took the train from Te Kuiti to stay with an old friend of Violet's now living in Auckland. Violet was about three months pregnant and looking forward to the birth. The next day they went for a drive and Violet noticed a sign advertising a Nurse Lyon's private hospital. She wondered if it was the same Nurse Lyon she had known from Te Kuiti, and went in to see her. It was indeed the same woman, and she thought it would be a nice place to go for her confinement in April.

That evening she did not feel very well and the next morning she had a small haemorrhage and went by herself to see Nurse Lyon. While she was there the bleeding increased alarmingly and Dr Alexander was called urgently. He found her miscarrying and asked Nurse Lyon to get another doctor immediately so that he could operate. Finding another doctor proved more difficult than expected and Dr Alexander was so concerned he commenced giving her chloroform himself as well as operating. She collapsed under the anaesthetic before the second doctor arrived. Together they tried to resuscitate her but to no avail. Her husband was expecting her to meet up with him in town and when she did not turn up he eventually phoned Nurse Lyon. Her death was a complete shock to all.

The post-mortem found she was carrying twins, a boy and a girl. The placenta was septic and she had haemorrhaged from this site. Bacteriology confirmed a streptococcal infection. The doctors concluded this was a natural event and not due to any interference. The coroner found the cause of death was 'streptococcal septicaemia following an incomplete abortion and the patient died while under an anaesthetic during the performance of a necessary operation.'

Police questioned Mrs Lydia Lyon a few days after the death and she employed Mr Singer to act as her lawyer. She was a fully qualified registered midwife, English trained, with nursing experience in England, Australia and New Zealand. She had emigrated to New Zealand in 1926 and married a farmer. Now widowed, she had been operating her private hospital for 18 months. Her actions were exonerated.

ಌ

In the pre-antibiotic period more women died from sepsis than any other cause and sometimes it was overwhelming, as in the following story, representative of a large number of fatalities.

Maud's story[16]
Deceased 21 August 1904, aged 23 years

Mrs Maud Pople was married to Albert, a motor man with the Tramway Company, and they lived in Onehunga. Maud had a 13-month-old child and had not long recovered from a gastric ulcer. She regularly used a syringe and had recently bought a new one. A fortnight before her death Maud visited Dr Murphy at the Friendly Society Dispensary in Auckland city with abdominal pains. She then developed a vaginal discharge and on Wednesday 17 August returned to the dispensary, where she was examined first by Dr Brockway and then by Dr Murphy, who diagnosed inflammation of the womb. He cleansed the vagina with antiseptic and inserted a cotton-wool plug with string attached, later removed by Albert. At the inquest both doctors emphasised they had used up-to-date antiseptic techniques when examining Maud.

Feeling well enough on Thursday, Maud went out in the evening to a show, but on Friday she became very ill. On Saturday morning Albert went to the dispensary to see Dr Murphy and was very angry when he found the dispensary closed. He created a fuss and eventually saw Dr Murphy, who sent him home with some medicine. At the inquest Albert maintained he had communicated his concern about Maud's condition to the doctor, but Dr Murphy denied he was aware it was a matter of life and death. Because of the distance between the dispensary in town and Onehunga, where Maud and Albert lived, a house call was not offered.

By Saturday evening Maud was semi-comatose and Albert's concern was magnified. He called in the local doctor, who immediately arranged admission to Auckland Hospital, but she died there the following day. Because he had seen Maud only in extremis, the local doctor could not provide a death certificate, hence the coroner's inquest.

The doctors remarked on the rapid onset and progression of the severe infection. The post-mortem confirmed Maud's pregnancy, miscarriage and acute septicaemia. Illegal interference was suspected but there were no signs of injury to the uterus. The jury of six men found that Maud had 'died from blood poisoning but there was not sufficient evidence to show how it was contracted.'

Maud's story demonstrates how quickly a fulminating infection could take hold, and even if medical help had been more readily available, it is doubtful her life would have been saved. These desperate situations were familiar to doctors in the pre-antibiotic era and must have been devastating for the relatives.

CR

Another less common cause of sepsis was gas gangrene, already mentioned as the cause of death in the case of Ada Legge. Infection is caused by the bacterium *Clostriduim perfringens*, which produces toxins and gas in the tissues and was the cause of death in the following case.

Doris's story[17]
Deceased 30 July 1934, age not stated but described as young

Doris was married to Arthur Geange, on relief work at Upper Hutt. They had three children aged four years, two years and ten months. Doris, still breastfeeding the baby, did not wish to be pregnant again. They could barely make ends meet, and when Doris became ill she refused to see the doctor because they already owed him money.

Shortly before her death Arthur borrowed £10 from a neighbouring farmer. This may have been used to pay the abortionist, but despite police enquiries no details of the abortion were ever divulged.

At the inquest it transpired that about a fortnight before her death Arthur took Doris into Wellington in his lorry and left her at the Central Hotel, the point at which they would meet again in two hours. What Doris did in those two hours was never revealed. She later miscarried at home and Arthur cleaned up the mess before calling the doctor. However, when the doctor arrived Doris was already dead.

Dr Lynch, Wellington pathologist, conducted the post-mortem and described a greatly swollen body with dark bluish green staining of the trunk. When he incised the skin, bubbles of gas escaped. The abdominal cavity contained a large quantity of gas. The womb, when touched, crackled from the bubbles of gas imprisoned in its substance. The cavity of the womb was ragged, although not perforated, and in it lay a fragment of afterbirth. The examination revealed a severe septic infection with gas gangrene in all the tissues of the body. The blood in all the organs contained numerous bubbles of gas. Microscopic examination confirmed the presence of *Clostridium perfringens*. Dr Lynch concluded this was most likely the result of a criminal abortion. The coroner, acting alone, found 'death was due to gas gangrene septicaemia associated with abortion.'

CR

The next case was unfortunate to suffer the two greatest risks of unprotected sexual intercourse – an unplanned pregnancy and a sexually transmitted infection – at the same time.

Ada's story[18]
Deceased 14 February 1903, aged 21 years

Miss Ada Timms was admitted to Christchurch Hospital suffering from septicaemia. Her mother said that on the evening of 9 February, Ada had had a miscarriage and had been attended by a nurse and doctor. Hospital doctors curetted the uterus to empty it of decomposing fragments of placenta. Gonorrhoea was diagnosed. There was no sign of any interference. The verdict was 'that she died from septicaemia the result of a miscarriage, the deceased being afflicted with gonorrhoea at the time of her miscarriage.'

౦౩

Improvements in sanitation and housing saw a reduction in typhoid fever, but at the turn of the century this was still a common illness, and a septic abortion could be misdiagnosed as typhoid, as in the following case.

Isabella's story[19]
Deceased 17 March 1908, aged 23 years

Miss Isabella McLiver, by all accounts quiet and shy, was the oldest sibling of six brothers and one sister. Her mother ran a boarding house in Auckland for about 20 boarders and Isabella carried out domestic duties in the bedrooms and kitchen. Since the death of her father ten years before, she had been close to her mother and they slept in the same bed. She had no boyfriends and her mother and sister did not believe she had ever had a sexual relationship with any male.

One of the boarders had been in hospital in December 1907 with typhoid fever, and when Isabella became ill on 6 March the doctor admitted her to hospital with suspected typhoid. She was febrile, weak and suffering from diarrhoea. However, tests for typhoid were all negative. Several doctors interviewed her and she told them her periods had always been regular and denied ever being pregnant. However examination confirmed a pregnancy.

Over the 11 days she spent in hospital she became increasingly ill and died of septic peritonitis. At the post-mortem, doctors found signs of a miscarriage at about three months' gestation, which they considered must have been induced, possibly self-induced. In their opinion, reflecting the wisdom of the day, a natural miscarriage would not have caused such a severe infection. Isabella's mother was adamant about her daughter's virginity and one of the doctors thought it possible for a miscarriage to take place at three months without the mother being aware of it.

The police were disappointed doctors did not notify them of the suspicious illness until after death. They were unable to bring any evidence to the inquest to assist the jury in identifying who or what had caused the abortion. One of the detectives suspected that one of the boarders was responsible for the pregnancy, and that because of the shame of such an occurrence, Isabella had carried out a self-induced abortion, but there was no evidence to support this. The jury of six men returned a verdict that 'the cause of death was peritonitis following on a septic abortion and that there is no evidence to enable the jury to determine by whom such abortion was procured.'

ଔ

Apart from sepsis, other causes of abortion deaths were haemorrhage, air embolism and poisoning. Haemorrhage, either visible or concealed, required treatment in a hospital and could leave women weak and in poor health from anaemia; it often contributed to a fatal outcome, as in the following stories concerning Rosina and Florence.

Rosina's story[20]
Deceased 20 November 1914, aged 38 years

Mrs Rosina Healey had been widowed for four years. She had a daughter aged five years and for the past year they had lived together in a family hotel in Wellington owned by Rosina's father. Her married sister Lucy was also part of the family business. Rosina enjoyed good health and spirits until one morning she was unexpectedly found dead under her bed by her little daughter.

The post-mortem found a four- to five-month-old fetus within the uterus. The placenta had been detached by a large haemorrhage, and the doctor conducting the post-mortem was unable to shed any light on whether it was natural or induced. Although there was inflammation about the dilated opening to the cervix there was no definite evidence of interference.

Rather unconvincingly, one of the doctors said the death may even have been due to shock. Lucy, who denied any knowledge of her sister's pregnancy, told the coroner that only the day before, Rosina had been in a state of shock when her little daughter had been brushed, fortunately not seriously, in an accident with a car. The coroner, acting alone, avoided controversy about the cause of death and simply returned a verdict of 'death caused by shock due to concealed haemorrhage.'

Florence's story[21]
Deceased 25 January 1924, aged 24 years

Florence Baynes had been married to Harold, a farmer of Temuka, for three years. They had two children, a girl aged two years and a son aged 11 months. Florence had always enjoyed good health. About a fortnight before her death she visited Dr Hogg, being about three months overdue for her period and worried that she might be pregnant. He examined her and confirmed her suspicions.

On 23 January she became unwell. She told Harold she had fallen against the verandah post and hurt herself and went to bed about 8 pm. She did not want him to call the doctor but on 25 January when she collapsed he sent for Dr Hogg at about 2.30 am. The doctor arrived about 3 am and found her in a very weak state, evidently suffering from the effects of blood loss. He examined her and found signs of a recent miscarriage. She was too weak at the time to be moved so Dr Hogg remained with her until 7 am. He returned again about 10.30 am and found her a little stronger but still too weak to travel to the hospital. He arranged for her admission to Timaru Hospital about 1 pm that day. He asked her about her miscarriage and she repeated the story about falling against the verandah, but he suspected she had done something to herself. After a good deal of persuasion Florence admitted that she had interfered with herself.

Dr Parr, Medical Superintendent of Timaru Hospital, stated at the inquest that he had examined Florence after her admission on 25 January. She was in a state of severe shock with signs of general peritonitis and bleeding from the uterus. The bleeding was severe and life-threatening, so although she was not in a very fit state for surgery Dr Parr operated at about 4 pm. He found general peritonitis and a large septic uterus with two small perforations through its wall. He decided that the only possible chance of saving her was to remove the uterus, although it was doubtful whether she could stand the operation. An emergency hysterectomy was carried out, but she collapsed and died at about 4.30 pm before the abdominal wound was closed. In Dr Parr's opinion the perforation of the uterus must have occurred several days previously and must have been caused by some blunt instrument.

The coroner, acting alone, found that 'death was due to sepsis and general peritonitis caused by infection on perforation of the uterus. The perforation had evidently been caused by the deceased using some blunt instrument on herself for the purpose of procuring a miscarriage.'

ଔ

Air embolism was usually fatal. When a syringe or catheter is used and the placenta is dislodged, venous spaces are opened up and air can enter the circulatory system, or air can be forced in by pressure on the syringe. It can then travel to the vital organs, the heart, lungs or brain. If there is a large amount of air, death is usually rapid due to cardio-pulmonary collapse, as in the stories of Adeline and Eileen.

Adeline's story[22]
Deceased 17 March 1935, aged 22 years

Miss Adeline Bradley enjoyed good health, but died suddenly at 266 Worcester Street, Christchurch, where she rented a room. At the coroner's inquest her mother, Jemima Finlay, said Adeline was her daughter from a former marriage but she knew nothing of the pregnancy. She knew Adeline had been keeping company with Joseph Clarkson for over a year. Clarkson, 34, was a draper's assistant in a big city department store, a position he had held for many years. He was married with an eight-year-old son, but had a court separation order and was seeking a divorce.

At the inquest, Mrs Magee, another occupant of the residence in Worcester Street, said Clarkson knocked on her door at 8.30 pm saying Adeline was ill. Clarkson then telephoned for Dr Orchard at 8.40 pm and the doctor came as soon as he could. When he arrived he found Adeline lying deeply unconscious on the bed. Her skin was a pale bluish colour. He applied restoratives (adrenaline and coramine) but she died at 9.12 pm. Clarkson admitted helping Adeline to use a syringe. The police searched Adeline's room and found several bottles containing medicines.

A post-mortem by the pathologist, Dr Pearson, revealed Adeline was pregnant and had died of an air embolism, the first such case he had encountered. The coroner returned a verdict that 'death was due to heart failure due to air embolism. This condition was brought about by the use of a syringe which had been inserted into the womb by one Joseph Frederick David Clarkson with the consent and assistance of the said Adeline May Bradley.' As a result of the evidence, police arrested Clarkson and charged him with manslaughter.

Trial of Joseph Clarkson, 1935

At the Magistrate's Court hearing Clarkson pleaded not guilty and was committed for trial. On 14 May, in the Christchurch Supreme Court presided over by Justice Johnston, Clarkson was described as a well-known citizen of good repute. The defence argued that the act was carried out by Adeline, who had some nursing experience. The jury retired at 3.15 pm and returned at 5.30 pm with a verdict of guilty and a strong recommendation for mercy. The sentence, deferred for four days, was two years' imprisonment with hard labour. The judge said the sentence would have been longer, but Clarkson had assisted with rather than been fully responsible for the abortion. So much for the recommendation for mercy.

Eileen's story[23]
Deceased 25 August 1936, aged 24 years

Eileen Watts, a tailoress, worked for a dressmaker in Palmerston North. During the week she boarded in Palmerston North and most weekends she travelled to her parents' home in Levin. Her father was the proprietor of a rural service bus and she often went with him. For the past three years she had been keeping company with Andrew Keen, 19, painter, of Palmerston North. They had gone on a tour together in a car at Easter time.

In June, Eileen found out she was pregnant. She confided in a woman friend, Imilda, whom she had known for about 12 years. Eileen told Imilda about Andrew Keen and the tour, and when she visited Imilda on 28 June she said she was very worried she was pregnant. She said she was trying to get rid of it and Andrew had supplied her with lots of pills, in bottles labelled 'Female Pills', but they did not work. Imilda saw the bottles and remembered a list of ingredients printed on the bottle but she did not remember what the ingredients were.

Eileen also spoke of having used some 'weed' (perhaps seaweed, used for dilating the cervix to induce miscarriage) but did not say how it was used. She said Andrew was expecting a visiting traveller and he hoped to get something from him to bring about an abortion. Andrew had also told Eileen about some woman in Wanganui, but Imilda did not know the woman's name or her address.

About a fortnight after this visit Imilda received a letter from Eileen to say Andrew had got her some crystals to be dissolved in water and used with a syringe. In a later letter she said she had used three lots of crystals and had three more lots left. She also said they awaited a reply from Wanganui in regard to what might be done there. The woman in Wanganui wanted £10 to carry out an 'operation'.

On Friday 21 August, Eileen arrived in Wanganui and went to the home of Mrs Elizabeth Clark in Liverpool Street. Mrs Clark lived with her husband, her daughter and her son-in-law, and took in boarders. Eileen introduced herself as 'Miss Margery Watson' from Palmerston North and requested board for about a week. She usually had her breakfast in bed but would get up and go out later on.

On Tuesday 25 August she was in good health and had a full lunch at Mrs Clark's. After lunch, at about 1.45 pm, Eileen went to the bathroom. On the bathroom wall hung two Higginson syringes, one used by Mrs Clark and one used by her daughter. Eileen took and used the one belonging to Mrs Clark. She came staggering out of the bathroom, frothing at the mouth. Mrs Clark thought she was having a fit. Dr Hutchison was called and he arrived within 15–20 minutes, but by that time Eileen was already dead.

The police were notified and enquiries were conducted. Among Eileen's belongings in Wanganui they found only Beecham's Pills. In Palmerston North they found a vaginal syringe and three packets of douching crystals. In her handbag was a letter about some powder, signed by A. S. Nalder, traveller, and addressed to Mr A. Keen.

Dr Hutchison and Dr Robertson conducted the post-mortem. A fetus of about four months' gestation lay within the uterus. The right side of Eileen's heart and pulmonary veins contained dark frothy blood. Specimens were forwarded to Dr Lynch, pathologist at Wellington, for confirmation of the findings. The cause of death was asphyxia following an air embolus travelling from the uterine veins to the lungs and heart, such air embolism having been caused by the use of the Higginson syringe. The coroner's report was in accordance with the medical evidence. At the inquest Andrew Keen denied everything.

ଔ

Alma's story[24]
Deceased 15 February 1935, aged 21 years

Alma Telfer was happily married to Archibald, 27, a farmer held in high esteem throughout the district of Te Awamutu. They already had a young family and when Alma became pregnant again she wanted to try a recipe of quinine in brandy that someone had given them. Archie purchased the ingredients, a bottle of brandy from the local barman and an ounce of quinine powder from a pharmacy in Te Awamutu. Quinine was not a classified poison under the Poisons Act.

Alma took half an ounce of quinine in brandy around midnight when they were retiring to bed. They chatted for about half an hour and then she became delirious. Dr Quin was called in but he could do little. She was taken with all speed to a private nursing home, but within three hours of taking the drug she died from quinine poisoning.

The dosage she had taken was well above the recommended safe dose. A medicinal dose would normally be from one to ten grains, or in the case of malaria up to 15 grains. In an ounce there are 437 grains, so Alma took a massive overdose, more than 200 grains. It was a tragic mistake. Analysis of the organs removed at post-mortem confirmed she had died of quinine poisoning.

Police charged Archie with the manslaughter of his young wife and after the Magistrate's Court hearing on 10 May he was committed for trial in the Hamilton Supreme Court on 30 May, presided over by Justice Reed. The jury, after a short retirement, compassionately returned a verdict of not guilty.[25] He was more fortunate than Joseph Clarkson.

ଔ

Shock, collapse or heart failure was sometimes the only explanation by doctors for a sudden death, as in the stories of Ellen and Gwen. Such explanations would be more critically appraised today.

Ellen's story[26]
Deceased 1 March 1926, aged 29 years

Mrs Ellen McGlinchy was married to John, a Christchurch City Council labourer, and they had one living child and one deceased. Ellen had had a very bad time with both deliveries and was fearful of another pregnancy. She attended her GP on 18 January 1926, complaining of being run down, and mentioned that she thought she was pregnant. He prescribed a general tonic.

About a month before her death John caught her taking some pills from a box labelled Ergoapiol. She took the entire box. She told John that about 20 February she had used a crochet needle on herself in order to bring on a miscarriage.

Ellen worked part-time at different places prior to her death, most recently, for the past six weeks, in Mrs Godfrey's tea-rooms. Ellen went to work as usual on Sunday 28 February but the following morning, Monday 1 March, John arranged for child care with an aunt and left Ellen at home in bed while he went to work. That evening she was pale but said she would go to Mrs Godfrey for tea and let her know she would be at work the next day.

After being at Mrs Godfrey's for about five minutes she complained of feeling unwell and lay down on a bed. She took her coat and hat off but left her other clothes on. Mrs Godfrey went on preparing tea and about two minutes later heard Ellen give two moans. About three minutes later Mrs Godfrey called out and asked if she was all right. There being no answer, she went in to her and shook her, but there was no response. Ellen was blue in the face. Mrs Godfrey called her husband and they tried to give her some brandy and water. Dr Louisson was summoned but Ellen was already dead by the time he arrived. When police removed the body a quantity of blood was discovered on the bedding where Ellen had been lying.

Dr Pearson, Christchurch Public Hospital pathologist, conducted the post-mortem. Ellen was approximately three and a half months pregnant and the gestational sac was unruptured. There was a haemorrhage with clots in the lower part of the uterus, with slight separation of the lower part of the placenta, and this appeared to be the site of the haemorrhage. However, the body was not bloodless.

In view of the patient's history, Dr Pearson was of the opinion that Ellen died of syncope – acute heart shock associated with various stimulants such as fear and terror following sudden haemorrhage from the womb. Because he was uncertain of the cause of death he retained portions of the organs for chemical analysis. No poison was found.

In answer to the coroner Dr Pearson stated that he thought the use of a crochet needle of the sort presented at the inquest could not have caused the abortion, and there was no evidence of injury to the vagina, cervix or uterus. Ergoapiol pills were frequently used in attempts to procure abortion and, in Dr Pearson's opinion, very large doses might attain that object, but they produce very few post-mortem signs. There was no evidence of air embolism.

The coroner, acting alone, found that 'the cause of death was syncope following sudden haemorrhage from the womb, the haemorrhage being due to an attempt by deceased to procure abortion.'

Gwen's story[27]
Deceased 25 February 1912, aged 35 years

When Miss Gwendoline Thompkins of Auckland suffered abdominal pains and vomiting she called in her GP, Dr Parkes. He first attended Gwen on 15 February and continued to visit her daily until she improved, then every other day. On Sunday morning 25 February he received an urgent call from Mr George Crichton, carpenter, at whose home Gwen was staying, to come immediately, but she died just moments before the doctor arrived. Because her death was wholly unexpected he could not provide a death certificate. She had recently given him her name as 'Mrs Crichton'.

At the inquest the following day, Dr McMaster, who conducted the post-mortem, said he could find nothing to explain her death. Painkillers were the only medicine Gwen admitted taking, but to exclude poisoning her stomach contents were sent for analysis. Tests were negative. In a search of her room detectives found eight bottles of medicine, one labelled 'Poison', containing tablets.

Although she was in early pregnancy, Dr McMaster found no evidence of interference. In his opinion, the most likely explanation for her sudden death was syncope and collapse due to intense pain. He described adhesions attached to the retroverted uterus; these may have caused severe pain as the uterus enlarged. The coroner's verdict read: 'the cause of her death was syncope resulting from intense pain' and 'Gwendoline Thompkins came to her death in a natural way.' *NZ Truth* was more suspicious and accused the coroner of handing out the grand old verdict of 'natural causes' to cover up an illegal abortion.

☙

In the early years of the 20th century, pregnancy was usually diagnosed by taking a menstrual history and examining for an enlarged uterus. No pregnancy tests were available. Women might recognise quickening (fetal movements) at about 18 weeks' gestation. Absence of periods did not always indicate pregnancy, as in the following story.

Rosie's story[28]
Deceased 5 October 1922, aged 23 years

Rosie Frew's parents were dead and she lived with her half-brother and sister at Riverton, Southland. Another half-brother, Herbert Boniface, who was an assistant manager in Willis Street, Wellington, had recently visited Riverton and Rosie had returned with him to Wellington on 24 September, staying with Herbert and his wife Myrtle for a month's holiday. When she arrived in Wellington she was in her usual state of health and remained so until Tuesday 3 October, two days before her death.

Soon after arriving in Wellington, Rosie had visited Mrs Nellie Natea, an old school friend from Riverton. A day or two later Rosie called to see Nellie again. She said she had 'gone and done it again'. Nellie knew that she had had a baby before and understood her to mean that she was pregnant again, not far gone. Rosie told Nellie that she had not had a period for two or three months. Her brother did not know and she did not wish him to know – she said that if he knew he would shoot her. She said she was taking pills. Rosie asked Nellie to buy her a syringe, which she did. The doctor in Riverton had once recommended she syringe twice a day for personal hygiene. At the coroner's inquest Rosie's sister-in-law, Myrtle, identified the enema syringe produced as an exhibit. She said it was left on the rail of Rosie's bed the day she was taken to hospital. Rosie had not concealed the fact that she used the syringe, three times a day for a week; she had said that it eased her pain. Rosie told Myrtle she had syringed before but not as frequently as this.

Rosie went to bed on Tuesday afternoon and at 4 am on Wednesday morning complained of pain. Herbert rang for Dr

Bowerbank at 5.30 am. The doctor arrived about 10 am and after an examination admitted her to Wellington Hospital.

Dr Harris, the house surgeon who admitted her, recognised the symptoms and signs of peritonitis. An operation was performed at 4.30 pm that afternoon. The surgeon found the abdomen full of altered blood and there was a large perforation in the fundus of the uterus. The uterus was removed. She gradually became weaker and died the next morning at 3.50 am. Before she died she told Dr Harris she did not do it herself, but she refused to tell him who did. When questioned by the police, who visited the hospital at about 10 pm on 4 October, Rosie refused to answer any questions. She said, 'If I die I'll take it with me.'

At the post-mortem there were signs of acute general septicaemia. The uterus removed during the operation was now in a sealed jar. There was a large perforation of the fundus. Cultures from the heart, pericardial fluid and abdominal fluid showed streptococci and staphylococci. There were no signs of pregnancy macroscopically or microscopically. In the opinion of the doctors, it would be possible but very difficult for the wound to be self-inflicted, and the syringe produced as evidence could not have caused the perforation unless the uterine wall had been softened by some previous disturbance, either mechanical or due to disease. The wound was an unusually large one, although the size of the wound would not necessarily indicate the size of the instrument that had been pushed through.

The coroner, acting alone, found the cause of her death 'was cardiac failure following acute septicaemia caused by a septic perforation of the uterus, but there was no evidence to show whether this perforation was done by herself or by someone else.'

The stigma and shame associated with her previous pregnancy and the mistaken fear that her delayed period was due to pregnancy precipitated the desperate remedies she used. It is not unusual for travel and changed circumstances to cause amenorrhoea (absence of periods).

ଔ

The 1920s saw the dawn of the antibiotic era, which would revolutionise the medical treatment of infections in the 1930s. One morning in September 1928, **Professor Alexander Fleming** (1881–1955) was tidying up his cluttered laboratory, sorting through a number of glass plates that had previously been coated with staphylococcus bacteria as part of his research in a London hospital.[29] One of the plates had mould on it. The mould was in the shape of a ring and the area around the ring was free of staphylococcus. The mould was *Penicillium notatum*. Fleming concluded that the bacteria in the ring had been killed off by some substance that had come from the mould, and he named the substance penicillin. However, it was difficult to produce enough penicillin for practical use, and the true potential of this discovery was not realised until the early 1940s. Eventually large-scale fermentation processes were developed in the USA for the production of penicillin, and it was first used in World War II.

In the meantime, research in another area was progressing in Germany. The Bayer team believed coal-tar dyes, which can bind preferentially to bacteria and parasites, might be used to attack harmful organisms in the body. After years of fruitless trial and error, and work on hundreds of dyes, a team led by physician/researcher **Gerhard Domagk** (1895–1964) finally found one that worked – a synthetic red dye that had a remarkable effect in stopping some bacterial infections in mice. Domagk received the Nobel Prize in 1939.[30]

Sulfonamides or sulfa drugs, as these new drugs were called, were the first antibiotics to be used systemically. Prontosil, the first medicine to effectively treat a range of bacterial infections, was patented in 1932 and the results of clinical trials were published in 1935. The drug protected against infections caused by streptococci, including blood infections, puerperal fever and erysipelas, but had a lesser effect on infections caused by other bacteria.

Further research showed that in the body Prontosil was metabolised into a smaller, colourless, active compound called sulfanilamide. This compound was first synthesised in 1906 and was widely used in the dye-making industry; its patent had since expired and the drug was therefore available to anyone. This research resulted in a sulfa craze. For several years in the late 1930s, hundreds of manufacturers produced myriad forms of sulfa, aiming for improved products with greater effectiveness and less toxicity. As the first and only effective antibiotics available in the years before penicillin, sulfa drugs continued to be used through the early years of World War II and are credited with saving the lives of tens of thousands of patients.

In June 1936 *The Lancet* reported exciting news regarding the successful treatment of puerperal fever patients in Queen Charlotte's Hospital, London, and subsequent papers confirmed the arrival of a remarkable breakthrough in the treatment of streptococcal infections. Cases of pneumonia and bacterial meningitis also responded to sulfanilamides. The era of antibiotics had arrived; newspapers spread the news and before long, hospitals in New Zealand were using these new drugs.[31]

Although the sulphonamide group of drugs changed the scene dramatically with regard to deaths from septic abortion, they were not always effective and fatalities still occurred. The following patient may well have received one of the sulphonamide drugs during her admission to hospital, but although she lingered in hospital for a month, the infection did not respond.

Gwen's story[32]
Deceased 15 May 1937, aged 22 years

Gwendoline Meale was brought up in Northern Wairoa but for the 12 months prior to her death she lived in Auckland, where her parents had shifted. Gwen worked as a cashier at the Farmers Trading Company, Hobson Street. She was very friendly with Wilfred (Fred) Blanchfield, a garage attendant at Drive Yourself Ltd in Lower Albert Street, who had known her from her earlier days in Wairoa. He was married but separated from his wife and they had no children.

Gwen and Fred had a sexual relationship and Gwen informed her lover she was pregnant sometime in February. Fred denied any knowledge of where or how she had an abortion but he knew when it was because Gwen had phoned him on 3 April to say she had had the operation to be 'fixed up'. She gave her lover the phone number of the house in which she was staying as 27-559. Fred did not visit the house but phoned several times to enquire how Gwen was and spoke to the woman of the house.

On 5 April Gwen sent a telephone message to say she would not be at work on account of illness. She returned home but left again on Saturday 10 April, telling her parents (untruthfully) she was going to Waiheke Island for the weekend to see her grandfather. She returned home on Monday 12 April but did not go to work as she was not feeling well. She did not tell her parents what she had done over the weekend.

On 13 April Dr Horton was called in to see her. She told him she had been about four months pregnant and was still bleeding from the vagina following a miscarriage eight days before. He returned the following morning with another doctor to administer an anaesthetic, while he curetted the womb of the retained placenta. This was followed by a douching of the uterus. He continued to pay several home visits over the next three days. On 16 April Dr Horton washed out the womb again. On 17 April Gwen appeared very ill with septicaemia and he admitted her to hospital. She told the house surgeon who admitted her she had used a rubber instrument on herself, but this was not consistent with other evidence. She remained in hospital until her death one month later on 15 May.

The post-mortem showed no injury to the uterus but there was pus in the pelvic cavity and adhesions among the pelvic organs and intestines. Toxic changes affected the liver, spleen and kidneys. Death was due to complications from a septic abortion.

The inquest was held on 17 May and reconvened on 28 May and on 14 and 16 July 1937. The police traced the occupants of the house through the phone number and interviewed a couple on 15 May. Mrs Yvonne Helen Mackie, 32, lived at 2 England Street with her husband, Leslie Ward Mackie, 40, who was a qualified chemist but was no longer practising or registered as a chemist. The couple refused to answer any questions at the inquest for fear of incriminating themselves, but it was intimated that he was a professional abortionist and sent young women to his home to be cared for by his wife while recovering from their operations. No incriminating evidence was found in a search of the house, and no prosecution ensued. However, 20 years later, in 1957, Mackie and his wife were both imprisoned for a year for another abortion offence, then in 1962 Mackie and his nurse were both charged with yet another abortion offence. On this occasion Mackie went to prison for three years and his nurse was fined and put on probation for three years.

෴

Even in the best possible circumstances of a planned therapeutic abortion carried out in a public hospital, the risk of death could not be eliminated.

Jean's story[33]
Deceased 21 December 1938, aged 42 years

Jean Holdsworth was married to Bernard, a sheep farmer residing at Waikohu, near Gisborne. They had three children aged nine, ten and eleven years. For a number of years Jean had not enjoyed good health and over the past ten years Dr Singer of Gisborne had treated her for high blood pressure. When she consulted him in October about her hay fever he discovered she was pregnant. He said if she continued the pregnancy her life and that of the child would be in danger. There was a risk she would not be able to carry the child to term, and the added strain of the pregnancy would imperil her life and would at least cause permanent injury to her own health. In his opinion, the pregnancy should be terminated. He discussed this with both Jean and Bernard. At first they did not like the idea of an operation but after some time they consented.

On 21 November Dr Singer discussed the case with his colleague Dr Brown, who agreed with the decision to carry out a therapeutic termination. Early in December Dr Singer admitted Jean to Rostrevor Hospital where he performed the termination. After the operation Jean appeared to recover quite well, then on about 10 December she developed a septic infection and doctors thought it necessary to empty the uterus.

Dr Singer carried out a second operation on 12 December but was then called away from Gisborne, leaving Dr Kahlenberg in charge. Because of Jean's deteriorating condition he called a case conference on 18 December with three other doctors. They agreed on the correct treatment (which almost certainly would have included one of the new sulfa drugs) but this was of no avail and Jean died of septicaemia. Bernard was satisfied everything was done for Jean and both operations had been performed in the best interests of her health. The coroner, acting alone, found 'death was due to septicaemia following an operation.'

༶

Another patient lingered in hospital for a month of treatment, but her infection was also fatal.

Eileen's story[34]
Deceased 27 April 1939, aged 35 years

Miss Eileen Fergus worked in hotels, usually as a housemaid. At the time of her death she was working at the Criterion Hotel in Wanganui and shared a room with another employee in a flat opposite the hotel. For the past year she had been keeping company with James Urquart Hay, 39, a single man employed by the Public Works Department at Fordell, near Wanganui. They were engaged to be married in April at an Easter wedding. About the end of January or the beginning of February Eileen told Jim about her pregnancy. He told her not to worry as it would make no difference to him.

When Jim visited Eileen after work on Wednesday 22 March he found her in bed. The following evening she was worse and suffering pain. He called Dr Cook to come and see her and he admitted her to Wanganui Hospital on 23 March. She was suffering from an incomplete abortion, and a day or two later, signs of general septicaemia appeared. The local condition cleared up with surgical treatment but a septic infection of the valves of the heart (ulcerative endocarditis), supervened. This was a direct sequel to the infection associated with the miscarriage. In 1939 the condition was almost invariably fatal and despite treatment she died on 27 April, one month after admission.

When questioned about her miscarriage she said she had taken about a dozen Apiol pills, obtained from a young woman in Wellington. This brought on her miscarriage, which she passed in the toilet of her flat on the evening of Wednesday 22 March. She denied having any illegal interference other than the pills and she impressed as being truthful in this respect.

A post-mortem showed active ulceration of the mitral valve with masses of septic clot formation. The kidneys and spleen also showed toxic changes. The coroner, acting alone, found in accordance with the medical evidence that 'the cause of death was ulcerative endocarditis following septic abortion.' The police were unable to obtain any significant information.

○3

It would be some years before the fear of sepsis was removed from women's lives.

4. CONTRACEPTION: MAINLY BARRIERS

Access to Information on Contraception

In a word, the McMillan Report was negative regarding contraception. It states:

> Evidence was given by responsible and representative women in support of a mother's right to say when she will bear children, and, although we agree that this privilege might well be conceded her, we are of the opinion that it is not the function of the State to undertake the dissemination of the knowledge and give the practical instruction necessary to enable the general adoption of this principle.

The committee made no mention of the different methods of contraception available to couples, with the exception of female sterilisation. However, the committee noted the widespread ignorance of effective methods of contraception as one of the important underlying causes of abortion. In excluding contraceptive information from the report, the committee missed an opportunity to correct misinformation.

In fairness, the committee may also have felt constrained by the Indecent Publications Act 1910, which made it an offence to sell, deliver, print, insert in a newspaper, send through the post, exhibit, leave on the premises of another, write, draw, affix or impress any indecent document. The Act did not define indecency but the police and magistrates had guidelines to determine whether material was indecent. In the guidelines, 'indecency' included references to any disease affecting the generative organs of either sex; any complaint or infirmity arising from or relating to sexual intercourse (i.e., venereal disease); the prevention or removal of irregularities in menstruation; or any drugs, medicines, appliances, treatments or methods for procuring abortion or miscarriage, or preventing conception. It was a defence, however, if the work was of 'literary, scientific, or artistic merit or importance', and if the act of the accused was not of 'an immoral or mischievous tendency'. The purpose, according to the Attorney-General, John Findlay, in 1910, was to protect the 'liberty which improves and ennobles a nation', while removing the 'license which degrades'. The committee could have relied on this defence if its members had been so inclined.

The Indecent Publications Act 1910 replaced the Offensive Publications Act 1892 and remained in force, with occasional amendments, until 1963. There was another complication. The Customs Act 1913 made it an offence to import documents within the meaning of the Indecent Publications Act 1910. This created, in effect, a dual system of censorship, with customs officers prohibiting items at the ports of entry and thereby acting as censors, and magistrates making decisions according to their views when cases came before the courts. Inconsistency prevailed, making decisions problematic for booksellers. A book might be imported, but it could still be the subject of a complaint.[1]

Whether or not a book was banned was the decision of the Comptroller of Customs, under the Minister of Customs, who had the authority to appoint an advisory committee to assist in decisions. Booksellers published lists of available books.

In 1924 the following advertisement appeared in *NZ Truth*:[2]

BOOKS BY POST FROM AITKEN'S BOOK ARCADE

> Sex knowledge judiciously imparted is the greatest insurance toward the development of sterling manhood and womanhood. It is the duty of every man and woman to be informed upon the subject of sex and the care of the body. It is a subject vitally important to every individual.
>
> 'Married Love' (complete cloth bound edition), by Marie Stopes. Price 9/6 post free.
> 'Mother, How Was I Born?' by Marie Stopes. 1/6 post free.
> 'Radiant Motherhood,' by Marie Stopes. 9/6 post free.
> 'Early Days of Birth Control,' Marie Stopes. 1/6 post free.
> 'Truth About Venereal Disease,' by Marie Stopes. 3/6 post free. . . .

Censors in New Zealand were liberal enough to allow Dr Marie Stopes's 1918 book, *Married Love,* to be imported, although it was banned in America and Australia.[3] Dr Truby King was strongly opposed to contraception, and in the years 1921–1927, when he was Director of Child Welfare, he strictly enforced a ban on publications with information on contraception.

In 1922 New Zealander Ettie Rout's book, *Safe Marriage*, was prohibited.[4] *The Press* in Christchurch responded with a blistering editorial:[5]

> During the discussion in the House at the end of last month on the estimates of the Internal Affairs Department, it was said that certain books which circulated freely among intelligent people in other countries were banned by the censor in New Zealand. A case of this kind has just occurred, a brief telegram from Wellington in yesterday's paper stating that Miss Ettie Rout's book, 'Safe Marriage' has been banned by the Customs Department, under the provisions of the Customs Act, 1913. That Act forbids the importation of all indecent documents within the meaning of the Indecent Publications Act 1910, which in turn provided that any document or matter referring to the subject dealt with in Miss Rout's book shall be deemed to be indecent. In the present instance, the banned book deals quite plainly and candidly with certain measures for preventing venereal disease and the use of contraceptives, and it has a strongly laudatory preface by Sir Arbuthnot Lane, consulting physician at Guy's Hospital and a man of international reputation. Such a book would, no doubt, offend the religious and moral scruples of many people, who would disapprove strongly of its teachings. Many others, again, equally reputable people, would praise the author for having the courage to deal so frankly with a matter of profound social importance. We need not discuss the question whether such a book can properly be condemned as indecent, but since the Customs authorities so regard it, we are entitled to ask how it is that books dealing with the same subject with equal frankness have been on sale in probably every bookseller's shop in the Dominion for years past, without any barrier to their importation being raised by the Customs Department or any objection to their open sale being made by the police. The truth is that the treatment accorded to this book is a typical instance of the very unsatisfactory nature of the censorship practised in New Zealand. The authority given

to the Customs Department by the Act enables it on the dictum of some unknown official to decide that any book dealing with certain subjects is indecent and therefore empowers the Department to prevent its importation into the Dominion. In the eyes of the law a book is not deemed to be indecent unless a Magistrate decides that it is so. In the present instance a book has been banned by the Customs after a certain number of copies have passed into the hands of the importers. If the police chose to take action, the latter might or might not be convicted; it would all depend upon the view of the Magistrate before whom the case was heard. But if every Magistrate in the country held that it was not an indecent publication and dismissed the case, the Customs authorities would still, apparently, have the power to prevent its being imported. Such a system, which places some obscure official above the law, is utterly preposterous, and is full warrant for the dislike felt by most people for the censorship, which, as we have shown, is not only wrong-headed but inconsistent, straining at a gnat and swallowing a camel. The only course for the Government to adopt, consistent with that individual liberty to which all have a right, is to sweep away the censorship and leave the law to deal with those whom it finds guilty of purveying indecent literature of any kind. For these the punishment can be so severe as to make a repetition of the offence most improbable.

A new Board of Appeal was proposed and had the support of booksellers. News of the ban reached England, and two eminent doctors, Sir Archdall Reid and Sir Bryan Donkin, both cabled support for release of Ettie Rout's book.[6] Booksellers began selling it at their own risk, arguing they had to stock such books for serious students and nurses.

Ettie Rout weighed in as well and was supported by the editor of the *Maoriland Worker*.[7] The author received a letter from the Comptroller of Customs asking her for a return address for the 45 copies of her book *Safe Marriage*. She cheekily replied:

> I have received letters from different members of the New Zealand Parliament, saying they are raising the matter in the House, but they wish to see the book itself before they can decide wisely and equitably what course to take. I am sure you will admit the reasonableness of this. Will you kindly, therefore send the parcel of 45 copies of *Safe Marriage* to the Hon the Speaker, New Zealand

Parliament, Wellington, New Zealand, for presentation to Parliament, for the use of the members of the Opposition (Labour and Liberal) first, and afterwards for the use of members of the Government and their supporters.

The editor presumed the request would not be granted and concluded 'We must root out this censorship, because if we allow it to say that we must not read this book or that, it is the end of all freedom to inform our minds about matters that seriously interest us.'

In 1924 Stopes's *Married Love* was temporarily banned. In 1929, police charged bookseller Norman Brown with selling another of Marie Stopes's books, *Enduring Passion*.[8] In the Wellington Magistrate's Court, supporting the police case, Dr T. Valintine, Director-General of Health, described the work as 'a perfectly beastly book'. Dr M. Watt, Assistant Director-General of Health, also condemned the book, saying it was of no scientific value and written in a crude way. In a reserved decision the magistrate, Mr E. Page, S.M., dismissed the case, saying the selling of the book to a detective of mature years was not an offence.

Contraceptive advertisements were assailed on all fronts, coming under the purview, not only of the Indecent Publications Act 1910 but also the Post Office Act 1883, amended in 1900 and 1906, and the Quackery Prevention Act 1908. Editors of newspapers could be accused of double standards, for carrying the harrowing account of an abortion tragedy alongside paid advertisements for abortifacients, as in the following story.

Mary's story[9]
Deceased 7 February 1904, aged 37 years

Mrs Mary Cook lived in Dunedin with a family of six children ranging in age from 18 months to 14 years. There was a gap of seven years between the two youngest children. Husband Robert, a confectioner, was away in Auckland for three weeks, and while he was away, about a fortnight before Mary's death, an elderly nurse came to stay. She used different names, being variously known as Mrs Johnston or Mrs Henderson, although her real name was Mrs Waddell. She stayed in the house, sleeping in the same bedroom as Mary. On the morning of Thursday 4 February Mary's daughter saw Mrs Waddell come into the washhouse carrying bloodstained clothing – two sheets, a blanket and a nightgown. Mrs Waddell left that day and did not return. During her stay she sometimes brought liquor into the house and at times was under its influence. Mary was not in the habit of taking drink and only did so to oblige Mrs Waddell.

During Mrs Waddell's stay, several visitors, friends and neighbours called and not all were made welcome. Mrs Smith, one of Mary's friends, thought Mary should see a doctor, but Mary refused. She told her friend she was going to have a miscarriage and she would be all right as Mrs Waddell was looking after her. However, on Friday 5 February, when left alone, she called for her friends. They could see how weak she was and immediately sent for Dr Evans. She told the doctor she had had a miscarriage carried out by herself. He ordered an ambulance to transfer her to Dunedin Hospital and Mrs Smith accompanied her.

When admitted to hospital she was semi-delirious and suffering from septicaemia. She gradually deteriorated and died on Sunday evening. She told the hospital doctors the same story, that she alone was responsible for the miscarriage, but the post-mortem revealed an internal wound to the uterus that was unlikely to have been self-inflicted.

Because of the suspicious circumstances, the police and the coroner were notified, and an inquest was held before six male jurors. Evidence at the inquest revealed that Mary had talked to other women about her experiences with self-abortion. She had used medicines and had operated on herself more than once in the seven-year gap between her last two children. She had seen Dr Macdonald in January when he confirmed the pregnancy. She had asked him for assistance, saying she had as many children as she could support, but he said he could not help her.

Mrs Waddell refused to answer any questions at the inquest, as was her right. When interviewed by the police she denied everything. In his summing up, the coroner said the evidence of the medical men indicated it was possible but very improbable that Mary had performed the operation herself. If she had induced another person to perform the operation, it was most probable she would be bound over by promises not to reveal the name of that person. He said if Mrs Waddell had given evidence it would most probably have been a blank denial.

After a short retirement the jury returned with the verdict that 'death was caused by blood poisoning, the result of an illegal operation, but by whom the operation was performed there was not sufficient evidence to show.' No further action was taken by the police.

The account of Mary's inquest in the *Otago Daily Times* of 15 February 1904 was incongruously placed next to a prominent advertisement for one Dr Elmslie, with the heading 'A Friend In Need'. Part of the advertisement reads:

> Ladies may consult Dr Elmslie at his Residence, No 13 Wellington Terrace, Wellington from 10 to 12, 2 to 4, 7 to 9 daily, who is a legally qualified Physician and Specialist, and whose up-to-date Treatment gives the greatest satisfaction. Strictly confidential. Call or write. Sole Agent for Famous Ladies' Corrective Tablets, 10s 6d (extra), 21s post free. Guaranteed safe and reliable. Moderate charges.

The Post Office Act empowered postmasters to detain and destroy posted packages of obscene or indecent publications, especially targeting advertisements for the treatment of diseases of the sexual organs. However, the public continued to place faith in folk medicine and traditional and alternative therapies, and politicians were not convinced of the desirability of total domination of the medical market by doctors.

MP John Hornsby introduced a Quackery and Other Frauds Prevention Bill in 1906, which aimed to put much-needed controls on the sale of patent medicines and health appliances that exploited the vulnerable, for example, the very common so-called cures for masturbation. During the parliamentary debate on this Bill, the emphasis shifted from extravagant or misleading advertising to the advertising and sale of contraceptives. Using an assumed name, Hornsby sent away for a sample of suspect literature from one of the 'abominable' advertisers:[10]

> The result of that was that I had sent to me a package of stuff from Melbourne, and I found that it consisted of diagrams principally, with a list of questions submitted to the person who was supposed to have been writing. The diagrams showed the human female body, cleft in twain and by alphabetical signs indicated certain portions of the human anatomy. One portion was the mouth of the womb, and on that there was a preventive. These things were being vended for the purpose of enticing women, more especially young women, to fly in the face of nature, and to destroy themselves body and soul.

A SUSPICIOUS DEATH

THE CORONER'S INQUEST

The inquest in connection with the circumstances surrounding the death of Mary Cook, a married woman, who died in the Hospital on February 7, was resumed at the Magistrate's Court on Saturday morning before Mr C. C. Graham, coroner.

Ethel Cook said she was the daughter of Mary Cook, the deceased. She remembered that about a fortnight ago someone came to stay at the house. The deceased was not then ill. This person called herself Mrs Johnston, and stayed at the house from Friday till the following Thursday, and part of the time deceased was ill in bed. Mrs Johnston told witness on the Wednesday that the deceased was going to give birth to twins. Deceased was then in bed. Witness never noticed Mrs Johnston doing anything to deceased, but she slept in the same room as deceased. On the morning of Thursday, February 4, Mrs Johnston came into the washhouse with blood-stained clothing —two sheets, a blanket, and a nightgown, all blood-stained. Witness examined the clothing. Mrs Johnston left that day, deceased remaining in bed, and Mrs Johnston did not again return to the house. Mrs Johnston had told witness her name was Mrs Waddell. Deceased remained in bed till she was taken to the Hospital on February 5. Witness recognised Mrs Waddell in court as the person she had known as Mrs Johnston.

To Mr Hanlon: Deceased had been ailing some considerable time; though not confined to her bed she was seriously ill. Mrs Waddell came to the house with deceased. Witness went out several times when Mrs Waddell was at the house, but did not go very far away. Witness went down town several evenings. Deceased was in the continual habit of taking medicine. There was a large number of medicine bottles in the house.

To Sub-inspector Green: A number of visitors came to the house, but none of them stopped any length of time while Mrs Waddell was there. Witness saw Mrs Waddell bring drink to the house, and she seemed at times to be under the influence of liquor. Deceased had never taken drink until it was given her by Mrs Waddell.

Mary Ellen Smith, wife of Robert George Smith, bootmaker, residing at Belleknowes, said she called on deceased on January 31, and deceased was then very ill, but not in bed. The nurse was with deceased. Witness was told the nurse's name was Johnston, but she (the nurse) said "No, Henderson." Witness

A FRIEND IN NEED.

DR ELMSLIE,

L.F. PHYS., ET SURG, GLASG., L.S.A., LOND., L.M., Etc.,

Registered by the Governments of Great Britain, New Zealand, and New South Wales,

No. 13 Wellington Terrace, WELLINGTON.

This Highly-qualified Physician and Surgeon from the Hospitals of London and Paris has, by 25 years of study and research, become an Expert and Specialist in CHRONIC, NERVOUS, BLOOD, SKIN, and SPECIAL DISEASES of Men and Women.

In his very successful treatment of the above class of difficult cases there is "No Experimenting and No Failures."

Consultations are Free to all, so that a friendly chat, either personally or by letter, costs nothing, and may save you years of misery, so none need despair. New Scientific Treatment and New Unfailing Remedies of the very best and purest are Honestly and Faithfully used. Moderate Charges.

Consultation Hours: 10 to 12, 2 to 4, 7 to 8.

YOUNG MEN! If you are suffering, or weak, or sad, call or write to Dr Elmslie, No. 13 Wellington terrace, Wellington, as he thoroughly understands your troubles and their causes. His Skilful Treatment and Scientific Remedies enable him to GUARANTEE a Complete Cure in every case undertaken, or he will make no charge. Strictly confidential. Moderate charges. Consulting Hours: 10 to 12, 2 to 4, 7 to 8.

LADIES may consult Dr Elmslie at his Residence, No. 13 Wellington terrace, Wellington, from 10 to 12, 2 to 4, 7 to 8 daily, who is a legally qualified Physician and Specialist, and whose up-to-date Treatment gives the greatest satisfaction. Strictly confidential. Call or write. Sole Agent for Famous Ladies' Corrective Tablets, 10s 6d (extra), 21s post free. Guaranteed safe and reliable. Moderate charges.

These two items were rather incongruously placed next to each other on page 7 of the *Otago Daily Times*, 15 February 1904.

During the debate, another member of Parliament, Anglican father-of-six James Allen (1855–1942), thought the problem of contraceptives was much more important than patent medicines,

> namely, the fact that there exists in this community, and in other communities, the habit – the horrible habit – of utilizing means, preventives and so on, which interfere even with nature itself. To find such growing here in a community like New Zealand is a startling fact, and one we ought to deal with promptly and effectively if we can, for there can be no healthy national life and growth unless we breed as we ought to breed – it is just as well to say so in plain English.

The Bill did not pass, and later, when Allen was Minister of Defence, he eventually approved the issue of free prophylactic kits to soldiers, as recommended by Ettie Rout.

Public health pioneer Dr James Mason was less repressive in his approach and supported the Quackery Prevention Act 1908. He told the parliamentary committee debating the Bill that it would be impossible to prevent the sale of contraceptives, but he nevertheless thought they should be prohibited to those who 'had not yet reached the age of discretion'. The Quackery Prevention Act did not single out contraceptives for special attention, as the majority of MPs considered this an unjustified interference with private lives.

Concern over the declining birth rate fuelled medical opposition to the use of contraceptives. In an article published in the *New Zealand Medical Journal* in 1905, Dr Herbert Barraclough condemned their use as unnatural, immoral and unpatriotic.

> We are confronted with a declining birth-rate in almost every civilised country in the world... There is undoubtedly an increasing number of women who shirk the cares of motherhood... I refer more especially to married women, who, for society reasons, or to shirk the domestic cares which the birth of children would bring upon them, deliberately use means to prevent conception. Apart from the disgusting nature of the practice, it seems to me to be in the highest degree immora... In some cases the matter is carried so far that even after conception has occurred abortion has been resorted to... When married women resort to practices of this kind, surely the ultimate abyss of moral degradation has been reached... I think it behoves the medical profession as a whole to rise up in condemnation of what is fast assuming the proportions of a national crime.

By 1922 the opinion of the medical profession had not changed. A *New Zealand Medical Journal* editorial said:[11]

> We have no words sufficient to express our contempt for people who are healthy and living in fairly good economic conditions who get married with the intention of having no children. The limitation of families among the poor has something to commend it, but it is hardly ever practised, and other classes of society, where there is no justification on medical grounds, it results from selfishness in its most revolting form on the part usually of the mother . . . We have read the arguments advanced by advocates of the general and extended use of contraceptives, and they do violence to everything that is sacred to the name of nature, morality, science and common-sense.

Ten years later, in 1932, another editorial used the words 'distasteful' and 'repulsive' to condemn contraception. However, a glimmer of hope is detected in the following statement: 'We hold it right that contraception should be practised by married people for just medical or even economic reasons.'[12] But Dr Doris Gordon and many others did not support socio-economic reasons for contraceptive use.

Not everyone agreed with this head-in-the-sand conservatism. In 1932, Dr Washbourn read a thought-provoking paper to the Nelson Clinical Society, which ended with the following assertion:[13]

> I personally believe in quality rather than quantity, and tell those who come to me for advice all that I know in regard to birth control, believing as I do that in that way lies safety for the future. A married couple have in almost everything else a freedom of choice, and to me it seems absurd that in one of the most important matters we should attempt to withhold from them that freedom of choice. Not only is it absurd but dangerous in the long run.

Widespread disapproval, plus the abundance of legislation, curtailed some of the worst excesses in advertising, but carefully worded advertisements, as inoffensive as possible but sufficiently creative so the public understood what was being purveyed, still reached a wide audience through newspapers and magazines. Suppliers were usually chemists but also patent medicine vendors, herbalists and other retailers.

Some examples from the turn of the century include:

1903 'A Ladies Department under the management of a Registered Lady Pharmacist, having been opened, Patrons may rely on having every care and attention. Williamson and Co, Chemists, Victoria Avenue, Wanganui.'[14]

1904 'Sponges! Sponges! We have an enormous assortment of bleached and unbleached Turkish sponges, a necessary adjunct to the toilet. Smith and Caughey, Ltd.'[15]

1909 'In All Ladies' Complaints consult Mrs Towler. All letters receive immediate attention. Strictly confidential. Advice Free. Stamped envelope for reply.'[16]

Bootmaker/abortionist Hyman Isaacs (*NZ Truth*, 17 March 1923) and one of Mrs Towler's advertisements (*Otago Daily Times*, 2 January 1915).

Mrs Towler ran a health business from 15 Royal Arcade, Dunedin. She advertised widely from 1898 to 1919 and provided a mail order service. The Arcade was known in Dunedin as the 'go to' place for advice on abortion. In the 1920s it contained a toiletry store run by Mrs Towler's daughter, Miss Edith Towler, who, like her mother, became a 'household name' in Dunedin. She was also an accomplice of the infamous abortionist Mrs Mary Jane Clark. Both women escaped conviction in 1923. In 1927 Mrs Clark was acquitted of the manslaughter of Jessie Smart. In

1929 a failed abortion found her again before the courts, but again she was acquitted. This is the same Mrs Clark who featured in connection with the case of Mora MacKenzie, whose death was one of the factors leading to the abortion inquiry of 1936. The Arcade also housed the premises of bootmaker/abortionist Mr Hyman Isaacs, who was acquitted after an abortion trial in 1923. He was rumoured to ask for sexual favours in return for abortion.[17]

Mail order chemists were very popular in the 1920s and 1930s:

1923 Hygienic Necessities For Women
      Omega Whirling Syringes . . . 30/– (Post Free)
      Eclipse Whirling Sprays . . . 21/–
      Douches, Enemas, etc, from 4/6 to 25/–
      Posted privately to any address in plain wrapper.
      Cox Gordon's Pharmacy, 70 Manners St., Wellington.[18]

1930 Mail Order Chemist. Write for Free Catalogue of Ladies and Gentlemen's Toilet and Rubber Goods, Every Description. All correspondence treated as strictly confidential, and parcels forwarded in plain sealed wrapper, post free. Mail Order Chemist P.O. Box 791, Christchurch.[19]

1935 Ralph's Reliable Remedies. (Ralph Sanft) Prompt Mail Order Chemist, Dept., S. 201 Symonds St., Auckland.[20]

1935 Free! Husbands And Wives Write for our Revised Free List of Hygienic Appliances and Chemist's Sundries; all orders promptly dispatched post free. The Dependable Mail Order Chemist. Mendel Spitz M.P.S., Dept. 5, 99 Richmond Road, Auckland W1.[21]

ଔ

In 1926 two men were prosecuted for distributing pamphlets on contraception.

Trial of Mr David Kennedy Pritchard, 1926[22]

Mr David Pritchard, an elderly gentleman, previously an auctioneer in Dunedin but now a market gardener of Lower Hutt, was sufficiently interested in public affairs to have at one time contested the Hutt electorate for Parliament. He carried on a sideline business, the Toilet Requisites Company, which operated out of P.O. Box 624. In the Wellington Magistrate's Court, police charged him with sending indecent matter through the post.

Obtaining names from the electoral roll, he had sent a pamphlet to married women, advertising prophylactics 'as recommended by Dr Marie Stopes'. Some women who received the circular were offended and complained to the police. Pritchard was not a chemist and merely purchased the goods from wholesale suppliers and sent them to customers. Defence counsel argued that attitudes to contraception had changed a great deal since the law was enacted, but the magistrate did not agree and fined Pritchard £10.

Trial of Mr James George Hanafin, 1926[23]

Following the prosecution and conviction of Pritchard for sending indecent matter through the post, Hanafin, a Christchurch chemist of Stanmore Road, was similarly charged. He had a large mail order business and advertised in newspapers for such items as whirling syringes, enemas and corrective pills, listed with their prices. He replied only to those requesting information. In November 1925 his P.O. Box was closed for a time while Post Office authorities investigated his mail order business.

His defence counsel argued that everything in Hanafin's catalogue was widely advertised and could be bought in any chemist shop; the authorities had not kept up with changed attitudes to contraception; and if the government really wanted to stop the sale of contraceptives they should ban their import. The Magistrate reserved his decision and, when delivering his judgment, said it appeared to him there had been a change in public and judicial opinion, especially since the war. He dismissed the case, which was a relief to legitimate businesses.

Birth Control Pioneers: Margaret Sanger, Marie Stopes and Ettie Rout

New Zealander Ettie Rout (1877–1936), mentioned in connection with the banning of her book *Safe Marriage*, was a contemporary of birth control pioneers Margaret Sanger (1879–1966) in the United States and Dr Marie Stopes (1880–1958) in England. All three women saw contraception as preferable to abortion, which at that time was a dangerous intervention. They were born within three years of each other and their careers intersected. All three knew each other and had mutual friends. At times they collaborated and supported each other, and at other times they disagreed fundamentally. All three were fiercely independent and passionate about improving the lives of women, but in their own ways.

Margaret Sanger[24] is the one who contributed most to 'birth control' over her long life; in fact it was she who first used that term. Born Margaret Higgins in the town of Corning, New York State, she was the sixth of eleven children in a working-class Irish-American family. Her mother also had seven miscarriages and Margaret believed all these pregnancies took a toll on her health. Her mother died at the age of 49 suffering from tuberculosis, which Margaret also contracted.

Portrait of Margaret Sanger. (Photograph by Underwood & Underwood, 1922. Reproduction Number: LC-USZ62-29808. Prints and Photographs Collection, Library of Congress, United States of America)

With the support of two elder sisters Margaret attended college and went on to study nursing. In 1902 she married William Sanger, an architect, and they had three children: sons born in 1903 and 1908 and a daughter born in 1910. In 1910 the Sanger family moved to Greenwich Village, New York City, where Margaret became involved with the radical politics of the time and supported the Industrial Workers of the World Union, but for 12 years she was primarily a wife and mother.

She then returned to work as a nurse in a poor neighbourhood on the Lower East Side. Here she saw women in poor health from frequent childbearing, and others who had tried to self-abort or had undergone illegal abortions. In her autobiography she describes how strongly motivated she was to improve access to contraception when one of her patients, Sadie Sachs, died of a septic abortion. Little information was available in libraries or elsewhere. She advocated vaginal suppositories and douching for women, and condoms for men, but not coitus interruptus (withdrawal).

In 1912 she started her campaign to educate women about sex by writing a column in a magazine called *What Every Mother Should Know*, followed by *What Every Girl Should Know*, which later became booklets. In 1913 she separated from her husband, although the divorce was not finalised until 1921.

In 1914 she wrote seven monthly issues of a publication called *The Woman Rebel*, which promoted a woman's right to birth control. This landed her in trouble, as it was illegal under the Comstock Act of 1873 to circulate 'obscene' material. In August 1914, rather than face a possible five-year prison sentence, she left her children behind and fled to England. While en route to England, her 16-page booklet *Family Limitation* was published in the USA. Her estranged husband spent 30 days in prison when he was entrapped for possessing a copy.

In England, she connected with various progressive movements and researched methods of birth control. Influenced by sexual psychologist Havelock Ellis, she embraced the idea of free love and had affairs with Ellis and other men, including writer H. G. Wells, who was also a close friend of Ettie Rout and Marie Stopes. In 1915 she visited a Dutch clinic and learned about the diaphragm, and she became convinced this method was more effective than the methods she had been advocating back in the USA. It was illegal to import these so she and her allies smuggled supplies back to her home country. In October 1915, after the charges against her were dropped, she returned to the USA; tragically, a few days later her five-year-old daughter Peggy died of pneumonia.

In 1916 Margaret opened the first birth control clinic in the USA, in Brooklyn, but nine days later police arrested her (along with her sister Ethel Byrne, who also worked at the clinic), and she spent 30 days in prison for breaking the Comstock laws. Margaret appealed her sentence and scored a victory for the birth control movement through a change that allowed doctors to prescribe contraception for medical reasons. Over the years she was arrested eight times for activism in challenging the Comstock laws. In February 1917 she published the first monthly issue of the *Birth Control Review*, and this publication continued until 1940.

In 1920 Margaret met Ettie Rout in London through their mutual friend H. G. Wells. Margaret introduced Ettie to her friend Rose Witcop, another birth control pioneer. Rose and her partner, the communist/anarchist Guy Aldred, published an English edition of Margaret Sanger's *Family Limitation*.

In 1921 Margaret established the American Birth Control League (ABCL), a precursor of today's Planned Parenthood Federation of America. The founding principles of the ABCL were as follows:

> We hold that children should be
> (1) Conceived in love;
> (2) Born of the mother's conscious desire;
> (3) And only begotten under conditions which render possible the heritage of health.
>
> Therefore we hold that every woman must possess the power and freedom to prevent conception except when these conditions can be satisfied.

In 1922, at the age of 43, she married James Noah H. Slee, a wealthy oil businessman who was able to provide funding for her campaigns and projects. She travelled widely to China, Korea and Japan promoting birth control.

In 1923 Margaret opened a birth control clinic, which she called the Birth Control Clinical Research Bureau (BCCRB), staffed by female doctors and social workers. The clinic received substantial funding from John D. Rockefeller Jr and family. That same year, Aldred and Witcop in England published a revised edition of Margaret's *Family Limitation*, this time with illustrations and a section on abortion. Copies were seized by police, and the publishers were charged with obscenity under English law. Margaret did not travel to England to attend the court case, but Ettie Rout became very involved, probably over-involved, to the extent of antagonising some of the defence team. In solidarity with Margaret, Ettie sent a copy of her own book, *Safe Marriage*, to the Director of Public Prosecutions, and invited him to take action on that too, since it was indiscriminately sold by shopkeepers in England although banned in New Zealand.

The magistrate held that *Family Limitation* was not obscene in itself but its publication had been indiscriminate. He ordered that the stock be destroyed. An appeal was lodged. Ettie had a lesser role in the appeal, which took place on 9 February 1923. Although she put herself forward as a witness, the judge ruled she was not an expert witness because she was not a doctor. The judge dismissed the appeal and the costs were met by Dora Russell, together with her husband Bertrand Russell, and the economist John Maynard Keynes. Aldred and Witcop were allowed to publish the booklet without the offending illustrations. Ettie was keen to continue the campaign and urged Margaret Sanger to come to London, but she replied she was preoccupied with other matters in the USA.

In 1927 Margaret organised the first World Population Conference, held in Geneva, which was a meeting of international scientists to discuss the environmental impact of population growth.

In 1928 conflict within the birth control movement leadership led her to resign as president of the ABCL and take full control of the BCCRB, marking the beginning of a schism in the movement that lasted until 1938.

In 1929 she formed the National Committee on Federal Legislation for Birth Control, which served as the focal point for her lobbying efforts to legalise contraception in the USA. Early in 1935 Ettie visited New York, as her book on exercises for women had been published in America as *Stand up and Slim Down*. While there, she was invited to be the guest editor of a special issue of *American Medicine* on contraception and disease prophylaxis. Running out of time, Ettie asked Margaret to contribute a segment on birth control, but she declined, suggesting two other women who could help. Ettie ended up not contacting them, but instead filled the pages with a severe critique of the ABCL. This led to an almighty row with Margaret Sanger, who terminated their correspondence, exclaiming, 'This woman is a pest!'

In 1936 a lengthy legal battle was won when the United States Court of Appeals allowed birth control devices to be imported into the country. In 1937, motivated by this victory, the American Medical Association adopted the policy that contraception was a normal medical service and a key component of medical school curricula. This was a significant breakthrough. New Zealand doctors did not follow suit; at that time they were preoccupied with the McMillan Inquiry.

In addition to her many articles and lectures, Margaret also wrote several books in the 1920s and two autobiographies in 1931 and 1938. Like Marie Stopes, she received hundreds of thousands of letters from women desperate for advice about birth control, and in 1928 a selection of these was published in the book *Motherhood in Bondage*.[25] The letters remain a powerful testament to the vulnerability of women without access to reliable contraception.

For the next three decades Margaret continued her commitment to birth control. In 1937, she became chairman of the newly formed Birth Control Council of America, and attempted to resolve the schism between the ABCL and the BCCRB. Her efforts were successful, and the two organisations merged in 1939 as the Birth Control Federation of America, which in 1942 became the Planned Parenthood Federation of America, a name Margaret considered too euphemistic.

In 1951 she was introduced to Dr Gregory Pincus, a biologist and reproductive physiologist, and she encouraged him with a small grant to begin hormonal contraceptive research. Her long-time friend, Katharine McCormick, who had inherited her husband's wealth (largely generated from combine harvesters), provided nearly $2 million for the development of the oral contraceptive pill.[26] Pincus worked closely with clinician Dr John Rock, a Catholic doctor who specialised in infertility. In 1955 the Caribbean Island of Puerto Rico, a self-governing territory of the USA, was selected as a suitable site for the first large-scale trial of the contraceptive pill in women, conducted under the supervision of Dr Edris Rice-Wray. Enovid, the first oral contraceptive pill, was approved by the Food and Drug Administration (FDA) for menstrual conditions in 1957, and as a contraceptive in June 1960. Without the foresight and dedication of Margaret Sanger this would not have happened when it did.

Meanwhile, in 1952, at a meeting in India, Margaret was one of the founders of the International Planned Parenthood

Federation (IPPF). This became the world's largest non-governmental international family planning organisation, which the New Zealand Family Planning Association joined in 1955 as an associate member and in 1959 as a full member.

In 1965 Margaret Sanger witnessed another important milestone in *Griswold v. Connecticut*, which made birth control legal for married couples; something for which she had spent many years campaigning. Estelle Griswold, Executive Director of the Planned Parenthood League of Connecticut, and Dr Buxton, a professor at Yale School of Medicine, opened a clinic in New Haven, Connecticut, to test the law against contraception. They were found guilty under state law and appealed to the Supreme Court. By a vote of 7-2 the Supreme Court invalidated the Connecticut law that prohibited the use of contraceptives. The court argued it violated the right to marital privacy.

In 1966 Margaret Sanger died of congestive heart failure in Tucson, Arizona. Her advocacy was not without controversy; like her contemporaries she was a supporter of the eugenics movement, popular with intellectuals at the time. However, for her great services in advancing women's reproductive rights, Margaret Sanger has been recognised with many important honours. Her great legacy was that 'Every child should be a wanted child.'

ଔ

Dr Marie Stopes (1880–1958)[27] was born in Edinburgh to an architect father whose hobby was archaeology and a scholarly mother who studied Shakespeare and was also a suffragist. Her upbringing was on the one hand loving (especially by her father) and on the other puritanical (especially by her mother), with no sex education from either.

Marie was not a medical doctor; her doctorates were obtained in palaeobotany. She had a PhD from Munich (1904) and a DSc from University College London (1905). Her studies took her to the University of Manchester, where she became the first female member of the science faculty. She conducted well-respected research on the history of ancient plants and the composition of coal, and wrote a number of papers and books on these topics. Her work earned her a grant from the British Royal Society, another first for a woman. The grant allowed her to travel to Japan to conduct research in 1907 and 1908. Her interest in Japan coincided with a five-year love affair with a Japanese professor of palaeobotany who she had met in Munich. He was 14 years older than Marie, married with one daughter, and an atheist. Because of her strict upbringing, the affair did not extend to a sexual relationship, and it ended in 1908. She continued to lecture in palaeobotany until 1920, when her scientific career was overtaken by her preoccupation with love, marriage and birth control.

In 1911 she married a Canadian botanist and geneticist, Reginald Ruggles Gates, but never changed her surname. As an independent person, she resented his wish to control her. The relationship was very unsatisfactory sexually and emotionally. In order to understand more about the reasons for the failure of her marriage, she adopted a scientific approach and read as much as she could find on the topic in the library of the British Museum. With the help of an older friend and lodger, Aylmer Maude, she reached the conclusion her husband was impotent and the marriage was unconsummated. It was finally annulled in 1916.

In 1914, when Margaret Sanger fled to Britain to escape being imprisoned, she met Marie Stopes. Margaret wrote about this meeting:

> She then explained to me that owing to her previous unfortunate marriage she had no experience in matters of contraception nor any occasion to inform herself of their use. Could I tell her exactly what methods were used? I replied that it would give me the greatest pleasure to bring to her home such devices as I had in my possession. Accordingly, we met again the following week for dinner at her home, and inspected and discussed the French pessary which she stated she then saw for the first time. I gave her my own pamphlets, all of which contained contraceptive information.

Marie's ignorance and her wish to rectify the dearth of knowledge for other women prompted her to write about her discoveries in her first book, *Married Love*, which was published in 1918. It was the first book to give advice on marital happiness and sexuality. Prior to this, the prevailing attitude was that it was the duty of a virtuous wife to submit to her husband's demands and she was not expected to feel sexual satisfaction, let alone pursue it.

In 1918 Marie married the wealthy Humphrey Verdon Roe, co-founder of the Avro aircraft company, who was very supportive of her views and able to finance the publication of her book. Although condemned by the churches, the medical establishment and the press, *Married Love* was immensely popular, selling 2,000 copies within a fortnight. Thousands of women wrote and asked her for advice. It was an overnight sensation, demonstrating the need for such information in plain language for the general public. Marie turned her disastrous first marriage into the central revelation of her life.

Inspired by Margaret's campaign in the USA, Marie started a birth control campaign in Britain. She used the publicity gained from *Married Love* to advance her cause, and this resulted in her second book, *Wise Parenthood* (1918), which included more specific advice on contraception. It says something about her self confidence that she wrote a book on married love when she was a virgin and a book on parenting before she was a parent.

In July 1919, at the age of 38, she delivered a stillborn son, a tragedy for which she held her doctors responsible. This event may have played a role in her strong distrust of doctors for the rest of her life. Despite her scientific training, Marie had some unusual beliefs. In 1920 she wrote *A New Gospel* and circulated it to all the bishops attending the Lambeth conference. She claimed it had been dictated to her by God.

Having achieved fame with her books on marriage and birth control, Marie now saw herself as the pre-eminent sexual health expert and condescendingly wished to use her influence to promote the cause of venereal disease prevention. She decided to write a book on venereal disease, and Sir William Arbuthnot Lane, a British surgeon who had supported Ettie Rout, arranged a meeting between Ettie and Marie in order for Ettie to share her extensive knowledge of the subject. In March 1920 the two met, and Ettie provided her with material, some of which she used. Marie's moral code was much stricter than Ettie's. She did not approve of sex outside marriage and it was not surprising they did not get on.

When *The Truth About Venereal Disease* came out in 1921, Ettie offered to endorse it for the New Zealand and Australian markets and to compile a list of potential reviewers. Marie was thankful and their correspondence resumed. However, when Ettie asked Marie for financial help for a preventive programme for the occupying forces in Germany and even offered to promote her book to the troops, Marie declined, on the advice of friends, not wishing her reputation to be sullied by association with the outspoken Ettie.

In 1922, when Ettie published her book *Safe Marriage*, the two sparred again. In her outline of the history of birth control, Ettie paid tribute to the early pioneers Annie Besant and Charles Bradlaugh, who were prosecuted in 1877 for publishing an American birth control pamphlet, *The Fruits of Philosophy or the Private Companion of Young Married People*, by Charles Knowlton. Marie grandly opined that it was she who had introduced birth control to Britain, to which Ettie replied 'But it is disinterested field-workers that are wanted, not Museum Hypatias or Prophetesses. You can write well, talk well, and I believe you could work well – if you would empty out the rubbishy emotionalism, the superstition, the vanity and egoism with which you becloud and degrade your work.'[28]

The Most Outspoken Book Published

"MARRIED LOVE," by Dr. Marie Stopes, is the first publication to break down the age-old barrier of prudery which has blocked the door of knowledge. Never before has such a frank, clean, and sensible book been written. If you are married or contemplate matrimony you must read "MARRIED LOVE"— you must own a copy, for it is a book that you may turn to again and again for advice upon important personal and matrimonial problems. It points the way to married happiness and health. It is a book of enlightenment, written by Dr. Stopes to kill for ever the demon ignorance. It is a straightforward discussion of the vital problems confronting every man and woman.

You Must Read
Married Love

"MARRIED LOVE" has helped thousands of men and women to know the real joys of married life. If Dr. Stopes could read some of the numerous letters we receive daily from grateful readers of her book—sincere letters of praise, thankfulness and enthusiasm—she would feel amply repaid for having devoted her life to tell men and women what they need to know.

1000 Copies of this Remarkable Book to be Sold at the Special Price of 7/6

There is a message for you in Dr. Stopes' book that will point the way to the happiness that you have always wanted. Send for it to-day. It's a revelation. No need to write a letter, just fill in coupon and enclose postal notes for 7/6, and the book will be sent packed in box in plain wrapper.

Advertisement for Marie Stopes's book *Married Love*.
(*NZ Truth*, 22 September 1923)

In 1923 Ettie and Marie took opposing views in the trial of Aldred and Witcop for republishing Margaret Sanger's *Family Limitation*. Marie Stopes had fallen out with Margaret Sanger when she had visited the USA, and in Marie's opinion the pamphlet was prurient and the suggestion that abortion was sometimes justifiable was wrong. Ettie, on the other hand, considered herself, Margaret and Marie to be equals, and if Margaret's books were banned, all should be similarly treated. Marie was furious and replied 'It didn't matter at all if Margaret's pamphlet was suppressed so long as other books (hers) on birth control were not.'

Marie Stopes at the time of her marriage with Mr. H.V. Roe, 1918, from *The authorized life of Marie C. Stopes* by Aylmer Maude (London: Williams and Moorgate Ltd, 1924), facing page 125. (General Collections Library reference no.: M0017375, slide number 6278, Wellcome Library, London)

On 17 March 1921, Marie opened the Mothers Clinic in Holloway, north London, the first birth control clinic in the country. It offered a free service to married women and also gathered data about contraception. In 1925 the clinic moved to central London, and others opened across the country. By 1930, other family planning organisations had been set up, and they joined forces with her to form the National Birth Control Council, which later became the Family Planning Association.

In 1923 Marie published *Contraception, Its Theory, History and Practice*, aimed at the medical and legal professions. It went through a number of editions and was used extensively by the pioneers of birth control in New Zealand. For contraception Marie advocated the use of the cervical cap, which fits snugly over the cervix, in contrast to Margaret, who preferred the diaphragm (or Dutch cap), which is placed in the vault of the vagina to cover the cervix. Doctors criticised her promotion of the cervical cap, claiming (incorrectly) that it was one of the most harmful methods of birth control for women. But her fiercest critic was the Catholic Church. In 1923 a Catholic doctor, Dr Halliday Sutherland, wrote a treatise accusing Marie of using poor women for birth control experiments. She vehemently denied the charges and sued Sutherland for libel. She lost, won at appeal and then lost again in the House of Lords, but the case generated huge publicity for her views. Marie wrote a number of other books on sexual health, including *A Letter to Working Mothers* (1919), *Radiant Motherhood* (1920), *The Human Body, Sex and the Young* (1926), *Enduring Passion* (1928), and *Roman Catholic Methods of Birth Control* (1933).

At the age of 43 Marie gave birth to a son, named Harry Stopes-Roe, who became a leader of the humanist movement in Britain. Sadly, the ideals of love, marital harmony and family happiness, which she publicly espoused, eluded her in her private life. She separated from Roe in 1938 and was estranged from her son because she disapproved of his marriage, ostensibly on eugenic grounds (because his wife was short-sighted). Her self-aggrandisement and her arrogance were traits that protected her from critical attacks but led to increasingly eccentric behaviour. In the last two decades of her life she retreated into literary pursuits, producing a number of poorly received collections of love poetry, plays, a novel and a film. When diagnosed with advanced breast cancer, she refused standard treatment and died on 2 October 1958.

Her name lives on. The clinics continued to operate after her death, but by the early 1970s they were in financial difficulties and in 1975 they went into voluntary receivership. A year later, the modern organisation Marie Stopes International was established by Dr Tim Black (1937–2014) and his wife Jean. Since then the organisation has grown steadily and today works in 41 countries and has clinics worldwide.

૱

Ettie Rout (1877–1936)[29] was born in Launceston, Tasmania, the daughter of an ironmonger. She had a twin sister and a sister two years younger. The Routs sailed for New Zealand at the end of 1884, when Ettie was nearly eight years old, and settled in Wellington, where her father opened a business in Manners Street. After the family moved to Christchurch around 1896, Ettie attended Charles Gilby's pioneering commercial college, where she excelled at shorthand and typing. She was one of the first shorthand writers appointed by the government to work in the Supreme Court and on commissions of inquiry, where she was exposed to a wide range of social issues, particularly for a woman of that era.

In 1904 she set up a public typing business, initially with Charles Gilby's son Horace. She also worked as a reporter for the *Lyttelton Times*. She had a reputation for working long hours, meeting deadlines and delivering completed documents on her bicycle. She was tall and fit, no doubt enhanced by attending gym classes run by her longtime friend and physical culturist, Fred Hornibrook. Ettie dressed unfashionably, shunning corsets and elaborate hats and opting for clothes more practical for cycling such as calf-length skirts and men's boots. Her opinions were also unconventional. She was a rationalist or freethinker and espoused liberal ideas on sexuality following those of the Swedish feminist Ellen Key, the social reformer Edward Carpenter, and the writer Havelock Ellis. The radical thinker Professor A. W. Bickerton was one of her close friends, and she attended some of his open classes at Canterbury University.

Ettie was committed to socialism, and she became involved in the labour movement in 1907, recording the proceedings of an inquiry into the working conditions of Canterbury farm labourers and acting as adviser to the union secretary. She founded the *Maoriland Worker* newspaper with the New Zealand Shearers' Union in 1910. She was an honorary member of the union, and edited the first six issues of the newspaper free of charge, until the shearers joined the New Zealand Federation of Labour in early 1911. The federation took over the newspaper and replaced her with another editor.

Ettie set up the New Zealand Volunteer Sisterhood in July 1915, during the Gallipoli campaign of World War I. The Sisterhood consisted of women between the ages of 30 and 50, who travelled to Egypt to care for New Zealand soldiers. The first 12 volunteers went to Cairo in October 1915, despite government opposition; they worked in the New Zealand YMCA canteen and in hospitals, and one of them ran a cookery school. Ettie arrived in Egypt in February 1916, and soon noticed the high venereal disease rate among the troops. She saw this as a medical problem rather than a moral one, to be treated like any other disease. To prevent the spread of venereal diseases she recommended that prophylactic kits be issued to soldiers and that brothels be inspected for hygiene. The New Zealand Medical Corps officers did not agree with her recommendations.

Most of the New Zealand Expeditionary Force (NZEF) left for France in April 1916, but Ettie stayed in Egypt to care for the soldiers fighting the desert campaign in Sinai and Palestine. She thought they needed better rest and recreation facilities and better food than the army had provided, so she opened the Tel El Kebir Soldiers' Club and later a canteen at El Qantara. For this work she was mentioned in dispatches and in the Australian official war history.

When the New Zealand Medical Corps had still not adopted prophylactic measures against the army's serious venereal disease problem by June 1917, Ettie went to London to apply more pressure to those in authority. She combined the work of several of the foremost doctors in the field to produce a prophylactic kit of her own design, containing calomel ointment, condoms and Condy's crystals (potassium permanganate). She then set up the New Zealand Medical Soldiers Club at Hornchurch, near the New Zealand Convalescent Hospital, and sold her kits to the soldiers there.

On 24 October 1917 one of her letters was published in the *New Zealand Times* giving venereal disease statistics to reinforce her plea for prophylaxis. This letter outraged the Women's Christian Temperance Union who accused her of trying to make 'vice' safe. Ironically the letter also helped to convince the defence minister, James Allen, to approve the issue of propylactic kits.

At the end of 1917 the NZEF finally introduced the compulsory distribution of free prophylactic kits to soldiers going on leave, but they gave Ettie no credit for the kit's development and adoption. In fact, for the remainder of the war the cabinet banned mention of venereal disease and Ettie's work from New Zealand newspapers under the emergency war regulations. Mention of this sensitive topic brought a possible £100 fine. In April 1918 venereal disease was debated in parliament, and Lady Stout led a deputation of women to ask the prime minister, William Massey, to shut down Ettie's Hornchurch club.

Ettie Annie Rout. (Ref: PAColl-4832. Alexander Turnbull Library, Wellington, New Zealand)

Undaunted, Ettie continued her work in Paris. She greeted New Zealand soldiers with her trademark kiss on the cheek as they arrived at the Gare du Nord on troop trains from the front, and handed them cards advertising a local brothel. The brothel was committed to high standards of hygiene, and was regularly inspected by Ettie to ensure that these standards were maintained. From 1919 to 1920 Ettie also ran a Red Cross depot at Villers Brettoneux, a ruined town in the Somme. For her work in Paris and in Villers Brettoneux, the French decorated her with the Médaille de la Reconnaissance Française (Medal of French Gratitude).

On 3 May 1920 Ettie married Fred Hornibrook in London, where he was developing his fashionable physiotherapy practice. The couple had no children. In 1922 Ettie was interested in finding a vaginal suppository that would release a chemical to kill both venereal disease microbes and sperm – a combined microbicide and spermicide. A manufacturing chemist came up with Chinosol as a disinfectant and Ettie tried the foaming tablets on herself. This, she believed, would give women more control over the prevention of venereal diseases. However, the tablets were expensive, and it was against the law for chemist shops to sell them with instructions on how to use them. Ettie solved this by writing a little book called *Safe Marriage: a return to sanity* (1922), but as already explained, this did not reach New Zealand couples due to a ban by Truby King. In her book, she gave instructions on safer sex (although that term was not used). She recommended a 'sexual toilet outfit' comprising an enamel bidet, soluble suppositories, a syringe and a properly fitted diaphragm, to be used with a spermicide. She dismissed the 'safe period' as unsafe and did not put faith in withdrawal (coitus interruptus), as it relied on the cooperation of the man and was less sexually satisfying for the woman.

Always primarily a campaigner, she wrote a number of books, among them *Safe Marriage* (1922), *Sex and Exercise* (1925), a vegetarian cookbook (1926), and a largely inaccurate book on Māori culture entitled *Maori Symbolism* (1926).[30] She returned briefly to New Zealand in 1936, by which time she had become estranged from her husband. On the way back to London she died of a self-administered overdose of quinine in Rarotonga on 17 September 1936. She was buried in Avarua, in the graveyard of the London Missionary Society Church (now the Cook Islands Christian Church).

The reactions to Ettie Rout's pioneering work to prevent the spread of venereal disease revealed the hypocritical attitudes of her day. Although her initiatives were of great benefit to New Zealand, she was not only largely ignored, but news of her work was suppressed in her own country. Even when the New Zealand Returned Soldiers' Association sent a post-war tribute of £100, this was not publicised. In her obituary she was called 'one of the best known of New Zealand women' but there was no mention of what she was best known for; the first paragraph of the obituary was devoted to her typing speed.[31]

Ettie's work polarised opinion. During her lifetime she was variously described as the 'guardian angel of the ANZACs' (by a French doctor), 'the most wicked woman in Britain' (by a bishop, speaking in the House of Lords), and an 'unforgettable heroine' (by her friend H. G. Wells, who mentioned her in one of his novels).[32] In 1922 she noted, in a letter to H. G. Wells, 'It's a mixed blessing to be born too soon.' Although New Zealand struggled to accept her during her lifetime, many of her ideas and methods have been accepted since.

ఌ

The main contraceptive methods used in the first half of the 20th century were abstinence, coitus interruptus (withdrawal), douching after sex, condoms and female barriers (cervical caps and vaginal diaphragms). On 31 December 1930, in response to the Lambeth Conference of the Anglican Church, which approved of contraception in certain circumstances, Pope Pius XI issued a papal encyclical titled *Casti connubii* (Latin for 'of chaste wedlock'). It stressed the sanctity of marriage, prohibited Catholics from using any form of artificial birth control, and reaffirmed the prohibition on abortion. The encyclical really only affirmed the Church's teachings and did not stop Catholic women resorting to abortion, as in the following story.

Kate's story[33]
Deceased 27 June 1915, aged 25 years

Kate Andrews was married to Leonard, the station master at Southbridge in Canterbury. They were Catholic and had seven children. Kate was well known throughout the district in musical circles as a vocalist, having assisted on numerous occasions at benefit concerts.

About a year before her death Kate had experienced a miscarriage from which she made a good recovery. With seven young children she did not keep robust health, and she told her husband they had enough children. She visited Christchurch a few days before having a miscarriage on 18 June. Whether there was any connection between these two events is not known, but the police were suspicious and conducted enquiries.

When she became ill she did not want Leonard to call a doctor and it was not until she became light-headed that he called in Dr Withers. The doctor prescribed medicine, and kind neighbours came in to help. Kate died suddenly after lapsing into a coma, which devastated Leonard as he had not realised how ill she was.

The post-mortem, carried out by Dr Volckman, revealed an incomplete abortion at about two months' gestation with remains of a septic placenta. The coroner, acting alone, found 'death was due to septic peritonitis caused by miscarriage.' No charges were laid.

ଔ

Abstinence within marriage was probably very common when circumstances dictated no more children. Marie Stopes had this to say on the topic:[34]

> Total abstention is in my opinion essential to be used in every home as a *temporary* measure during the ill-health of either wife or husband. I think, on the other hand, it should not be used by normal persons as a measure extended over long periods of time, for its subsidiary ill-effects more than counterbalance any 'moral' advantages if it is used for long periods. It is, moreover, the *most* 'unnatural' of all methods of contraception which can be used by a loving pair.

Abstinence before marriage was the expected code, not only for Catholics but for all women. For those who transgressed this code the social stigma and disapproval was often profound enough for women to commit desperate acts, and in the following tragedy Mary was supported by her lover.

Mary's story[35]
Deceased 2 May 1935, aged 21 years

Mary Raymond was part Māori and lived in Auckland. Her badly decomposed body was found floating in the Tamaki Basin on 2 June 1935, one month after she went missing. The body was naked except for a portion of a cotton singlet about the shoulders. A rope held her body in position under the Panmure Wharf and at the other end of the rope were two sacks and a piece of canvas. It was at first difficult to identify the body because of the length of time it had been in the water before being washed by the tide to its resting place, where it was found by two men working on their boat.

The press followed the mystery very closely and the following story emerged. Mary, an attractive, dark-haired young woman with a beautiful voice, came from Te Puke, where her parents still lived. She left Te Puke to work in Auckland and stayed with relatives. At Christmas time in 1934, when holidaying in Rotorua, she met and fell in love with Edward Henry Dudley Bennett, 25, a young Māori from a well-known Wellington family, on track to developing a publishing business. On New Year's Eve they declared their love for each other and talked of marriage at Easter time.

On 27 January Mary came to Wellington and stayed with Dudley's relatives, who welcomed her as one of the family. Early in February she informed Dudley she was pregnant and she did not want to bring shame to his family. They both agreed it would be best to have the pregnancy aborted. She stayed in Wellington until 25 April, when she returned to Auckland by herself for this purpose. Dudley gave her £3 and arranged for her to collect £8.10s that he had owing to him from a firm in Auckland.

They communicated by letters and telegrams, and she told him she was staying with a Mrs Wilson but this woman would not operate because Mary did not have the required £12. The firm that owed Dudley money had given her only £5. She confided in a girlfriend, Peggy, and asked her for money. Peggy could not give her any money but said she knew a doctor who would charge only £6. Mary left Mrs Wilson's place to stay with Mr and Mrs Hughes, distant relatives who lived in Wellington Street.

Mary let Dudley know of the change in plans and as far as Dudley knew Mary had gone ahead with the operation at Dr Hewer's rooms in Queen Street about 1 May. It was a huge shock and surprise to receive a telegram on 2 May which read 'Mary missing. Come at once. Serious. Hughes.' That evening Dudley caught the train for Auckland and went straight to see the Hugheses. He met up with other relatives of Mary, all searching for her, and he called upon Dr Hewer, who denied having seen Mary. Dudley also put a series of advertisements in the *Auckland Star:*

> Mary. Letters at G.P.O. I am waiting at Peggy's. Love, Dud. (11 May)
>
> Mary. Must know how you are by Friday, or else. Dud. Write W 4357, Star. (15 May)
>
> Mary. Imperative you let me know something by Friday, otherwise you may regret. Dud 9251 Star. (16 May)

Dr Hewer took the precaution of engaging a top criminal lawyer, Mr Singer, in case of further enquiries, and arranged for letters between Mary and Dudley to be destroyed, because they mentioned his name.

A month later the gruesome discovery of Mary's body led to an inquest. A young woman acquaintance, Miss Dagmar von Zglinicki, saw Mary walking with Dr Hewer in Queen Street on 1 May. A mystery man telephoned *NZ Truth* with information about his wife meeting Mary on 1 May. The coroner was frustrated by the efforts of Hewer and his accomplices to interfere with witnesses and to destroy letters containing evidence. Dudley stood out as an honest victim of this tragedy.

The coroner found the cause of death was shock following an illegal operation. George Hewer described himself as an electrotherapist and endocrinologist, calling himself 'Dr' Hewer although he was not a registered medical professional. He practised from rooms in Queen Street, Auckland. The assumption was that something had gone very wrong with the abortion and he had dumped Mary's body in the sea. He was not charged on this occasion but police kept him under surveillance, and in August 1935 he was arrested on another charge of illegally procuring abortion. On this occasion, despite a spirited defence by Mr Singer, he was found guilty and imprisoned for two years with hard labour.

ଓ

Periodic abstinence to avoid fertile times in the cycle was a hit and miss affair, with some instructions actually increasing the chance of pregnancy. Scientists working independently in Japan (Kyusaku Ogino) and Austria (Hermann Knaus) in the 1920s finally figured out an effective method and published their definitive papers in 1932 and 1933. Ogino had published his first findings in Japanese as early as 1924 and Knaus his first findings in 1929. Both are credited with the discovery.[36]

The method relies on understanding the physiology of the menstrual cycle and identifying the 'fertile window', or the days in the menstrual cycle when intercourse is most likely to result in a pregnancy. It is based on a calculation of the time of ovulation (usually 14 days before the next period) and the survival time of the sperm (up to five days). In 1939, two French doctors described the shift in temperature that occurs immediately after ovulation, and this became an additional sign to be incorporated into the calculation. However, for the time period covered in this book it was not yet a method relied on by many New Zealand women. Even the Pope did not refer to it in his 1930 encyclical.

In 1920 Marie Stopes mistakenly thought fertility coincided with menstruation. In her textbook in 1934 she corrected this but thought the method unnatural and unreliable and did not advocate its use.[37] It became known by various names: safe times, fertility awareness, the calendar method, the rhythm method and later the symptothermal method. Because it is the main method approved of by the Catholic Church, it is sometimes referred to as 'Vatican roulette'. If properly taught and practised diligently, it is now an acceptable method.

Coitus interruptus, or withdrawal, was a common contraceptive method (and still is), relying on the male ejaculating outside the vagina. Marie Stopes described it as harmful and unreliable and believed absorption of the seminal fluid was somehow beneficial. She wrote 'I condemn the method both on the grounds of its harmfulness to the male central nervous system, and its local effect, and because it deprives the female of the proper completion of the physiological reactions set in motion by the onset of the coital act.'[38]

Breastfeeding was recognised by women as an activity that delayed conception, but Marie Stopes disapproved of using prolonged suckling as a contraceptive method. Modern guidelines (established by world experts after a review of its effectiveness in Bellagio, Italy, in 1995) have improved its usefulness, and the name Lactational Amenorrhea Method or LAM enhances its credibility.

Condoms (also known as French letters, sheaths, rubbers and many other names) suffered through their association with prostitution and venereal disease prevention. Marie Stopes did not recommend them for married couples, although she regarded them as useful for protection from venereal disease, in cases of premature ejaculation and in the first two weeks of marriage. When pregnancy was a great risk to the woman, she recommended condoms in addition to a female method. She thought them unreliable, unsatisfactory and unaesthetic, stating 'It robs the woman of contact with the seminal secretions' and 'It is inadvisable for regular use, as are all methods used by the male.'[39]

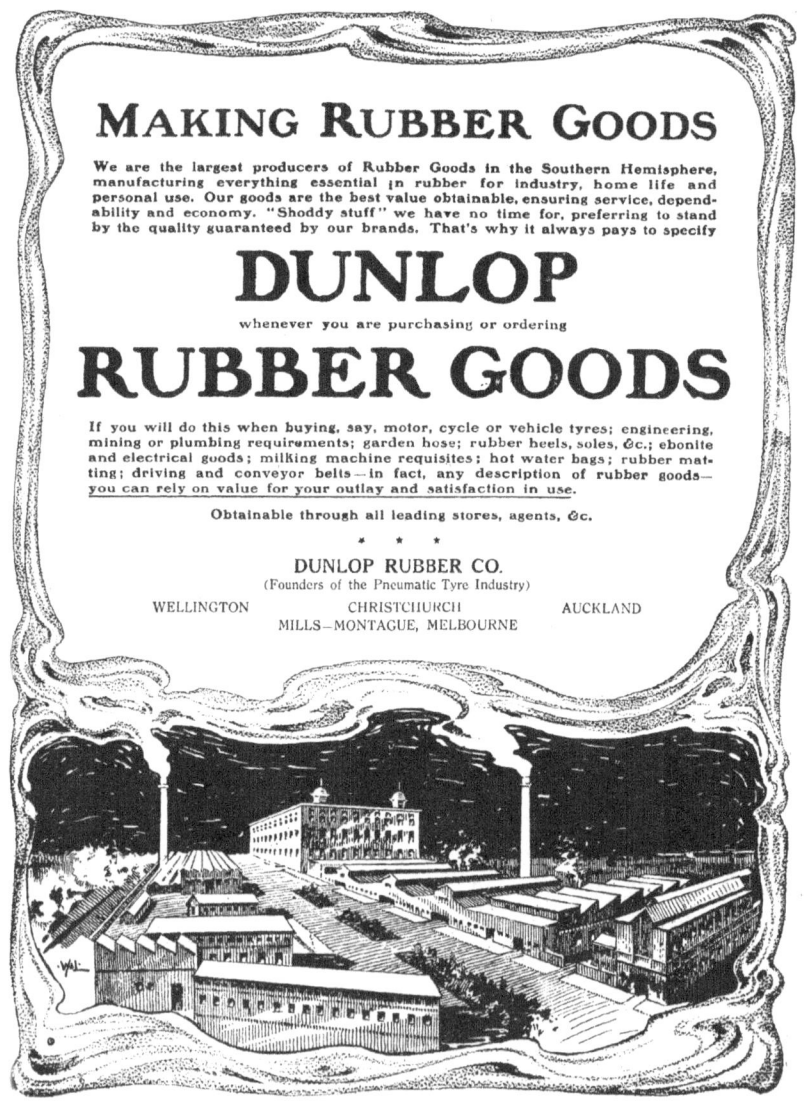

Dunlop Rubber advertisement (*Observer*, 6 December 1920). No mention of condoms, just goods for 'home life and personal use'.

Because of the stigma surrounding condoms, they were not as popular with women as female barriers. Although they were not openly advertised in New Zealand, imported rubber condoms were available from chemists and other outlets, such as garages and fruiterers. Mail order services were popular, as in this *NZ Truth* advertisement from 1924:[40]

> Toilet And Rubber Goods of every description.
> Write For Full Price List.
> We claim the largest mail order business in N.Z.
> Correspondence Strictly Private.
> Everything sent in plain sealed wrapper, Post Free, from
> Mail Order Chemist
> Box 791 Christchurch.

Condoms were of two types: rubber and animal membrane. Rubber condoms were thicker, while animal membrane condoms, usually made from sheep gut or fish bladders, were thinner but more expensive. We know condoms were used because in 1914 they featured as one of the causes of blocked sewerage systems.[41]

Spermicidal pessaries, combined with a rubber cervical cap, were Marie Stopes's favoured method of contraception. Her advice was 'cap and chemical are best'. ('Suppository' and 'pessary' are just fancy names for a large tablet; 'spermicidal' means that they contain chemicals that kill sperm.) She advocated any number of proprietary preparations containing quinine, alum or 'Chinosol' (a proprietary chemical spermicide from Germany).

Various spermicides were available at the time. Rendell's pessaries ('the wife's friend') were made of quinine and salicylic acid in cocoa butter. Foaming tablets, the majority of them manufactured in Germany, released chemicals such as carbon dioxide or hydrogen peroxide. Gelatine suppositories were less likely to damage rubber caps than greasy or oily ones. Jellies or pastes came in tubes, to be used with a rubber cap. In the Marie Stopes Clinic, non-quinine suppositories were used, as some women found quinine irritating.

When members of the Sex Hygiene and Birth Regulation Society (which later became the Family Planning Association of New Zealand) presented the results of the Married Women's Questionnaire to the McMillan Inquiry, soluble pessaries, either proprietary or homemade, featured as a common method of contraception. Women reportedly swapped recipes, such as those using cocoa butter and quinine, and cooked them up on their stoves.

Sponges and other vaginal barriers. Since ancient times, sea sponges have been used for menstrual hygiene and as a vaginal barrier.[42] Cleopatra was reputed to have used a sponge soaked in vinegar. The Ebers Papyrus, dating back to 1550 BC, contains the following prescription for a vaginal suppository: 'To make a woman cease to become pregnant for one year, two years or three years, tips of acacia and dates are triturated with honey. Seed wool is moistened therewith and placed in the vulva.' Marie Stopes's third-ranked contraceptive method was the vaginal sponge, and she advocated squeezing and filling the sponge with plain olive oil. Her clinic sold sponges, larger in size than the sponges used for sanitary protection. Other substances used in conjunction with the sponge were alum powder, quinine powder, quinine ointment, soap powder or a weak vinegar solution. These were the forerunners of cervical caps (developed in 1838) and diaphragms (1882).

READ THIS!
WHIRLING SPRAYS—The best English makes. A special line of high pressure sprays. No. 1 ordinary 15/-, No. 2 strong 17/6; No. 2 extra high pressure 25/-. Other Brands Ingrams etc 12/6, 15/6 and 17/6; Wonder Spray 17/6.
Hygienic Spray Antiseptic Tablets for use with above sprays (invaluable to ladies) 100 for 10/6, 50 for 6/6.
All rubber goods called check Pro-race paragon and unique 7/6.
Our Special Safe Check highly recommended by the Faculty 25/-.
Corrective Pills (Guaranteed) No. 1 10/6, No. 2 15/6, Three in a tin 2/6, one dozen 7/6, Our Special 2/6 each, 3 for 5/-. Pills. No. 501 the best Vitality pill ever made gives you liquid life. Try a box. Small 5/-, large 10/6. · Write for anything. Everything sent in plain wrapper strictly private. POST FREE from
CHEMIST
P.O. Box 421 - - WELLINGTON

Advertisement for Whirling Sprays and other items. The Pro-race checks were the cervical caps used by Marie Stopes in her London clinic. (*NZ Truth* 9 May 1925)

Douching. Marie Stopes was one of the first to speak against douching, or washing out the vagina, and here she would be aligned with modern medical opinion. She thought it inconvenient, impractical and harmful, and strongly objected to instructions that advised daily douching for personal hygiene, stating 'The natural contents of the vagina should not be thus intruded upon.'[43] As a contraceptive she found it unreliable, unwholesome and psychologically harmful. However, douching with potassium permanganate was recommended generally as a treatment for gonorrhea.

Douche cans, syringes and enema equipment were commonly sold by New Zealand chemists and stockists and found in most homes in the early part of the 20th century. The douche can or bag was hung high on a hook on the bathroom or bedroom wall to allow gravity to assist the flow of water into the uterus (an alternative was the compressible rubber douche). A woman would sometimes douche in her bedroom, lying on her back on the bed with buttocks on the edge of the bed and legs draped downwards. She would then insert the tube into her vagina and open the tap to allow the water to flow in. The outflow would be collected by a waterproof channel to fall into a basin or bucket on the floor. The same procedure could be performed over the bath. Plain water was sufficient, but many additives were recommended, such as salt, vinegar, soap, alum or quinine. Disinfectants or spermicides were also used, depending on the circumstances. Dushol, Lysol and Epsom salts (magnesium sulphate) were popular brands used for douching.

Women used douching for personal hygiene after menstruation or when suffering from vaginal discharge or vaginal odour. Vaginal discharge, commonly referred to as 'the whites', may or may not have been due to infection, but symptoms were usually treated with a vaginal douche. Douching is no longer recommended as it interferes with the normal protective bacteria that inhabit the vagina.

Douching after intercourse as a method of contraception was based on the commonsense assumption that removing semen would lessen the chance of conception. It could also be used to eliminate traces of semen odour after an extramarital affair. Contraceptively speaking, douching was unnecessary for most of the menstrual cycle and relatively ineffective for the short time a woman was fertile. During the infertile times of the menstrual cycle the plug of sticky mucus in the cervix is impenetrable by

Advertisements for items that were often used as contraceptives or abortifacients, such as enemas, 'corrective' pills, and whirling sprays and syringes, in the *New Zealand Herald*, 5 July 1930 (left) *Maoriland Worker*, 18 April 1913 (top), and *NZ Truth*, 14 March 1925 (above).

sperm, and in the fertile times of the cycle when the cervical mucus is wet and slippery, it takes only 15 seconds for fast moving sperm to swim beyond the reach of the douche. However, the science of conception was not fully worked out until the 1930s, so much unnecessary douching took place in the early 20th century.

ଔ

The procedures used for personal hygiene or contraception could be adapted for use in self-abortion, as in the following story.

Elizabeth's story[44]
Deceased 11 November 1928, aged 35 years

Elizabeth Bradney was married to Fred, a mariner, and they lived with their two children in Kingsland, Auckland. In connection with work, Fred was away most nights. He left home about 2 pm, Sunday 11 November and returned at 8 am on Monday 12 November. When he left, Elizabeth was in good health and spirits; when he returned she was dead.

Elizabeth's story is told through the evidence given at the inquest by her 11-year-old daughter, Betty:

> My father left to go to work on Sunday as usual. We had dinner about 1 pm. Mummy got the dinner ready. My mother, my brother Joseph (aged five years) and I had tea about 5.30 pm. I got the tea ready. My mother told me to get the tea ready. She was sitting on the kitchen doorstep when I was getting the tea ready. I washed the dishes when tea was over. My brother Joe and I went to bed about 5.40 pm. We both sleep in the one room. That is the room next to my father and mother's bedroom. About 5.45 or 5.50 pm my mother came into our bedroom to get undressed. She usually undresses in our room before she goes to bed. After my mother got undressed she went out to the kitchen and after she was there some time I heard her call out 'Betty'. I got out of bed and went out to see what my mother wanted and when I got to our bedroom door she stumbled in the passageway and fell on the floor. I thought that there must have been something wrong with my mother but I did not know what it was. When she fell on the floor she said 'Oh Betty. Oh Betty. Mrs Christmas.' I tried to get her into the bed but was unable to do so and I put a pillow under her head and went for Mrs Christmas (a neighbour).

After my mother had undressed and went out into the kitchen, she came back into the room again, and put something under our bed. I did not see what it was as I was facing my brother in the bed talking to him. After I got up when my mother called out to me I saw an earthenware basin and an enema under the bed, I think that is what I heard my mother put under the bed. After I dressed I ran across for Mrs Christmas and when she came back with me I emptied the po and there was only wee in the po. The po was in my mother's room in the front of the house. I did not hear my mother in the front room after she undressed.

For the past week I heard my mother using something almost every night in our room. We used to go into her room every night last week and after she had finished we used to come out of her room and get into bed. I used to hear a noise. I think that it was the enema that I heard my mother using on those occasions. My mother kept the enema and the bowl behind our bedroom door. My father is away every night except Saturdays. He was never at home when she was using the enema.

The basin and the syringe was half under the bed at the time that Mrs Christmas came into the house. The po was just near the basin. I did not see any blood on the floor before I went out for Mrs Christmas but I saw blood afterwards. I noticed that the blood ran along the passage and into the kitchen. My father and mother were on good terms when he left to go to work. I know that my mother went to see Dr Reid about a month ago. No person came to the house to see my mother after my father went to work until I went for Mrs Christmas.

Mrs Christmas lived opposite the Bradneys. She had been there for 14 years and the Bradneys for four years. She knew Elizabeth fairly well and had last seen her on Friday 9 November when she appeared well. About a week before that, she said she had been to see Dr Reid and he told her she was two months' pregnant. Elizabeth did not say what she intended to do about it but Mrs Christmas understood she did not want to give birth to another baby. She said Elizabeth and her husband did not get on too well.

When Mrs Christmas came at Betty's request, she found Elizabeth on her back on the floor in the passage, partly across the children's bedroom door, near the kitchen. She had on a singlet and nightdress, stockings and slippers. She was dressed for bed and the children were also dressed for bed. Mrs Christmas knelt down beside Elizabeth and spoke to her but she did not answer.

She was lying in a pool of blood and her body was quite cold. Mrs Christmas asked Betty to run for another friend at Grey Lynn and also to get her friend to ring for a doctor.

The doctor moved the body into the bedroom before the police arrived. Mrs Christmas said that last November Elizabeth had sent for her, and when she came to the house she found her lying on the floor in the passageway in about the same place. She later went to the public hospital. On about three occasions she had sent for Mrs Christmas and she had always helped her. Each time she was pregnant, she said it was a miscarriage. Mrs Christmas had never heard of her buying any drugs or having equipment to induce a miscarriage.

The police took as evidence the earthenware bowl containing an enema. The tube of the enema contained a small quantity of fluid. There was also a small quantity of liquid in the bowl. In a chest of drawers in the front room was a small tin box containing vulcanite and glass tubes for the enema and a bottle of pennyroyal pills in the top drawer. There were 10 pills left in the bottle. In another drawer were three ebonite and two glass tubes for use with a douche can. The two glass tubes were six inches long and one of the ebonite tubes six and a half inches long. In another drawer was an empty tin labelled Ergotin and Apiol Capsules. On the dresser was a bottle of Lysol containing a small quantity in the bottom of the bottle. On the kitchen dresser was a half a bottle of Dushol and in the fire grate four empty Epsom salts packets, which from their appearance appeared to have been placed there recently. On the mantelpiece was a packet containing five packets of Epsom salts and in a niche below the mantelpiece a further half packet of the same salts. The house was clean and tidy and neatly but modestly furnished.

After Dr Murray had viewed the body, police removed it to the public morgue. Dr Murray and pathologist Dr Gilmour conducted a post-mortem. The uterus was enlarged and contained a four-month-old fetus and placenta. Septic matter covered the inner surface of the uterus. Death was due to acute septicaemia following an incomplete abortion. Elizabeth had apparently been douching with Epsom salts. The coroner, acting alone, found the cause of her death was 'septicaemia following on an incomplete abortion brought about by herself.'

Intrauterine devices (IUDs). According to folklore, intrauterine contraception dates back to ancient Arabs, who inserted pebbles in the wombs of camels to prevent pregnancies during long treks. The precursors of IUDs were stem pessaries used in Europe since the mid-1800s and fashioned from gold. However, these devices were inserted into the cervix and were not wholly within the uterine cavity. In the Married Women's Questionnaire presented to the McMillan Inquiry, one New Zealand woman reported using a silver stud.

The earliest intrauterine device was a ring-shaped device fashioned from silkworm gut (a suture material) devised by Dr Richard Richter in Germany at the turn of the 20th century. He published his results in 1909; at that time he was the lone exponent of the method.

In the 1920s, Dr Ernst Gräfenberg (1881–1957) of Berlin used rings made first of gut, then of silver and gold, with traces of copper.[45] In the pre-antibiotic era, uterine infections were a significant risk with this method; few practitioners supported Gräfenberg's work, and textbooks and medical professionals condemned the method outright. When he left Germany to live in the USA, Gräfenberg was warned by colleagues not to use IUDs, and over the next two decades the method lapsed. In her book on contraception Marie Stopes describes IUDs, but they were not used in her clinic and no doctor would have inserted them in New Zealand.

Sterilisation. In the early 20th century sterilisation was seen as a fairly drastic measure, to be used more for punishment or eliminating 'degenerates' from the gene pool than for contraception. Some countries enacted eugenic or punitive sterilisation laws in the early 20th century, but New Zealand had no specific laws regulating sterilisation. However, we were not immune from quackery. In 1906 Ettie Rout learned of unscientific ill-treatment when she spent three months as a secretary reporting on the Royal Commission into the Burnham Industrial School, a borstal where Dr William Henry Symes recommended vasectomy for chronic masturbators when his other 'treatments' failed.[46]

The Mental Defectives Act 1911 (amended in 1928 and 1935) did not include sterilisation as a management option for mental defectives.[47] Although some women's groups wanted sterilisation to be included, this was not supported by Dr T. G. Gray, Inspector-General of Mental Hospitals, based on his study tour of England, Europe and America in 1923.

In 1934 the National Council of Women discussed the issue of sterilisation of mental defectives at their annual conference and Dr Emily Siedeberg McKinnon was appointed to consult with branches and prepare a report.[48] No remit was passed supporting sterilisation.

Male sterilisation, or vasectomy, was not used for contraception in the first half of the 20th century. Surgeons were restrained by a common law edict based on a 13th-century English law which held that any person who injured a man, rendering him unfit to fight for the king, could be charged with maim or mayhem. A non-contraceptive vasectomy was often carried out to prevent the spread of infection in older men undergoing a prostate operation. Before the advent of antibiotics, infection could spread from the prostate area, down the tubes to the epididymis and testicle. This painful and potentially dangerous complication was prevented by tying the tubes at the time of the prostate operation.

Female sterilisation was uncommon until antibiotics increased the safety of the procedure, but there was no law against it. Dr Doris Gordon advocated sterilisation for women in poor health after multiple pregnancies, and the McMillan Report approved of this method 'in exceptional cases in which a woman's life is likely to be endangered or her health gravely impaired by further pregnancy.'

సౌ

Many types of contraceptives were available in the early 1900s, but most were defective or dangerous, and laws based on the prudish morals of that era prevented people from accessing accurate information about contraception. For the majority of women, reliable contraception was unimaginable.

5. A FLAWED LAW

Like most other Commonwealth countries, New Zealand inherited its abortion laws from England. The first New Zealand statute, the Offences Against the Person Act 1866, was an exact replica of the 1861 English law.[1] Abortion by any means (including self-abortion) led to life imprisonment or a lesser term, usually three to ten years. Supplying the means to carry out an abortion led to imprisonment for up to three years.

In 1905 an amendment to the Criminal Code Act gave judges more general powers to clear courts and to forbid the reporting of proceedings, measures which were frequently adopted.

In 1908 an amendment to the Crimes Act protected the obstetrician who might have to sacrifice the child to save the mother before or during birth. 'No one is guilty of any crime who before or during the birth of any child causes its death by means employed in good faith for the preservation of the life of the mother.'

The 1908 Juries Act brought changes to the conduct of the Coroner's Court and cases no longer had to be heard before six male jurors. Although coroners had the right to decide cases without a jury, the practice of employing a jury of four or six men persisted in some areas until 1914.

Only deaths that were sudden, unexpected or suspicious were referred to the coroner, and the inquest usually took place in the Magistrate's Court. An official verdict on the cause of death was arrived at after hearing all the relevant evidence from interested parties – relatives, friends, medical professionals and the police. Witnesses could decline to answer questions if the evidence was incriminating and they could employ a lawyer to represent their interests.

After hearing all the witnesses, the coroner decided if further evidence was required, and hearings were sometimes adjourned until, for instance, the results of tests or post-mortem findings were available, or until the result of a court trial was known.

Establishing the cause of death was not always easy. Medical professionals sometimes gave conflicting opinions. Witnesses would often lie or not tell the whole truth, to protect the privacy of the woman or to protect the abortionist who had helped her. The primary function of the Coroner's Court was not to establish guilt but to determine the cause of death. Evidential standards were less rigorous than in a criminal court.

The following story demonstrates how merely ascertaining the cause of death left many questions unanswered.

Sarah's story[2]
Deceased 30 March 1903, aged 33 years

Sarah Bennett was married to Alfred, a painter in Auckland. They had three children, one stillborn. Sarah was ill in bed for about a fortnight before Dr Moir was called on Wednesday 25 March. He suspected her abdominal pains were the result of illegal interference but Sarah denied that she was pregnant or that she had done anything. However, she did tell Dr Moir that she and her husband had had an argument about seeing Mrs So and So (he had forgotten her name), reputedly the local abortionist. Dr Moir also recalled that two years ago and four years ago, he had attended Sarah with similar abdominal symptoms, but on these two previous occasions the symptoms were less severe and she had recovered.

Over the next few days her condition deteriorated, and on Sunday morning she was transferred to Auckland Hospital, where doctors operated to empty the uterus. The pregnancy was about two to three months' gestation. On the cervix were two wounds and bruising, signs of illegal instrumentation.

A post-mortem examination confirmed injuries to the uterus and septic peritonitis. At the coroner's inquest Alfred denied any knowledge of his wife's pregnancy, any argument between them or any knowledge of an abortionist. For lack of evidence the jury returned a verdict that 'death was the result of acute blood poisoning, arising through an improper operation which had been performed for the purpose of procuring a miscarriage, but that there was no evidence before them to enable them to decide by whom the operation was performed.'

One exasperated coroner, Mr Mosley S.M., denounced the witnesses in a scathing indictment of their behaviour.

Queenie's story[3]
Deceased 21 March 1931, aged 15 years

Queenie Burley was an adopted daughter. She did not live at home and her mother knew nothing of her pregnancy. She had recently lost her job as a domestic servant in a private home. On Tuesday 17 March, because she had nowhere else to stay, a dressmaker friend Helen Williamson, 29, took Queenie to a house in Hereford Street, where she stayed until Friday 20 March.

She was then taken by Dick Harker, a young taxi driver, to spend the weekend at a bach at North Beach. She was accompanied by two friends, Hazel Flannery, 19, and Joan Lawson, 22, both domestics. Her boyfriend Charles Trillo, 19, a clerk who worked in the office of his father's Gold Band Taxi firm, joined her at the bach. On Saturday 21 March, she became seriously ill and Harker took her by taxi to Christchurch Hospital, where she died the same evening.

Dr Pearson, the pathologist at Christchurch Hospital who conducted the post-mortem, found a large perforation of the uterus. In his opinion the interference could not have been self-inflicted. The coroner found 'that death was due to general peritonitis with septic inflammation of the uterus and perforation of the uterus. This condition was the result of an illegal operation performed for the purpose of procuring a miscarriage by some person unknown.'

Her young friends attended the inquest into her death. Her female friends knew of her pregnancy and said she had taken pills and medicine. Charles Trillo refused to answer questions. The coroner was frustrated by the attitude of these uncooperative witnesses. He said:

> This girl has been nothing more or less deliberately done to death and it is a very sad thing that someone cannot be brought to book for the outrage. Most of the witnesses have told deliberate untruths or failed deliberately to tell the whole truth. That applies to the men who gave evidence and to some of the women witnesses. They have not assisted the cause of justice one iota and if their consciences do not prick them, they are not worth much.

Police enquiries led nowhere. It was never established who was responsible for the pregnancy or who carried out the operation.

Queenie was disadvantaged in many ways, but septicaemia was no respecter of class, and truth could be just as elusive in more affluent circumstances. The following case is unusual in that wealthy women rarely feature in coroner's reports or court cases.

Marjorie's story[4]
Deceased 4 April 1932, aged 27 years

Marjorie Potter lived in Mt Eden, Auckland with her father, stepmother and family. Her mother had died and her father, a prominent Auckland identity and former Mayor of Mt Eden, had remarried 13 years before. There were four children from the first marriage and one son from the second marriage. Marjorie was the only daughter. The family had a lady's help.

Marjorie did not need to work and spent most of her time playing tennis and golf. Her father gave her an allowance and paid for her clothing. She was the lady champion tennis player at the Parnell Tennis Club and enjoyed playing in tournaments. She was of slim build and usually kept very good health. However, recently she had had to retire from a tournament because she felt ill.

She was away from home on Friday 1 April and Saturday 2 April, and the family presumed she was staying with friends. It is possible she visited an abortionist. At home, she had her own room and kept very much to herself. On the morning of 4 April, her brother Ralph, 24, at her request, took her two cups of tea and some buttered toast and jam. He noticed she looked unwell and asked if he should call a doctor. She said she was recovering from stomach trouble and didn't need a doctor.

Ralph then left for work, arriving home about 6 pm. Marjorie's stepmother had been in the house in the morning and the lady's help had been in the house all day, but neither of them had heard anything or suspected anything was wrong, as Marjorie was independent and usually looked after herself. When Ralph went into her bedroom to see how she was getting on, he found her sitting in a chair with her back to the open window. She was dressed in her underclothing with bare arms, legs and feet. She had been dead for several hours. He immediately called Dr Moore.

The post-mortem found an enlarged uterus and signs that a miscarriage had taken place. Cultures grown from the uterine samples revealed staphylococci and streptococci, and the coroner found 'death was due to heart failure following a septic abortion'. Marjorie's doubles partner, Ken, denied any responsibility for her pregnancy, and any knowledge of her pregnancy or abortion. When interviewed by the police he refused to answer any questions.

Before returning his verdict, the coroner said 'Some day the police will find where the girl stayed and then some more will be known of the case. These things always come out sooner or later.' But that prediction proved wrong. Marjorie took her story to the grave.

ଔ

When warranted, coroners recommended that police further investigate any criminal activity. If police felt there was sufficient evidence, the offender would be charged with a criminal offence, such as procuring an abortion, aiding and abetting an abortion, or supplying the means to procure an abortion. Because of doctor–patient confidentiality, doctors were usually reluctant to involve police, but since 1920 doctors also had a duty to report cases of septicaemia to the Health Department, and through that route police sometimes became involved.

The offender would be charged and, in serious cases, arrested. The police prepared depositions to be heard in the Magistrate's Court, sometimes called the Lower Court or Police Court. If there was insufficient evidence, the offender would be discharged by the magistrate. If not, nearly all alleged abortion crimes were regarded as serious and were referred for trial in the Supreme Court (the equivalent of the High Court in today's justice system).

Here, a Supreme Court judge and a grand jury of 12 men (sometimes more) from the community examined the case for the prosecution in a closed sitting to decide if there was a reasonable suspicion that a crime had been committed. If there was a case to answer, the decision was a 'true bill', and if not, the decision was a 'no bill' and the case was dismissed. 'True bills' were referred for a jury trial in the Supreme Court. The grand jury system was abolished in 1961.

In the Supreme Court, the jury of 12 men had to reach a unanimous verdict of guilty or not guilty. If they could not agree (i.e., a hung jury) the presiding judge ordered a retrial. If the second jury could not agree, the judge ordered a third trial. If the third jury could not agree, the judge usually applied to the Solicitor-General or Attorney-General for a stay of proceedings (*nolle prosequi*). Rarely, a fourth trial was ordered, as in the case of Mrs Annie Aves, who underwent four trials in 1936 and 1937 before being acquitted of a charge of procuring abortion (see Chapter 9 for more details).

Any decision made in the Supreme Court could be referred to the Court of Appeal for a ruling on points of law. Sometimes the presiding judge made the referral, and at other times the prosecution or defence counsel lodged an appeal.

The question of whether an abortion was lawful or unlawful was a problem for doctors, but in 1938 a significant trial took place in London that helped to clarify matters.

Trial of Dr Aleck Bourne, 1938[5]

Dr Bourne (1886–1974), a prominent London gynaecologist, brought a test case after the rape of a 14-year-old girl, referred to him by Dr Joan Malleson. The rape, by three Horse Guardsmen, occurred in April 1938, and resulted in the girl becoming pregnant; Dr Bourne carried out an abortion for no fee in St Mary's London Hospital in June, and the trial was conducted at the Old Bailey in July. The prosecution pointed out that both Dr Malleson and Dr Bourne were members of the Medical Legal Council of the Abortion Law Reform Association, but Dr Bourne said his motive was compassion and he had acted openly and honestly. His aim was not to change the law but to clarify what was permissible under the existing law, which allowed abortion only to save the life of the mother.

Ruling in favour of Dr Bourne, Justice Macnaghten accepted the defence's argument that the abortion had been carried out in good faith because continuing the pregnancy would make the girl a 'physical or mental wreck'. This judgment helped to clarify what was lawful and unlawful with respect to abortion. The judge's ruling, although not directly applicable in New Zealand, was influential in changing medico-legal opinion in this country.

03

The criminal law was spectacularly ineffective in dealing with abortion. Police often suspected abortionists but had difficulty finding corroborative evidence that would stand up to the intense scrutiny of defence lawyers. The presence of abortion instruments on the premises did not necessarily mean they had been used, and in the case of doctors, the instruments had multiple legitimate uses.

Crown prosecutors also faced a number of hurdles. The abortionist could easily deny any involvement. If the woman visited an abortionist on her own, there could be no-one to corroborate evidence. Accompanying a woman to the abortionist's premises was insufficient to prove anything had taken place. Only the woman and the abortionist knew what had taken place, and if neither was able nor willing to say anything, it remained a secret. Letters, telegrams and money transfers were sometimes used as corroborative evidence.

Defence lawyers were often crucial to the outcome of a case. Typically, they did not call witnesses for the defence but relied on cross-examination of Crown witnesses and, in addressing the jury after all the evidence had been presented, exploited all the weaknesses of the Crown case. Two of the most prominent defence lawyers of the era were Alfred Charles Hanlon (1866–1944),[6] based in Dunedin, and Richard Arnold Singer (1878–1961),[7] who practised in Auckland for three decades.

Alfred Charles Hanlon was born in Dunedin, of Irish parents. At the age of 15 he was articled as a law clerk, and after six years he was admitted as a barrister and solicitor, then established his own legal practice. While based in Dunedin he also accepted cases from afar. In 1894 he married Polly, and the couple had three daughters and a son. His son, Jack, was gassed in World War I and suffered chronic lung disease.

Alf Hanlon was an impressive figure both in stature (he was over six feet tall) and in manner, blending passion and oratory with dignity. He habitually wore a sprig of boronia in his buttonhole. He loved the sea and belonged to yachting and boating clubs. He was passionate about sport, particularly horse racing, rugby, cricket and golf. He was a lifelong member of the Dunedin Shakespeare Society, and declaiming dramatic roles gave him as much satisfaction as courtroom oratory. His career and reputation were enhanced through the 1895 trial of Minnie Dean, the Winton 'baby farmer'. Although she was found guilty and hanged, the judge praised Hanlon for his able defence.

In 15 murder trials where he acted as senior counsel, Minnie Dean was one of three sentenced to death. In six of the other murder trials the accused were found guilty of manslaughter, and in the remaining six cases (including abortionist Mrs Glegg in 1920), the accused were found not guilty. In 1930 he became a King's Counsel, but he had no ambitions for higher office.

Alfred Charles Hanlon appeared regularly in the newspapers; here he is seen in the *Otago Daily Times*, 19 September 1930 (top left); *New Zealand Herald*, 7 February 1944 (bottom left); and *New Zealand Truth*, 27 June 1929 (top right) and 3 September 1910 (bottom right).

Hanlon defended many notable abortion cases:

1901 – Mrs Charlotte Bradbury, abortionist
1901 – Mr Thomas Whiteman, lover
1904 – Mr John Richards, lover
1906, 1919, 1923 – Mr Jimmy Hayne and Miss Elisabeth Inglis, abortionist and accomplice
1917 – Mrs Ethel Eadie, for using instrument
1917 – Mr John Blake, whose daughter had an abortion
1920 – Mrs Helen Glegg, abortionist
1922 – Mr and Mrs Harland, infanticide
1923 – Mrs Rosina McFie, subverting the course of justice
1923 – Mr Hyman Isaacs, abortionist
1923 – Mr Albert Harris, putative father
1923, 1928, 1929 – Mrs Mary Jane Clark and Miss Edith Towler, abortionist and accomplice
1929 – Mr Martin Melville, putative father

Richard Arnold Singer of Auckland, known to his friends as Dick, had a more robust style than Hanlon, and aggressively defended his clients. He was born in Camberwell, South London, where his father was a rabbi. Singer trained as a barrister in London, immigrated to New Zealand in 1902 and was admitted to the bar in 1904. He married Dorothy, and they had a son and a daughter. He was a connoisseur of the arts and music and wrote two books of poetry: *Dreams in Exile* (1908) and *The Years Go Round* (1928). He took an active part in city life and gained a reputation as a criminal and divorce lawyer.

In 1929 Singer was in court himself, for failing to file tax returns. In 1930 his wife died tragically when one night she took a lethal dose of Lysol. The coroner's verdict was accidental poisoning, not suicide. Singer himself survived a murder attempt in July 1937, when a home-made bomb was thrown at him as he arrived home from work in a taxi. He was hospitalised with serious injuries but resumed court work after seven weeks' convalescence. The perpetrator was never found. Anti-Semitism may have been the trigger. After the accident, his health declined and he suffered a nervous breakdown. In July 1941, his name was struck off the roll of barristers and solicitors of the Supreme Court of New Zealand by the disciplinary committee of the New Zealand Law Society. He had appropriated for his own purposes a debenture left in his custody, and was censured even though he paid it back.

A Flawed Law • 137

Richard Arnold Singer also featured regularly in the *NZ Truth*; these pictures of him appeared in the newspaper on 7 May 1910 (top right), 4 August 1923 (top left) and 17 May 1928 (bottom left).

The 1910 picture was captioned:
'Mr R. A. Singer
(Solicitor and Poet, Auckland).
His law is good, and others know it;
A smart young man, though he does not show it;
A lawyer sharp, and a medium poet,
Is Singer.'

In 1944 Singer published a book, *24 Notable Crimes*, based on a series of radio broadcasts he had made for the New Zealand Broadcasting Service.[8] He then moved to Australia, but his application to practice there as a barrister was refused. He died in Australia in 1961.

Singer's notable abortion cases included:

1910 – Mrs Martha Maxwell, abortionist
1911, 1925, 1926 – Mrs Martha O'Shaughnessy, abortionist
1912 – Miss Emmil Warner, abortionist
1915 – Mr Gifford Bowern, putative father
1917, 1922 – Mrs Hannah Dalton, nurse
1917, 1923 – Mrs Jessie Armstrong, abortionist
1918 – Mr Charles Christey, supplier of medicine
1922 – Mr David and Mrs Jean Imrie and Mrs O'Shaughnessy, accomplices and abortionist
1924 – Mrs Maud Herbert, abortionist
1928 – Dr Joseph Hennessy, abortionist
1929 – Mrs Jessie Morris, abortionist
1929 – Mrs Georgina Colnett, abortionist
1929, 1939 – Mrs Adeline Pyle, abortionist
1930 – Mrs Edith Beagles, abortionist
1930 – Mrs Lydia Lyon, nurse
1931 – Mrs Hilda Richardson, nurse
1931 – Mr Alfred Woodley, lover/alleged amateur abortionist
1932, 1935 – 'Dr' George Hewer, abortionist
1932 – Mrs Margaret Arnott, abortionist
1932 – Mr Ralph Sanft, chemist
1932 – Mr Raymond Grigg, abortionist
1933 – Mr Robert and Mrs Mary Campbell, abortionist and accomplice
1935 – Mrs Adelaide Porter (aka Mrs Thornton), abortionist
1936 – Mr Alfred Sanft, chemist assistant
1937 – Mrs Louisa Beuth, abortionist

Abortion was a serious crime, but the sentences imposed by judges, most commonly up to seven years' imprisonment, failed to deter. Juries often failed to convict. There was considerable public sympathy for abortionists whose main motivation was to help women in distress, and many jurors would have been aware of situations in their personal lives where a woman had benefited from the services of an abortionist.

Women were usually given immunity from prosecution in return for information about an alleged abortionist, and the unfairness of this strategy was not lost on male jurists. However, the woman's evidence was often ruled inadmissible because she was an accomplice to the crime. Judges routinely cautioned juries about accepting uncorroborated evidence from an accomplice, and defence counsel made the most of this.

Immunity could be complicated. In the following case, a couple who refused to testify at the trial of an abortionist were subsequently charged themselves. The man was convicted but not the woman. The abortionist was then retried and this time convicted, when the couple testified against him.

Trials of Charles McPherson and John Pascoe, 1906[9]

Charles McPherson, foundry fitter, was a prominent young West Coast footballer from a highly respected family. He had known Miss Mary McCormick for three years, and when she told him in February 1906 that she was pregnant, he contacted John Pascoe, a Reefton veterinary surgeon who had a reputation in the district as an abortionist.

For a fee of £15, two operations, a week apart, were alleged to have taken place in a railway station on the outskirts of Greymouth between 1 and 13 March 1906. On 15 March, Mary miscarried and was attended to by a chemist, who referred her to a nurse, who referred her to a doctor. She recovered, and married Charles on 3 April.

Police interviewed both Charles and Mary, and as a result Pascoe was charged with procuring abortion. In April, Pascoe appeared in the Greymouth Magistrate's Court. Charles and Mary were both called as witnesses but they refused to swear to statements previously made to the police, pleading they would incriminate themselves. Without their evidence, there was nothing to connect Pascoe to the offences and he was discharged.

However, when the court resumed later that afternoon, the McPhersons were both charged – Charles with employing Pascoe to carry out an abortion and Mary with allowing this to happen. Had they answered questions in Pascoe's case they would not have been charged, as they would have been given immunity in return for supplying crucial evidence.

Due to legal delays the McPhersons were kept on remand with bail for months, but eventually in September 1906 both were tried in the Hokitika Supreme Court. The jury found Charles guilty but made a strong recommendation for mercy, citing his good name, that this was his first and unlikely to be repeated offence, and that he had married Mary. Dismissing the defence's plea for probation, Justice Edwards imposed a sentence of two years' imprisonment with hard labour. The Crown did not proceed with the case against Mary.

As a result of Charles's conviction, Pascoe was then charged in the Magistrate's Court in October 1906, and this time the McPhersons gave evidence against him. Pascoe was committed for trial in the Christchurch Supreme Court in November 1906. The jury found him guilty and Justice Denniston sentenced him to seven years' imprisonment, remarking as he did so that this was not the first time Pascoe had been charged with the offence of abortion.

Justice Sir John Denniston. (*Sun*, 13 February 1917)

In fact, on 10 March 1905, one year before operating on Mary, he had faced a similar charge in the Westland Supreme Court, Hokitika. At his first trial, presided over by Justice Cooper, the jury could not agree and a fresh trial was ordered. When the second jury also found him not guilty, the judge could not refrain from saying, 'Although not convicted with the crime with which you are charged you leave the dock a disgraced man. Go!' One year later, he was not so lucky.

୧୨

The man suspected of being responsible for a pregnancy (husband, lover, friend or rapist) could easily deny any involvement, and tests were not available to prove or disprove paternity. Husbands frequently denied any knowledge their wife's pregnancy. Because of the privacy and confidentiality of sexual relationships, such matters were not easily discussed even in the intimacy of the home, so it was not surprising that such information was withheld in a doctor's consulting room, and that there was an even greater reluctance to divulge such intimate details to police or in the glare of the courtroom. However, men who shirked their responsibility came in for criticism.

Mary Ann's story[10]
Deceased 18 March 1914, aged 23 years

Mary Ann Hegarty lived in Christchurch with her mother and worked as an assistant in a drapery shop. She did not confide in her family about her pregnancy or her abortion. One Saturday night she went to the home of her sister-in-law, Catherine, and had a miscarriage in the chamber pot in the middle of the night. Catherine stayed up most of the night caring for Mary Ann and by the morning she was so worried she called in Dr Simpson.

Mary Ann's condition worsened and on Monday she was admitted to the Alexandra Nursing Home. She was operated on at 8.30 that night and died on Wednesday night. On the day before she died police questioned her, but she refused to divulge any information. She told the doctors she had only taken pills and quinine, but they suspected she had been interfered with.

Dr Fenwick, who conducted the post-mortem, found extensive peritonitis and, in his opinion, this was almost certainly caused by the use of a dirty instrument. The coroner, acting alone, found Mary Ann had 'died from peritonitis caused by inflammation in the uterine cavity due to an illegal operation.'

The headline in *NZ Truth* scathingly proclaimed 'One More Unfortunate. Mary Ann Hegarty's Mysterious Death. Values Seducer's Honor More Than Her Life.' The reporter wrote:

> The atmosphere of mystery and tragic circumstances which characterised the death of Mary Ann Hegarty at Christchurch last week cannot fail to strike a dual chord of sympathy in the feelings of the broad-minded public. This sympathy for the unfortunate girl whose lips, during her dying hours, were sealed on the names responsible for her untimely death will be equalled only by the contempt felt for the girl's seducer, whose name and personality we are unable to disclose. In consequence of this the blackguard will be permitted to follow his way through life and take his stand among his fellows with a smug equanimity coupled with a

feeling of satisfaction at having denied other innocent girls in the country of the danger signal the publicity of his name would have provided. *Truth* insists sincerely that the rascal will soon receive his just dues instead of the protection he hoped for from the silence maintained by the girl whom he killed. Whilst *Truth* fully appreciates the admirable spirit which prompted Miss Hegarty to keep silent when she realised that she was dying and that whatever she could say might wreck other lives and other homes than her own, it is equally obvious that such splendid charity was far more than the conscienceless seducer, who religiously held aloof from the girl during the whole time of her trouble, deserved.

The mystery was never solved and the rascal never received his just dues.

଄

In the following story, five years later, the grand jury went as far as recommending a law change to hold men more accountable by removing the immunity to arrest in exchange for evidence.

Friede's story[11]
Deceased 4 March 1919, aged 22 years

Miss Friede Sandel worked as a waitress in the Trafalgar Hotel, Nelson. She was having an affair with a married man, Jack Richard, who would climb the fire escape to see her. Friede confided in her waitress friend, Emily Newport, that Jack had slept with her nearly every night for the last four months and now she was about ten weeks pregnant. She had already taken Apioloid pills and had tried to use a catheter but needed help. Together one afternoon they took a taxi to visit the local abortionist, Mrs Fletcher.

Mrs Fletcher said she would not do the abortion on a Wednesday because it was unlucky. Friede said she had a catheter and equipment in her room at the hotel, and Mrs Fletcher returned with Friede and Emily in the taxi to see it. In her evidence Emily alleged that Mrs Fletcher advised Friede to get some washing soda and Sunlight soap. Money changed hands, Friede giving a £1 note to Mrs Fletcher, who then syringed her with soap and warm water. After the operation Friede gave Mrs Fletcher another £4. Emily kept an eye on Friede because she had fainted twice during the procedure. The next day she had a miscarriage in the chamber pot.

When she became unwell with abdominal pain, Dr Lucas was summoned. He diagnosed an incomplete miscarriage and admitted Friede to Nelson Hospital under the care of the superintendent, Dr Jamieson. Dr Lucas and Dr Jamieson examined her under anaesthetic and found that the abortion had been completed but the uterus was exceedingly inflamed. Later Friede told Dr Jamieson that something had been done to terminate the pregnancy. Her condition rapidly deteriorated and she died at 2 am on 4 March.

The post-mortem revealed a large tear in her uterus and in the opinion of the doctors this had not been caused by self-use of a catheter but by some other unskilled person wielding an instrument with considerable force. The abdomen was full of pus. The coroner concluded that Friede 'had died from peritonitis and septic poisoning following on criminal abortion performed on her on Thursday 27 February 1919.'

Trial of Mrs Emma Caroline Fletcher, 1919

Jack Richard was not charged but Mrs Fletcher, 38, was brought to trial. A grand jury deliberated for two hours before returning with a 'true bill' on both indictments – for murder, and for unlawfully using an instrument. They added the following rider to their verdict: 'That in the opinion of this Grand Jury the criminal law in New Zealand should be so amended as to do away with the present immunity from arrest and indictment of the male offender whose action is the primary cause of the trouble.' His Honour Justice Hosking thanked the grand jury and said he would forward the presentment to the proper authorities. The law was not altered.

Friede's friend Emily Newport refused to answer questions until she was granted immunity by the Crown. She had made a detailed statement to the constable in charge of the case, which described the events leading up to Friede's death. The judge considered that the Crown should have given her a free pardon, and offered to adjourn the case for the Crown to wire to Wellington for such a pardon. This was done.

At the first trial in the Nelson Supreme Court, the jury was out from 5.45 pm to 9.40 pm and failed to agree. A second trial was set to take place the next day with a new jury. The jury retired at 3.30 pm and after five hours announced that it was impossible for them to agree. A third trial was ordered to take place on 22 July 1919, but this was delayed until 5 August, then until 29 August, then until 25 September, when it was conducted by Justice Stringer. This time the jury returned a verdict of not guilty of using an instrument with intent to procure a miscarriage. Justice Stringer recommended the Crown enter a *nolle prosequi* (no prosecution), but as the Crown Prosecutor had no authority to do this, his Honour decided the matter should be held over till the December sitting of the Supreme Court. Meanwhile, Mrs Fletcher was freed on bail.

In December, the Crown Prosecutor intimated that the Crown did not intend to proceed with the murder charge. Justice Stringer, addressing the accused, explained that this did not necessarily mean that the Crown did not intend to proceed further. Mrs Fletcher was now at liberty, but if further evidence arose, and the Crown considered they were justified in proceeding, they could do so. It was not the same as a discharge after a verdict of not guilty.

☙

Some men were chivalrous. Harold refused to testify against his lover, Alma.

Trials of Harold George Holland and Alma Green, 1917[12]

Harold Holland was a hop grower from Belgrove, in the Nelson-Marlborough area. He had been friends with Alma for about eight years. When she terminated an unplanned pregnancy, a family friend, purporting to be acting in her best interests, went to the police. Harold was charged with procuring and unlawfully supplying an instrument on or about the month of November 1916. Alma was also charged, and both cases were heard together in the Nelson Magistrate's Court. The public were asked to leave the court.

Mrs Louisa Jackson and her husband Thomas, of Tory Channel, testified they had known Alma for many years. She had a standing invitation to come and stay with them and Alma did so at the end of 1916, staying for 11 weeks. She was about six months pregnant at the time. Mrs Jackson wrote to Harold suggesting he marry Alma, but Alma's mother disapproved, as Harold suffered from tuberculosis.

The story that unfolded in court was that Harold sent Alma two parcels. One of these contained a rubber instrument with a wire insert (a catheter and stilette) and the other contained a long silvery instrument, pointed at one end and hollow, which Harold had had fashioned by George Brown, a manufacturing jeweller in Nelson. Alma was annoyed to receive these gifts and showed them to Mrs Jackson, who strongly disapproved of Alma doing anything with them. Harold sent Mrs Jackson £10 for looking after Alma and £60 for Alma.

Soon after receiving the money, Alma left for Wellington and gave her forwarding address as 'Mrs Anstice, Sydney Street', reputedly one of Wellington's abortionists. The next time Mrs Jackson saw Alma, she had resumed her slim shape and was childless. One of her letters, written about a fortnight after she left for Wellington, from a nursing home in Wadestown where she was convalescing, said 'It was a baby boy and it cried.' Upon receiving this news, Mrs Jackson went to the police with other incriminating letters and telegrams sent and received while Alma was staying with her.

Mrs Jackson said in evidence that Alma told her she had been to Mrs Anstice in Wellington and, for a fee of £160, she had used an instrument not unlike the one that Harold sent her, but larger. A doctor visited her the next day in Nurse Jenner's nursing home and took the instrument away. Shortly after that, the child was born prematurely but did not live long. It would have been about seven months' gestation.

When the cases were referred to the Nelson Supreme Court in March 1917, they were treated separately by Justice Chapman. In the first case, against Harold, the public and all witnesses were cleared from the court. After deliberating for four hours the jury found him guilty of two of the three charges (procuring and supplying) but not the alleged contact with the Wellington abortionist. His defence lawyer, Mr Wilford, made a strong plea for special consideration,

Justice Frederick Revans Chapman.
(*NZ Truth*, 11 February 1911)

as Harold was a first offender and of good character. He also objected to the detective's questioning and asked for a referral to the Court of Appeal. Justice Chapman rejected this and sentenced Harold to three years' imprisonment with hard labour.

Alma's case was then heard before Justice Chapman. Harold was called as a Crown witness but he refused to answer any questions and was regarded as a hostile witness. The judge warned him more than once that there would be consequences unless he answered the questions. Harold maintained his silence, and for his flagrant contempt of court Justice Chapman added 18 months to his original sentence of three years. In Alma's case the jury returned in less than an hour with a verdict of not guilty.

ɊЯ

Sometimes the man did not believe he was responsible for the pregnancy and suspected, rightly or wrongly, that he was being blackmailed. It was frequently a case of one person's word against another.

Trial of Bertram Bunn, 1915[13]

Bertram Bunn, 31, was a soldier with the Expeditionary Force at Trentham. In civilian life he was a civic-minded grain merchant from Christchurch. In the last election he had stood as a Reform Party candidate for the Riccarton electorate. He was charged with eight counts of supplying Mrs Eliza O'Donnell, 24, with the means to procure miscarriage between the months of July and October 1914.

Eliza lived with her parents, having separated from her husband a fortnight after her marriage three years before. She had known Bunn for about a year, under the false impression he was a single man. In her evidence she said Bunn had supplied her with several lots of pills and medicine to bring on a miscarriage. The pills made her sick, so she stopped taking them and her mother confiscated them. She also tried hot mustard baths and eating boiled onions, with no effect. She said Bunn told her he could arrange for her to have an operation and made several dangerous suggestions, which she declined. One was to see a woman 'doctor' who would perform an operation 'round the river bed or anywhere' and another was to visit a 'doctor' who required clients to be blindfolded when taken there and back.

On 13 March Eliza delivered a child, which lived for four hours. The charges against Bunn arose out of an investigation into the death of her illegitimate child. In the Christchurch Supreme Court, presided over by Justice Denniston, Bunn was ably defended by Mr Hanlon, who demolished much of the evidence given by Eliza and her mother, father and sister. Most damning was the allegation that Eliza's mother had offered to make Eliza leave Christchurch and keep things quiet in return for £400 or £500 from Bunn. The jury deliberated for one hour and forty minutes before finding Bunn not guilty.

Subsequently Eliza sued for maternity expenses in connection with her illegitimate child, but the magistrate dismissed the case. By the end of the year Eliza's husband sued for divorce on the grounds of adultery.

ଛ

Except for purveyors of abortifacients, most abortionists did not seek out clients but, at considerable risk to themselves, provided an on-request service. Those who flaunted their reputation, exploited vulnerable women, demanded sexual favours, used dangerous methods, charged high fees or caused death were generally disapproved of by the public, the police and the judiciary. Sometimes investigation of one crime led to another, as in the following story.

Eileen's story[14]
Deceased 22 December 1922, aged 29 years

Eileen O'Donoghue was born in Napier and lived with her mother practically all her life. About seven months before her death she left home to go and live with friends of the family, Mr and Mrs Martin of Shannon Station, about 35 miles from Wairoa. Mrs Martin was pregnant and Eileen was going to help out at the station during her pregnancy and confinement. When Mrs Martin was away from June to October, Mr Martin had become intimate with Eileen and got her pregnant as well.

In December, Eileen came to Gisborne with a letter and a cheque for £40 addressed to Andrew Sheerin, barman at the Royal Hotel and a cousin of Mr Martin. He made arrangements for Eileen to see Mrs Quinn. Eileen first stayed at the Albion Hotel and then at the Arcadia. She was taken by taxi to Mrs

Quinn's house and later had a miscarriage at the Arcadia. When she became ill, Dr Singer was called in. He gave Eileen a referral letter to Cook Hospital but she refused to go there, and three or four days later she left by the *Arahura* sailing for Napier.

Eileen wrote to say she would be home for Christmas and arrived on 21 December. However, when she arrived she was very ill and hardly able to speak. Her mother put her to bed and gave her a cup of tea. Eileen said she had indigestion and it had turned to ulceration of the stomach. Next morning she was worse and her mother called in Dr Moore. Eileen confided in Dr Moore that she had miscarried when she was two months pregnant, and he strongly suspected it was a case of an illegal abortion, although no details were divulged.

Dr Moore diagnosed peritonitis and admitted her straight away to Napier Hospital. Her mother accompanied her there in the ambulance. Within four hours of her arrival, doctors operated to empty the womb and evacuate a large quantity of pus from the abdomen. Her condition deteriorated and she died that same evening. The coroner, acting alone, found the cause of death was 'acute general septic poisoning and exhaustion following acute general peritonitis, the result of a pelvic abscess secondary to acute septic infection of the womb and Fallopian tubes.'

Police enquiries led to charges against Mrs Quinn, not only for the death of Eileen, but also for unlawfully using an instrument on another young woman, Mona Hamon. Albert Harris, who was responsible for Mona's pregnancy, was also charged.

Trial of Mrs Frances Quinn and Mr Albert Ernest Harris, 1923[15]

In February 1923, Mrs Frances Quinn, 30, abortionist of McLean Street, Gisborne, and the man responsible for Mona's pregnancy, Mr Albert Ernest Harris, 41, a well-known sheep farmer, were both charged with unlawfully using an instrument for the purposes of performing an illegal operation. Mrs Quinn was also charged with Eileen O'Donoghue's death. The Magistrate's Court was cleared for the hearing.

Mona said she had known Harris for about 12 months and for the last nine months had been going out in his car. In November she found she was pregnant and Harris obtained pills for her, which did not work. He then arranged for her to see Mrs Quinn and accompanied her on visits to Mrs Quinn's home, where an instrument was used on Mona four times. On the fourth occasion, a fortnight before Christmas, Mona met up with Harris in town at midday and he took her to Mrs Quinn's. Three women were there at the time and another operation could not be carried out on account of the visitors. Mrs Quinn asked Mona to stay for the afternoon, stating she did not think she would have time to 'fix her up' that day because she was 'fixing up' Miss O'Donoghue, who was staying at the Arcadia.

Shortly before 8 pm Mona and Harris saw Mrs Quinn and Eileen in a taxi, and Mona and Harris were invited to join them. When they had gone a certain distance Mrs Quinn asked the taxi driver to stop the car and Mona and Mrs Quinn got out and went over to a ditch, where Mrs Quinn carried out the fourth operation. The car was about 200 yards ahead of them. They walked back to the car and later drove to Mona's home. Harris paid for the taxi.

Mona haemorrhaged and ended up having to go to Sister Brewer's private hospital to be operated on by Dr Collins. He concluded Mona was septic due to an illegal abortion and admitted her to Cook Hospital, Gisborne. She was treated and eventually recovered after six weeks in hospital. After depositions in the Magistrate's Court along these lines, both Mrs Quinn and Albert Harris were committed for trial in the Supreme Court.

Much to the disappointment of the crowd that had turned up to watch the proceedings, Justice Reed cleared the court. On the first charge, the manslaughter of Eileen by Mrs Quinn, the jury retired for only 50 minutes and returned a verdict of guilty. She was sentenced severely to seven years in gaol with hard labour, to be followed by a period of five years' reformative detention. On the second charge, of unlawfully using an instrument on Mona Hamon, the jury could not agree and the judge ordered a retrial. No increase in the sentence is recorded.

Mr Hanlon, coming all the way from Dunedin, defended Harris. The jury found Harris guilty on three charges as an accomplice. In her evidence Mona produced letters written to her by Harris and signed 'J. O. Tricks'. The letters revealed Mona was not the only one he was intimate with. Detective McLeod confirmed that it was a matter of common knowledge that Harris was in the habit of joyriding with young unmarried women by day and night.

The jury was out for only 15 minutes and returned with a verdict of guilty on three charges. In sentencing Harris, the judge said 'You are simply a lustful man prepared to take advantage of any young girl you can get hold of. Your case is different from that of a professional abortionist. You did not do it for money. Therefore your penalty is lighter.' Harris was sentenced to five years' imprisonment with hard labour.

His Honour then made a public pronouncement in regard to juries:[16]

> For some extraordinary reason there is a certain type of man whose sympathies are with abortionists in this class of case. For that reason it is sometimes difficult to secure conviction. Although no man desires to be complimented on doing his duty, I think Gisborne is to be congratulated on the way in which the juries in these cases have done their duty and thus wiped out an unclean spot in the town. If all juries did their duty in a similar manner we should hear less of this class of case. An acquittal when the evidence is clear is only an encouragement to this class of person to carry on her nefarious trade.

Justice John Ranken Reed (left: *New Zealand Herald*, 19 October 1928; right: *Observer*, 12 June 1915).

Police and Crown prosecutors frequently had difficulty presenting corroborative evidence, especially from accomplices. In the following case, the solution to this problem was not well received.

Trial of Thomas Brown and Edward Arthur Raven, 1904[17]

On 10 September in the Magistrate's Court, New Plymouth, police charged Thomas Brown and Edward Arthur Raven with the procurement of the miscarriage of a young tailoress, Fanny Coombes, 21, on 5 September. Both men pleaded guilty and were committed for sentencing in the Supreme Court.

On 26 September, in the New Plymouth Supreme Court, Thomas Brown, 68, herbalist of Opunake, was sentenced to five years' gaol for procuring abortion. For obtaining the services of Brown on behalf of his girlfriend, Raven, a young draper's assistant, was sentenced to two years' hard labour, but he was immediately remanded while the particulars of his turning King's evidence were submitted to Wellington. Raven turned King's evidence on the condition that any sentence imposed on him would be remitted. He was remanded to gaol for a few hours and thereupon reprieved.

The Minister of Justice, Mr McGowan, was asked to justify the Crown's actions. He explained that the police suspected Brown was a professional abortionist who had been operating for many years, but for lack of evidence they were never able to lay charges. Miss Coombes had undergone her operation in the dark in the recreation grounds and was unable to identify the operator. It was only through Raven's evidence that a prosecution against Brown would succeed, and Brown's guilty plea was made only in the knowledge that Raven would testify against him.

There was nothing unusual at the time in granting a pardon or remission of sentence to people who turned King's evidence, but this explanation inflamed the citizens of Taranaki. Raven was a Sunday School teacher and a strong advocate of Christian Endeavour, but many saw him as morally bankrupt. He had seduced the young woman while engaged to another, offered £10 to Brown to perform the operation, then, to save his own skin, turned on the man who had helped him out of his predicament. The young woman suffered serious complications, was admitted to hospital and could have died. It seemed unfair that Brown be condemned to five years' penal servitude when the Minister of Justice had intervened and released Raven for giving King's evidence when, in the opinion of many, there was ample other evidence to convict. Letters to the editor flowed freely over this whole affair.

ଔ

Sometimes, unfairly, police found it easier to charge the lesser participant and let others go free.

Katie's story[18]
Deceased 6 October 1915, aged 34

Mrs Catherine Stanley, or Katie, as she was known in the family, was married to Percival Stanley, a storeman at Dalgety's in Dunedin. They had been married for six years and had two sons, aged four and two. Katie's mother thought Percy drank too much and treated his wife badly.

When Katie became pregnant again, Percy got a box of 'Female Pills' from his friend, Mr Walter Towler, who was the son of the infamous Mrs Elizabeth Towler in the Arcade. Mrs Towler carried on a business as a 'ladies specialist' although she had no qualifications. She made the pills and sold them to approved customers. They made Katie feel sick and did not work, so Percy suggested she see Mrs Towler herself. The two met, as arranged, at Halligan's butcher's shop and Mrs Towler took her to see the abortionist Mrs Maud Turner, whose husband was in the asylum. Mrs Turner would not do anything until £5 was paid. She then operated, but this too was unsuccessful, and after three visits Katie requested her money back. Percy had to intervene and bully Mrs Turner into refunding the money, which was paid in two instalments.

Katie did not miscarry after these alleged operations, but about four or five weeks later she became unwell. Dr Williams visited her and thought she had a threatened miscarriage. On 30 September, when her condition deteriorated, he admitted her to Dunedin Hospital by ambulance. She was about four months pregnant, and bleeding. Dr Bowie operated and initially thought she had a bicornuate uterus, but in fact she had a large laceration. He removed a dead fetus, but shortly after she collapsed and died.

At the post-mortem, the pathologist, Dr Roberts, found extensive peritonitis and considered the laceration in the uterus had most likely been caused by the forceful use of a blunt instrument by an unskilled person. This intervention had probably occurred at least a week before her death, but there was no history confirming this. At the inquest, the Towlers (mother, daughter, son and daughter-in-law) and Mrs Turner denied everything. In accordance with the evidence of the pathologist, the coroner's verdict was that the 'deceased died from sudden heart failure consequent upon toxic absorption from pelvic lesions caused by the use of an instrument in an illegal operation on deceased to procure a miscarriage.'

Much against Percy's wishes, it was Katie's brother, James Houston, who reported her death to the police. Percy was subsequently charged with attempting to supply a noxious thing to his wife in order to procure a miscarriage, but the two women, Mrs Towler and Mrs Turner, were not charged. Percy was found not guilty.

ଔ

Judges frequently delivered homilies that were repeated in the press for the benefit of the public. In the following case, Justice Cooper expressed his views at length when sentencing a young man.

Trials of William Henry Sutcliffe, 1904, and Thomas Lawrence, 1905[19]

Pansy Butterfield, unemployed, and Thomas Lawrence had been companions for six months. When Pansy became pregnant Lawrence obtained pills for her to take, and when these did not work he took her on six occasions to see William Sutcliffe at a house in Hereford Street, Christchurch, where she was operated upon until a miscarriage occurred. Lawrence paid Sutcliffe £10.

When Pansy became ill a doctor was called and Pansy disclosed what had happened. Police charged Sutcliffe with unlawful use of an instrument to procure abortion in June and July 1904. Lawrence was arrested by police on board a steamer to Wellington, travelling under an assumed name, and police charged him with counselling another to procure abortion. Sutcliffe and Lawrence were tried separately in the Christchurch Supreme Court presided over by Justice Denniston. In November 1904 the jury took only a quarter of an hour to find Sutcliffe guilty. He was sentenced to six years' imprisonment.

Theophilis Cooper, Auckland barrister (*Observer*, 29 June 1895).
He became Justice Cooper in 1901.

Lawrence pleaded guilty but his sentence was postponed, Justice Denniston reserving a point for consideration of the Court of Appeal. This concerned the admissibility of a telegram purported to have been sent by Lawrence to Pansy under a false name. In April 1905, the Court of Appeal, comprising the Chief Justice Sir Robert Stout and four learned judges, unanimously agreed the telegram was not admissible and the conviction could not stand. The court ordered a new trial, which took place in May 1905 with Justice Cooper presiding. Lawrence had by this time spent six months in prison.

This time, Lawrence at first pleaded not guilty but then changed his plea to guilty. Witnesses testified to his good character and unblemished record. His defence counsel pleaded for probation, but the judge dismissed this. *The Press* reported fully the remarks of the judge when sentencing Lawrence:[20]

> He was quite sure that the accused had hitherto borne a good character, and that must, to some extent, perhaps, in a case of the present description, weigh with him in determining the measure of punishment that would be inflicted upon the accused. But the offence was one of an extremely serious nature, so serious indeed that although the accused had not actually committed the offence of procuring the miscarriage, the Legislature had placed him in the same category as the person who actually committed the offence. He was afraid that there was not sufficient consideration or sufficient thought on the part of young men when they indulged in vicious practices, and wished to get rid of the consequences of their vicious acts. He was afraid that there was not sufficient consideration shown first for the girl, and secondly for the example which such men set to the community. He was afraid some people thought the procuring of the miscarriage of a girl was a venial offence. He entirely disagreed with that, for he considered it to be a serious offence, one of the most serious a man could commit. It had been suggested that the accused's degree of guilt, although in the eye of the law it was the same as that of a man who actually committed the offence, was of a lesser nature. That was a matter of opinion. When a girl who had fallen and was under a strong temptation to get rid of the consequences of her fall, fell into that temptation and obtained or persuaded another person to commit the offence, there might be something to be said in favour of the girl, because she wished to cover her shame and to get rid of the consequences of what was as much the act of the person

who seduced her as her own act. But where a man got a girl into trouble and declined to marry that girl and persuaded another person to commit the offence of abortion upon that girl, he was very much afraid the reason why the offence was committed was not so much to save the girl from shame as to get the man himself out of the trouble and expense of supporting the child. The principal offender, that was the man who actually performed the operation, had been sentenced by the Court to six years' imprisonment. It might be said, and had been said by the accused's counsel, that the principal's act differed from that of the accused inasmuch as he performed the act for reward, but the principal offender would not have been in trouble in which he had been, and he would not have been expiating the consequences of his crime had he not been persuaded to commit that crime by the accused. It was always a very painful thing to any judge, and to him especially, to see a young man in the accused's position. It was very painful to have to administer the law as one who in his conscience thought it ought to be administered, but he could not pass over that offence either by admitting the accused to probation or by sentencing him to a short term of imprisonment. He failed to see any material difference between the accused's guilt and that of Sutcliffe, the principal offender. He would take into consideration one or two matters. First he would take into consideration the time during which the accused had been in gaol, and secondly that he did not persist in his defence the previous day. Taking all the circumstances into consideration and the accused's previous good character, he could not impose upon him a less sentence than four years' imprisonment with hard labour, to take effect from the present time.

ଓଃ

Sometimes even the judges showed mercy, albeit for unusual reasons.

Trial of Charles Raymond Christey, 1918[21]

Charles Christey, a middle-aged proprietor of the billiard saloon at Tuakau, was disabled and confined to a wheelchair. He developed a platonic friendship with 17-year-old Julia Booker and told her one day if she was ever in trouble to get in touch, because in such matters he was as good as a doctor. When she became pregnant that is exactly what she did, writing to ask for help. She later called on him and he gave her a small bottle of medicine with typewritten instructions to take a dessertspoonful as directed. She took two doses and became sick. She wrote to Christey again and he replied, sending the letter by a boy care of her employer, who, intending no wrong, sent it on care of her mother. When her mother opened the letter and read the contents she immediately informed the police. The boy, the employer and Julia's mother all testified to this in the Magistrate's Court.

The government analyst identified the liquid as a compound of mercury used for the prevention of abortion in cattle and in the treatment of syphilis. The analyst said this particular preparation was double strength and dangerous to use internally. It was a violent poison which could cause gastric irritation and purging. If used correctly the dose would be thirty drops, or half a teaspoonful, not the dessertspoonful Christey had advised.

Justice Stringer presided over the case in the Auckland Supreme Court on 13 December 1918. Christey was defended by Mr Singer, who did not call any witnesses to give evidence. Addressing the jury, he emphasised that Julia, who had given evidence, was an accomplice to the crime. He stressed Christey's disabilities and the fact he had a ten-year-old daughter who depended upon him. After a retirement lasting over the lunch hour, the jury returned a verdict of guilty. Sentence was deferred until the following morning.

Justice Stringer expressed satisfaction in the jury exercising sufficient moral courage to find a verdict in accordance with the evidence. He said there had been a tendency among certain juries to look upon the procuring of abortion as a more or less legitimate employment, which was, of course, a deplorable state of affairs. In addressing the accused, he stated:[22]

> I think in my experience that this is almost the first time a conviction has been recorded. In this case you are – unfortunately for yourself – a cripple and have been so for many years, and that is going to afford you protection. I realise sending you to gaol would not be any great punishment for you and would be extremely inconvenient for the gaol officials. I have therefore come to the conclusion that it is not desirable to send you to gaol. I have strong suspicions from the evidence that this is not the only case in which you have been implicated, but I am not going to consider that in sentencing you. I will assume it is your

only case. I order you to come up for sentence when called upon. That means that you escape the punishment which you richly deserve, and which I would have administered to you but for your physical disability; but if you are brought up on a similar charge you may rely upon it you will receive considerable punishment and you will do well to take warning.

All the accused said was, 'Thank you, your Honour.'

ଓ

Prosecution was possible even if the woman was not pregnant, as in the following story.

Catherine's story[23]
Deceased 28 March 1912, aged 24 years

Catherine McGill was married to John, a carpenter of Auckland, and they had two children, the youngest five months old. Dr Bernardi delivered Catherine's youngest child but had not seen her since, until he was called in urgently on Monday morning, 25 March. He found her in bed with a high fever, passing blood clots vaginally. He advised immediate transfer to Auckland Hospital, but Catherine refused to go. He then telephoned another doctor to come and administer an anaesthetic at 2 pm while he examined the womb. Dr Bernardi discovered a perforation and he refrained from any further exploration. He insisted Catherine go to the hospital and the following morning she was admitted, but she died two days later.

At the inquest Dr Bull, who conducted the post-mortem, said he found three wounds in the uterus, one of which had perforated the wall. He considered the perforating wound had probably occurred before Dr Bernardi saw her and thought it impossible for Catherine to have made it herself. Dr Bernardi, however, disagreed. Dr McGuire, chief medical officer at the hospital, agreed with Dr Bull about the improbability of Catherine using an instrument on herself. Death was due to septicaemia, the result of peritonitis caused by the perforation. Sadly, there was no evidence of pregnancy.

Dr Bull and Dr McGuire presumed Catherine, believing herself to be pregnant, went to some unskilled person who operated upon her. The coroner directed the jury of six men to find a verdict of manslaughter against some person or persons unknown, and this verdict was returned accordingly. The callous headline in the *New Zealand Herald* read 'Woman's Fatal Delusion'.

Trial of Mrs Harriet Garaway Mincham, 1912[24]

The police continued their enquiries and as a result charged Mrs Mincham, 23, with supplying an instrument for the deceased to perform the act of abortion on herself. Catherine's husband, who was not charged, gave evidence in the Auckland Magistrate's Court and provided information not available at the coroner's inquest. He now admitted providing his wife with pills and confirmed that Mrs Mincham had visited their house, supplying his wife with a catheter but neglecting to give her instructions on how to use it. The evening before being admitted to hospital his wife asked a woman friend to dispose of the pills and the catheter, the latter burnt in the fireplace. Police submitted as an exhibit a reinforced catheter similar to the one used.

In June 1912 Mrs Mincham, described as being very stylishly dressed and very composed, faced trial in the Auckland Supreme Court, presided over by Justice Sim. After hearing the evidence, the jury, after one hour's retirement, found Mrs Mincham not guilty.

☙

From left: Justice Sim, Justice Stringer, Justice Herdman. (*New Zealand Herald*, 8 April 1927)

Women could be charged with permitting someone else to procure an abortion. Judges tended to be lenient and women were typically given two years' probation.

Trial of Gladys Harriet Prout, 1934[25]

Miss Gladys Prout, 22, described as an attractive young woman, worked as a domestic at one of the hotels in Hawera, and was accused following investigations into the suicide of a married man, Mr John James Dowdle, 49, custodian of the Hawera Borough Public Baths for the past 13 years. On the evening of 30 December his body was found by his sons. One of the sons, Clive, had come home from Wellington about 9.30 pm and told his mother he would go down to the baths to find out what was delaying his father. He found his hat and coat in the office but there was no sign of him. Clive went away and returned with his brother. They turned on the lights and discovered their father, fully clothed, drowned at the deep end of the baths. He left a suicide note in the office for his wife saying 'Good bye'.

Dowdle was a well-known figure in Hawera, and further afield in swimming circles he was known as the designer of a successful swimming instruction device, used throughout the Dominion. For a long period he had been a prominent member of the Salvation Army and held the rank of Sergeant Major in the Hawera Corps.

At the inquest it transpired that earlier that evening Gladys's parents had visited the Dowdle home and Mr Dowdle had gone out to the car to speak with them. Daisy Prout, Gladys's younger sister, had told her parents that about a fortnight before, Gladys had seen Dowdle and paid him £5 to have an abortion. The angry mother threatened Dowdle, told him she had been to his employer, the Borough Council, and said she would give him one week to leave town. He came inside, told his wife Josephine about the accusation, had tea and left for the baths at 7.30 pm. Mrs Dowdle said she would challenge Gladys's mother and did so that evening, in disbelief that her husband had committed a crime.

As a result of these sensational findings at the inquest, Gladys was charged in the Hawera Magistrate's Court that on 8 December she had permitted to be unlawfully used upon her an instrument to procure abortion. An important side issue was raised at the hearing when a doctor who had been consulted by Gladys refused to give evidence, on the basis that to do so would be a breach of patient confidentiality. This discussion was widely taken up by the medical and legal fraternity.

In the Magistrate's Court Gladys pleaded not guilty, but when the case came before the New Plymouth Supreme Court she pleaded guilty of permitting an unlawful operation to be performed upon her. Justice McGregor ordered probation and for Gladys to come up for sentence if called upon within three years. She was also ordered to pay £5 in court costs. The verdict of the coroner was that Dowdle committed suicide by drowning, subsequent to an accusation being made against him of a criminal offence.

Bench of judges, from left to right: Justice Ostler, Justice Adams, Justice Herdman, Late Justice Sim, Late Chief Justice Sir Charles Skerrett, Justice Stringer, Justice Reed, Justice McGregor, Justice Blair. (*Auckland Star*, 9 January 1930)

ଔ

Intention to cause miscarriage was deemed criminal even if the means used was harmless.

Trial of Hugh Austin, 1905[26]

Hugh Austin, 19, was charged that on 15 August 1904 he gave his girlfriend Beatrice Dennis a bottle containing a mixture of perchloride of iron, which he had obtained from a friend, with the intention of procuring a miscarriage. The pregnancy continued and in September 1904 he was ordered to find surety of £100 as a precaution against his leaving the colony without making provision for the maintenance of his unborn illegitimate child.

On 10 October 1904, he was charged in the Wellington Magistrate's Court that on 15 August he had unlawfully supplied a drug (perchloride of iron) to a young girl for an unlawful purpose. He pleaded not guilty. On 4 February 1905 in the Wellington Supreme Court he was found guilty, but the jury returned a strong recommendation for mercy on account of the prisoner's youth and his ignorance as to the possible consequences of his action. Certain law points were referred by Justice Denniston for argument before the Court of Appeal, Austin being granted bail meantime.

On 31 March the Court of Appeal deliberated. The fact that perchloride of iron was an innocuous substance, ineffective in producing a miscarriage, was one of the matters on appeal. The Court of Appeal upheld two of the four charges and the conviction remained. Although the substance was not a 'noxious thing', the supplying with intent to procure a miscarriage was deemed criminal.

When Austin came up for sentencing in April 1905, Justice Denniston said 'The primary object of the State in inflicting punishment is neither retribution nor reformation, but to deter.' He took account of Austin's age and his previous good behaviour and sentenced him to six months' imprisonment, asking that he be kept from contact with ordinary prisoners. Austin was then removed, weeping bitterly.

꽁

Perverting the course of justice was also a punishable offence.

Trial of Mrs Jessie Morris and Mr William Bobbett, 1929[27]

On 3 July 1929, police arrested Mrs Jessie ('Jean') Morris, 40, dressmaker, and charged her with unlawfully using an instrument upon Mrs Ivy Moselen from Kaeo. She was remanded on bail until 12 September, when she appeared in the Magistrate's Court. She pleaded not guilty and was committed to the Auckland Supreme Court for trial, where she was defended by Mr Singer.

The alleged offence took place in the upstairs fitting room of Mrs Morris's dressmaking shop in Upper Queen Street, Auckland, about 28 April 1929. Ivy said she went to Auckland with a companion from Kaeo, Mrs Hinemoa Hughes, who introduced her to Mrs Morris. Mrs Hughes denied everything and refused to give evidence in court, however Ivy intimated that she was in similar circumstances.

Ivy said she visited Mrs Morris twice and on the second occasion an operation was successfully performed for a fee of £5.

She returned home to Kaeo and on 7 June haemorrhaged badly. Her doctor admitted her to Whangaroa Hospital, where she developed septicaemia and received treatment as an inpatient for three months.

On 4 November in the Auckland Supreme Court, Justice Herdman said it was a perfectly simple case, and the jury returned, after a retirement of 40 minutes, with a guilty verdict. His Honour sentenced Mrs Morris to four years' imprisonment with hard labour. In pleading for his client, Mr Singer said her husband was an inmate of the mental hospital and she was forced to earn her own living. This was her first offence.

On 11 September 1929, in the Magistrate's Court, police charged Mr Bobbett (36, a labourer and a married man with five children) with attempting to obstruct, pervert or defeat the course of justice by endeavouring to persuade Ivy Moselen to give false evidence at the hearing of a charge against Mrs Jessie Morris. He was remanded on bail until 19 September.

Justice Alexander Lawrence Herdman (*NZ Truth*, 11 January 1919)

Bobbett knew the Moselens from when he lived in Kaeo some 20 years ago. In August, while Ivy was still an inpatient in Whangaroa Hospital, he wrote to her husband, who handed the letter to the constable at Whangaroa. The letter read:

> Dear Roy,
>
> I imagine you will be surprised to receive this from me, but when you read it you will understand. Of course, I do not know your feelings in the matter and it is rather a delicate matter to write about. The lady (you know who I mean) is very worried, of course, as she does not know what course of action you and Mrs Moselen are going to take, whether to help her or against her. I know her fairly well, and found her to be a good sort, always ready to give help in trouble.

Well Roy, the position is that if you are going to try and help her the best, the only thing to do is for Ivy not to be able to recognise her in the course of the proceedings. The lady will be in the room with several women, and Ivy will be asked to pick her out, and if she makes up her mind not to recognise her, it will squash the whole business and end it as far as Ivy is concerned. On the other hand, it means seven years for the woman. The reason I am writing this is because I am sorry for her. She did me a good turn when I was in a mess. Well Roy, as I have already explained I do not know your feelings about this matter, but I sincerely hope it all ends without trouble and worry for you. I know for sure this can happen so long as Ivy is positive that she does not know her and cannot recognise her.

Wishing you all the best of luck,
Yours sincerely,
Bill (of Kaeo long ago)

Bobbett admitted writing the letter but denied any instruction from Mrs Morris. Instead he tried to blame his wife, saying it was she who suggested he write the letter and dictated what he should write.

The case was heard in the Auckland Supreme Court on 29 October 1929, with Justice Herdman presiding. In his summing up, the judge said stupidity was no excuse for the commission of a crime. After retiring for half an hour the jury returned a verdict of guilty with a recommendation for mercy. The judge said that in view of Bobbett's good character the sentence would be a fairly light one, and sentenced him to a term of six months' imprisonment. He received his deferred sentence on the same day Mrs Morris received hers.

☙

Sometimes abortionists were prosecuted based on the evidence provided by clients just before they died, in what are known as dying depositions. A dying deposition is considered credible and trustworthy based on the supposition that most people who know they are about to die do not lie. It is an exception to the hearsay rule, which prohibits the use of a statement made by someone other than the person who made it. In abortion cases, even when a woman made a dying deposition her evidence was often inadmissible if it did not stand up to challenges from the defence.

The statement had to be made by the woman while conscious and competent, but with the certain knowledge that death was imminent. The statement had to be about what she believed to be the cause of her death, in a form that could be introduced into evidence during a trial in her absence. If the woman had the slightest hope of recovery, no matter how unreasonable, the statement was inadmissible. Other safeguards were that the statement be made in the presence of the accused and witnessed by a legal authority such as a magistrate.

These strict conditions were frequently unmet. In most cases, the woman would not reveal who did the abortion, or even how or when it was done. The woman would sometimes be sworn to secrecy; she usually felt a strong sense of loyalty to someone who had helped her and would not divulge information even on her deathbed. Sometimes, however, she would feel it necessary to break this confidence, and doctors and police sometimes used coercion to extract a confession.

In the following story, the dying deposition was of no help.

Myrtle's story[28]
Deceased 8 November 1925, aged 18 years 11 months

Myrtle Thomson (also known as Myrtle Thorpe), third daughter of James and Lucy Thomson, lived at home in Cashel Street, Christchurch. Her boyfriend, Don Baker, had been taking her out for about ten weeks when she became pregnant. On 28 October, Don took her to an address in Essex Street and they were met outside by two women, Mrs Lena Gray and Mrs Amy Glenn. Don was asked to stay outside on the footpath while the three women went inside. He was later invited inside and was asked to pay the remainder of the fee, amounting to £10.

On 22 October, Myrtle became ill. At first her parents thought she was having a nervous breakdown and arranged for her to see Dr Bevan Brown for psychological help. Later, on 3 November, the family doctor admitted her to Christchurch Hospital. She was suffering from acute sepsis but the doctors did not operate.

The day before she died, she gave her dying deposition in the presence of the coroner and a magistrate, stating:

> My name is Myrtle Veronica Thomson. I know the accused (Mrs Glenn). She operated on me. I have been ill since I was operated on. I cannot tell you how it was done. I did not

really know. I was lying on a bed. I did not see what was done myself. I went to the accused because I was pregnant. She told me she would take away the child. I paid her £7. Someone paid it for me. Don Baker was responsible for my condition. I went to Lena's house – that is Lena Gray. It was at Lena's house that the operation took place but Lena did not do it. I lay on my back on my left side when the accused operated.

At the inquest, Mrs Gray refused to answer questions. The coroner's report gave the cause of death as 'acute inflammation of the womb associated with blood poisoning, the result of an illegal operation.'

Trial of Mrs Maud Amy Glenn, 1926

Police arrested Mrs Glenn, 28, and when Myrtle died they charged her with manslaughter. Bail was refused while she awaited the Supreme Court trial, which took place on 10 February, presided over by Justice Adams. A whole afternoon was spent on legal arguments over whether the dying deposition was admissible. Because it did not strictly conform to the rules laid down in the Justices of the Peace Act, the judge ruled it was inadmissible. From that point the case collapsed and the judge in his direction asked the jury to acquit the prisoner, which they did.

ଔ

Dying depositions were not always truthful, as in the following story.

Agnes's story[29]
Deceased 7 November 1906, aged 26

Mrs Agnes Moughan (née Dawson), 26, of Palmerston North, was married two days before she died. John Moughan, commission agent, had been living with her since January, boarding in her house. When she was gravely ill he said marrying her was the least he could do. She took her marriage vows on the same day she made her dying deposition.

Agnes already had a young infant to care for and could not face another pregnancy. To avoid social embarrassment she sometimes went under the name of Mrs or Miss Smith. When she consulted

Dr O'Brien on 30 October, he found her both seriously ill and pregnant with a prolapsed uterus. He conferred with Dr Stowe for a second opinion. The two doctors assisted in the delivery of a premature infant in a critical condition but alive at the birth. Agnes was terminally ill from septicaemia. She died in Nurse Dender's private nursing home in Palmerston North, having been admitted there a few days before by Dr O'Brien, when the public hospital could not take her.

> **THE PALMERSTON SENSATION**
>
> (Press Association.)
> PALMERSTON NORTH, This day.
> Susan Cole and John Moughan were charged at the S M. Court with having in July last caused bodily harm to Agnes Moughan, wife of the accused Moughan, from which death resulted, and also that during the same period, accused, with intent to procure the miscarriage of Agnes Moughan, used an instrument upon the latter. The dying depositions of deceased were taken before Mr Thomson, S.M., and put in evidence, in which deceased stated accused (Coles) twice operated upon her.
> The medical evidence was to the effect that death was due to septic poisoning, caused by the laceration of the internal organs.
> Accused were each committed for trial on the second count, and bail was refused.

Bush Advocate, 22 November 1906.

Her dying deposition was taken by Mr Thomson S.M. in the presence of her husband and Dr O'Brien, but subsequent findings differed from what she said. She stated that in June or July she had been operated on twice by Mrs Susan Cole, who used a catheter in an attempt to perform an abortion, but she had not seen her since. There had been no payment, although John had given Mrs Cole a bookcase and a stool.

Dr O'Brien was present at the post-mortem conducted by Dr Wilson, who said the septicaemia was of recent origin, within the last fortnight, and could not possibly have been due to the attempted abortion in June or July that Agnes had described in her dying deposition. He considered that the fatal septic peritonitis had been caused by the recent forceful use of an instrument by an inexperienced person, causing severe lacerations.

The coroner's inquest concluded 'that the deceased Agnes Moughan came to her death as the result of an operation to procure abortion performed on her by some unskilled person or persons a short time prior to her death.'

While Agnes was still lying critically ill, police arrested Mrs Cole and detained her in the Wanganui gaol. Mrs Cole was a Palmerston North resident who went out washing and cleaning. She had been married twice but both husbands had left her. On 12 November, John Moughan was also arrested and taken into custody.

Trial of Mr John Moughan and Mrs Susan Cole, 1906

On 22 November, both Mrs Cole and Agnes's husband John Moughan were charged in the Palmerston North Magistrate's Court with using an instrument to procure abortion and causing bodily harm which resulted in death. There was animosity between the two accused and they applied to have separate trials, but the judge refused, saying they had cooperated in the commission of the crime.

The trial took place in the Palmerston North Supreme Court on 27 February, with Justice Chapman presiding. Both were acquitted on the grounds that there was no direct evidence to attach them to the crime. Agnes's dying deposition did not relate to the events that led to her death and was deemed inadmissible. John gave evidence that she had been to Wellington in the fortnight before her death, but whoever caused the lacerations remained unknown.

ଔ

Sometimes obtaining a dying deposition was difficult.

Eva's story[30]
Deceased 21 February 1914, aged 25 years

Eva Wackrow was married to Wilfred, a railway engine driver of Palmerston North, and they had three children. She was about three months pregnant when she visited her sister in Upper Hutt, returning to Palmerston North on 9 February. She told Wilfred that while she was away she had miscarried one evening after playing tennis. She became ill and stayed at her mother's place for a while. On her return home, Wilfred thought she needed medical attention, but she said she was getting along fine. However, she took a turn for the worse on 18 February and at this stage Wilfred called in the doctor, who admitted her to hospital.

On 20 February Mr Cecil Hewlett, clerk of the court at Palmerston North, visited Eva in the hospital as she lay seriously ill and wrote down the statement made by Eva in answer to questions from the stipendiary magistrate, in the presence of two police officers and a friend, Mrs Larsen. The following is an example of the sort of interrogation women were subjected to:

> Q. Do you feel strong enough to make a statement?
> A. What do you mean?
> Q. Do you know where you are?
> A. I am in bed in the hospital.
> Q. How did you get ill?
> A. By a miscarriage.
> Q. What brought it about?
> A. I don't know.
> Q. Don't you know what caused it?
> A. I can't understand you.
> Q. What caused the miscarriage?
> A. I don't know how it came about. I think I got a cold. That's all.
> Q. Don't you know of any other cause?
> A. I was half silly. I don't know. Mrs Larsen and I did take ergot which Mr Hepworth used to sell us. He sold it to Mrs Larsen.
> Q. Where did you get it from?
> A. Mrs Larsen, the one here got it for me. Mrs Larsen interjects 'It was her money'.
> Q. How long before your miscarriage did you take this ergot?
> A. I don't know. I was silly the other night when I was talking. Mrs Larsen interjects 'It was two months ago.' Don't cry Mrs Larsen. We are both as bad as one another.
> Q. How much did you take?
> A. About an egg-cupful.
> Q. You say Mrs Larsen took it too?
> A. Mrs Larsen's husband ran away and she ran out of money and she asked me if I would stand good for her until she got some from her washing.

Q. Do you think that brought about your trouble drinking the ergot?
A. I don't know. It affects my head.
Q. Mrs Larsen says it was two months ago since she got it for you and took it with you. Is that correct?
A. I don't think it was two months ago. I have not seen her since.
Q. Did you get any from anyone else?
A. No.
Q. Which Hepworth was it you got from?
A. The old gentleman.
Q. That is the herbalist?
A. To Mrs Larsen 'Is it?' Mrs Larsen says 'Yes'.
Q. Was the ergot ordered by a doctor?
A. It was just black stuff and I took about a teaspoonful.
Q. For what purpose did you take it?
A. I took it to try and bring it on.
Q. To bring what on?
A. Our monthlies.
Q. Did you know you were pregnant then?
A. It took no effect on me at all. I only took it now and again. I could not afford buying it.
Q. Did you know you were pregnant then?
A. Of course.
Q. Do you realise how seriously ill you are?
A. Yes, for every time I stand on my feet I fall. I don't think it is good stuff that Mrs Larsen took.
Q. Do you expect to get over this illness?
A. No because I have been naughty.
Q. Do you believe you are going to die?
A. No, don't tell me that. (Witness cries.)
Q. You have no expectation of dying?
A. No.

Eva died the following day. At the post-mortem, placental fragments, which had caused the fatal sepsis, were found in the uterus. The verdict of the coroner and a jury of six men was simply that she had 'died from septicaemia or blood poisoning following a miscarriage.'

ଔ

It can be seen that, despite the numerous problems faced in obtaining a successful prosecution, no one suggested abortion was a health matter and not a crime; a legacy that remains to this day.

6. DOCTORS

Officially, the medical profession did not regard abortion as a legitimate practice, except in cases when a therapeutic abortion was necessary to save the life or preserve the health of the mother. Such cases were carried out in a hospital, usually after seeking the opinion of another doctor. Because of the fear of prosecution, many doctors refused to have anything to do with abortion. Others provided them discreetly, in the knowledge that they were better equipped to safely carry out the procedure than an untrained person. Although righteous persons and organisations condemned the practice of abortion and denounced doctors who carried out abortions as a disgrace to their profession, the general public was less condemnatory, as in the following two cases.

Two Trials of Dr Alfred John Leggatt, 1900–1901[1]

Dr Leggatt immigrated to New Zealand in 1882, after spending 34 years in the Indian Medical Service, and settled in Nelson. He took an active role in the community, including support for the local Friendly Societies. Before he lost one of his hands in a gun accident, he was Captain of the H Battery. He was appointed honorary surgeon to the Fire Brigade and was also the Port Health Officer. He was married, with three sons and two daughters.

For some time, the police suspected he was providing abortions for the women in the area. In July 1899, police searched his premises and confiscated a book containing the names of his patients. Police questioned three women, who subsequently featured in criminal trials. In two of these, Dr Leggatt faced a Supreme Court trial, and in the other, the police charged the woman herself. The public condemned this police handling of confidential patient information.

In July 1900, Dr Leggatt was accused in the Magistrate's Court of offences against Katherine Prussing, 21, of Collingwood, dating back to June 1899. In the meantime, Katherine had married in June 1900 and was now Mrs Smith. Dr Leggatt was committed to trial on a charge of having performed an illegal operation when Katherine was about six months pregnant using a metal uterine sound, an instrument commonly used in gynaecological practice. The fetus, which had been buried in the garden, was exhumed. The Chief Justice, Sir Robert Stout, refused Dr Leggatt's request for the Supreme Court trial to take place in Wellington. Justice Edwards presided over the case in the Nelson Supreme Court on 12–13 December 1900. Dr Leggatt maintained the abortion was therapeutic. Prosecution witnesses were unreliable. The jury took only 28 minutes to deliver a not guilty verdict.

At the same session of the Nelson Supreme Court, Dr Leggatt featured in another trial, that of Kate Vincent, recently divorced and accused of unlawfully allowing Dr Leggatt to perform an abortion on her in July 1899. Her name was one of those in Dr Leggatt's record book. Dr Leggatt did not testify. The jury came back after a retirement of 20 minutes with a not guilty verdict.

On Saturday afternoon, 15 December 1900, police arrested Dr Leggatt and charged him with having performed on 5 May 1900 an illegal operation on a young woman who had attended him under the name of 'Miss Spencer'. Police accused a young man, Reuben Snowden, of paying the young woman £5 for the purpose of procuring the operation. Both Dr Leggatt and Snowden were committed for trial.

In the Magistrate's Court on 21 December 1900, the case against Snowden was heard first, and then the case against Dr Leggatt proceeded. However, the hearing was not concluded and had to be rescheduled to after the summer break. Both men were committed for trial before Justice Connolly in the Nelson Supreme Court on 5–6 March 1901. In his summing up the judge expressed strong views against abortion, but the jury was not persuaded. Both men were acquitted and, on hearing this, a slight applause erupted from the back of the room. This demonstration was quickly suppressed by the judge.

On 3 January 1902, the residents of Nelson were shocked at the untimely death of Dr Leggatt at the age of 57. The principal cause of death was anaemia, attributed to the malarial fever he had contracted during his residence in India, but some wondered whether the stress of his confidential records being seized and the consequent trials contributed to his demise. His funeral was well attended despite the rain.

Trial of Dr James Alexander Fullarton, 1903[2]

Dr Fullarton was a prominent and popular doctor in Invercargill. His arrest, on a charge of using an instrument with intent to procure the miscarriage of a young woman named Margaret Bates, caused quite a sensation.

On 5 January Dr Fullarton confirmed Margaret's pregnancy, and she discussed it with her boyfriend William Campbell, a coal merchant of Invercargill. The couple called on Dr Fullarton a few nights later to ask him for help. Dr Fullarton expected £20 cash before he would do anything. On the following Tuesday, William paid him £16 and arranged for Margaret to call an hour later, when the alleged offence took place. Later on, he paid the remainder of the fee. Margaret then went to stay with a friend at Ryal Bush, and miscarried the next day.

On 4 March 1903, in the Invercargill Supreme Court before Justice Williams, true bills were returned in all cases, but subsequently it was revealed that in Dr Fullarton's case, ten of the 19 grand jurymen had voted for a true bill and nine had voted against it. In law, a true bill required 12 votes. The defence argued that the indictment should be quashed, but the judge decided the case must go ahead and, if Dr Fullarton was found guilty, be referred to the Court of Appeal.

Margaret Bates testified that William had provided her with pills to take. Other witnesses testified that Dr Fullarton was present on the night the alleged offence took place. The jury, after a retirement of less than five minutes, returned a verdict of not guilty. The result was received with loud applause.

ख

In 1896, **Dr Emily Hancock Siedeberg** CBE (1873–1968)[3] became the first woman doctor to graduate from the University of Otago. She was born at Clyde in Central Otago. Her German architect father had prospered through mining operations and contracting. Her Irish mother came from a family of lawyers and doctors. Emily was an outstanding pupil at George Street School and Otago Girls' High School, but showed no inclination for teaching, which at that time was almost the only acceptable career for a girl of her talents.

Her father dreamed of a medical career for his gifted daughter and urged her to apply to the Dean of the Medical School, Professor J. H. Scott. Scott was less than enthusiastic, but agreed. The University Council gave grudging approval, and Emily next approached the medical staff at the hospital where she would have to do her clinical work. Six were against the proposal, two were in favour, and one thought women should be allowed to take a medical course – but in Britain.

Emily enrolled despite the hardly favourable omens. Fellow students resented her intrusion into their all-male domain and initially gave her a hard time, not fraternising with her or even sitting beside her at lectures. In the dissecting room, they sometimes threw bits of body at her, and obstacles were put in her way when it came to studying 'certain pieces of anatomy'. She had to go to the dissecting rooms on her own at night. On one occasion, she was frightened when she saw a dismembered hand at the window.

Dr Emily Siedeberg McKinnon.
(*The Press*, 22 December 1937)

Dr Emily Siedeberg, Superintendent at St Helens, Dunedin, with matron Miss Alice Holford and sub-matron Miss E. Trott. (*Otago Witness*, 11 October 1905)

It was a lonely time until her second year, when another woman, Margaret Cruickshank, enrolled. By the time she completed her course at the end of 1895, she had earned respect and admiration as well as her medical degree. Opportunities were still limited for New Zealand's first woman doctor, so she set out for Europe to engage in postgraduate work, first in Dublin, studying midwifery at the Rotunda Hospital, then in Berlin, studying gynaecological and skin diseases. In 1898 she returned to establish a general practice in Dunedin, and made a significant contribution to the health of women and children. Over her lifetime she became involved in a number of social causes.

In 1899 Dr Siedeberg was a founding member of the Dunedin branch of the New Zealand Society for the Protection of Women and Children (Plunket), although she was critical of some of Dr Truby King's ideas. From 1905 to 1938 she was the Medical Superintendent of the Dunedin St Helens Hospital. She took an active role in the National Council of Women, serving three terms as president. She continued her private practice until 1928, when she married a retired banker, James McKinnon, and thereafter used the name Dr Siedeberg McKinnon.

The following is a personal recollection (abridged) from one of her caregivers towards the end of her long life:[4]

In her old age, she was dainty, strong, well dressed and walked erect. Always pleasant, she spoke quietly with no unnecessary chatter. Well-mannered (the first person I met to use a finger bowl at table), she, with all the indignities of old age, was always a Lady.

I remember reading Doris Gordon's books *Backblocks Baby Doctor* and *Doctor Down Under* and saying to Dr Siedeberg I hoped someday someone would write about her. 'I should hope not' she replied and then made a comment about Doris Gordon 'just being above herself and blowing her own trumpet'.

She told me of the appalling number of backyard abortions and not only for the unmarried; many men demanded marital rights whatever the health of their wives. 'Women need to take precautions', she counselled. She was the first woman to own and drive a car in Dunedin and often drove around the Dunedin foreshore looking for women in need.

Dr Siedeberg believed strongly that women had more to give society than they had the chance to give. She had some stirring battles with such leading Doctors as Truby King and Ferdinand Batchelor. Nowadays, they would be called male chauvinists; they firmly believed careers for women would destroy home life.

She often expressed her views in print. She advocated for women police, factory health inspections and equal opportunities for women. In 1949, after she retired from medicine, but not from social work, she was awarded the CBE. She died in Iona Home and Hospital, Oamaru in 1968 aged 95.

Here is one story in which Dr Siedeberg was involved as the anaesthetist.

Kathleen's story[5]
Deceased 7 May 1906, aged 25 years

Kathleen Matthewson was a domestic servant; when not in service she lived at home with her parents in Port Chalmers. She was strong and healthy. She had a number of boyfriends, and sometimes she and her sister Annie, or other girlfriends, would meet up with them at a small camping house at Browns Bay. Occasionally they would stay there overnight. Three of these young men – William Brown, clerk; Stanley Irwin, warehouse clerk; and Edwin Newman, Drainage Board draughtsman – all testified at her inquest.

Kathleen left home on 18 April, saying she was going to Mosgiel for a holiday with a girlfriend from Dunedin and she would be back in a week's time. Edwin Newman said he knew her as Miss Smith and he had seen her in Dunedin on that day, when she had seemed despondent. When he teased her about putting on weight, she burst into tears and confided she was 'in trouble' and she would have to 'get rid of it'. He advised her to go up country to be confined and if possible get the man who got her pregnant to take some responsibility. He offered to help if she needed money. He admitted he had been intimate with her in February but did not consider himself responsible for the pregnancy.

The following night, 19 April, Edwin saw her again by chance on his way to the theatre. They did not speak for long, but she said she was going to Mosgiel and then Balclutha, because she had heard of a woman there who was very good with maternity cases. The girlfriend who was supposed to have accompanied her on holiday said she had seen her in Dunedin on 21 April, when she appeared particularly melancholy.

From that time until 3 May, a period of 12 days, the police were unable to trace her movements. When she did not return home, her mother sent her sister Annie to Dunedin to make enquiries. The girlfriend who was supposed to have gone on holiday with her said there was absolutely no truth to that story. Kathleen's mother wrote an accusatory letter to William Brown, holding him responsible for Kathleen's absence and wanting an answer. Indignant, he told her he knew nothing about Kathleen's whereabouts and demanded an apology.

Kathleen arrived back in Dunedin on Thursday 3 May, but did not get in touch with her family. Instead she went to see Dr Church at his house. That was the first time he had seen her. She told him her name was Kathleen Smith and she had met with a mishap the previous Monday, 30 April, in Mosgiel. She had just come back to Dunedin by train and had stayed at the Leviathan Hotel (which had a reputation as a venue for women having abortions).

Dr Church found her feverish and very ill with diarrhoea and vomiting. He strongly suspected an illegal operation had been performed, but she vehemently denied this. She said, 'I have brought this trouble on myself. I have been taking drugs for a long time.' She later said the man who had got her into trouble had paid for the drugs but she steadfastly refused to say what she had taken, who had supplied the drugs, or who her boyfriend was.

Dr Church advised admission to hospital but she absolutely refused. An acceptable alternative was to go to Mrs Norman's home at 2 Serpentine Avenue. Mrs Norman, an unregistered nurse and a widow, worked mainly outside her home but from time to time took in patients, mainly maternity cases. She had 23 years' experience as a nurse and Dr Church had used her services in the past.

Dr Church visited Kathleen frequently and on Saturday 5 May called in Dr Siedeberg to assist with chloroform anaesthesia while he carried out a curetting of the uterus, removing as much of the foul tissue as he could. Mrs Norman paid one guinea to Dr Siedeberg and Kathleen said she would repay her when she could.

Dr Church's examination confirmed his suspicions that an illegal operation had been performed. Repeated efforts by the doctor and the nurse to gain more information were unrewarded. After the curetting Kathleen improved temporarily, but on Monday afternoon she collapsed, and she died about 9 pm. Kathleen told Mrs Norman her true name and address only on Monday afternoon, and that evening Mrs Norman dispatched her maid to inform Kathleen's parents of her illness.

The first intimation her parents received as to Kathleen's whereabouts was the message from Mrs Norman's maid to say she was lying very ill at Mrs Norman's home in Serpentine Avenue. They did not go that evening to see her. The maid returned the following morning, this time with the sad news that Kathleen had died during the night. Kathleen's mother accompanied her back to Mrs Norman's. The maid thought Kathleen's mother seemed aware of her daughter's problem, although at the inquest this was denied. Her mother said if she had known she would have looked after her and sent her to a different part of the colony, where she had friends. Kathleen's death created a sensation and was referred to in the newspapers as 'The Serpentine Avenue Case'.

The post-mortem found she had died of acute peritonitis caused by the rupture of an abscess in the right Fallopian tube. After her death, a few pills containing ergot were found in her belongings. Her sister Annie recalled that on one occasion she had gone into a chemist's shop to get pills recommended by William Brown.

Dr Roberts, pathologist at Dunedin Hospital, conducted the post-mortem in the presence of Dr Church and Dr Siedeberg, and all three testified at the inquest. When asked if the police should have been notified, Dr Roberts ventured his opinion:[6]

> If the patient had been moribund or expected to die, I should have communicated with the police. That has been my feeling for some time, for the reason that we have to attend cases of grave suspicion and we have an idea that this sort of thing is going on, and I have a feeling that if we could bring it home to anyone I would be willing to take a little risk in doing so – the risk being that the patient might recover and that I might be accused of a betrayal of professional confidence. That is what I would do but I would not quarrel with another doctor who thought otherwise. It was a question for each medical man to determine for himself. If I knew that an illegal operation had been performed I would not deem it my duty to inform the police while there was still hope of recovery.

The inquest was long and detailed, and fully reported in the press. In his summing up, the coroner asserted that the police should have been notified before Kathleen's death. He said it was very much regretted that information had not been given to the police at the proper time, to allow the girl's dying deposition to be taken, which might have thrown some light upon the matter. He accused Dr Church of making a great error of judgement in not calling upon the police, and during the inquest Dr Church apologised.

The jury of six men, after a brief retirement, returned a verdict that 'the cause of death was septicaemia, the result of an illegal operation, but by whom performed there was not sufficient evidence to show.' The jury expressed regret that the police had not been informed by the doctor or nurse of the circumstances of the case immediately after the examination had proved that an illegal operation had been performed.

☙

Sir Frederic Truby King CMG (1858–1938) was the Medical Superintendent of Seacliff Asylum, but he is better known as the founder of the Plunket Society.[7] He embraced the views of the social purity reformers. In 1890 he wrote an article, published in the *New Zealand Medical Journal*, entitled 'A Plea for Stringent Legislation in the Matter of Corrupt and Immoral Publications',[8] in which he attacked the following categories of 'useless and pernicious' publications:

(1) Books of distinctly corrupt and immoral tendencies (purporting, usually, to be the guides, philosophers, and friends of humanity in general, and youths in particular), e.g., *The Elements of Social Science.*
(2) Pamphlets of similar tendencies (mostly quack advertisements) e.g., 'Health, Strength, Vigour, Manhood.'
(3) Corrupt and indecent advertisements.
(4) Corrupt and immoral literature, e.g., *Nana.*
(5) Corrupt and indecent newspapers, or newspaper articles, and printed or pictorial sheets of any kind calculated to pervert public morals, or to furnish what *The Lancet* aptly calls 'Pictorial Education in Crime' e.g., *The Police News, The Dead Bird,* indecent reports of rape or divorce cases, etc.

King expressed particular concern over the vulnerability of boys and young men exposed to material containing false or misleading information about male sexuality. He attacked what he considered to be fallacious and immoral ideas spread by 'quacks' and 'vile charlatans' about men's need for sexual release and about the alleged dangers of male masturbation.

During his tenure as Director of Child Welfare, King was responsible for a strict enforcing of the Indecent Publications Act 1910. Under his watch, Customs seized Ettie Rout's book *Safe Marriage: A Return to Sanity* in 1922 and Marie Stopes's book *Married Love* in 1924. When he retired in 1927, the ban on these two books was lifted. King considered George Drysdale's *Elements of Social Science* a particularly pernicious text. The book, first published in 1854 and regularly reissued until 1914, controversially argued that the suppression of natural sexual instincts caused more harm to an individual's health than did sexual excess. If society would allow the 'natural' expression of the sexual appetite, the result, proclaimed Drysdale, would be a diminution of such 'perverse' activities as masturbation and prostitution and such medical problems as syphilis, gonorrhoea, and hysteria. Drysdale, an English physician and leader of the Malthusian League, promoted a gospel of 'preventive intercourse': early marriage with the use of contraceptives. His book discussed five methods of contraception: the 'safe period', coitus interruptus, the sheath, the sponge and douching. King primarily opposed the book because he believed it encouraged immorality and sexual

Sir Frederick Truby King, photographed circa 1913 by Henry Herbert Clifford of Christchurch. (Ref: PAColl-3861-31-01. Alexander Turnbull Library, Wellington)

precocity in the young. He adhered to a social purity and medical ideology that equated sexual health with sexual self-control.

King believed in sexual abstinence until marriage and a limitation of sex within it. He wrote that all female mammals found the sexual act repugnant and this was a natural safeguard to precocity. His views on contraception were equally unenlightened: he believed that contraceptive information should be kept out of the hands of the populace, as it reduced the sexual act to mere pleasure with no burden of responsibility. He was opposed to abortion. King and his wife were childless but cared for other children and adopted a daughter in 1904.

Seacliff Mental Asylum was situated in a farming estate of 900 acres, and it was King's interest in animal husbandry that led him into the field of infant welfare. In 1907, King founded the Royal New Zealand Society for the Health of Women and Children, better known as the Plunket Society, or simply Plunket. Plunket was named after the inaugural patron of the Society, Lady Victoria Alexandrina Plunket, mother of eight and wife of then Governor of New Zealand, Lord William Plunket (1864–1920). King believed that scientifically formulated doctrines on nutrition and infant care were the key to reducing infant mortality and promoting the future health of the nation, and that motherhood was the most important calling for girls. He founded Karitane Hospitals, which were the first of their kind and soon spread rapidly around the country. They were known as a safe and caring environment for new and expectant mothers, and babies who were failing to thrive. Dunedin's Karitane Hospital also operated as the sole training centre for Plunket nurses.

King wrote and published several manuals, among them *Feeding and Care of Baby* (1913) and *The Expectant Mother and Baby's First Months* (1916). This latter publication was given to every applicant for a marriage licence. King was regarded as somewhat eccentric by his medical colleagues, but his contributions to society were recognised with a Companion of the Order of St Michael and St George (CMG) medal in 1917 and a knighthood in 1925. When he passed away in 1938 at the age of 79, he was the first private citizen to be given a state funeral. King's legacy lives on in the Plunket society, although many of his original teachings do not. The strict regime of care and directive advice from the Plunket nurse has been replaced by a flexible model of care and support for parents and their children.

Although he was authoritarian in manner, King's care and compassion is demonstrated in this case of abortion involving one of his nurses.

Minnie's story[9]
Deceased 12 September 1907, age not recorded

Minnie Landsberry came from Sydney with her friend Sadie Hopkins in October 1906. From January 1907, they were both employed as nurses at the Seacliff Mental Hospital, although

Minnie had just handed in her resignation a short time before she became ill, and was planning to return to Sydney. Since March she had been friendly with John Melville, who was employed at Seacliff Mental Hospital as an electrician. Dr King had visited John on the evening of Sunday 1 September, the day before Minnie left, because he was convalescing from influenza. Dr King found Minnie in John's room with something that she had brought him to eat. He reported her to the Matron for fraternising with another staff member.

The next day, Monday 2 September, Minnie left Seacliff and stayed for a few days in Dunedin. She said that she had stayed at the Leviathan Hotel, which had a reputation as a venue for illegal operations. On Thursday 5 September, she returned to stay at the Seacliff Hotel to be near her friends. She had told John six to eight weeks earlier that she was pregnant, and on her return from Dunedin told him she had used a crochet needle on herself to procure a miscarriage. When her friend Sadie visited Minnie, she found her febrile and very ill. Minnie never mentioned the pregnancy to Sadie but told her that she thought she had influenza. She did not wish to be seen by a doctor, but by Sunday she was so ill that Sadie and John both called in Dr Tizard, who recommended that she go to Dunedin Hospital the next morning.

When Dr Tizard reported to Dr King his suspicion that Minnie was suffering from a septic condition probably associated with miscarriage, they agreed that the best course of action was admission to Dunedin Hospital. Dr King, Sadie and John accompanied Minnie on the train trip. At the Seacliff station, Dr King took Minnie aside into the ladies waiting room and pressed her for more information about her condition. She told him what she had told John, that she had used a crochet needle on herself. When they arrived in Dunedin Dr King ordered a cab and Minnie begged that John be allowed to accompany them. In the eyes of Dr King, John needed a severe reprimand, but he agreed to his coming.

On arrival at the hospital at 1.30 pm on Monday 9 September, Dr King took charge and informed the admitting doctor of Minnie's situation. His explanation was that it was to save her having to repeat her own story. After the examination was over and he had left, one of the nurses came to Dr King and said that Minnie would like to see him again. He returned, assuming that she would want to know the gravity of her illness and what her prognosis was. Instead she told him that he had been too hard on

John Melville and she hoped that this would not interfere with his prospects. Soon after, John decided to leave Seacliff Mental Hospital anyway.

In Dunedin Hospital, Minnie was under the care of Dr Batchelor. On Tuesday 10 September he examined her under anaesthesia, confirming sepsis from a recent miscarriage. Because she had no relatives in New Zealand, she was asked if she wished the police to be informed, but Minnie said that she did not want anyone to know. Her condition deteriorated and she died two days later.

At the post-mortem, the Dunedin Hospital pathologist, Dr Roberts, found pelvic peritonitis and signs of a recent pregnancy of about three months' gestation. Bacteriological examination confirmed septicaemia. In his opinion an abortion had probably taken place between 2 and 5 September, when Minnie had gone to Dunedin.

At the coroner's inquest the jury of six men found that the cause of death was 'blood poisoning, the result of a miscarriage self-induced by the deceased.' We only have Minnie's word that this is what had happened. It is just as probable she was protecting someone else who had operated on her in Dunedin.

ଔ

Sometimes an unregistered doctor masqueraded as a medical abortionist.

Trial of John Pearson, 1908[10]

'Dr' John Pearson claimed he was a registered practitioner from Sydney, but the New South Wales police said he was unregistered and, furthermore, well known as an abortionist. He had deserted his wife and family and lived with a domiciliary nurse, Mrs Bridget Chalk, who in 1893 received a four-year sentence for procuring abortion. In August 1908, at the Christchurch Supreme Court, Pearson was acquitted on a charge of illegally using an instrument to procure abortion, but found guilty of indecent assault, and was sentenced to six months' imprisonment. In 1912, Mrs Chalk was sentenced to eight years' imprisonment by Justice Denniston following the death of Mrs Martha Henderson from air embolism.[11]

Under section 143 of the Hospitals and Charitable Institutions Act 1926, private hospitals had to be licensed. The Department of Health had the power to initiate an inspection if it suspected the premises were being used for illegal purposes. However, the difficulty lay in proving illegal operations had been performed when doctors falsified records as dilatation and curettage (D&C). The following story concerning Dr Temple illustrates how private hospitals or nursing homes were used as a shelter for abortion activities.

Agnes's story[12]
Deceased 9 October 1921, aged 24 years

Miss Agnes Cook immigrated to New Zealand in December with workmate Elizabeth Ellis, and for six months both women were employed as second cooks at the Christchurch Club. Agnes applied for two weeks' leave on 20 September, saying she wished to visit her brother in Auckland. She did have a brother in New Zealand, but he was a miner in Huntly. She withdrew £30 from her savings account on 24 September and at the time of her death only £2 remained.

When she was about three months pregnant she visited a Christchurch doctor, Dr Adolph Temple, under the name of 'Mrs West', telling him her husband was a seafaring man, away on a coastal boat. She visited Dr Temple three times, but there were no records of her visits in his book. According to Dr Temple she complained of vomiting and haemorrhage, for which he prescribed a tonic and bed rest. On 24 September he advised her to go into Mrs Barson's nursing home.

Mrs Eliza Barson was a nurse who had run a maternity nursing home in Linwood for 30 years. Dr Temple frequently sent patients to her, although it was not a registered home. When Agnes arrived she told Mrs Barson she had fallen and was threatening to miscarry. When first interviewed by police, Dr Temple signed an untrue statement saying he had sent Agnes to Mrs Barson's home on 28 September (not 24 September). He admitted he had told lies, but only to protect the girl.

He visited her on the day of admission and was attentive throughout. She was bleeding and he attempted to stop the bleeding by plugging the vagina. For the persistent vomiting he gave an injection and for pain a morphia suppository. In a few days he personally got her some medicine from Steed's Chemist to try and induce uterine contractions, but Agnes was unable to take it. He told the chemist's assistant he did not want it known for whom the medicine was obtained or where she was. Arthur Griffin, chemist's assistant at Steed's Chemist, Ferry Road, testified he had made up prescriptions for Mrs West (for quinine sulphate and ergot), Mrs Barson (for lead and opium) and another pseudonym, Mrs Wood (for bismuth mixture).

On Tuesday, Dr Temple told his colleague Dr Bates that he was worried about an abortion case. He said the patient would probably require curetting and asked Dr Bates if he would see the case with him the following day. Dr Bates agreed but did not come until Thursday morning. Agnes was still retching. During the operation, Dr Temple encountered difficulties. He found the cervix soft and friable and was unable to apply forceps or dilators. He handed over to Dr Bates, who had been giving the anaesthetic. Bates was more successful and managed to get the fetus away using a sharp curette followed by his fingers.

Dr Temple visited Agnes two or three times a day, and on the following Thursday he called in Dr Bates again, as Agnes's condition was far from satisfactory. Dr Bates decided to put her under anaesthetic and sweep around with a blunt curette and give her a good douche out with Lysol.

After the second curetting Agnes did not improve. On the morning of Saturday 8 October, Dr Morkane, a specialist in women's diseases, was called in. It was only then that Agnes agreed to hospital admission. She then told Dr Temple she had deceived him and she was really Agnes Cook, not Mrs West. She asked Dr Temple to ring her employer at the Christchurch Club. Nurse Barson accompanied her to Christchurch Hospital. Agnes told the hospital doctors she had been taking medicines other than those prescribed by Dr Temple to get rid of the pregnancy. Another patient in the bed next to Agnes testified at the inquest that she overheard a visitor (Nurse Barson) telling Agnes to 'Keep quiet. Don't say anything to anybody.'

Nothing could be done to save her, and Agnes died the following day. At the post-mortem, six tears in the uterus were described, with gangrenous edges. The verdict of the coroner, acting alone, was that death was due to 'acute suppurative peritonitis following perforation of the uterus and vagina.' He added that there was no proof the perforations were the result of the operative work of either Dr Temple or Dr Bates, and although it would have been preferable for her to have been admitted to hospital at an earlier stage, he acknowledged that Agnes had refused to do so. As required by health authorities, Dr Temple notified the Medical Officer of Health of Agnes's illness as a case of puerperal septicaemia.

☙

Medical practitioners also came under the purview of the Medical Council, as in the following case.

Trial of Dr George Oscar Jacobsen, 1927[13]

Dr Jacobsen, 60, of English background and practising from Sussex Street, Wellington, was accused by the Medical Council of New Zealand of infamous conduct in a professional respect. The motion to have his name removed from the Medical Register was heard in the Wellington Supreme Court by Justice Reed in April 1927.

He was arrested on 23 August 1926, charged with inciting a young woman, Miss Brown, to procure an abortion, but the case was dismissed in the Wellington Magistrate's Court on 16 September 1926 through lack of evidence.

The motion by the Medical Council alleged that on 13 June 1926 he gave another pregnant woman, Mrs Davis, seeking to terminate her pregnancy, the name and address of Mrs Nevill, 150 Queen's Drive, Lyall Bay, Wellington.

The first witness called was Miss Brown, 18, a domestic servant from Greytown, described as an attractive young woman, neatly attired in a black velvet coat and smart dress. In April 1926, her boyfriend Frank Maher, 23, a painter, suggested she take pills from the chemist, but these did not work. He then went to see Dr Jacobsen on her behalf, pretending to seek help for his sister. For a fee of one guinea the doctor said he would provide a prescription, but only when Maher returned with the money. This he did, but the prescription did not help.

Miss Brown then consulted Dr Jacobsen, but because she was four months pregnant he said he could do nothing for her, adding that if she had come earlier he might have been able to help. He suggested she get married, but she told him this was out of the question as she was too young and did not like her boyfriend enough to get married. Dr Jacobsen then gave her the name and address of Mrs Nevill (whose correct name was Mrs Wylie), as someone who might be able to help. She saw Mrs Nevill, who told her it would cost £25 and instructed her to provide cotton wool, butter muslin and a change of clothing. She had to wear a catheter internally and take plenty of exercise. She visited Mrs Nevill several times, but on the last occasion police intercepted and questioned her. She never returned and gave birth to her baby on 15 December 1926.

In the other case, Mrs Davis, 31, mother of three, died in July 1926 after visiting Mrs Nevill, allegedly on the advice of Dr Jacobsen. Lawyers debated at length about the admissibility of evidence from the deceased woman. Mrs Nevill was now serving a three-year sentence for this crime.

His Honour said he would not be justified in finding a person guilty on evidence that was not absolutely clear, cogent and convincing. It was a case of the young woman's word against the doctor's. He dismissed the motion of the Medical Council to have the doctor's name removed from the Medical Register.

ଔ

In the years 1900 to 1939, few doctors came before the courts, but an exception was **Dr Joseph Hennessy** of Wellington. He was born in India in 1896, the son of an Irish doctor serving there with the British Army Medical Corps. He was educated in Ireland, graduating with a medical degree from the National University of Cork. From 1917 to 1920 he served in the Royal Air Force Medical Service. He went to Persia as medical officer for the Anglo-Persian Oil Company for about two years, on a salary of £900 per year, then he returned to London. In 1923 he came to New Zealand and purchased a practice in Tuakau, in the Waikato area, but left after 18 months for Auckland. He did not stay there very long before shifting to Wellington in 1926. The Wellington United Medical Institute employed him on a salary of £750 per year for two and a half years.

He was a debonair young man about town who enjoyed alcohol and an active social life. His drink-driving offences led to fines in Auckland and Wellington and eventually the cancellation of his driving licence for two and a half years; a great disadvantage for his professional practice. His excuse was that since being in the East he had recurrent bouts of malaria, for which he took quinine. When he felt another attack coming on he took whisky to ward off the symptoms.[14] More serious than traffic infringements were the charges against him regarding abortion.

Trial of Dr Joseph Patrick Hennessy, 1928[15]

In April and May 1928, Dr Hennessy, 32, received much publicity when he stood trial in Wellington for procuring an abortion on 24 March. The charge came about as a result of a police raid on a private nursing home run by Mrs Jean Potter, Broomhedge Street, Wellington. Mrs Potter, an elderly, alcoholic, retired nurse, was suspected of involvement in receiving abortion cases.

The police found a young Wairarapa woman convalescing on the premises and interviewed her and, later, her boyfriend. As a precaution, police admitted the young woman to Wellington Hospital, where she made an uneventful recovery. In a statement she described in detail how she had attended Dr Hennessy in his rooms at Kent Terrace, and how her boyfriend had paid £50 for the operation. Afterwards, on the advice of Dr Hennessy, she had gone to the nursing home for convalescence, where Dr Hennessy had supervised her care.

JURY FINDS YOUNG DOCTOR INNOCENT OF MALPRACTICE

Headline and images from the trial of Dr Joseph Patrick Hennessy in *NZ Truth*, 17 May 1928. Left: 'A "Brief" Consultation – Dr. Joseph Patrick Hennessy (left), found innocent of malpractice, chatting with his counsel, Lawyer Singer, of Auckland.' Right: Portrait of Dr Hennessy.

The subsequent hearings in the Magistrate's Court and the Wellington Supreme Court, presided over by Justice Reed, were followed closely by a curious public disappointed that the judge cleared the court of all but the participants. Dr Hennessy made a striking appearance – short in stature but immaculately groomed and wearing full morning dress with patent leather shoes. Confident in manner, he seemed mildly indifferent to the proceedings. For most of the time he was allowed to leave the dock and take a seat behind his counsel, Mr Singer from Auckland, who had been engaged because of his considerable experience in abortion cases.

The legal arguments centred on the use by the police of the two young accomplices, male and female, who were given name suppression and immunity from prosecution. In an eloquent address to the jury, Mr Singer strongly deprecated the police officers' tactics in obtaining their information, especially their surprise raid at 2.30 am on the boyfriend's home in the country, merely to take a statement. He also elaborated on the Minister of Justice pardoning the accomplices in return for incriminating evidence. The jury took only half an hour to return a verdict of not guilty.

Dr Hennessy was acquitted on 9 May 1928, but exactly three months later, Adrienne Stouppe lay dead.

Adrienne's story[16]
Deceased 10 August 1928, aged 20 years

Miss Adrienne Stouppe lived with her parents in Jackson Street, Island Bay, Wellington. Two months before she died, her mother was concerned about her health and took her to see Dr Hardwick Smith for 'treatment of her nerves'. He prescribed a tonic. For the past two years she had worked as a typist in the sales department of the National Electric Company, where Ralph Wear worked as an engineer. He was married and resided at Lyall Bay. When interviewed by the police in connection with Adrienne's death, he said he was on friendly terms with her and sometimes took her part-way home in his car, but he denied being responsible for her pregnancy. However he admitted going to Waikanae to visit Adrienne when she was there. At the inquest Mr O. C. Mazengarb represented Wear.

On Wednesday 1 August, Adrienne left home with a suitcase, telling her mother she was going to Mahara House, Waikanae, for ten days' rest. On Monday night 6 August she phoned home and spoke to her brother, but exactly where she was when she made the phone call remained a mystery. She returned home on Wednesday 8 August about 12.40 pm, arriving by taxi. Although her temperature was not raised, she appeared very ill and Dr Clay was summoned. He was very suspicious and when he questioned her Adrienne said 'You can guess can't you?' He replied he could not guess and she said 'Dr Hennessy'. When he examined her he immediately ordered her transfer to the hospital. Adrienne's mother said she was unaware of the pregnancy.

Dr Rhind, assistant surgeon at Wellington Hospital, examined Adrienne and found her seriously ill, with signs of acute generalised peritonitis. He asked her what had happened and she told him she had been interfered with first on Wednesday 1 August, and again on Sunday 5 August, as nothing had happened the first time. He considered her only chance was an immediate operation under a general anaesthetic, and this was performed about an hour after admission. In her uterus he found the remains of a recent incomplete abortion. He cleaned the interior of the uterus and then opened the abdomen and found it full of pus. He then closed the wound, providing drainage for the purulent fluid. Adrienne also received a blood transfusion. The next day her general condition improved slightly and a detective visited her to take a statement. She refused to comply as she said she did not want to get anyone into trouble.

In the small hours of the next morning, Friday 10 August, she died. Dr Rhind initially thought a depression in the wall of the uterus was an instrumental injury, but seeing the specimen post-mortem he thought it more likely to be an area of softening caused by abscess formation. He could not say whether an instrument had been inserted into the uterus.

Pathologist Dr Philip Patrick Lynch. (*NZ Truth*, 12 July 1924)

Dr Lynch, Wellington Hospital pathologist, conducted the post-mortem. He also could not say whether an instrument had been used, but diagnosed pyaemia, a severe form of septicaemia with abscesses in distant organs, in this case in the lungs. He could not say whether the miscarriage was natural or induced. However, on this occasion the coroner, acting alone, had no such reservations – he found 'the cause of death was pyaemia following a septic abortion, criminally produced.'

On 17 August, one week after her death and before any proceedings were initiated, Dr Hennessy fled New Zealand on the *Maheno*, bound for Sydney. When interviewed by reporters about the death, he said he knew nothing about it and refused to discuss it. After a spell he set up an expensive practice in Castlereagh Street, Sydney, as a Medical Electrical Specialist. To equip his rooms he purchased electrical apparatus from Watson and Son costing about £400. The terms were £125 cash deposit and promissory notes for £30 a month under a hire purchase agreement. A dispute ensued over the equipment and he landed in the hands of the receiver, bankrupt. He moved to less expensive rooms in Macquarie Street.

His lifestyle continued to attract scandal, as both he and his partner Iris Cullen (known as 'Mrs Hennessy') indulged in alcohol, drugs and parties. They were both required to testify at the inquest into the death of one of their social set, a pretty socialite named Dell Hutton, wife of a Sydney optician, who died in a haze of drugs and alcohol.[17] After that, news of Hennessy's whereabouts seemingly no longer interested the New Zealand public.

ଓ

Dr Walter Granville Carew, general practitioner of Auckland, was well known for providing assistance in abortion cases, two of which resulted in fatalities.

Mabel's story[18]
Deceased 9 February 1931, aged 37 years

Miss Mabel McKenzie worked as an accounting clerk in the National Bank of New Zealand. She joined the bank in 1915 in Wanganui and was transferred to the Auckland branch in 1924. On 15 December 1930 she took sick leave and the medical certificate, signed by Dr Grant, stated she was suffering from a thrombosed vein of the left leg, requiring three weeks in a nursing home.

She also attended Dr Carew. At the inquest he said Mabel consulted him on 16 January complaining of shortness of breath. Her periods were very irregular but she denied any possibility of pregnancy. The medicine he prescribed did not help her and she returned to see him more than once. He diagnosed a displacement of the uterus and recommended dilatation of the cervix, which she agreed to have carried out privately.

On 29 January he admitted her to the Aratonga Nursing Home and on Saturday 31 January he operated on her under anaesthetic. He visited her each day, and on 3 February, in great pain, she passed a fetus at two months' gestation. This was reported as a surprise finding. Dr Carew arranged for the anaesthetist to assist him again that evening while he performed a curettage. The next day Mabel developed a fever and had trouble passing urine, so on 5 February Dr Carew admitted her to Auckland Public Hospital. On the morning of 8 February, hospital staff diagnosed acute peritonitis and operated to drain pus from the abdominal cavity. Surgeons found a perforation passing from the vagina through to the bladder. The following day she died.

At the post-mortem examination, the abdominal organs, liver, spleen and kidneys all showed toxic changes. The cervix was torn and the uterus was septic. The coroner, acting alone, presented an unusually full report:

> Deceased had been operated on by Dr Carew for dilatation of the cervix on 30 January at a private hospital. She was at that time in a condition of early pregnancy but Dr Carew was unaware of that condition, the possibility of the existence of which deceased had denied. In the course of the operation the upper anterior part of the vagina was, owing to the struggling of the patient, accidentally injured by a perforation which penetrated into the bladder. Peritonitis supervened on this injury. The deceased was removed to the Public Hospital on the 5 February. Death was due to peritonitis caused by the injury to the vagina. No blame is attachable to any person.

A more skeptical observer would have questioned the doctor's actions from start to finish, but his evidence was not challenged and was corroborated by the other medical staff.

Rose's story[19]
Deceased 7 September 1938, aged 27 years

Miss Rose Hogan came to Auckland from Melbourne and had no relatives in New Zealand. Her boyfriend, Howard Strickland, 27, worked as a porter at the Auckland Railway Station. Since February 1938, Rose had worked in the machine room at Modern Shoes Ltd. She did not turn up for work on Monday 29 August; as it later transpired, she had had a miscarriage on Sunday 28 August, from which she never recovered.

Rose rented a room at an apartment house run by Mrs Hansen and on 2 September, when she became ill with abdominal pain, her landlady called in Dr McDougall. Rose told him (untruthfully) her periods were regular and he did not suspect a pregnancy. He thought she had anaemia and influenza and prescribed a tonic. Rose did not confide in her landlady.

Rose sent Strickland a telegram saying she wanted another doctor, but instead he went to Mr Teape, the chemist, saying his girlfriend needed help. Mr Teape phoned Dr Carew, asking him to visit Rose. Rose told Dr Carew a different story – that she had had a miscarriage after taking two lots of pills bought from a chemist. Dr Carew examined her and arranged for her to go to Mrs Kaye's private home, where she took in cases for nursing care. Mrs Kaye was an English-trained nurse, not registered in New Zealand. When Dr Carew told her about Rose's miscarriage she did not wish her to stay and thought she should be in hospital. However, Dr Carew persuaded her to let Rose stay, and that evening, with the assistance of another doctor, he performed a hot uterine douche under a light anaesthetic in Mrs Kaye's house.

On 3 September, in the evening, Strickland came to collect Rose in his car and take her back to her room, but her landlady refused to let her stay as she did not want an abortion case on her premises. Strickland returned to Mrs Kaye, who reluctantly let Rose stay another night. She said she had a case of measles and did not want it to spread. On 4 September Strickland arranged alternative accommodation for Rose at Mrs Webb's apartment house in Hobson Street. However Rose was obviously very ill and Mrs Webb told Strickland she should be in the public hospital. Rose was thin with little reserves and in a lot of pain. Dr Carew was telephoned but he did not visit and did not want Rose admitted to the public hospital. On 6 September Mrs Webb took the initiative and phoned a St John's Ambulance nurse to take Rose to hospital in the ambulance. Rose told the hospital doctor her last menstrual period was on 30 May and she miscarried on Sunday 28 August after taking pills. She was diagnosed as suffering from septicaemia and peritonitis. Despite treatment, including a blood transfusion, she never rallied and died at 1 pm on 7 September.

At the post-mortem, carried out by Dr Gilmour, pathologist at Auckland Hospital, he found a large amount of pus in the pelvis, some bleeding into the pelvic cavity and toxic changes in the liver, spleen and kidneys. An abscess had formed adjacent to the right ovary. In Dr Gilmour's opinion, a septic tract in the uterus had been created by the passage of an instrument.

Frederick Knight Hunt, Auckland magistrate and coroner. (*NZ Truth*, 23 February 1928)

At the inquest, Strickland was less than truthful but admitted he may have been responsible for the pregnancy. The coroner, acting alone, found 'death was due to septic abortion.' After returning his formal verdict, Mr Hunt could not restrain himself from delivering a scathing attack on the treatment Rose received:

> This poor friendless girl was allowed to die. It is a case on another young life thrown away to one of these abortionists. There are certain circumstances that should be referred to. Here is a friendless young girl, living in an apartment house alone. She becomes ill; she is taken to Mrs Kaye's place. I am satisfied Mrs Kaye did not want her there. It is somewhat curious that Mrs Kaye shelters behind Dr Carew. He says the girl's temperature was normal and she was fit to leave. Mrs Kaye is an experienced nurse, yet she did not notice the girl's serious condition, although two apartment housekeepers saw how bad she was. Mrs Kaye should have ascertained where the girl was going, and if she was not satisfied, should have taken her back

or notified the authorities. She could have sent for the ambulance as the Hobson Street boarding housekeeper did. There was carelessness there. As regards the young man Strickland, he is deserving of the severest censure in the strongest words that I can use. He was responsible for her condition. He takes her from Mrs Kaye's place to an apartment house. The woman there says she is too ill, and to take her to the hospital. He takes her back to Mrs Kaye's and then later, to an apartment house in Hobson Street and dumps her there without any attention or care. It was fortunate that the woman of the house sent for help. It is possible that if she had proper attention sooner she would not have died. It is to be hoped we never have such a bad case again.

No charges ensued.

Dr Carew's career came to an ignominious end.[20] In 1952 he was called as a witness in a Supreme Court trial after he had referred a young woman to another Auckland abortionist. The elderly woman abortionist, Mrs Snowden, was found guilty. Dr Carew died in highly unusual circumstances on 8 December 1952. He was addicted to morphine and was found dead at his home after returning from visiting a patient. He had been widowed for some four years, and his longstanding housekeeper died 12 hours later, in equally unusual circumstances, from heart failure.

಼

Dr Doris Gordon MBE (1890–1956), a general practitioner obstetrician from Stratford and a mother of four, played an important role in improving maternity services for New Zealand women. She championed pain relief in childbirth and promoted the soon-to-be-superseded 'Twilight Sleep' using two drugs, morphine and scopolamine. In 1927 she was instrumental in establishing the New Zealand Obstetrical Society (which in 1932 became the New Zealand Obstetrical and Gynaecological Society) to promote the scientific study and practice of obstetrics and to protect the interests of general practitioner obstetricians from intrusive Health Department policies. Dr Doris, as she was known, became its long-serving secretary. Canvassing business, community and women's groups, she spearheaded a national campaign to endow a full-time Chair of Obstetrics and Gynaecology in the Medical School at the University of Otago, for undergraduate education. Professor J. B. Dawson was appointed in 1931. She also established an endowment fund for a post-graduate School of Obstetrics and Gynaecology in the University of Auckland.[21]

Because of her strict upbringing and personal beliefs, Doris was unable to challenge the prevailing negative views of the medical profession regarding contraception and abortion. She did not support the liberal views expressed by other New Zealand medical practitioners like Dr H. E. A. Washbourn or Dr Sophia De La Mare. Birth control promoters elsewhere, especially Margaret Sanger in the USA and Dr Marie Stopes in England, fully recognised the advantages of birth control to prevent unplanned pregnancies and unsafe abortion, advantages which Doris could not accept. In disparaging the work of Marie Stopes, whose work was very popular in New Zealand, Doris wrote in 1937, 'Worst result of all, there crept into feminine psychology the thought, "If it is not wrong to prevent it, is it wrong to abort it?"'[22] Her attitudes were pronatalist, racist and eugenicist. She disapproved of the increasing emancipation of women. In her submission to the McMillan Inquiry she stated, 'Until we bring women back to that old fundamental Eastern idea that motherhood is their mission, barrenness their disgrace, until we do that, or unless we do that, we can be prepared to write RIP over the short lived race at present known as New Zealanders.'

However, on another topic in her submission she challenged the orthodoxy of her colleagues in recommending female sterilisation after multiple pregnancies if repeated child bearing seriously affected the woman's health. She approved of contraception only if it was medically necessary.

In *Gentlemen of the Jury*[23] she wrote:

> Birth control information, which was meant to benefit the few, has become a way of escape from duty for the majority. Individually and collectively the best elements of civilisation are hastening to exterminate themselves with their new-found knowledge. It is not the purpose of this book to maintain that birth control is at all times wrong. There are times and occasions when it is right and justifiable. It is worth remembering, however, that the abuse of birth control knowledge in New Zealand has already reduced this country to a dangerous state of stagnation, and, coupled with the rising tide of abortions, threatens in a very few years to extinguish its white people.

Doris was appalled at the failure of the courts to punish abortionist Mrs Annie Aves, lambasting the jury system for what she regarded as a clear dereliction of their duty.[24]

Unusually, the case went on to four Supreme Court trials, and all failed to convict. This was one of the reasons that motivated Doris to publish her polemic against abortion, *Gentlemen of the Jury*.

Her co-author was general practitioner Dr Francis Bennett, who later distanced himself from the publication, writing in his autobiography:[25]

> She [Doris] once wrote a lengthy denunciation of the abortionist and sent it to me for literary criticism. I thought it was awful and wrote and said so. She then appeared guest-like on my doorstep and was taken in. All the spare time of the next week was spent in literary conference. It was a hopeless collaboration. She amended the text behind my back. I did the same to her. Eventually we sent it to Professor Dawson. It came back, reduced to half and red-pencilled on every page. It next went to the advertising firm in Wellington which was going to publish it. Here it was re-written by a member of the staff. In its published form it was a very bad book.

Trials of Isabel Annie Aves, 1936 and 1937[26]

Mrs Annie Aves (1887–1938), 51, previously Mrs Craike, was a well-known abortionist from a respectable middle-class street in Hastings. Her usual technique was to insert sea-tangle tents to dilate the cervical canal. When police raided her Fitzroy Avenue premises in June 1936, they found two infant bodies and 20 separate collections of fetal remains buried in the fowl yard and kitchen garden.

When police searched the house they found detailed financial records, address lists and inventories of equipment purchased either from a traveller or by direct sales from Wellington. Her solicitors sent IOUs to defaulters. Using the telephone and address lists, police interrogated a number of women and selected five young single women as witnesses to support the Crown case. Mrs Aves faced seven charges of using an instrument to procure abortion, all alleged to have taken place between May 1935 and June 1936. Two women gave evidence relating to two events each, and three women gave evidence relating to a single event. Some male partners were also interviewed, and a total of 26 witnesses gave evidence for the prosecution. The defence called no witnesses, but relied on exposing weaknesses in the Crown case. Bail was refused.

Chief Justice Sir Michael Myers. (S P Andrew Ltd :Portrait negatives. Ref: 1/1-018601-F. Alexander Turnbull Library, Wellington)

Despite damning evidence Mrs Aves survived four trials, each time the jury failing to agree. The first trial was held in the Napier Supreme Court, presided over by Justice Blair. Subsequent trials were held in the Wellington Supreme Court, presided over by the Chief Justice, Sir Michael Myers. At the third trial, the foreman disclosed that two jurors were immovable. At the fourth trial, in February 1937, the judge did not want to know how they were divided:

> His Honour: Do you think it is of any use my keeping you together a little longer?

The Foreman: No use whatever.
His Honour: Well, Mr Lusk [Napier Crown Prosecutor], I shall of course have to discharge the jury.
Mr Lusk: I have the authority of the Solicitor-General that a stay of proceedings will be filed.

That was the end of the case and Mrs Aves continued her practice. Her husband Charles Aves died soon after, in April 1937, and she moved to Westshore, Napier. The following year she was murdered.

Trial of Colin Herbert Hercock, 1938 [27]

Miss Dorothy Stafford, 19, a home help employed in Otane, had been going out with her boyfriend Colin Hercock, 21, a grocer's assistant from Waipawa, for two years. When she became pregnant, he vowed his love and wanted to marry her, but she did not feel ready for marriage and suggested an abortion. He strongly opposed this but eventually, on Thursday 29 September 1938, he borrowed his mother's car and took Dorothy to Napier to see Mrs Aves.

For a fee of £20 Mrs Aves took her in and that evening performed the abortion. Dorothy stayed with Mrs Aves until Saturday, when she returned to the home where she worked. On Sunday, Dorothy was very ill. Hercock insisted she see a doctor and returned that evening with Dr Allen, who admitted her to Waipukurau Hospital. Hercock believed his loved one was about to die and, in his distraught state, acted rashly. Collecting a rifle he owned, he drove to Napier, knocked on Mrs Ave's door at 11.30 pm and, when she answered, shot her in the abdomen. She died at 10.30 pm the next day, 3 October 1938, at Napier Hospital. Her funeral was very well attended.

Hercock claimed he had only wished to frighten her, but his actions were premeditated and he was fortunate not to be convicted of murder. After shooting Mrs Aves he fled the scene, threw the rifle into the harbour and then reported to the police station. Dorothy recovered and gave evidence at Hercock's trial. Depositions were made in the Napier Magistrate's Court and the charge of murder was heard in the Napier Supreme Court, presided over by the Chief Justice Sir Michael Myers. The jury returned after two and a half hours with a verdict of manslaughter and His Honour imposed a sentence of 12 years' imprisonment with hard labour.

In sentencing Hercock, His Honour said:

> We know that Mrs Aves had performed an illegal operation on a girl and you took her there for that purpose. I know that some two years ago she was charged with a series of those offences and in the face of the most convincing and conclusive evidence four juries were unable to agree. I do not hesitate to say that the few – I hope only a few – who refused to do their duty in that case undertook a serious responsibility as events have turned out, as it appears this woman came back and continued her previous course. If she had been dealt with as she should have been, this tragedy would not have happened. Nevertheless she is entitled to her life and that you have destroyed.

On appeal the sentence was reduced to seven years with hard labour. Mitigating circumstances were his state of mind at the time, his youth and his previously unblemished record.

ଓଃ

With few exceptions, from 1900 to 1939 doctors were unhelpful in providing women with reliable contraception and safe abortion care, principally for moral, racist or legal reasons. Doris Gordon is recognised for doing much to improve the practice of obstetrics in her time but in hindsight she also did great harm. She was a forceful and influential woman and progress on the essential matters of contraception and abortion was delayed by many decades, at least in part, because of her negative attitudes.[28]

7. CHEMISTS

Chemists were the mainstay of abortion services, being present in most localities and, in some cases, offering confidential mail order services. Women often went to the pharmacist for advice on irregular menstruation, and there was an unwritten code that confidentiality prevailed. Chemists also commonly prescribed tonics for anaemia and treated vaginal discharge. A woman, or in many cases her partner, often went to a chemist for advice when an unplanned pregnancy was suspected.

Abortifacients such as pennyroyal, apiol, ergot and quinine sometimes worked, and this enhanced their reputation. Some of this success was no doubt due to a placebo effect when periods resumed in non-pregnant women: if worry about a pregnancy caused a delay in menstruation, the mere taking of a corrective was sometimes enough to bring on the flow.

Lawyers often debated the relative effectiveness of purported abortifacients. Defence lawyers could always find one or more doctors to testify that such and such a preparation did no harm or in legal terms was not noxious. Potency varied according to the raw material used, leading to variations either over or under the recommended dosage. Unscrupulous vendors sold worthless remedies to a vulnerable clientele at inflated prices.

The commonly purveyed abortifacients of the time were relatively safe in healthy women, with some notable exceptions; for example, a recognised unwanted side effect of apiol was damage to the nervous system (peripheral neuropathy). In 1904, Parliament passed regulations under the Public Health Act 1900 requiring the composition of proprietary medicines to be displayed on the label and a warning to be displayed if the contents contained a poison. Four years later, pursuant to the Noxious Weeds Act 1908, many local authorities issued a warning that pennyroyal (*Mentha pulegium*) was a noxious weed and offenders were liable to prosecution.[1] However, it was not until 1942 that the government introduced legislation which prohibited the advertising of treatments for amenorrhoea or female irregularities, and prohibited the sale of ergot preparations without a prescription. Until then, Ergoapiol and other ergot compounds could be bought over the counter, and the *Kai Tiaki* nursing journal regularly advertised Ergoapiol throughout the 1920s.

Advertisements for abortion were constrained in the same way as contraceptive advertisements – by the Offensive Publications Act 1892, the Indecent Publications Act 1910, the Post Office Act 1883 (amended in 1900 and 1906), and the Quackery Prevention Act 1908. Nevertheless, discreet promotion continued, such as the following examples:

> Consult Mrs Louisa Hawkins, 106 George Street. By letter, 5s; personally, free. Female Pills, 3s 6d and 5s box.[2]

(Most suppliers were chemists, but Mrs Hawkins, who advertised widely, described herself as a herbalist specialising in female complaints.)

> FREDERIC JAMES RAY
> DISPENSING AND FAMILY CHEMIST (*London Qualifications)*
> Pollen Street, Thames
> List includes:
> Essence of Pennyroyal, 8d per oz
> Tincture of quinine, 6d per oz.[3]

> SEE THAT YOU GET IT.
> APIOL & STEEL PILLS FOR LADIES
> Are the acknowledged leading remedy for all Female complaints. Recommended by the Medical faculty. The genuine bear the signature of Wm. MARTIN (registered without which none are genuine). No Lady should be without them. Of all Chemists throughout the World MARTIN, Pharm Chemist, SOUTHAMPTON, ENGLAND.
> Agents – SHARLAND & CO. Ltd., Auckland and Wellington, and NEW ZEALAND DRUG CO., Christchurch.[4]

A WONDERFUL MEDICINE

BEECHAM'S PILLS

ARE universally admitted to be worth a Guinea a Box for Bilious and Nervous Disorders, such as Wind and Pain in the Stomach, Sick Headache, Giddiness, Fulness and Swelling after Meals, Dizziness and Drowsiness, Cold Chills, Flushings of Heat, Loss of Appetite, Shortness of Breath, Costiveness, Scurvy and Blotches on the Skin, Disturbed Sleep, Frightful Dreams, and all Nervous and Trembling Sensations, etc. The first dose will give relief in twenty minutes. Every sufferer is earnestly invited to try one Box of these Pills, and they will be acknowledged to be

WORTH A GUINEA A BOX.

For Females of all ages these Pills are invaluable, as a few doses of them carry off all humours and bring about all that is required. No female should be without them. There is no medicine to be found equal to Beecham's Pills for removing any obstruction or irregularity of the system. If taken according to the directions given with each box, they will soon restore females of all ages to sound and robust health. This has been proved by thousands who have tried them and found the benefits which are ensured by their use.

For a Weak Stomach, Impaired Digestion, and all Disorders of the Liver, they act like magic, and a few doses will be found to work wonders on the most important organs in the human machine. They strengthen the whole muscular system, restore the long-lost complexion, bring back the keen edge of appetite, and arouse into action with the rosebud of health the whole physical energy of the human frame. These are FACTS testified continually by members of all classes of society, and one of the best guarantees to the Nervous and Debilitated is—

BEECHAM'S PILLS HAVE THE LARGEST SALE OF ANY PATENT MEDICINE IN THE WORLD.

Prepared only by the Proprietor, THOMAS BEECHAM, St. Helens, England, in Boxes, 9½d, 1s 1½d, and 2s 9d each.

Sold by all Druggists and Patent Medicine Dealers everywhere.

N.B.—Full directions are given with each box.

WOMAN'S UNFAILING FRIEND,

TOWLE'S PILLS
FOR FEMALES.
PENNYROYAL AND STEEL.

86 years Reputation. Are the oldest, Safest and only Reliable Remedy for all Ladies' Ailments. Quickly correct and relieve the Distress Symptons so prevalent with the Sex. PREPARED ONLY BY E. T. TOWLE & CO., LTD., NOTTINGHAM, ENGLAND. Sold by all Chemists and Stores throughout New Zealand.

FORTNIGHTLY DANCES.

A Meeting will be held in Duvauchelle Hall on THURSDAY, April 24th with the object of forming a Fortnightly Dance, or Euchre and Dance.

All those interested are requested to attend.

FREE OFFER FOR TWO WEEKS.

Every woman who sends a stamped addressed envelope to the New Zealand Chemical Co., Box 133, Dunedin, will receive a free sample of Bett's Improved Female Pills. These have been proved to be the best and most reliable on the market.

PROGRESSIVE EUCHRE PARTY AND DANCE.

GOOD AGGREGATE PRIZE.

THE first of a series of fortnightly euchre parties and dances will be held in St. Peter's Sunday Schoolroom on FRIDAY, May 1st 1925. In addition to ordinary prizes a good aggregate prize is offered for the winter months.
Prices: Ladies 1/-; Ladies without basket 2/-. Men 2/-.

Advertisements for Beecham's Pills in the *Auckland Star*, 2 January 1900 (left), Towle's Pills in the *Observer*, 12 July 1919 (top right) and special offer for Bett's Improved Female Pills in the *Akaroa Mail and Banks Peninsula Advertiser*, 21 April 1925 (bottom right), cunningly placed between two advertisements for local dances.

SPECIAL IMPORTATIONS
Dr Bonjean's Female Regulating Pills
Tansy, Pennyroyal and Cotton Root Female Pills
2/6 per box, obtainable from the lady in charge of the
Ladies' Department
WM. C. FITZGERALD,
CONSULTING CHEMIST, WELLINGTON.[5]

J.W. HALL, PHARMACEUTICAL CHEMIST
J. W. Hall, having had more than fifty years' experience
as a Pharmaceutical Chemist, is prepared to give advice
to the best of his ability on all minor ailments, and on the
use and administration of medicines.
The following are some of his best known preparations:
Steel and Pennyroyal Pills. The best known
emmenagogues.
J.W. HALL, CHEMIST, POLLEN STREET, THAMES[6]

(Emmenagogue is a rather old-fashioned term for a medicine to restore menstruation.)

C. & G. KEARSLEY'S ORIGINAL
WIDOW WELCH'S FEMALE PILLS
Prompt & Reliable, For Ladies. The only Genuine
AWARDED CERTIFICATE OF MERIT AT THE
TASMANIAN EXHIBITION, 1891.
100 Years' Reputation
Ordered by Specialists for the cure of all Female
Complaints.
Sold in bottles, 1/1½ and 2/9 of all chemists
CATHERINE KEARSLEY, 42 WATERLOO RD,
LOND, ENG.[7]

DR MCINTYRE'S Extra Strong FEMALE PILLS, are a
boon to women; 4s 6d.
Also DR BONJEAN'S Female Pills – Obtained at J. R.
SEWELL, Chemist.[8]

WOMAN'S UNFAILING FRIEND
TOWLE'S PENNYROYAL and STEEL PILLS FOR
FEMALES
Are the Oldest, Safest and only Reliable Remedy for
all Ladies' Ailments. Quickly correct all Irregularities,
remove all Obstructions, and relieve the Distressing
Symptoms so prevalent with the sex.
PREPARED ONLY By E.T. TOWLE & Co.,
NOTTINGHAM, ENGLAND

And Sold by all Chemists and Stores throughout Australasia.⁹

MARTIN'S PILLS APIOL & STEEL.
Sure and certain for all Female complaints. Every lady should keep a box in the house.
Chemists and Stores sell them throughout the world.
Proprietor: MARTIN, Chemist, Southampton, England.¹¹

Otago Witness, 26 April 1905.

Pills and potions were often combined with other methods if they did not appear to work. Chemists supplied enema equipment, also known as irrigators, for washing out the bowel, a common procedure. Dr Truby King even developed a special infant-sized enema, regarded as an essential household item and routinely used to ensure an infant had daily bowel movements. Adult enema equipment, such as a reservoir can held up high on a hook, was easily adapted for douching, or women could purchase special feminine douching equipment, such as hand-held rubber balloons. Chemists also supplied catheters for bladder care in cases such as urinary retention due to an enlarged prostate. They were made of glass, metal, rubber or gum-elastic. Bougies or dilators were sold for the home treatment of urinary tract strictures, which could be caused in a number of ways, but often occurred as the aftermath of a sexually transmitted infection, especially gonorrhoea. These instruments could be adapted to dilate the cervix, the first stage in an instrumental abortion.

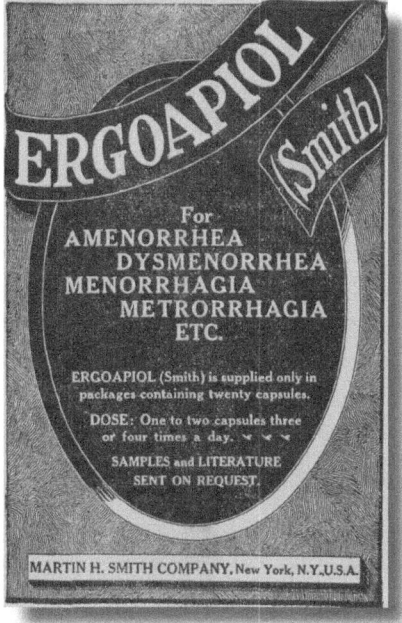

Advertisements for the notorious Mrs Towler in the *Otago Witness*, 26 April 1905 (top left), the chemist J.W. Hall in the *Thames Star*, 27 August 1904 (bottom left) and the abortifacient Ergoapiol in the nursing journal *Kai Tiaki*, 1 October 1921 (above).

Rubber catheters bend very easily and need an introducer or wire inserter for correct placement. In the case of the cervix and the uterus, if an instrument does not align with the direction of the internal organs, the risk of perforation is great. In some women the uterus tilts forwards, in others it tilts backwards, and the skill of the operator lies in correctly determining the anatomy. Doctors and midwives are trained to recognise these variations.

Some pharmacists stocked what were known as 'tents' or 'pencils' to dilate the cervix. Tents were made of an absorbent material which expanded in the presence of moisture. If placed in the cervical canal, the material would gradually swell and dilate the canal, sometimes enough to cause a miscarriage and at the very least making it easier to insert an instrument into the uterus. Sea-tangle tents were made of dried seaweed and sponge tents were made of a mucilaginous plant material. A string was attached to enable the device to be removed.

One well-equipped woman obtained a full range of chemist's goods.

Norah's story[12]
Deceased 16 October 1930, middle-aged

Norah Forgeson, also known as 'Mrs Carlyle', was separated from her husband. She had two children, a boy and a girl. She was housekeeper for Mr Smith, a widower with three children, who farmed near Ashburton. Norah planned to leave on 24 October for the North Island to be near her mother, and handed in her notice.

A neighbour, Mr Ernest Mills, 31, was very friendly with Norah and for the past six months had been a frequent visitor to the homestead, sometimes staying to play cards with Norah. They had an intimate relationship. Norah informed him of her pregnancy and discussed with him her plans to procure a miscarriage. First he purchased pills for her – Beecham's and Bonjean's. Then she went to Christchurch to obtain seaweed pencils, which she showed him. In August, she asked him to purchase an enema syringe, which he obtained from the United Friendly Society Chemist.

On Thursday 16 October, Norah had lunch as usual with her employer and his eldest son. When Mr Smith returned that evening about 5.30 pm, the children said they had not seen 'Mrs Carlyle'. He knocked at her door but got no answer. When he went in, he found her dead on the floor beside her bed, lying on her side with her knees bent up, with the new enema syringe and a jug of water placed nearby. At the post-mortem examination, she was found to be about three and a half months pregnant. The pelvic veins contained numerous air bubbles. Death was due to air embolism.

ɞ

A sympathetic pharmacist would naturally want to help women; such was the distress with which they presented. Most chemists carried on their business with a local reputation that inevitably spread through community networks; a woman who received help would often pass on the knowledge confidentially to help another woman in the same predicament. Only when misfortune occurred would the police become involved and the wider community become aware of illegal practices.

In Wanganui, James Nosworthy, an elderly herbalist, was the 'go-to' chemist who came to public notice after the death of a young woman.

Martha's story[13]
Deceased 26 December 1901, age not recorded but described as young

Martha Reader was a domestic servant in the private home of Mr and Mrs Jones, Wanganui. Her boyfriend, Robert Crane, was a young blacksmith who lived with his parents. They had been going together for eight or nine months and intended to get married in April. Martha became unwell, but because she had just had a dental extraction using gas, some of her symptoms were attributed to that.

She refused to see any doctor until she was seriously ill and admitted to hospital. Before she died, she told Dr Connolly she had obtained an 'instrument', which she described as a brown tube with a wire running through it, from Mr Nosworthy the chemist, and he had instructed her how to use it. This was a male catheter costing two shillings and sixpence. She also confided in two hospital nurses, who confirmed this story. One of the nurses said that Crane had advised Martha to get rid of the child as they could not afford to marry just yet.

The post-mortem confirmed a recent miscarriage and signs of septic peritonitis. There was a perforation at the junction of the body and neck of the womb, which was consistent with the use of a blunt instrument.

At the inquest Crane was less than forthcoming about his role in obtaining the abortion. He said Martha took some medicine (powder) obtained from the local chemist, Mr Williamson, but this only made her sick. Crane also mentioned Martha taking medicine from Mr Nosworthy, but nothing about a catheter. Nosworthy denied everything.

The jury criticised the hospital for not taking her dying depositions. The verdict read:

> That the deceased met her death from septic peritonitis, brought on by the perforation of the womb with an instrument used by herself. The jury considers that it is to be regretted that the rules of the Hospital do not provide for the dying depositions being taken in suspected criminal cases.

The hospital replied that the Board knew of no rule which would interfere with the taking of dying depositions at the hospital and the jury was evidently misinformed on this matter.

No charges were laid but the police kept Nosworthy under surveillance, and five years later they brought a case against him.

Trial of James Nosworthy, 1907[14]

On 2 October 1906, police charged Nosworthy with unlawfully supplying an instrument to Charles Snow, knowing that the same was intended for an illegal purpose. Snow was an undercover policeman.

Depositions in the Magistrate's Court alleged the supply took place in Nosworthy's shop on 1 September, when Snow, attired in plain clothes, said he had got a girl into trouble. Snow asked for a particular medicine and Nosworthy told him if the medicine was not successful he could then obtain an instrument (a sea-tangle tent). On 22 September, Snow returned, stating the medicine had not been successful, and he was then supplied with the sea-tangle tent and full instructions for its use.

Herbalist in Trouble

(Per Press Association).

Wanganui, October 2
In the Police Court this morning, James Nosworthy, herbalist, was remanded for a week on a charge of attempting to commit a crime by unlawfully supplying an instrument or thing to one James Snow, knowing the same to be intended to procure a miscarrirge.

Hastings Standard, 2 October 1906

At a subsequent raid of Nosworthy's shop, police found 26 illegal instruments and in Nosworthy's books no less than 22 entries of sales made on credit during a short period. A number of these were to local married women. In addition, police alleged there would have been a number of cash sales. Doctors gave evidence that sea-tangle tents were not used in legitimate medical practice, but Nosworthy claimed he stocked them for veterinarians and farmers.

The case was heard in the Wanganui Supreme Court, presided over by Justice Chapman, on 11 March. The defence argued that, as the constable had no intention of using the instrument, Nosworthy could not be convicted. The judge did not accept this argument and, relying on a precedent in England, directed the jury accordingly. The jury returned a guilty verdict, and to ensure justice, the judge referred the case to the Court of Appeal. Nosworthy, in poor health and described as practically a cripple, was released on bail until 15 April, when the Court of Appeal upheld the conviction. Nosworthy was sent to the Wellington Supreme Court for sentencing, where Justice Chapman sentenced him to two years' imprisonment.

The case elicited considerable public discussion on the role of government in allowing sea-tangle tents to be imported and sold, and the use of an undercover constable in making the arrest. Nosworthy's business was sold to an experienced herbalist who extensively renovated the premises and advertised all kinds of herbal and homeopathic medicines. It is not known whether he continued the abortion service.

☙

At the turn of the century, the registration of chemists was controlled by the Pharmacy Act 1880. Registration was by examination, but those already in practice for a number of years gained recognition through their years of experience. Nosworthy was in this category, and so was Mr Thomas Moore, 68, unmarried, who lived in his Waipawa pharmacy premises with his housekeeper Mrs Mary Ann Mills, also 68. His reputation as an abortionist reached Lottie Ancell.

Lottie's story[15]
Deceased 30 October 1902, aged 23 years

Lottie Ancell enjoyed good health and worked as a bookkeeper at the Clarendon Hotel in Napier. Her employer described her as of bright disposition, accomplished and well-esteemed. Her friends and family, who thought she was travelling from Napier to Wellington to visit her step-mother and sick brother, were devastated at the news of her sudden death, en route, in the town of Waipawa on Thursday 30 October.

Her mysterious death occurred in Thomas Moore's premises, in an upstairs room that he used for dental extractions. Dr Ross was summoned immediately and carried out a post-mortem examination on the Thursday afternoon. Lottie had been between four and five months pregnant, but there were no signs of interference. Dr Ross thought her sudden death was probably due to a convulsion, and the coroner's verdict, in rather convoluted and archaic language, determined that she:

> did labor and languish under a grievous disease of body to wit asphyxia caused by convulsions and on the 30th day of October 1902 the said Lottie Ancell by the visitation of God in a natural way of the disease and distemper aforesaid and not by any violent means whatsoever in the knowledge of the said jurors did die.

But those who knew her well rejected this 'visitation of God', questioned the coronial findings and encouraged the police to investigate further. As a result, police charged Moore with murdering Lottie on 30 October, and Mills with aiding and abetting.

Trial of Thomas Frederick Moore and Mary Ann Mills, 1902

As it transpired, Lottie intentionally visited Mr Moore, a qualified and registered chemist. The Crown produced five doctors to testify in the Napier Supreme Court hearing and they were subjected to detailed cross-examination. The allegation of the Crown was that death was due to air embolism caused by the application of certain instruments by Moore, assisted by Mrs Mills – not convulsions, as ascertained by the coroner.

When called to give evidence in the Supreme Court, Mrs Mills surprised the court by retracting evidence she had given in the Magistrate's Court and signing a declaration incriminating Moore. She was obviously torn between loyalty and honesty:[16]

> I, Mary Ann Mills, have been living with Moore for 26 years. I know that he used to operate on young women for abortion, but I don't think that he has for two or three years. I want to tell the whole truth about the matter. On October 30th I did not see Lottie Ancell come into the shop at all. I heard Mr Moore upstairs in the little room. I was in the shop and kitchen, back and forth all the morning. I could hear Moore moving about upstairs. Doody Ferguson was in the shop and kitchen with me. At about 12 noon, I was in the kitchen with Doody Ferguson. Moore came to

the door and beckoned me with his finger. I went out of the kitchen to him. He said 'The young woman upstairs is foaming at the mouth.' I said 'What woman?' He said 'The person up there.' I ran upstairs and he came with me. As soon as I got to the room I saw a girl lying on the couch. I think she was still alive. I could see her tongue moving. She was lying partly on her back and partly on her side. I turned to Mr Moore and said 'Now, what have you been doing to her?' He said 'Nothing; I have done nothing.' I said to him 'Go and fetch the doctor quick' and he went down and soon Dr Ross came. I noticed that the girl's stays were loosened and her clothes disarranged. I was called as a witness at the inquest. Before going there Mr Moore urged me to say that he had not seen the girl. I told at the inquest what was not true. I did so as I wanted to save Mr Moore. I have on two or three occasions warned Mr Moore about taking women for operations. I know he used to do it. I have not seen him. About three years ago I read Dr Orpen's case in Auckland. I then warned Moore and he promised me faithfully that he would not do it anymore. I am telling this entirely of my own free will, as an honest woman. I don't know why I should suffer for what Moore does. I must have been mad to screen him. I pulled the girl's clothes straight before the doctor came.

The jury enquired if they could bring in a verdict with regard to one accused while they disagreed about the other. Justice Edwards refused to accept such a verdict. The jury could not agree and the judge ordered a fresh trial. The Crown Prosecutor, acting under instructions of the Solicitor-General, entered a *nolle prosequi* (do not prosecute) in respect of the charge against Mrs Mills, but proceeded with the charge against Moore. The outcome of the retrial was that Moore was found guilty of manslaughter and sentenced to seven years' hard labour.

Mrs Mills was tried in the Supreme Court for perjury and was awarded 12 months' probation and ordered to pay 10 guineas in costs. In sentencing her, the Chief Justice, Sir Robert Stout, said:[17]

> I do not ordinarily grant probation in perjury cases, because I think it one of the worst of crimes, one which tends to destroy the foundation of justice. If people are allowed to come into Court and give false testimony no one could say what might be done. It might destroy altogether the foundation of the administration of justice, which after all is the basis of every civilised community.

Arthur Lindop, 35, chemist, provided an abortion service in the Wairarapa.

Trials of George William Hulley and Arthur Lindop, 1907[18]

George Hulley 19, a butcher's assistant in Carterton, was having sexual relations with his 16-year-old girlfriend Lena Reid. When she found she was pregnant, she told George and he sought advice from the chemist Arthur Lindop. Lindop sold George a bottle of Blaud's pills, and when these did not work, George went back and Lindop gave him some more pills and another decoction containing chlorate of iron, myrrh and carbonate of potash. When those medications did not work, George went back again two weeks later, and Lindop handed him a box of sea-tangle tents, with instructions on how to insert them into the cervix. He said he stocked these for use by veterinarians and farmers. Lena refused to use any of the tents and threw them away. She later confided in her mother, who remonstrated with George about not telling her sooner about her daughter's condition.

Mrs Reid, accompanied by another woman, took Lena to an abortionist in Masterton. At that stage she was four-and-a-half to five months pregnant. After the abortion she became ill, and police intervened. They did not obtain evidence about the person who had carried out the abortion but tricked George into making a confession, by not warning him about making incriminating statements. When he appeared in the Magistrate's Court the jury was out for only 15 minutes before returning a guilty verdict, but with a strong recommendation for mercy. The judge, in sentencing George, spoke of his good character and did not send him to prison. Instead he gave him probation and fined him £10 towards the cost of prosecution.

Lindop was arrested on a charge of supplying the means to procure an abortion. He was described as a highly respectable person, esteemed in hockey and cricket circles, the son of a borough councillor, and a native of the Wairarapa.

In November/December his case was heard in the Masterton District Court. Defence argued that it was not uncommon for young men to visit the chemist for the purpose of restoring a girl's natural functions, and that the medicines Lindop prescribed were innocuous tonics incapable of causing an abortion, while the tents were not used. The precedent of Nosworthy was raised in proceedings, but the outcome was different. After a retirement of half an hour the jury returned a verdict of not guilty.

ଔ

Supplying abortifacient drugs was a disputed area, and the following two stories – one in Auckland, the other in Christchurch – illustrate the typical role of the chemist in advising women.

Alice's story[19]
Deceased 27 May 1911, aged 22 years

Miss Alice Hart, typist, lived with her widowed mother in Auckland. Her mother said she came home ill on 9 May. Dr Bull attended her and also sought the opinion of his colleague, Dr Roberton. At some stage Alice told the doctors she had been operated upon by a nurse. On 25 May both doctors agreed the correct course of action was to admit Alice to Auckland Hospital.

Alice confided in the hospital doctor, Dr Macdiarmid, that she had been taking pills and medicines from Mr Eccles the chemist, but when these did not work she had seen a nurse in Beach Road on the North Shore, who performed an operation, and she had also seen another nurse in Devonport. To the detective who took her dying depositions, she said she would only reveal the identities of these two women and the man who got her into trouble if he would give her an undertaking the information would not be used against them. He could not give that reassurance and did not question her further. Despite treatment, she died two days after admission.

The post-mortem, carried out by Dr Macdiarmid, found her death to be due to sepsis following an illegal operation. The inquest was heard by the coroner and six male jurors. At the inquest Dr Ardagh, senior house physician at the hospital, stated that Alice told him she had seen Mr Eccles for pills and medicine to cure 'her condition', whereas Mr Eccles testified that he did not know of 'her condition' and had given Alice a quinine and iron tonic to restore her health. The jury believed Mr Eccles and not Dr Ardagh, and even added a rider to the verdict expressing the opinion that Mr Eccles was entirely free from blame.

Charlotte's story[20]
Deceased 13 February 1923, aged 25–30 years

Miss Charlotte Jervois immigrated to New Zealand from Ireland in 1922 and had no known relatives in this country. From time to time she stayed at the YWCA in Christchurch. Staff described her as shy and reserved, but during her last stay she seemed depressed and stayed in bed a good deal. A week before her death, she left the YWCA to go to work and live in at the Christchurch Club.

Dorothy Gordon, pantry maid at the Christchurch Club, occupied the same bedroom as Charlotte. On Tuesday 13 February, Dorothy returned home at about 10 pm. The light was on in the bedroom but Charlotte was not there. Her underclothing lay on the bed but her dressing gown was gone. When she had not returned by about 11.20 pm, Dorothy became concerned. The light was on in the bathroom but there was no response to calling or knocking on the locked door. Dorothy notified the warden on duty and he came and climbed up and looked over the door and discovered Charlotte on the floor, dressed in a nightdress. There were no towels in the room and no water in the bath. They clambered around to the balcony door, forced it open and carried her lifeless body back to her room.

Her body was later removed to the morgue at Christchurch Hospital, where Dr Pearson, pathologist, conducted the post-mortem. He determined heart failure as the primary cause of death and a septic condition of the pregnant uterus as the secondary cause. In his opinion, the stimulus to the heart failure may have been a very hot bath, or it may have been the insertion of an instrument such as a catheter or an enema. Microscopy confirmed a streptococcal infection. In Dr Pearson's opinion, the appearances strongly suggested interference, possibly by the use of contaminated instruments some days before death, although there were no signs of injury or perforation. The pills found in her room (Ergoapiol) might, if given in large doses, cause abortion, but Dr Pearson said they were mainly used for regulating menstruation.

At the inquest into her death, Henry Shaw, manager for W. R. Cooke and Sons, Chemists, High Street, Christchurch, testified that he had supplied pills and an enema to Charlotte. In January, Charlotte seemed very anxious to get work and Mr Shaw told her he would see what he could do. A few days later he received a note from her, asking if she could come alone and see him about her health. He replied positively and a day or so later she came in. She did not look well, and Mr Shaw asked her what her trouble was. She told him she had not menstruated in the previous month, but denied being pregnant. He asked if she knew of any reason why her periods had stopped and she said she had been suffering from 'the whites' (vaginal discharge). He told her she was probably run down and that was why she had not come on. He said he would give her some pills and if she were not pregnant they would probably fix her up, as they were the ordinary regulating pills. For 'the whites' he told her to douche and supplied an enema for that purpose. He did not supply her with a catheter, explaining that catheters were only supplied to a registered nurse or on a doctor's prescription. He denied supplying the Ergoapiol pills that were found in her possession.

Christchurch pathologist Dr Arthur B. Pearson. (*The Press*, 20 September 1932)

The coroner, acting alone, found 'the cause of death was heart failure associated with a septic condition of the pregnant uterus.'

ଔ

Most cities had at least one well-known abortionist. In Dunedin, it was **James Reynolds Hayne** (1852–1926), known as Jimmy. At the age of 28 he married Elisabeth, 20, and four years later they had a daughter. He established a business as a pharmaceutical chemist in Dunedin city, first in Princes Street, then in Moray Place. When abortifacient drugs failed to bring about the desired results, he provided an operative solution in a room at the back of his premises, believing that in so doing he was providing a necessary service. Miss **Elizabeth Inglis** (1880–1961) was his long-time assistant and mistress. She operated a boarding house and nursing home in nearby Hope Street, where Hayne sent cases for convalescence. She had no nursing training; in fact, she trained as a hairdresser. Throughout his various trials, Hayne was ably defended by Dunedin lawyer Mr Hanlon.

Hayne first came to public attention in 1906, when he was charged with the death of Miss Margaret Kendrick. The jury on this occasion found him not guilty. In 1913, Miss Margaret Donnelly died in Miss Inglis's nursing home, but neither Hayne nor Miss Inglis were prosecuted. In 1919, Miss Gladys Batchelor became a cause célèbre when she refused to testify against Hayne or her lover Norman Neylon in yet another abortion case. After three well-publicised trials, her case was abandoned. In 1921, Hayne and Miss Inglis were charged following the death of Mrs Violet Atkins; after three trials that case, too, was abandoned. In 1923, Hayne and Inglis were charged with procuring the abortion of 22-year-old Miss A (who was given name suppression in return for testifying at the trial). Inglis was found not guilty, but this time Hayne was found guilty and sentenced to seven years' imprisonment. Because of ill health, he was released after serving two years of his sentence and he died the following year at the age of 74. Miss Inglis never married, and died at the age of 80. Further details of these stories are as follows.

Maggie's story[21]
Deceased 22 September 1906, aged 35 years

Miss Margaret Kendrick, known as Maggie, was of small build and not very robust. She kept house for her brother Thomas, a coach builder in Mornington, Dunedin, and cared for their invalid mother, who lived with them. Maggie and her brother-in-law John Lilburne, a shipping clerk who also lived in Mornington, were close friends. For the past eight or nine months she had been in a sexual relationship with Alexander Goudie of Port Chalmers, a boilermaker employed on the steamship *Moeraki*. When Maggie found she was pregnant, Alex said he offered to marry her but was refused.

On Tuesday evening 11 September, she allegedly visited Hayne in his Princes Street shop, telling him she was 'wrong' and wanting him to make her 'right'. He asked her to return the following evening. She told her brother she was leaving for a holiday, but on Wednesday 12 September at 5.15 pm she went to see Hayne, and an operation took place in one of the three rooms behind his shop. He used an instrument (catheter) and charged her £25.

After the operation, she fainted and was escorted by his assistant to recuperate at a boarding house at 342 George Street run by Mrs Christina Biessel, living apart from her husband. Maggie stayed there for six days under an assumed name. Most of that time was spent in bed. On Saturday 15 September, when she felt really unwell, Hayne visited her and prescribed some medicine, which Mrs Biessel obtained for her. On Sunday, she had a miscarriage.

On Tuesday evening 18 September, of her own accord, she left the boarding house and Mrs Biessel escorted her in a horse-drawn cab to the home of her brother-in-law Mr Lilburne. She was feverish and in a collapsed state. He called immediately for Dr Evans, but the doctor was busy and could not attend until the following morning. She was in great pain and her family stayed up all night doing what they could to make her feel comfortable. When Dr Evans saw her in the morning, he at once suspected she had had an illegal operation, although she strenuously denied even being pregnant.

By the next day she was suffering severe abdominal pain, and Dr Evans diagnosed peritonitis. Initially she said she had taken drugs, but after he told her it was very unlikely that drugs alone would have caused her condition, she confided she had been to Mr Hayne. Dr Evans admitted her to Dunedin Hospital on Friday 21 September, and suggested that if friends or relatives asked, she should just say she had appendicitis.

Lilburne accompanied her to hospital and advised her to make a dying deposition before a magistrate, which she did, describing her experience in great detail and naming Hayne as the abortionist. She died at 3 am on Saturday morning 22 September. Her death caused a sensation in Dunedin when Hayne was arrested and charged.

The post-mortem, carried out by Dr Roberts, pathologist at Dunedin Hospital, found acute generalised peritonitis and a ruptured abscess on the right Fallopian tube. There were signs of a recent pregnancy of about two months' gestation. The uterus was gangrenous and there was another abscess on the wall of the uterus. At one site in the uterus there was an area of ulceration, possibly due to laceration from an instrument. In Dr Roberts's opinion, her septic condition had indubitably been brought about by external means.

An inquest into her death was held in the Coroner's Court before a jury of six men. Hayne's lawyer, Mr Solomon, attended on his behalf, with the permission of the coroner. He interjected a number of times, pointing out the different rules of evidence that applied in the Coroner's Court and the effect that evidence given there might have on Hayne's later trial in the criminal court. This applied particularly to hearsay evidence.

In his summing up, the coroner said if the jury was satisfied as to who performed the operation it was their duty to say so, even though the only evidence would be that of the deceased. The jury retired for a very short time and returned the verdict that Margaret Kendrick 'died of peritonitis caused by an illegal operation performed by James Reynolds Hayne.'

Trial of James Reynolds Hayne, 1906

In October 1906, before a crowded court, Hayne was charged with the manslaughter of Margaret Kendrick. He was committed for trial in the Dunedin Supreme Court. An argument ensued over whether he should be granted bail for the six weeks while awaiting trial. The magistrate refused bail, pointing out that Hayne had a loaded revolver in his possession when he was arrested.

In November 1906 in the Supreme Court, before Justice Cooper, Hayne was defended by Mr Solomon and Mr Hanlon. The defence argued about the admissibility of Maggie's dying deposition, claiming that it had not been taken correctly, with the magistrate paraphrasing some of Maggie's replies to questions; that Hayne had not been present to defend any of the statements made; and that there was doubt about whether Maggie knew she was dying, even though she died three hours after the deposition was taken. As well as focusing on these deficiencies, the defence persuasively argued that the deposition was made by an accomplice, and corroboration was essential. The judge allowed the deposition to be read, but said if Hayne was convicted, the matter should be considered by the Court of Appeal. In the end this was not necessary, as the jury was out for only ten minutes and returned a verdict of not guilty.

Margaret's story[22]
Deceased 3 October 1913, aged 25 years

Miss Margaret Donnelly lived in Invercargill, where she was employed as bookkeeper and typist for two brothers who were auctioneers. She had served them for eight years and was due for a promotion and salary increase. She asked for a few days' leave and told them she was going to see friends in Dunedin and would be back for work on Saturday. It was alleged she went on Tuesday to Dunedin to see Hayne, had an abortion, miscarried on Wednesday and took ill on Thursday, but Hayne did not call in a doctor until Friday morning. By this time Margaret was jaundiced and near death.

Hayne went to Dr Macpherson's house at 6 am, saying he wanted to take him into confidence, and asked him to see a dangerously ill patient. Dr Macpherson refused to go, saying he did not want to be mixed up in any of Hayne's cases. Then, about 7 am, Dr Macpherson got a ring from Dr Fleming, asking him to come and see a dying patient in a boarding house. At Dr Fleming's request, Dr Macpherson went to Miss Inglis's boarding house at 49 Hope Street. The patient was Margaret, who died later that morning. Dr Fleming initially claimed her rapid death was due to toxaemia of pregnancy, but this was disproved by the autopsy findings, which showed she died of a particularly virulent form of septicaemia.

At the coroner's inquest Mr Hanlon acted for Miss Inglis. In summing up the case, the coroner reportedly said:[23]

> this was one of those painful cases which occasionally cropped up and which were always shrouded with a certain amount of mystery, as the witnesses were all more or less interested in stifling the truth. This young woman had unfortunately become pregnant and a short time afterwards a miscarriage occurred. There was a suspicious circumstance in her leaving Invercargill to come to Dunedin. She was on the point of promotion in her employment but she came to Dunedin and went to an obscure boarding house in Hope St which had neither been advertised, nor had any notice to say it was a lodging house. How did she know of the place? She was to have left on Thursday but she suddenly decided to leave on Tuesday and started off first thing in the morning. She went to the place in Hope St where the miscarriage took place and she died under the circumstances mentioned by the doctor.

The coroner said he could only conclude that the immediate cause of death was acute septicaemia, the result of a miscarriage. There was not sufficient evidence to show how the miscarriage was brought about – whether by natural or by artificial means – because the only witnesses who could throw light on the subject refused to give evidence, on the grounds that such evidence would incriminate them. No prosecution ensued.

DUNEDIN SEPTICAEMIA MYSTERY.
REMARKABLE DEVELOPMENTS AT THE INQUEST.
WITNESSES DECLINE TO ANSWER.

Dr. Macpherson's Disclosures—He took Legal Advice—Invercargill Auctioneer's Strange Attitude — Declined to Answer Questions which might Incriminate — No Information from Chemist "Jimmy" Hayne—The Significant Silence of Miss Inglis—Is there a Mrs. Ritchie or Not?—The Coroner's Conclusions.

James Reynolds ('Jimmy') Hayne and Elizabeth Simpson Inglis at the inquest on the death of Margaret Donnelly. (*NZ Truth*, 25 October 1913)

Trials of James Reynolds Hayne, Elizabeth Simpson Inglis and Norman Neylon, October–November 1919; February and August 1920[24]

The headlines in NZ *Truth* summarise the case:

> Their Third Trial: Alleged Abortionists Arraigned: Hayne and Neylon Indicted on Grave Charge: Venue of Trial Changed to Wellington: Extraordinary Attitude of Principal Witness: Is it a 'Conspiracy Of Silence?'

> Case Adjourned Till Next Criminal Session. 'Mum's The Word!': Gladys Batchelor Still Silent: Hayne-Neylon Abortion Case Again Undecided: Judge Herdman Gives Girl Nine Months For Contempt Of Court.

> Remarkable Case: Hayne-Neylon Criminal Prosecution: No Evidence Offered Against Neylon. Gladys Batchelor Again Refuses to Speak.

> Trial of J.R. Hayne: Crown Enters *Nolle Prosequi*: Caustic Comment by Justice Edwards.

> A Cause Célèbre: The Silence of Gladys Batchelor: Hayne-Neylon Abortion Charge Collapses: Sensational Conclusion to Remarkable Trials.

Police charged Hayne and Miss Inglis with illegally using an instrument on Gladys Batchelor, aged 20 years, in Dunedin on 15 September 1919.

Gladys lived in Waimate and kept company with Norman Neylon, butcher and returned soldier. On 27 August, concerned about being pregnant, she approached Dr Pitt, who had cared for her since childhood. He merely asked her to return in one month. Her anxiety was such she could not wait for a month and returned to see him again on 5 September. This time he examined her and confirmed a pregnancy of about two months' gestation. When she asked if he could do anything for her, he replied that medical men did not do such things and advised her to confide in her mother. In the meantime, Neylon had written to Hayne in Dunedin, and advised Gladys to go and see him. Gladys told her mother she was going to Timaru.

When Gladys saw Hayne at his rooms in Moray Place, she did not take any money with her and he said he could do nothing until she paid £30. Miss Inglis arranged for her to stay in a private

(One Woman Who Can Hold Her Tongue.)

Gladys Batchelor.
(*NZ Truth*, 29 May 1920)

hotel in Princes Street until the money arrived. Neylon sent her £30 and Hayne accepted £25. She stayed in Dunedin from 12 to 15 September, the returned home to Waimate. The following Tuesday she was admitted to Waimate Hospital, and when she became seriously ill, she made a statement to the hospital doctor, after he told her she might die. However, she recovered. Hayne was arrested on 3 October and Miss Inglis on 4 October.

Hayne and Neylon appeared first in the Waimate District Court on 6 October 1919. After a hearing in the Dunedin Magistrate's Court on 17 October, they were committed for trial at the November sittings of the Dunedin Supreme Court. Both accused were represented by Mr Hanlon.

Two trials were held in Dunedin, and the juries disagreed in both cases. The first trial resulted in a hung jury. At the second trial Miss Inglis was found not guilty. The charges against Hayne and Neylon were then transferred to Wellington. Here the accused were defended by Mr Wilford. Gladys refused to give evidence. Justice Edwards, in desperation, adjourned the case to the May sessions, and in the meantime Gladys was charged with complicity in the abortion. At the May sessions Gladys received a sentence of nine months' imprisonment from Justice Herdman for contempt of court in refusing to give evidence. Neither cajoling, explanations, nor threats had any effect on Gladys – she took her punishment with composure and earned a certain respect from the public for her determined stand. The seal of silence on Gladys's lips was never broken.

The case was heard again in the Wellington Supreme Court in August 1920. In a dramatic turn of events, the Crown prosecutor announced that no evidence would be called against Neylon, and he was discharged. The trial of Hayne continued, but both Neylon and Gladys refused to answer further questions, and Justice

THEIR THIRD TRIAL

ALLEGED ABORTIONISTS ARRAIGNED

Hayne and Neylon Indicted on Grave Charge

VENUE OF TRIAL CHANGED TO WELLINGTON

Extraordinary Attitude of Principal Witness—Is it a "Conspiracy of Silence"?—Case Adjourned Till Next Criminal Sessions

HAYNE AND NEYLON
(The Two Accused)

"MUM'S THE WORD!"

GLADYS BATCHELOR STILL SILENT

Hayne-Neylon Abortion Case Again Undecided

JUDGE HERDMAN GIVES GIRL NINE MONTHS FOR CONTEMPT OF COURT

Headlines about the Hayne-Neylon case in *NZ Truth*, 7 February and 29 May 1920.

Edwards adjourned the court to consult with fellow judges. On resuming the following morning, Gladys stead-fastly refused to answer questions. The Crown prosecutor then announced a stay of proceedings. The ends of justice, he said, had been defeated by a conspiracy of silence.

Hayne was discharged. No further punishment was imposed upon Gladys. Neylon could still have been prosecuted for perjury but was not.

Violet's story[25]
Deceased 5 November 1921, aged 35 years

Mrs Violet Atkins was married but living apart from her husband Charles. There were three children of the marriage, aged four, six and ten – two girls and a boy. For over a year Violet had been living with her father, a fruiterer, in Timaru. On Thursday 6 October, she left home, saying she was going to Dunedin for a holiday. That day she sent a telegram to her brother Fred Hilton, a draper's assistant in Dunedin, asking him to meet her at the railway station.

Fred accompanied Violet to the Leviathan Hotel, where she booked a room. He left, but returned again at 6.30 pm. Violet told Fred she was pregnant and she had come to see Mr Hayne. Fred told her the best thing she could do was return home by the first express next morning. He asked her who had got her into trouble, but she refused to say.

The following morning, Friday 7 October, Violet came to see Fred at his workplace. She told him she had been to see Hayne, who told her to bring just a toothbrush and leave her luggage at the station. Fred strongly advised her to go home and not continue with the operation. She said the charge was 50 guineas, and opened her purse to show Fred she had the money. Whether this was her own savings or given to her, as she said, by the man responsible for her pregnancy, was a matter for later dispute. When she left Fred that morning he did not know where she went. She sent him a postcard on 10 October: 'Just writing to say having a good time and feeling all right. Will ring you up when I arrive in town.' This card was to feature prominently in the subsequent trials.

On Wednesday evening, 12 October, Fred was walking along Princes Street, Dunedin, and Miss Grace Wilson, a young woman whom he recognised from Timaru, stopped and chatted with him. Grace was a dressmaker who knew Hayne's assistant, Miss Inglis; Miss Inglis had written to Grace asking her to do some sewing for her in Dunedin. From 22 September until 18 October, Grace had sewed for Miss Inglis, and slept at Hayne's shop on a couch at the end of the dispensary.

Grace told Fred that Violet was also staying at Hayne's place, recovering from the operation. Grace said she cleared Mr Hayne's mail from the Post Office every night and she would meet Fred at the Post Office the following night. On Thursday they met and Grace said Violet was doing all right and she would be leaving Hayne's place the following night (Friday 14 October). She asked Fred to arrange a room for Violet, which he did, at Woods Hotel in Rattray Street.

On Friday night, Fred was in the vicinity of Hayne's place at about 7 pm to meet Violet as arranged. He waited until five minutes past 7 pm and when Violet did not come out, he impatiently went into Hayne's shop. Grace and Hayne were inside, and Fred said he was supposed to meet his sister in the vicinity of the shop at 7 pm. Hayne said, 'Yes, but you were not supposed to come in here.' Fred said, 'You have my sister here and I demand to see her.' Haynes went back through a door and returned with Violet. Violet shook hands with Hayne and left with Fred. Whether Violet had stayed at Hayne's between 7 and 14 October was disputed at the trial.

The following morning, Fred saw Violet at Woods Hotel and thought she looked unwell. He went with her to the station and saw her off on the train. She returned to her father's house briefly on Saturday 15 October, and then went to her married sister's place in Timaru. Two days later she was admitted to the Timaru Public Hospital. She told the hospital doctor she had recently aborted a fetus at about four months' gestation following a procedure several days before. Her condition did not improve, and on Thursday 20 October she was examined under anaesthetic and her uterus was emptied of the remnants of an incomplete abortion. Police arrested Hayne on 25 October. On 28 October, Violet gave evidence before a stipendiary magistrate; she was quite rational and described in detail her dealings with Hayne, who was present at the depositions. She died on 5 November.

The coroner, acting alone, found death 'due to pyaemia the result of an illegal operation performed on her at Dunedin for the purpose of procuring abortion by one James Reynolds Hayne.'

Trials of James Reynolds Hayne, 1923

Police charged Hayne with procuring an abortion on 7 October and with the manslaughter of Mrs Violet Atkins on 5 November. Mr Hanlon called no defence witnesses and exploited every weakness in the Crown's case. The first trial took place on 17 February 1923, in the Dunedin Supreme Court before Justice Adams. The jury was out from 3.45 pm until after 8 pm and was unable to agree. A retrial was ordered for 27 February, again before Justice Adams. The jury retired at 5.24 pm and returned at 9.35 pm, unable to agree; another retrial was ordered to take place at the May sittings. The third trial took place before Justice Chapman. The jury retired at 4.18 pm and returned at 8.44 pm, and the judge requested them to continue their deliberations. They did so, but were still unable to agree when they returned at 10 pm.

The case was referred to the Minister of Justice and the Solicitor-General. It was exceptional for four trials to be held, although not unknown in New Zealand legal history. In this instance, the recommendation was that the case should not proceed, and Hayne was discharged.

Miss A and the trials of James Reynolds Hayne and Miss Elizabeth Simpson Inglis, 1923[26]

Police accused Hayne and his assistant, Miss Inglis, that on or about 19 May 1923 they unlawfully used an instrument or other means to procure an abortion on 22-year-old Miss A (she was given name suppression). Mr Hanlon again defended both accused. The case was heard in the Magistrate's Court in July 1923 and in the Dunedin Supreme Court in August 1923, before Justice Sim.

When arrested, Hayne remarked, 'More trouble'. Police inspected his premises. He had a room marked 'workroom' immediately behind the shop, which contained a number of bottles typical of any chemist's dispensary, as well as a table, couch, gas griller and oven. In the corner near the window was a water closet. Off this room was the bathroom, and on shelves around the bath were a large number of empty medicine bottles. From the bathroom police confiscated exhibits used in the trials: a douche, two catheters and a bougie (a type of dilator). Immediately off the bathroom, a bedroom faced Moray Place, and contained two single iron beds. Off the dining room was another small room, curtained off, where there were another two single beds for Hayne and his female assistant. Pekinese dogs inhabited the dining room, and in the yard below, two cats roamed.

Miss A became pregnant to her lover, Charlie Stewart. Charlie had come to New Zealand from Scotland about two and a half years before, and worked as a tram conductor. They discussed what to do, and arrangements were made for Miss A to see Hayne. Miss A told her mother on 18 May that she was going on holiday for a few days. Charlie made the arrangements and found out Hayne would only perform the operation for £30 and would not accept less. Hayne said one case had cost him £1400 and another £1500.

The instructions Hayne gave to Charlie sounded something like the secret signs of a Druids' meeting. His girlfriend was to come alone and approach the door as the Town Hall clock struck eight. The door would be left slightly ajar. She was to ring the bell, enter and slam the door hard behind her. Hayne demonstrated how it was to be done.

On the night of her appointment, Miss A visited Hayne at his shop at 8 pm, as per instructions. He took her through the shop and into a long room, then through two doors to another room, which contained two beds, one for Miss Inglis and the other for Miss A. That night a vaginal douche was performed, and the following day Hayne, assisted by Miss Inglis, carried out an operation. When Miss A asked for pain relief later, she was told medication would hinder the process. When Charlie visited on Sunday night he was told the miscarriage had occurred, but he was not allowed to see Miss A until the following day.

Miss A remained at Hayne's premises for a few days and when she became ill, Dr De Lautour was called in. Hayne was reluctant to have her admitted to hospital from his premises and so Miss A was taken home in a taxi, accompanied by Miss Inglis, on 24 May. She was seriously ill and her parents called in Dr Fitzgerald, who insisted on her admission to Dunedin Hospital. Her mother accompanied her in the ambulance.

Miss A was dangerously ill with peritonitis and septicaemia, and initially the doctors feared for her life. She was examined under anaesthesia and found to have been delivered of a two-to-three-month-old fetus. There was a perforation on the right side of her uterus. She made a statement in hospital, and as a result Hayne and Miss Inglis were both arrested and charged on

25 May. Bail was allowed while they awaited trial. Miss A spent seven weeks in hospital, and suffered great pain, but fortunately she recovered.

In the Dunedin Supreme Court trial, the jury was out for only 25 minutes and returned a verdict of not guilty for Miss Inglis and guilty for Hayne, with a recommendation for mercy because of his age (he was 71 years old) and his health (he was crippled with rheumatism and suffered from a bad heart). Justice Sim said he always treated a jury's recommendation with respect, but in view of the police report and Hayne's previous offences, on this occasion it was his plain duty to impose a substantial term, and he sentenced Hayne to seven years' imprisonment, which he said would have been much longer but for the jury's recommendation. The maximum sentence was life imprisonment.

THE HEINOUSNESS OF HAYNE
DUNEDIN'S CELEBRATED CHEMIST CONVICTED

A Notorious Abortionist

SEVEN YEARS' HARD LABOR

JAMES REYNOLD HAYNE
(Who Goes Into Retirement for Seven Years.)

MISS INGLIS
(Hayne's Housekeeper and Attendant—Acquitted.)

NZ *Truth*, 18 August 1923

In addressing Hayne, His Honour said:[27]

> Hitherto juries have displayed a curious reluctance to convict in your case, however complete the evidence might have been. Happily that reluctance has been overcome, and at length twelve men have been found prepared to observe the oath taken and return a verdict according to the evidence. Dunedin has been redeemed from the reproach of being the city where a notorious abortionist was able to carry on with impunity and laugh at the law.

Hayne's career came to an end, and there was some protestation when he was released in June 1925 after serving only two years of his seven-year sentence.[28] He suffered ill health and was admitted to a nursing home in the North Island. A condition of his release was that he did not return to the South Island. He died in the nursing home in 1926, aged 74.

ଔ

One curious aftermath of Miss A's trial was the accusation that Miss A had been bribed not to testify against the accused.

Trial of Mrs Rosina Sarah McFie, 1923

Mrs McFie was a prominent Dunedinite, who at the end of World War I had been offered an OBE for her community service among soldiers and others (she declined to accept the award). The man in the street, or the women over the teacups, couldn't understand how such a woman would get involved in the Hayne affair, but she did. Police charged her with attempting to defeat the course of justice by bribing the principal witness, Miss A, not to give evidence.

On 11 June, when Miss A was in hospital, her brother visited her, and while he was with her Mrs McFie came in. She asked Miss A's brother to leave the room and then gave Miss A a bag of cakes and offered to give her money if

Mrs Rosina McFie.
(*NZ Truth*, 18 August 1923)

she would not testify against Miss Inglis, who had been arrested. Miss A had had an operation that day and was seriously ill. The visit upset her very much, and when Mrs McFie left, the senior nurse found Miss A sobbing and near hysterical.

The aggressive Police Superintendent Marsack prosecuted the case, Mr Hanlon defended, and Justice Sim presided. The jury was out for only 20 minutes before returning a verdict of not guilty.

☙

Obtaining a catheter from a chemist was not too difficult, and although in the following case the use of the catheter was unrelated to the cause of death, that did not stop a prosecution going ahead.

Ada's story[29]
Deceased 31 May 1929, age not recorded

Ada Heron, a young widow with children, of Temuka, died suddenly in 1929, and Martin Joseph Melville, 47, bachelor of Temuka, well known in the district as a former South Canterbury rugby representative, was committed to trial following her death. The two were neighbours for eight years, and for nearly two years Melville had eaten his meals at Ada's house. Earlier in the year, when faced with a pregnancy, Ada had asked Melville to obtain an instrument from the chemist in order to procure an abortion. When told by the chemist it was not customary to sell such articles without a doctor's order, Melville replied he wanted it for his father. Ada, when attending her doctor for another medical complaint, confided she had used the article (a catheter), and so when she died suddenly, police were informed.

Dr McInnes testified at the inquest. He had attended Ada for the past seven years. She consulted him six weeks before her death, complaining of chest pain, and he found her anaemic. When he was called to her home on 30 May, she was in bed and admitted using the catheter on the previous evening. The following day when he called, she was pale and shocked and not in a fit state to move to hospital. She died later that night.

Dr McInnes carried out a post-mortem and found no signs of pregnancy in the uterus, but an unsuspected ruptured ectopic pregnancy had haemorrhaged into the abdominal cavity. The coroner found that she 'died of internal bleeding caused by a ruptured ectopic pregnancy.'

Trial of Martin Joseph Melville, 1929

Within a week of Ada's death, Melville was charged with supplying an instrument for an unlawful purpose. He was defended by Mr Hanlon. At the first trial in the Timaru Supreme Court in July, the jury could not agree. At the retrial in November, after a short retirement, the jury returned a verdict of not guilty. Hanlon criticised the unfair methods used by the police in obtaining information from Melville.

ॐ

Hayne was the 'go-to' chemist in Dunedin; his counterpart in Auckland was Ralph Walter Frank Sanft. Ralph's Reliable Remedies were widely advertised and popular with women with menstrual irregularities. Sanft had a chemist shop in Upper Symonds Street in which he employed his younger brother, Alfred.

> RALPH'S Reliable Remedies (Ralph Sanft).—Prompt Mail Order Chemist.—Dept. H, 201 Symonds St., Auckland.

New Zealand Herald, 26 June 1935

Gladys's story[30]
Deceased 29 December 1932, aged 23 years

Miss Gladys Williams lived with her parents in Auckland. For the past five years she had been keeping company with Edward Longville, 25, and they were engaged to be married. In November, Gladys told Edward she thought she was pregnant, and early in December they both went to Sanft's shop. Gladys told her mother she was about two months pregnant and was taking pills.

Sanft, 37, sold the couple a black rubber enema, a bottle of Dushol and a box of Periodic Pills to ease menstrual pains, and Flopil to strengthen the muscles of the womb. He gave instructions to take two pills night and morning with water, and to syringe night and morning with a teaspoon of Dushol in a pint of warm water. He charged £1.19s.6d. On Christmas Eve, the couple returned and told him nothing had happened after taking two boxes of pills. He gave them two boxes of Dr Davis's Mega Pills, sold as a tonic for women's 'nerve troubles', which cost £2.2s.

At Christmas time, Edward stayed at the Williamses' home. On 27 December, about 8.30 am, he heard a fall and then heard Gladys groaning. He tried to open the bathroom door but could not. He called out to Gladys's mother and she got up. Edward clambered to the side window and got into the bathroom, where he found Gladys lying against the bathroom door, unconscious. Beside her was a syringe and bowl. They carried her to bed and called for Dr Kenrick. When he arrived, Gladys was having convulsions at short intervals, for which Dr Kenrick administered an injection of morphia. Later that morning she was still having convulsions and was admitted to hospital. Two days later she died.

The post-mortem found multiple bruises on her body from the fall and from being restrained during convulsions. Her uterus was enlarged, consistent with a pregnancy of three months' gestation. The placenta was lying in the vagina. Her brain was congested and oedematous. There were toxic changes in other organs and in the opinion of the pathologist, death was due to acute septicaemia. The coroner, acting alone, found in accordance with the medical evidence. No charges were laid.

ଔ

Sanft supplied the equipment in another case with a fatal outcome.

Eunice's story[31]
Deceased 1 May 1935, aged 22 years

Eunice Francis had been happily married to Bonython (Bon), 23, for three years. Since the marriage, Bon had not been in permanent employment, and the most he had earned was £2 10s a week on relief work at Kawakawa Bay Camp, near Auckland. They had three young children, the youngest ten and a half months old. Eunice had been in indifferent health, mainly through bad teeth, which were extracted a few days before her death.

On 1 May she carried out the usual duties of a young mother. That evening she had a bath and retired to the bedroom just before 11 pm, while Bon carried on reading his book. At about 11.15 pm, Eunice called out, saying she had hurt herself, and this was followed by a bump, as if she had fallen on the bed. When Bon entered the room, she was lying on the bed, distressed and gasping for breath. He tried to give her a little gin but that did not help. He bathed her forehead with cold towels, then at

11.50 pm went to phone for a doctor, the nearest telephone being at a neighbour's place about half a mile away.

When he returned with the neighbour, Eunice was lifeless. The doctor arrived soon after and confirmed her death. By Eunice's side were a syringe and catheter and a cup of kerosene, which were exhibited at the inquest. Eunice had been misinformed by two girlfriends about what to do to disrupt her pregnancy. At the post-mortem, a 14-week-old fetus was present in the uterus, with membranes unruptured. There was bloodstained fluid in the cavity of the uterus, smelling of kerosene, and the membranes had been lifted from the wall of the uterus posteriorly, leaving a raw area. The pathologist determined death was due to shock, following an injury to the interior of the uterus and the injection of kerosene into the uterine cavity.

The police arrested Eunice's husband and he pleaded guilty to supplying an instrument with unlawful intent to procure a miscarriage. He said he bought the syringe from Sanft at the request of his wife, even though he didn't approve of how she intended to use it. In the Auckland Supreme Court, Mr Spence defended Bon, saying he had already been heavily punished by the loss his young wife, to whom he was devoted, and the anguish of raising his little children, now motherless. The couple was in a desperate financial situation due to the economic depression and could not face the prospect of another mouth to feed. In sentencing him, Justice Fair said this was not the usual sort of abortion case, and admitted him to probation for two years.

Ralph Sanft was not charged over the death of Eunice, but the following year his younger brother Alfred, employed as an assistant, had to defend his actions in court.

Trial of Alfred Sanft, 1936[32]

Police charged Alfred in 1936 with supplying the means to procure an abortion. In the Magistrate's Court he pleaded not guilty to two charges and was defended by Mr Singer. He was committed for trial in the Auckland Supreme Court, presided over by Justice Fair. Melva Lilly, 20, told the court she was single and lived in Whangarei. She said she had come to Auckland at the end of August 1935, when she was pregnant, and had purchased drugs from Albert at Sanft's chemist shop in order induce a miscarriage. The defence successfully cast doubts on the young woman's evidence, and Mr Singer said, 'Every chemist in New

Zealand supplies such drugs and if this young man, who is merely an assistant, is found guilty, then every chemist in the Dominion will be liable to be brought before the court and sentenced to a long term of imprisonment.' The jury agreed and returned a verdict of not guilty in barely six minutes.

Trial of Ralph Sanft, 1954[33]

Ironically, nearly 20 years later, in December 1954, Ralph Sanft was committed for trial in the Auckland Supreme Court for false pretences, claiming his 'famous pills' were capable of procuring abortion. He also provided an extensive mail order service covering the whole of New Zealand and beyond, even reaching Tonga. He charged £5 for a bottle of his pills. Several women provided evidence at his trial. He was fined £400.

ଔ

Chemists knew that supplying drugs for the purpose of procuring a miscarriage was illegal, but those purchasing the medications did not usually complain. An aggrieved lover brought the following case.

Trial of Kenneth Patrick Blair, 1937[34]

Blair, a well-known Hamilton chemist, was charged with supplying drugs for unlawful use. In her evidence, Mrs Eileen Jerrard said Blair had supplied her with pills for her step-sister, Ellen Champness, 18, who was about eight weeks pregnant. The young woman assistant told Mrs Jerrard that she was not allowed to sell such preparations and that Mrs Jerrard would have to return and see Mr Blair, which she did, accompanied by Ellen. Ellen's mother, Mrs Ivy Champness, also knew of the pregnancy and the purchase.

However, Ellen's young man Billie Sigley, 22, panel beater, who had been courting her for about 18 months, wished to marry her despite her parents' objections. Billie and Ellen attempted to elope, but they were stopped at the railway station. Billie said he did not want Ellen to take the pills and went to the police.

In the Magistrate's Court, Blair said he only sold the preparation for lawful use and did not know of the pregnancy when the sale was made; however, the magistrate thought the case should be heard by a jury, and accordingly he committed Blair for trial in the Hamilton Supreme Court. In August the case was heard before Justice Callan. The foreman of the jury expressed the view that it was unnecessary to unduly stress the young woman, but His Honour replied that the jury must hear all the evidence. After hearing the evidence, the jury retired for 15 minutes and returned with a verdict of not guilty.

This happened soon after the Committee of Inquiry into Abortion and was the sort of case that frustrated Dr Doris Gordon, who berated the lenience of juries. While maintaining the professional standards expected by the community and the authorities, chemists walked a fine line between helping women and providing a legitimate service.

8. NURSES

Between 1900 and 1939 the nursing profession in New Zealand was well served by four senior nurse administrators – Grace Neill, Hester Maclean, Jessie Bicknell and Mary Lambie.

Mrs Grace Neill (1846–1926)[1] was born in Scotland and trained as a nurse and midwife in England. In New Zealand, she was responsible for the establishment of compulsory registration of nurses to protect the public and the profession from malpractice by unqualified persons. The Nurses' Registration Act 1901 was the first in the world that provided for training, examinations and a register of nurses. She did the same for midwives in the Midwives' Registration Act 1904. She inspected St Helens Hospitals.

Miss Hester Maclean (1859–1932),[2] an Australian-trained nurse and midwife, was Assistant Inspector of Hospitals from 1906 until she retired in 1923. Following the Health Act 1920, she was Director of Nursing in the new Department of Health. She was the first president of the New Zealand Trained Nurses Association and established and edited the nursing journal *Kai Tiaki* ('Guardian') for many years. During the war, she was in charge of the New Zealand Army Nursing Service, and immediately after the war, she was acting chief health officer during the influenza epidemic of 1918.

Miss Jessie Bicknell (1871–1956)[3] was the first nurse born and trained in New Zealand to be appointed Director of Nursing in the Department of Health, in 1923. She was committed to improving the standard of nurse training. In 1923 a deputation of nurses lobbied the New Zealand Branch of the British Medical Association to reduce doctors' reliance on untrained nurses and single-bed unregistered nursing homes.⁴ Nurse Bicknell supported the Nurses and Midwives Registration Act 1925, which, as well as providing for the registration of nurses and midwives on the same basis, established two classes of maternity training: one for midwives, who were sole practitioners, and one for maternity nurses, who assisted doctors. Untrained midwives who had been allowed to continue their practice based on experience were now barred from practising. In the mid-1930s she suggested that nurses and the National Council of Women (NCW) should work together to address the high incidence of septic abortion in New Zealand.

Miss Mary Lambie (1889–1971),⁵ another New Zealand-born nurse, succeeded Jessie Bicknell as Director of Nursing. She also trained as a Plunket nurse, spent a year studying Public Health at the University of Toronto, and trained as a midwife at St Helens Hospital in Wellington. She organised an emergency hospital in Napier after the disastrous 1931 earthquake. She had to cope with funding cuts during the Depression years, and made preventive medicine a priority.

ଔ

Nurses were respected in the community and were often sought after for advice. It was not surprising that a number of nurses became involved in abortion care. And not all nurses lived up to the high standards set by Neill, Maclean, Bicknell and Lambie. One notorious example was Mrs Martha O'Shaughnessy, whose family and associates reigned as a dynasty in the abortion business over three decades.

Mrs Martha Jane Maxwell (aka Mrs Martha O'Shaughnessy; aka Mrs Jean Imrie)

Here is a summary of the complicated abortion career of the most infamous Auckland abortionist of her time, who ran a nursing establishment from her private home. Her second husband, John Maxwell, was an alcoholic and prohibited from drinking, but Martha kept him well supplied with drink; he died in November 1909, at the age of 36. She then married her third husband, Mr James Edward O'Shaughnessy, who was 16 years her junior. The O'Shaughnessys had a confectionery and green grocery shop, a short distance from the back of their house.

ABORTION IN AUCKLAND.
AWFUL ACTS ALLEGED.
WHOLESALE SLAUGHTER CHARGES.
Kingsland Nursing Home Implicated.
GIRLS REFUSE TO GIVE EVIDENCE.
Detectives Denounced—Sensational Developments.

NZ *Truth*, 15 January 1910

Police first charged Martha Maxwell with procuring abortion in 1910, but after two trials she was acquitted. 'Ma' O'Shaughnessy, as she became known, discreetly distributed visiting cards to local chemists. Her standard technique was to insert a rubber catheter, to be left in place for 24 hours. In 1911, after the death of Elsie Holland, she was found guilty and sentenced to seven years in prison. Upon release, unrepentant, she continued her practice. In 1922, both she and her daughter-in-law, Kathleen Imrie, faced criminal charges after the death of Elsie Fraider. When her daughter-in-law died, the police withdrew the charges against Mrs O'Shaughnessy. In 1926, after more criminal charges, she received a sentence of ten years in prison. She died in 1942 at the age of 78.

The O'Shaughnessy home in Kingsland, Auckland. (*NZ Truth*, 12 August 1911)

Auckland Chief Detective Richard Marsack aggressively pursued suspected abortionists and kept them under police surveillance. Mrs Maxwell had long been in his sights. Largely through following up cases admitted to hospital, the Chief Detective compiled a list of women suspected of being her clients between 1 June and 17 November 1909. One of these young women was Mrs Mary Hassall, aged about 26.

Trial of Mary Hassall, 1910[6]

Mrs Hassall, mother of four, was seen by Dr Carolan after suffering a suspected epileptic fit. The doctor found a catheter inserted 24 hours previously and reported this to the police. Chief Detective Marsack wanted Mrs Hassall to testify against Mrs Maxwell. When she refused, he promised immunity if she testified and warned her that if she didn't testify she would be liable to prosecution.

As well as being Mrs Maxwell's client, Mrs Hassall was also her friend and accomplice, and refused to incriminate her. She told the Chief Detective she had performed the abortion upon herself, whereupon he charged her with the crime of self-abortion. After depositions in the Magistrate's Court, she was committed for trial in the Auckland Supreme Court, presided over by Justice Edwards. She pleaded not guilty and unsurprisingly, after a retirement of ten minutes, the jury returned a verdict of not guilty.

Trial of Mrs Martha Jane Maxwell, 1910[7]

Mrs Maxwell, widow, was charged with abortion offences in the Auckland Magistrate's Court. Police alleged five women each paid £5 for her services and two of them ended up seriously ill in hospital. Chief Detective Marsack clashed on several occasions with the Magistrate, Mr Haselden, and the defence lawyer, Mr Singer, a robust defender who relished abortion cases. The Magistrate's Court trial was described as extremely trying, with scenes of bedlam when the women refused to answer questions. At one stage, two of the police witnesses, both women, had a hair-pulling match in the court room during a luncheon adjournment. In the end, only one case, concerning Miss Mary Ellen Taylor, was sent for trial in the Supreme Court.

Mary, 26, an attractive machinist, lived with her parents in Auckland. She was loyal to her lover even though he abandoned her; she steadfastly refused to name him and described him as a 'decent fellow' of whom she was very fond. She dated her pregnancy from the night of 26 July 1909, her first and only act of intimacy with him or anyone else. (This evidence was unchivalrously queried by the magistrate.) Six weeks later, when she missed her period, he provided her with a bottle of medicine, but she took only three doses. After suggesting she resort to an operation, he forsook her and left the colony in October, seeking work elsewhere. He said he would write but never did.

Mary visited Mrs Maxwell at her residence on the evening of Friday 5 November. Mrs Maxwell told her to come back on Saturday, as she was superstitious of Friday. They did not discuss money. She returned on Saturday and was only on the bed for a few minutes before going home. On Wednesday 10 November, she became ill and her mother called in Dr Keith. At first Mary lied to Dr Keith, saying she had used an instrument on herself, as she did not want to incriminate Mrs Maxwell. On 18 November, with another doctor, Dr Keith operated on her at her home and removed a catheter (later produced as evidence). Mary was then admitted to Nurse Jones's private hospital, where doctors operated again. She developed a near fatal peritonitis and septicaemia, and remained in bed for five weeks. On 19 November, two detectives interrogated her for one and a half hours when she lay seriously ill, and this intrusion was severely criticised by Justice Edwards in the subsequent Supreme Court trial.

At the Magistrate's Court trial in January 1910, the magistrate asked Mary to remove the dark blue veil which covered her face, and she was then interrogated for over two hours. She caused a sensation when she stated that she had told the detectives she would only tell them the truth if they promised not to prosecute Mrs Maxwell. She said the detectives agreed that Mrs Maxwell would only receive a warning. They did not warn her she might also be prosecuted, and she felt tricked into giving evidence. Their actions were denounced by the defence and also later by Justice Edwards.

Mrs Maxwell pleaded not guilty and was committed for trial in the Auckland Supreme Court. At the first trial the jury was unable to agree, and a new trial was ordered for the following day. This time she was acquitted. She went on practising as an abortionist but remained under surveillance by the police. In July 1911, as Mrs O'Shaughnessy, she was again prosecuted, after the death of Elsie Holland.

Elsie's story[8]
Deceased 13 or 14 June (around midnight) 1911, aged 24 years

Miss Elsie Holland, young and attractive, worked as a lady-help providing domestic services in private homes in the Auckland area. At the time of her death she was between jobs. For the benefit of her family she fabricated a story about going away for a short time but told her friend James Warner, clerk, 35, she had made arrangements with Mrs O'Shaughnessy for 'treatment'. Elsie and James had been lovers for about 18 months and he went with her on the fateful night, leaving her just before they reached Mrs O'Shaughnessy's at about 8 pm.

Elsie was found dead on a blood-saturated sheet in a bed in the house on 14 June. A faint blue dye stained her mouth. No doctor attended her before her death and the doctor who saw her after her death, Dr Brockway, was unable to provide a death certificate. Police were notified, and the detective who attended was suspicious about tablets and a phial of dark liquid by the bedside that made it look as though Elsie had taken poison. Mrs O'Shaughnessy, her husband, her daughter Mrs Jane Hartley, and three other occupants did not provide reliable evidence and refused to answer questions at the inquest for fear of incrimination. The conduct of the witnesses and the robust defence of Mr Singer, the lawyer engaged by the family, frustrated the coroner.

The post-mortem showed Elsie died of acute septicaemia following an instrumental abortion – an unusual feature was the speed with which the infection occurred, within 28 hours of the alleged interference. She had not ingested any poison. The coroner and six male jurors could only conclude Elsie had died 'following an illegal operation performed by some unknown person.'

The jury added a rider to their verdict noting that the corrosive sublimate (perchloride of mercury) was placed in the mouth of the deceased in order to mislead and so defeat the ends of justice. (Mercuric chloride is a poisonous white soluble crystalline salt of mercury with many uses. It was formerly used in insecticides, batteries and metallurgy, and as an antiseptic, disinfectant, preservative and photographic fixative. It is a toxic form of mercury and is water soluble. The blue dye was added to the poison for reasons of safety.)

Trials of Mrs Martha Jane O'Shaughnessy and accomplices, 1911

The subsequent trials of those prosecuted kept the public intrigued from July to December. Crowds turned up to the hearings. Detailed sordid evidence sold newspapers. Large headlines proclaimed:

> Strange and Sensational Death of Elsie Holland.
> The Mystery of The Kingsland Home.
> Four Arrests Made, Another Pending.
> Mrs O'Shaughnessy Charged with Murder.
> Martha O'Shaughnessy Found Guilty, Seven Years Hard Labour.
> The Elsie Holland Mystery Solved.
> Mrs Hassall and Mrs Campbell Imprisoned.

It was described as the biggest case in Auckland's history. After depositions in the Magistrate's Court, three lengthy trials took place in the Auckland Supreme Court, all presided over by Justice Chapman. On the first two, the jury disagreed. The third trial lasted three days, commencing on 30 November 1911. The jury on this occasion took four hours to reach their guilty verdict.

Mrs O'Shaughnessy denied that her house was used for abortions, but Mrs Minnie Whittington testified that she had used Mrs O'Shaughnessy's services on two occasions. Two letters were also produced from persons seeking her services. Dubious evidence was provided by several other occupants of the house. For aiding and abetting the crime, the police charged two married women with children, Mrs Mary Hassall and Mrs Charlotte (Lottie) Campbell, who were present in the house on the night in question. Both women were fond of a drink and talked too much to their friend Mrs Elizabeth Sindlen, a brothel owner who made some extravagant disclosures. Mrs Hassall, previously charged in connection with the 1910 case,

Mrs Elizabeth Sindlen.
(*NZ Truth*, 19 August 1911)

The Kingsland Case, Auckland Magistrate's Court. (*Observer*, 12 August 1911)

was the person who probably put the poison in Elsie's mouth. Mr Albert (Bert) Herbert Williams, assistant barman, was a lodger who told lies to protect Mrs O'Shaughnessy. He was imprisoned after the second trial, when he was found trying to leave the country.

Mr O'Shaughnessy, Mrs Hassall and Mrs Campbell were all charged as accomplices. At the third trial, Mrs O'Shaughnessy was found guilty of manslaughter, with a recommendation for mercy. His Honour sentenced her to seven years' imprisonment with hard labour. Mrs Hassall and Mrs Campbell were also found guilty and sentenced to 12 months' imprisonment. Mr O'Shaughnessy was found not guilty.

On 3 May 1912, the Court of Appeal looked at the admissibility of certain pieces of evidence; that of Mrs Whittington and two letters found in Mrs O'Shaughnessy's house. The Court of Appeal confirmed this evidence was admissible and upheld all three convictions. The Chief Justice, Sir Robert Stout, said the case was clear beyond question and the only surprise was that there should have been one or two jurymen who had not the intelligence in the former trials to understand the evidence. The headline in the *Evening Post* provocatively announced: 'Convictions Affirmed. Chief Justice on Unintelligent Jurymen'.

Another Elsie died under the care of Mrs O'Shaughnessy's daughter-in-law, Mrs Imrie.

Elsie's story[9]
Deceased 16 August 1922, aged 24 years

Mrs Elsie Fraider lived in Whangarei with her husband Lornel, a driver for the Farmers' Union Company, and their four children, the eldest six years of age. She arrived unexpectedly at her parents' home in Mangere, Auckland, on Sunday 13 August, travelling on a coastal ship. She hadn't visited them for nearly two years; she said her husband thought she needed a holiday, and she had come down for a rest after having had influenza. Her sister had agreed to look after the children while she was away.

She told her mother she was going into town to see some people from Waihi and the next morning caught a train to Otahuhu. She planned to stay at Wellesley House that night and come back to her parents on Tuesday, then return to Whangarei on Wednesday. While she was in her parents' house, Elsie's handbag accidentally fell open, and when her mother commented on the amount of

Mrs Mary Hassall (top left) and Mrs Charlotte (Lottie) Campbell (top right) were both accomplices to Mrs O'Shaughnessy (*NZ Truth*, 8 July 1911). They were found guilty and sentenced by Justice Chapman to one year's imprisonment. Mrs O'Shaughnessy's third husband, Mr James Edward O'Shaughnessy (bottom left), was found not guilty of the charges laid against him (*NZ Truth*, 8 July 1911). Mrs O'Shaughnessy's daughter, Mrs Jane Hartley (bottom right), refused to cooperate with the police but was not charged (*NZ Truth*, 22 July 1911).

money it contained, about £20, Elsie was reticent about the need for cash. Her mother said later she had her suspicions that Elsie was pregnant, but did not mention it at the time.

Elsie did not return on Tuesday or Wednesday. On Wednesday evening her father received a telegram from Elsie's husband in Whangarei, asking him to go to the home of Mr David Imrie, 75 The Drive, Epsom. When he went there on Thursday morning he was greeted with the shocking news of Elsie's death. Two women in the house spoke to him and said 'You don't want a scandal, do you?'

Elsie, it transpired at the inquest, had attended the house to have an abortion. David Imrie, carrier, and owner of the house, lived there with his wife Kathleen (Kitty), their baby and his mother, the well-known abortionist Mrs O'Shaughnessy. She had been living with the Imries for some years following her release from prison and now preferred to be known as 'Mrs Jean Imrie'. Mr Singer represented the Imries and Mrs O'Shaughnessy at the inquest, and all of them refused to answer questions.

Dr Abbott of Epsom said Kitty Imrie had asked him to come to the house on Wednesday morning, 16 August, to see a friend who was ill. She said the woman was throwing herself about in a funny way. He found Elsie, who was of small build, on the bed, obviously very ill, pale and semi-conscious. Mrs Imrie said she had kept vigil all night. At 3 am something had come away and she had thrown it away.

Elsie had answered a few words to the doctor which provided no enlightenment. He found her bleeding from the uterus and advised her transfer to the public hospital. He drove to the chemist close by and phoned for an ambulance. He then attempted to stem the bleeding, but by the time he had finished, Elsie was dead. Dr Abbott said he could not provide a death certificate and believed if he had been called sooner he may have been able to save her life.

At the post-mortem Elsie was found to be exsanguinated. Her uterus was enlarged, reaching nearly to her umbilicus. Placental tissue had adhered to the wall of the uterus and she had haemorrhaged from the placental site. There were no signs of injury and no evidence to show what had caused the miscarriage.

The police made enquiries at the four-bedroom house where Elsie had died. Mrs Imrie said Elsie was an acquaintance, but her mother-in-law interrupted: 'Say nothing Kitty till we see a solicitor'. Police found bloodstained clothing and sheets. Letters headed 'Dear Nurse' were also found. Elsie's handbag contained a one-pound note, a ten-shilling note and the return half of a steamer ticket between Whangarei and Auckland.

The coroner, acting alone, found the cause of death was 'haemorrhage from the uterus following a miscarriage.' He added a rider that 'if medical aid had been obtained earlier the deceased's life could have been saved. No evidence was provided to show how the deceased came to be in the house in which she died or what occurred to her therein, the occupants of the house refusing to give evidence thereon.' The adjourned inquest was concluded on 4 September 1922.

On 7 September, in the Magistrate's Court, the police charged Mrs O'Shaughnessy, 58, and her daughter-in-law Mrs Kathleen Imrie, 29, with the death of Elsie May Fraider, by omission to perform or observe a legal duty. The accused, defended by Mr Singer, were remanded on bail. The case was set for 29 September but it was adjourned, as Mrs Imrie was dangerously ill in Auckland Public Hospital. Unfortunately, she died that day and the case collapsed. Mr Singer argued there had been no neglect and the magistrate agreed that the charge against Mrs O'Shaughnessy should be withdrawn.

Mrs O'Shaughnessy was again before the court in January 1925, November 1925 and February 1926.

Trials of Mrs Martha Jane O'Shaughnessy, 1925–1926[10]

The police charged Mrs O'Shaughnessy with the unlawful use of an instrument on a girl of 19 years on 14 December 1924, and in the Auckland Magistrate's Court on 22 January 1925 she pleaded not guilty to the charge. The young woman said she paid two visits to Mrs O'Shaughnessy in the company of her boyfriend and a girlfriend. After the operation, she stayed for three days with a Mrs Green, then returned home and became ill. When Dr Parkes visited, he immediately admitted her to hospital, where she remained for 11 days.

Mrs O'Shaughnessy, neatly dressed in a blue serge costume, appeared in the Supreme Court, presided over by Justice Reed, on 16 February 1925. She walked with a slight limp because of a leg wound that needed dressing several times daily. Mr Singer defended her. His Honour warned the jury about convicting on uncorroborated evidence, and after a retirement of three quarters of an hour the jury returned a verdict of not guilty.

Mrs Martha O'Shaughnessy. (*NZ Truth*, 12 August 1911)

Mrs O'Shaughnessy appeared in the Magistrate's Court again on 19 November 1925, charged with having unlawfully used an instrument on a female and having unlawfully supplied an instrument to another female. Mr Singer again defended her and obtained bail.

A married woman, Mrs A, 22, said she went to Mrs O'Shaughnessy's house at 75 The Drive, Epsom, on 20 October, accompanied by her sister-in-law, a girl aged 16, who used the name 'Miss Brown'. Mrs O'Shaughnessy told her the price of the operation, performed in the bedroom, would be £1. She was asked to purchase a catheter and return. When 'Miss Brown' returned with her boyfriend, a married man, to have the operation, the police were there conducting a raid.

Another married woman suffered complications in Auckland Hospital, but she was recovering at the time of the court hearing. When police visited the Imrie house to gather evidence for her case, they discovered another woman, Dorothy O'Brien, in bed. Mrs O'Shaughnessy said this woman was her niece. The following day, when police called, she had gone.

When these cases were heard in the Magistrate's Court, Mrs O'Shaughnessy was denied bail, the magistrate saying he could not take the risk, as there might be a death and he would feel responsible. Mr Singer said Mrs O'Shaughnessy's leg required hospital treatment, but the magistrate declared the prison could provide medical attention. One of the detectives snidely remarked that alcohol did not improve the condition of her leg.

Mrs O'Shaughnessy was committed to appear in the Supreme Court in January on three charges, but by the time the hearing came in February 1926 a fourth charge was added to her list of crimes.

The Supreme Court trial on 6 February before Justice Stringer dealt with only two of the charges, but the Crown said evidence could be produced by four other women in similar circumstances. The first case, Mrs Doris Hanlon, wished to have an abortion as she and her husband had planned a trip to Melbourne in connection with his business and they could not afford another child. Mrs O'Shaughnessy told her to come back at a certain date and to bring with her a catheter and the fee of £2. When she went to the house, her husband waited outside. Two detectives, also waiting outside, intercepted her when she emerged and took her to the police station, then to the hospital, where doctors found evidence of the illegal operation. This abortion happened while Mrs O'Shaughnessy was out on bail. The second case, 'Miss Brown', 16, had become pregnant to a married man, Mr Richard Hammond. He accompanied her when she went on the second occasion to see Mrs O'Shaughnessy. He also purchased the necessary catheter and paid a fee of £5. 'Miss Brown' said she stayed at Mrs O'Shaughnessy's from Saturday to Tuesday, when the abortion was finally accomplished. While she was staying there, Mrs O'Shaughnessy told her there were two other women waiting to receive attention.

The Crown called six other women as witnesses to prove Mrs O'Shaughnessy was operating a system. The sixth fainted in court and her evidence was dispensed with. The jury retired at 3.50 pm and returned at 5.20 pm with a verdict of guilty, and a strong recommendation of mercy on account of the prisoner's age (61) and poor health.

'Prisoner,' said Justice Stringer,[11]

> anxious as I am to give the fullest effect to the recommendation of the jury, I must say that having regard to your past history I cannot do very much in the way of mitigating the sentence I am compelled to pass. You have already been convicted of a similar offence several years ago, when you were sentenced to seven years' imprisonment. You have been tried several times, but you have not taken warning. While you were on remand upon the first two of these charges, while the sword of justice was hanging over your head, you go back to your home and commit several more offences, the audacity of which is to say the least, remarkable. In my opinion you are a menace to society and it is my duty to put you beyond the power of doing further harm. To my knowledge two young women who were foolish enough to place themselves in your bungling hands have met their deaths through it. We do not know how many others have done likewise. I should not be doing my duty to the public if I did not pass a very severe sentence. Not-withstanding your age I can do no less than sentence you to ten years' imprisonment.

This was the longest sentence for any abortionist in New Zealand in the 20th century.

Justice Stringer suggested a stay of proceedings be applied for, as hearing the other cases would make no difference to her punishment. The Crown solicitor said he would apply to the Attorney-General for a stay of proceedings. Mrs O'Shaughnessy, who had been weeping quietly as she stood in the dock, was helped out of the court by a wardress. So ended her career.

The following week Mr Richard Hammond, a young married man of good character, was sentenced by Justice Stringer to 12 months' reformative treatment when he pleaded guilty to the unlawful use of an instrument in connection with 'Miss Brown', one of the principal witnesses for the prosecution.

ଓ୨

In the following stories, nurses feature prominently as abortionists. Mrs Mary Henderson, Mrs Susan Wilson, Mrs Hannah Dalton and Mrs Maud Herbert received harsh sentences of seven years' imprisonment. Mrs Sarah Skellon and Mrs Reubena

Shirley received terms of two years and 18 months, respectively. Mrs Edith Gerraty was lucky to escape a conviction in 1920 and 1932, and must have been providing abortion services throughout that time. Mrs Georgina Colnett was luckier still and was never charged, even after the death of a client in 1928. Mrs Marjorie Pickering narrowly escaped conviction in 1938.

The first story is from the turn of the century.

Winnie's story[12]
Deceased 6 September 1900, aged 17 years

Mary Alice Winifred Luke, known as Winnie, lived with her parents in Wellington. Her unwanted pregnancy was diagnosed by Dr Anson on 27 August and she confided in her mother, who was absolutely distraught. That evening her mother went to see the herbalist and midwife, Mrs Henderson, who had a shop and adjoining rooms in Vivian Street. Mrs Luke had not seen her before, but she had been recommended as someone who was sympathetic to girls in trouble. Mrs Luke told her of Winnie's predicament and Mrs Henderson said she would need to see her. Her fee was £7 but Mrs Luke said she could afford only £5 and this was the amount paid.

The following day, Tuesday 28 August, mother and daughter came to Mrs Henderson's rooms. Winnie's mother was anxious, but Mrs Henderson said she had 'treated a minister's daughter and a doctor's daughter and had never lost a case.' She did not say what she had done to Winnie but advised she must go home to bed, take some gin and stay in bed until 11 am the next day.

That night, at about 1 am, Winnie became ill, so in the morning her mother visited Mrs Henderson. She advised oil and a poultice and visited Winnie later in the day. She continued to attend her over the next few days. On Wednesday evening Winnie passed the fetus, which was burnt. Only part of the placenta came away, so Mrs Henderson returned the next day with instruments, and again the following day with a large tin and a syringe. She repeated that there was no danger, but Winnie's parents were not reassured and on Friday 31 August her father called in Dr Scott.

Dr Scott saw Winnie together with her mother and Mrs Henderson, who was introduced as the midwife who had assisted at Winnie's recent miscarriage. Dr Scott was suspicious and asked if Winnie had been tampered with. He diagnosed acute septic peritonitis and was extremely concerned at her condition.

He ordered a nurse be sent to care for her. He saw Winnie on several occasions but she remained very ill. He consulted with Dr Ewart at Wellington Hospital and they decided to perform a curettage to remove any remains of the placenta. This they did in her home, with Dr Scott performing the curettage and Dr Ewart administering the anaesthetic. The material they obtained was highly infected. Dr Ewart said in his position over the last 12 years at Wellington Hospital he had seen half a dozen deaths from abortion. He said after curetting most women got better. Winnie did not.

On Sunday 2 September, Winnie made her dying depositions to the Stipendiary Magistrate, giving details of the abortion carried out by Mrs Henderson. The police immediately visited Mrs Henderson's rooms and found two other young women on the premises, having just had abortions. The young women were taken to hospital and remained there for some weeks.

Police arrested Mrs Henderson and removed some of her bloodied instruments as evidence of her activities. The following articles were among those exhibited at her trial: can and tubing, two glass syringes, a rubber syringe, a pair of large curling tongs (used as forceps to remove material from the womb), scissors, a vaginal speculum (for finding the cervix), and a tin containing tents (laminaria or sea-tangles).

Winnie died at her parent's home at 3 am on Thursday 6 September. A post-mortem found the womb enlarged to about four months' gestation with a large ragged tear, three fingers wide, in the upper part, consistent with force having being applied through the use of an instrument. The uterus and abdominal cavity contained pus. Infective organisms were found on the instruments used by Mrs Henderson.

At the inquest, held on 6–7 September before the coroner and six male jurors, Mrs Henderson denied everything and said girls were often getting stuff from the chemist and coming to her for relief. The coroner was scathing in his condemnation of Winnie's mother. He said he considered the evidence he had just listened to was simply amazing in its utter ignorance of the law, morality and all the attributes of motherhood. He concluded by pointing to the evidence Mrs Luke had just given and saying, 'Sign it, madam and go home and pray to your God to forgive you.' The editor of the *Free Lance* accused the coroner of abusing his office for making these remarks:[13]

It would be difficult to imagine anything more unwarrantable or unfair than the behaviour of the Coroner towards the witness, Mrs Luke, at the conclusion of the inquest on the woman's deceased daughter, the other day. The position in which Mrs Luke stood was a most painful and trying one. She had come forward and told frankly, and without reservation, the story of how, after the discovery of her daughter's shame, she had taken the girl to the female herbalist and arranged for the operation that subsequently proved fatal.

That the woman was suffering from extreme agony of mind and poignant distress was apparent to everyone in the court. Therefore, in view of her unhappy situation, common humanity should have prompted the Coroner to treat her with delicacy, and avoid as far as possible from harrowing her feelings further. But Mr Ashcroft is nothing if not dramatic and here was an opportunity for theatrical effect that could not be lightly sacrificed. Pointing to the evidence that had just been given, he said, 'Sign it, madam, and go home and pray to your God to forgive you.'

Such a sentiment as this, uttered under such circumstance, was absolutely indecent, as well as cruel. This was a preliminary and formal enquiry, and, if Mrs Luke had done wrong, the Coroner knew perfectly well that she would have to stand her trial before the proper tribunal for her behaviour. How wrong, therefore, apart from the unnecessary violence done to her feelings, that he should inflame public prejudice against her by his snuffling self-righteous sentiments. It was not the duty of Mr Ashcroft to judge this woman. How much less was it his duty to humiliate and wound her, before an assemblage of unsympathetic men, in the hour of her supreme trial. The thing was heartless.

We are not surprised that the unfortunate episode has aroused a perfect tornado of indignation in Wellington. The woman was so utterly helpless, she stood in such a pitiable position, and the Pecksniffian thrust from the Coroner was so utterly wanton and superfluous. Moreover, at that stage of a preliminary enquiry of a serious character, it was utterly unjustifiable, and calculated to prejudice the public mind against the woman. We don't know whether Mr Ashcroft ever prays to his God, but, if he does, it is to be hoped that next time he goes on his knees he will ask to be endowed with some of the virtue of Christian charity.

But the coroner had his supporters. The jury found Winnie had died 'on the sixth day of September at her father's residence, Wellington from peritonitis the result of a puncture of the womb caused by an illegal operation by Mrs Mary Henderson', and added a rider censuring Mrs Luke for her part in the matter.

Trial of Mrs Mary Henderson, 1900

On Monday 17 September, police charged Mrs Henderson in the Magistrate's Court with procuring an abortion and murder. She was a registered midwife, separated from her husband and left to her own resources. She had a heart complaint. Her children were sent to her brother in Sydney, who was not in the best position to help them.

Court officers took depositions from the two young women admitted to hospital, and they were granted immunity from prosecution. Maude, single, 23, stayed at Mrs Henderson's place for a week, during which time she had an operation for a fee of £7. Florence, single, 18, from Napier, attended Mrs Henderson in the back room of her shop. Mrs Henderson asked to see her boyfriend the following morning, and charged £20 because she said she was running a great risk. In fact, this money was never paid. Mrs Henderson swore both young women to secrecy, saying if anything happened and they needed to see a doctor they should say they had had a bicycle accident.

SUPREME COURT.

VERDICT OF MANSLAUGHTER AGAINST MRS HENDERSON.

(PER PRESS ASSOCIATION.)

WELLINGTON, December 5.
The jury returned a verdict of manslaughter against Mary Henderson, charged with the murder, by means of illegal operation, of Mary Luke. They added a recommendation of mercy to the finding. Sentence was deferred until Friday.

Mrs Mary Henderson (*Free Lance*, 1 December 1900) was sentenced to seven years' imprisonment with hard labour (*Hawera & Normanby Star*, 6 December 1900).

Mrs Henderson, defended by Mr Wilford, faced a three-day trial in the Wellington Supreme Court, commencing on 26 November 1900, on the charge of murder. She was not tried for procuring abortion. Lawyers argued about the admissibility of the depositions made by Winnie, and in the end they were ruled inadmissible, on the grounds that Mrs Henderson had not been served proper notice of the intention to take them. Another contentious point was how Winnie had become so seriously ill within 24 hours of the alleged operation, and whether the curetting might have caused injury to the uterus. Doctors for both sides testified.

After deliberating from 5.50 pm until 10.15 pm, the jury could not agree, and the judge ordered a retrial with a new judge and jury. One week later, the Chief Justice, Sir Robert Stout, presided and the jury returned a verdict of guilty of manslaughter. Mrs Henderson was sentenced to seven years' imprisonment with hard labour, to be served in the Terrace Gaol. In passing sentence, His Honour dwelt upon the gross ignorance shown by Mrs Henderson in connection with the operation. He said the use of curling tongs as an instrument after a miscarriage was a horrible atrocity, and a life had been lost through her ignorance. However, the jury recommended mercy. It was acknowledged that people went to her; she did not go to them. Leave to appeal was refused. Although she was described in the court proceedings as kind and gentle, her use of non-sterile instruments made Mrs Henderson a hazardous operator.

‱

Mrs Wilson has the distinction of being the only nurse to have received a seven-year sentence twice.

Trial of Mrs Susan (Nurse) Wilson, 1912[14]

Mrs Wilson was well known in Dunedin as an abortionist and practised from her home in Maitland Street. Women came from as far away as Invercargill for her services. She had practised without prosecution until March 1912. The case that brought her to the attention of the police was Kate, barely 16 years of age. Kate came to Dunedin about 19 March and was operated on twice. Subsequently she became ill, was admitted to hospital and recovered.

Although the case against Mrs Wilson lacked corroborative evidence, the jury found her guilty, but they recommended mercy. She was also known as a drunkard, and a report from the police surgeon stated that she had simulated madness for her own purposes. The judge, Sir Joshua Williams, did not think she deserved mercy and sentenced her to seven years' imprisonment with hard labour. Unrepentant, she was before the courts again in 1925.

Trial of Mrs Susan Wilson, 1925[15]

Mrs Wilson, now 55, was described as a small, wizened woman who had had a hard life. In the Dunedin Magistrate's Court, she was charged with malpractice on 26 May 1924 and 19 January 1925. We do not know much about this case, as all details were suppressed. A young woman, 18, related how she had gone to Mrs Wilson's house on the dates mentioned, and detailed what happened there and how much it had cost.

At first Mrs Wilson denied the charges, but then she pleaded guilty. Justice Sim surmised that she had been carrying on her abortion business since her discharge from her previous sentence. In the Dunedin Supreme Court, he sentenced her to another seven years' imprisonment.

෴

In the following story, a girl of 16 made a dying deposition that led to the conviction of Mrs Skellon.

Minotaur's story[16]
Deceased 20 February 1913, aged 16 years

Minotaur Bush lived with her parents in Auckland. For the past year, she had been in a relationship with Thomas Mackay, a young motor driver. The two had known each other for about six years. When she became pregnant Tom sought help, at a cost of £4, from

ON TRIAL FOR HER LIFE.
ACQUITTED OF MURDER : CONVICTED OF ATTEMPTED ABORTION.
THE DEATH, AT AUCKLAND, OF SIXTEEN-YEAR-OLD MINOTAUR BUSH.

NZ *Truth*, 31 May 1913

Mrs Skellon, 64, also known as Nurse Skellon. Tom brought Minotaur to Mrs Skellon's place in Freeman's Bay and waited in the dining room while Mrs Skellon took Minotaur into the bedroom. Minotaur lied to her mother, saying she was going to stay with friends. After the operation she needed somewhere to stay, so Mrs Skellon introduced the couple to a neighbour, Mrs Morris, and Minotaur stayed with her for a few days until Tom took her back home.

When she became ill, Dr Barber visited on 3 February and immediately sent her to the public hospital, where she was operated on that evening.

Mrs Sarah Eliza Skellon. (NZ *Truth*, 31 May 1913)

Whilst being treated in hospital she made a dying deposition, and as a result Mrs Skellon was charged with attempting to procure abortion; when Minotaur died on 20 February, the charge was increased to murder or manslaughter. The post-mortem found the cause of death was peritonitis due to interference.

Trial of Sarah Eliza Skellon, 1913

Mrs Skellon was tried in the Auckland Supreme Court, with Justice Cooper presiding. There were two charges: murder or manslaughter, and attempting to procure abortion. In May 1913, the jury found her not guilty of murder or manslaughter, but later, in August 1913, found her guilty of supplying pills of ergot and apiol with intent to procure miscarriage. The case was referred to the Court of Appeal, on the grounds that the wording in the indictment referred to 'unlawfully using an instrument or other means' and defence queried whether this included pills. The Court of Appeal upheld her conviction, and Mrs Skellon was sentenced to two years' imprisonment.

ଔ

Mrs Dalton was a maternity nurse who provided nursing services in her home in Ponsonby, Auckland, where she lived with her husband.

Vera's story[17]
Deceased 5 November 1917, aged 23 years

Vera Baker worked as a domestic servant in a home in Mount Eden Road, Auckland. Her parents were both dead. Her nearest relative was her Uncle Fred, a waterside worker, who identified her body at the inquest. They were not close, and until visiting her in her final illness, he had not seen her for about nine months.

When Vera became pregnant to Percy Henry, 26, he said he was not in a position to marry and agreed with her having an abortion. He accompanied Vera to see Mrs Dalton. At the first visit Mrs Dalton was not at home, but Vera returned later for an operation and was then admitted to Mrs Dalton's for care. Percy visited several times and brought with him the money requested. He paid £10 plus £1.10s for extras.

When Vera suffered complications, Mrs Dalton took her to see Dr Florence Keller in her rooms. The doctor recommended admission to hospital, but Vera refused, saying she wished to stay at Mrs Dalton's. Because of abdominal tenderness, Dr Keller was unable to examine her properly and arranged to examine her under anaesthesia provided by her husband, Dr Martin Keller. What she found alarmed her. A decaying limb was protruding from the cervix and also a piece of the mother's bowel. There were signs of sepsis and a laceration. She immediately called for more expert surgical help, and Dr Drier came within half an hour. He performed an abdominal operation and found that Vera had two uteri, each with its own cervix (a congenital anomaly). The pregnancy was in the right uterus, which was damaged by a large laceration. Both uteri were removed. Some more fetal parts, the size of a three-month pregnancy, were removed from the abdominal cavity and the damaged bowel was repaired. However, septic peritonitis was extensive, and Vera died two days later.

Dr Florence Keller was present when Vera made her dying depositions, and at her post-mortem. Vera stated before a magistrate that she had used an instrument upon herself. Dr Drier thought this was possible, but very unlikely. Dr McDougall, who conducted the post-mortem, also thought self-infliction very unlikely. The coroner's verdict stated that the cause of death was 'acute septic peritonitis induced by laceration of the right uterus and laceration of the great bowel', and added:[18]

There is evidence sufficient to warrant one Hannah Matilda Dalton being placed on her trial on a charge of unlawfully using an instrument on the said Vera Baker, with the intent to procure her miscarriage thereby causing the said laceration, and also to warrant one Percy Norman Henry being placed on his trial on a charge of aiding and abetting the said Hannah Matilda Dalton in the commission of such offence.

As a result of the inquest police made further enquiries and laid charges on 9 November 1917 against Mrs Dalton, 43, and Percy Henry. The charges were increased after death to include murder or manslaughter. Mr Singer defended Mrs Dalton and the cases were heard separately.

Trials of Mrs Hannah Matilda Dalton and Mr Percy Norman Henry, 1917–1918

The trial against Mrs Dalton took place in the Auckland Supreme Court on 28 November, with Justice Cooper presiding. After four hours, the jury announced they were unable to reach a verdict. The judge ordered a retrial at the February sittings. The case against Percy Henry was adjourned until the charges against Mrs Dalton were concluded.

In February, Justice Hosking presided in the Supreme Court, and once again, after four hours' deliberation, the jury could not reach a verdict. The judge ordered a third trial to take place immediately. This time, after deliberating for one hour, the jury returned a verdict of not guilty.

The case against Percy Henry then took place before Justice Hosking in the Auckland Supreme Court. In his defence he gave a rather different story to Vera's, saying he wanted to marry Vera but she refused. He also said the operation was performed much against his will. After a retirement of 20 minutes the jury returned a verdict of not guilty.

Ten years later, Mrs Dalton was again before the courts, but this time she was not so lucky.

Trial of Mrs Hannah Matilda Dalton, 1927[19]

Mrs Dalton, now 54, of 3 Surrey Street, Grey Lynn, Auckland, was paralysed in one leg and was described as a short, very bulky woman. The magistrate allowed her to remain seated during the taking of depositions when she was charged with, on three occasions, having unlawfully used an instrument to procure abortion. All three witnesses received name suppression.

A young woman, 20, from a country district, told of her partner calling to see Nurse Dalton and making arrangements for the abortion. When she called at the home, she was told Nurse Dalton was away in Thames but would return in a few days. She stayed in the house until Nurse Dalton returned. She testified about what happened and stated that other women were also there for the same reason. Mrs Dalton charged £50.

A married woman from Hamilton stated that in 1925, she had paid Nurse Dalton £25 to have an operation. When she found herself in the same predicament in January 1927, she wired 'Can you do a repeat order for me same as before?' The reply came back 'Everything all right.' However, the police intervened before the young woman left town.

The third witness was a married woman, with three children, in less prosperous circumstances. She could only find £6, and although Mrs Dalton wanted £10, she did it for the £6. The police searched her premises and found letters and telegrams, plus two catheters, which Mrs Dalton tried to hide.

In the Auckland Supreme Court, Mr Singer defended Mrs Dalton. He stressed that all the witnesses were accomplices in crime and their accounts were uncorroborated. However, the direction from the judge was clearly in favour of guilt. The jury retired for one hour and returned a verdict of guilty, with a strong recommendation for mercy on account of the prisoner's age and physical disability.

Addressing Mrs Dalton, Justice Stringer said, 'You had a warning some years ago which you do not seem to have availed yourself of. Although you were pitied on that occasion there is very good reason to suppose you caused the death of —.' Mr Singer objected to this remark, as Mrs Dalton had been found not guilty of the murder or manslaughter of Vera Baker in 1917. However, the judge continued:[20]

> I am not going to let that sway me. The fact that you were tried should have been sufficient warning. I cannot disguise from myself that you have been carrying on a systematic trade, and it is evident that women of all classes were resorting to you. Taking into consideration the recommendation of the jury, I cannot do less in the

interests of society – to which I think you and women like you are a menace – than impose the sentence I now do of seven years' imprisonment.

◊

Mrs Herbert provided abortions from her home in Auckland.

Jean's story[21]
Deceased 22 January 1930, aged 28 years

Jean Burdis (née Munn) had been keeping company with John Burdis, 30, for three years. They were engaged to be married and a marriage ceremony took place in Auckland Hospital a few days after her admission, when she was lying seriously ill. In September, she found she was pregnant and took abortifacient pills that did not work. John sought out Mrs Maud Herbert, 41, who lived in a two-bedroom house in Denbeigh Avenue, Mount Roskill. He visited her alone on Thursday 19 December 1929, and was informed by Mrs Herbert that an operation would cost £10. The following day he accompanied Jean to see Mrs Herbert.

On Sunday 22 December, Jean left her parents' home in Auckland with a suitcase, saying she was going to Hamilton, but instead went to Mrs Herbert's. John accompanied her. After having a procedure, Mrs Herbert asked her to take a walk for about an hour. She returned to stay at Mrs Herbert's home and the following night had a miscarriage, estimated to be about three or four months' gestation.

On Tuesday 24 December, Mrs Herbert was concerned about Jean's condition and called in Dr Miller. He diagnosed an incomplete abortion and arranged for another doctor and nurse to assist him while he performed a curettage, to empty the uterus. At that stage she did not have a fever, but the following day, Christmas Day, she had a high temperature.

On Thursday 26 December, Dr Miller admitted Jean to Awanui Private Hospital. Her condition fluctuated. Dr Miller consulted with Dr Moore, and as a result, Jean was transferred to the public hospital on Saturday 28 December. On Monday 30 December, a detective visited Jean in hospital with a Justice of the Peace to take a statement from her.

The dying deposition, before Mr Hunt S.M. and in the presence of Mrs Herbert and her counsel, Mr Moody, said:

> I left home for the last time on the Sunday before Christmas and went to a friend's place. She wasn't exactly a friend but she turned out to be a friend. She is present today. She helped to relieve me of my condition. I paid her something, about £9 in notes. She just said she was a trained nurse. I had been sick before I went to the place, off and on for about six weeks. I had been taking some medicine which caused the sickness. I felt very bad.

The police visited Mrs Herbert to make enquiries and to collect any incriminating evidence. They found bloodstained linen, towels and an unused catheter. The bath was blood splattered. In the back bedroom was a basin containing bloodstained fluid, which Mrs Herbert violently spilled on the floor. In the fire grate, they found the charred remains of a fetus wrapped in paper, and a charred catheter. On finding this, Mrs Herbert became hysterical and was taken into custody.

Jean remained in Auckland Hospital for over three weeks before finally succumbing to septic peritonitis. The post-mortem found the infection had spread to multiple organs, with toxic changes in the liver, kidneys and spleen. In the lungs were several abscesses. The coroner, acting alone, found 'death was due to blood poisoning due to a septic condition following an abortion.'

Trial of Mrs Maud Herbert, 1930

There was great public interest in this case. The grand jury hearing the initial charge reduced it from murder to manslaughter. The judge, Sir Alexander Herdman, said that in his many years' experience he had never tried a case where the evidence was so shocking. When the sordid details were presented by the police, Justice Herdman glanced at the women's gallery, where a number of women leaned against the rail. He said quietly, 'I notice up in the gallery a number of women listening to these disgusting details. If they have any self-respect they will go out.' Most of the women did not move until the court orderly directed them to leave.

The judge, in his lengthy summing up, said the evidence had hardly been challenged except in one respect, that of the admissibility of Jean's statement as an accomplice. Other than that, he considered the evidence was clear and definite. The jury retired for one and a half hours and returned a verdict of guilty.

Mrs Herbert was remanded for sentence and received seven years' hard labour.

ଓ

Mrs Shirley provided an abortion service from her home in Christchurch.

Catterina's story[22]
Deceased 27 March 1936, aged 26 years

Mrs Catterina Hill had been married for nearly eight years to Edward, a commission agent, and they lived in Greymouth, with one child. In January, Catterina suspected she was pregnant and sought remedies from the local chemist, Mr Bluett. When these did not work, Bluett suggested they contact Mrs Ruebena Shirley, in Papanui, Christchurch, a married woman aged 40 years with a 14-year-old son and a husband on relief work. She had nursing experience but was not a registered midwife. Edward phoned Mrs Shirley early in March, and the Hills arranged to go to Christchurch, leaving by train on Saturday 14 March.

Initially they stayed at the White Hart Hotel, and the abortion was carried out on Sunday 15 March at Mrs Shirley's home. The next day, Catterina was ill. Edward had a row with Mrs Shirley and things went from bad to worse, with Edward eventually removing Catterina from Mrs Shirley's place, by asking to take his wife for a drive and not returning. He took her to see Dr Francis Bennett. Dr Bennett co-authored *Gentlemen of the Jury*, which argued the case against abortion, with Dr Doris Gordon in 1937. He had met the Hills three years before, when he practised in Greymouth, but had not seen them since moving to Christchurch. He later testified at the inquest and at the trial. Edward also consulted a private detective with the Arrow Detective Agency, to help reclaim the £15 they had paid Mrs Shirley.

On Friday 20 March, Catterina was in pain and Dr Bennett was telephoned. He arranged for her to go to Mrs Roberts's private maternity hospital, and here the miscarriage occurred, with delivery of the afterbirth about an hour later. Catterina was at Mrs Roberts's place for only a few hours, as Dr Bennett advised admission to the Christchurch Public Hospital.

For the next few days, Catterina was treated in the hospital, but she did not like being there; she discharged herself, against the doctors' advice, and went to be with Edward at the Ambassador Hotel. On Wednesday night, Catterina developed pains and on Thursday, Dr Bennett readmitted her to the hospital, where she died from septicaemia and peritonitis the following day.

The police made enquiries and searched Mrs Shirley's premises. They found a syringe, Lysol, ergot, iodine, enamel basins, a rubber sheet, cotton wool and a board to place on the bed to keep the buttocks steady.

Trial of Mrs Reubena Shirley, 1936

The Christchurch Supreme Court trial, presided over by Justice Northcroft, was followed with the closest attention by a crowded public gallery, including many women, some of whom knitted busily throughout the hearing. Mrs Shirley was defended by Mr McMenamin. It became known as the 'Shirley case'. No fewer than 27 witnesses were called.

A sensational development was the evidence given by two other young women, given name suppression, who came forward to support the case incriminating Mrs Shirley. On the original charge, relating to the manslaughter of Catterina, the jury returned a verdict of not guilty, but on the subsequent charges, relating to the two young women, she was found guilty of procuring abortion and sentenced to 18 months' imprisonment on each charge, to be served concurrently. So much for a justice system that valued the life of a woman less than that of two witnesses who lived to tell their story.

ଔ

Mrs Gerraty provided an abortion service in provincial Thames, and on two occasions, in 1920 and 1932, escaped conviction.

Trial of Mrs Edith May Gerraty, 1920[23]

Mrs Gerraty, 50, a midwife and a miner's wife with a grown family, lived in Thames. Police charged her with unlawfully using an instrument with intent to procure abortion on 4 May. Two young men, Daniel Fisher and Kenneth Casey, were also charged in relation to the offence. All were remanded for eight days. When they reappeared before two Justices of the Peace, the charges were dismissed on the grounds of insufficient corroborative evidence, but the police successfully appealed. The case against Mrs

Gerraty was heard in the Auckland Supreme Court, presided over by Justice Stringer, on 20 August 1920.

Miss Ivy Bilman, a domestic servant employed by Dr Liggins, said that in April 1920, when employed in Thames, she found herself in trouble due to sex with her previous boyfriend, Kenneth Casey. She asked him to marry her, but he refused and asked her to see Mrs Gerraty for an operation. She refused and again asked him to marry her, but he said he could not afford to. He later admitted that he was afraid she might be playing a game on him.

Later, on the evening of 4 May, she did go to Mrs Gerraty, accompanied by her current boyfriend, Daniel Fisher, who waited outside. She was taken into a back room, where Mrs Gerraty used an instrument. Fisher promised to bring the money the next day.

Two nights later, accompanied by a woman friend, Ivy returned to see Mrs Gerraty, who was in bed with the flu. She told her to come back the following Monday, but in the meantime Ivy became ill and was admitted to hospital on 11 May suffering from an incomplete septic abortion. An immediate operation was performed, the surgeon noting a laceration caused by some interference. The operation was a success; Ivy survived and gave evidence at the subsequent trial.

On 15 May, police arrested Mrs Gerraty and searched her house, but found nothing. She denied all accusations. At her trial, the judge warned the jury about convicting upon uncorroborated testimony, and after a short retirement the jury returned a verdict of not guilty. The two young men, Casey and Fisher, also faced charges, but after a short retirement the jury returned with a verdict of not guilty in both cases.

Mrs Gerraty was before the courts again in 1932, after the death of Mrs Emma Gaylor in Waikato Hospital from septicaemia. After two trials in the Hamilton Supreme Court, she was found not guilty.

ଔ

Mrs Colnett practised in Auckland.

Freda's story[24]
Deceased 1 November 1928, aged 29 years

Miss Freda Clark worked as a clerk in the Te Aroha Borough Council Office. She lived with Mr and Mrs Reader in Te Aroha from June 1927 until Saturday 27 October 1928, when she left to go to Auckland by the 5 am train. She told Mrs Reader she was going to Auckland because she had received a wire from her sister's neighbour, saying her sister, Mrs Doris Dannefeard, was ill and undergoing an operation.

Freda was friends with Percy Sowerby, 38, a farmer who lived outside Morrinsville. He had been separated from his wife for 12 months and they had one adopted child. Sowerby often came to see Freda at the Readers' home, although he had not visited in the two months prior to her departure. However, in the publicity surrounding Freda's death, he was referred to as 'the man in the case'.

On Thursday 1 November, at about 10.50 am, Dr Horton of Auckland received a telephone message from a man, asking him to call urgently. When he arrived at the house about 11 am, Mr and Mrs Colnett met him and said something dreadful had happened to Freda, who had been staying with them. At about 8.30 am, Mrs Colnett had brought Freda a breakfast of bacon and fillet steak, which she had eaten, then at about 10.30 am, she had found Freda dead.

Dr Horton confirmed Freda's death, but made no further examination. She lay on her bed, in a nightdress, her arms by her sides and her legs stretched straight. The body appeared to have been laid out after death. Mrs Colnett asked Dr Horton if he could certify her death and he said that was impossible. He told her it was her or her husband's duty to report the matter to the police, but in any case, he would report it. Dr Horton had never seen Freda before and could offer no opinion as to the cause of death. Before Dr Horton left the Colnett's house, Mr Singer, their solicitor, had already arrived at the house.

Mrs Georgina Colnett lived with her husband George at 88 Williamson Avenue, Auckland. He was a tutor of French, with about 20 pupils. Mrs Colnett trained as a nurse in Sydney, but failed her last exam at the Women's Hospital there. She had been in New Zealand about 25 years and nursing in Auckland for the last 17 years, although she was not registered. Nursing mainly took place in the homes of patients, and she was allowed one patient per month in her own home.

The police investigated the case as far as they could, with everyone declining to answer questions. They found Freda had a diaper cloth between her thighs and the bottom sheet was bloodstained. Two bloodstained diaper cloths lay alongside the bed. On the dressing table was a handbag containing £15, a railway

Mrs Colnett's house in Williamson Avenue, Grey Lynn, where Freda Clark died. (*NZ Truth*, 6 December 1928)

second-class return ticket from Te Aroha to Auckland dated 27 October, a partly used packet of Aspro, and sundry accounts in the name of Miss Clark. In the washhouse, the copper was full of water and contained a bloodstained bedsheet and 13 bloodstained towels. In the bathroom were three hot water bags, an ordinary douche can with rubber attachment, and two waterproof sheets.

Mrs Dannefeard (Freda's sister), Mr Clark (Freda's brother) and Percy Sowerby were at the Auckland mortuary on the morning of 2 November to identify the body. Dr Murray conducted the post-mortem. Fingertip marks were present on the lower part of the abdomen, five inches from the top of the vulva and in the middle line and to the right of the middle line. These marks were due to someone exerting strong pressure with their fingers over the lower part of the abdomen in the region of the womb. Two inches below the navel were five small recent bruises. Striae on the lower abdomen indicated a previous pregnancy. The body organs were congested and the heart muscle showed toxic myocarditis. The enlarged uterus contained a four-month-old fetus and placenta. Pus was found between the placental membranes and the uterine wall. Death was due to acute septicaemia following a septic incomplete abortion.

The coroner, Mr Hunt, was exasperated by the wall of silence created when the key witnesses, the Colnetts and Sowerby, refused to answer questions on the advice of their lawyer. Fiery exchanges took place between Mr Singer, the coroner and the Crown Solicitor. The coroner and the police demanded that the law be satisfied by the divulgence of all the facts, but the same law entitled the witnesses to decline to answer questions that might incriminate them. The result was a stalemate.

Acting alone, the coroner convened three hearings; the first immediately following the death, the second on 26 November 1928, and the third on 9 July 1929. The latter was held in the coroner's room, beyond the public gaze. His only finding was that 'the cause of death was acute septicaemia following a septic incomplete abortion.' The Colnetts were not charged.

ෲ

Having a tenacious defence counsel definitely helped, as in the following case.

Trial of Mrs Marjorie Pickering, 1938 and 1939[25]

In the Wellington Magistrate's Court on 29 September 1938, police charged Nurse Pickering, 42, mother of four, with unlawfully using an instrument on a young woman, 19, with intent to procure miscarriage. Mrs Pickering was defended by Mr Ongley. When the magistrate refused bail, Mrs Pickering collapsed and had to be assisted from the dock. Defence then applied to the Supreme Court for bail, which was granted by Justice Reed, with the proviso that Mrs Pickering report daily to the police.

However, at the resumption of the case on 12 October, Mrs Pickering failed to appear. Mr Ongley said she was suffering from a nervous condition. This did not impress the magistrate, who ordered the police to escort her to court, accompanied by the police doctor. At this hearing, police added another abortion charge, concerning a married woman. Mrs Pickering had charged £15 in one case and £20 in the other, and had refused to proceed until paid. She was committed for trial in the Supreme Court and bail was refused.

On 25 October in the Wellington Supreme Court, presided over by Justice Quilliam, Mrs Pickering pleaded not guilty. The defence questioned the Crown witnesses' identification of the accused and stressed the fact that the evidence was from accomplices. The jury deliberated for over five hours and returned a verdict of guilty, adding a strong recommendation for mercy on the grounds that those who procured the commission of offences were equally guilty.

Mr Ongley applied for leave to appeal on the question of whether the jury had been misdirected on the nature of the corroborative evidence. On 28 October, when Justice Quilliam imposed a sentence of three years' imprisonment with hard labour, Mrs Pickering wept, and asked, 'What about my children?' She had to be assisted from the dock. At the sentencing, Mr Ongley outlined other concerns. There were two charges and the jury had returned one verdict. He argued the two cases should have been considered separately.

Despite being put down in a peremptory manner by the judge, Mr Ongley persisted, and the Court of Appeal heard his arguments on 27 March 1939. Meanwhile, since her sentencing, Mrs Pickering had remained in prison. The Court of Appeal, consisting of Chief Justice Sir Michael Myers, Justice Ostler and Justice Fair, ordered a retrial. This took place in the Wellington Supreme Court on 2 May, presided over by Justice Smith. The jury took an hour and three quarters to reach a verdict of not guilty on both charges.

☙

Women sometimes turned to nurses for care and support when they found themselves in difficulty after an abortion elsewhere. For her trouble, Mrs Durston received a fine for breaching regulations.

Jennie's story[26]
Deceased 25 March 1910, aged 30 years

Miss Janet McColl, or Jennie to her family, kept house for her brother Dugald, a miner in Waitahuna Gully. She left for a holiday on 12 March, accompanied by her boyfriend, Thomas Carr, 30, and went to the house of Mrs Annie Durston in Dunedin on 15 March. Mrs Durston, an unregistered ladies' nurse, was widowed and took in cases for nursing care in her seven-bedroom home in the suburb of Mornington. Jennie arrived on her doorstep, identifying herself as 'Mrs Carr' and asking for a bed for a week or so.

That night, she told Mrs Durston she had been taking pills and medicines for the past four months and was expecting to miscarry, which she did in the early hours of the morning. On 16 March she was delivered of premature twins about three to four months' gestation and the bodies were burnt in the copper fireplace by Mrs Durston. Jennie died nine days later in Mrs Durston's house.

At first Jennie's family did not know where she was staying, but in the few days before she died she was visited by her three sisters and her brother Dugald. At the inquest Mrs Durston was criticised by the coroner for her management of the case, but not by Jennie's family. Although Jennie was unusual in not developing a fever, Mrs Durston failed to recognise other signs of infection and did not appreciate the seriousness of the fainting turns Jennie experienced. She delayed calling a doctor, and in the end the doctor arrived only ten minutes before Jennie died.

The post-mortem findings were a perforated uterus and septic peritonitis. Jennie shed no light on who might have used an instrument upon her and there was no accounting for her whereabouts in the few days before arriving at Mrs Durston's. At the inquest an important witness was missing – Jennie's boyfriend, Thomas Carr. He was 'the boy next door', the two families having lived side by side for many years. The police conducted an extensive search but could not trace him. He left his work at the Railways without collecting his pay.

The coroner's inquest took place before six male jurors. They concluded:

> the cause of death being general septic peritonitis due to puerperal infection following a miscarriage, and the jury is of opinion that the puerperal infection was caused by an instrument having been used for the purpose of procuring abortion but by whom the instrument was so used the evidence does not show. And the jury is also of opinion that Mrs Durston greatly erred in her duty in neglecting to call in a doctor at an earlier period.

In the Magistrate's Court on 24 May, Mrs Durston was fined £5 for a breach of the Midwives Act, for practising without being registered.

ଔ

In 1914, public health and nursing regulations were being implemented to improve maternal health. In the following case, health inspectors closed Mrs Llewellyn's private hospital while they investigated May's death.

May's story[27]
Deceased 1 February 1914, aged 25–30 years

May Otto lived and worked in Auckland as a domestic servant. Although her mother disapproved, for the past six months May had been keeping company with Charles Clifford. When she found herself pregnant, she talked with him several times about 'getting rid of it' and visited two women abortionists. The first wanted to charge £10 and the second was away on holiday when they called. May had also taken pills of ergot and pennyroyal, and apiol and steel, but these had not worked. She had also tried douching and this was a disaster; much to her embarrassment, she burned her external genitals and vagina by using water that was too hot, and had to visit her doctor with painful ulceration. There was also a mysterious visit to Te Aroha shortly before her miscarriage.

About a week before her death, she went to the Auckland private hospital of Mrs Charlotte Llewellyn, asking for employment and using the name 'Miss Charles'. On 23 January, she confided to Nurse Llewellyn that she was pregnant, and during the night of 24 January she had a miscarriage, passing a four-and-a-half-month-old fetus. The following day, Dr Caldicott attended her. Nurse Llewellyn was later reprimanded for assisting at a miscarriage without obtaining medical supervision. Dr Caldicott recommended transfer to Auckland Hospital, but May refused.

Dr Caldicott examined May under an anaesthetic, and douched and drained her womb. From the history May gave him of passing copious amounts of fluid, he concluded this was a natural miscarriage caused by an excess of amniotic fluid (an unusual diagnosis). After a few days of treating her, he insisted on her transfer to hospital and she was admitted in a critical condition with a high fever on 29 January. May was reluctant to give details about her family, so the hospital doctor notified the police. As a result, her mother visited her just before she died on 1 February.

Dr Bull carried out the post-mortem, confirming a recent miscarriage but no sign of injury, other than the vaginal ulceration caused by the hot douche. He diagnosed a septic pneumonia with numerous abscesses in both lungs.

The case was heard by a coroner without a jury, and the lengthy verdict read:

the cause of death was puerperal septicaemia following a miscarriage. There is evidence that the girl desired to bring about a miscarriage but there is no evidence that the miscarriage was due to anything other than her general illness. It is also a fact that the nurse at whose home the girl had the miscarriage failed to comply with the regulations in that she herself attended to the girl and did not call in medical assistance. Medical assistance was however called in the day after and there is nothing to suggest that this slight delay in calling medical assistance in any way affected the girl's chances of recovery.

ଔ

Marguerite turned to her trusted midwife, Nurse Davidson, when she needed help.

Marguerite's story[28]
Deceased 24 January 1929, aged 30 years

Marguerite Downes was married to Joseph, 56, a labourer, and they had three children, aged eleven, nine and three years. He had only just moved to Ashburton from Christchurch, and was in the process of shifting his wife and family to be with him. Marguerite visited him from 12 to 14 January, when she was in good health. On Wednesday 23 January, Joseph returned to Christchurch to pack up some things, and was surprised to find Marguerite at Nurse Davidson's, having had a miscarriage. Marguerite told him she had fallen down the steps at the back door. George Austin, linotype operator, boarded with the Downes family in Christchurch. He had known them for five years. When Marguerite became unwell, George carried her bag to Nurse Davidson's nursing home. He visited her on the Wednesday afternoon and took one of the children along. He later denied any knowledge of her illness.

Mrs Josephine Davidson was a registered nurse who had a maternity home in Addington. Marguerite had been there for the confinement of her last child three years before. Marguerite saw Nurse Davidson again in December and made arrangements to be confined about the first week of May. She called again on Tuesday 22 January in the afternoon, accompanied by George and looking very miserable, in pain and feeling very sick. Nurse Davidson took her in, gave her a cup of tea and put her to bed. That night her condition became worse, and Nurse Davidson called in a doctor. Dr Stringer arrived before 2 am on Wednesday morning. About 20 minutes after the arrival of the doctor Marguerite delivered a five-month-old dead fetus. From its condition, the doctor assumed it had probably died in utero some days before. The afterbirth came away shortly afterwards and the delivery appeared complete. However, Marguerite continued to vomit and Dr Stringer admitted her to hospital on the afternoon of Thursday 24 January, about 4.45 pm.

Dr Davidson, an Assistant Medical Superintendent at Christchurch Public Hospital, saw Marguerite after admission and described her condition as serious. She was deeply jaundiced, was vomiting incessantly and complained of abdominal pain. Her toxic condition was attributed to the effects of her miscarriage. She was not in a fit condition to make any statement, and gradually sank and died about 9 pm that day.

Dr Pearson, Christchurch Hospital pathologist, carried out the post-mortem. The peritoneal cavity contained a considerable quantity of bloodstained fluid. There was an intense degree of general peritonitis, with thick purulent fluid in the abdominal cavity, and toxic changes in the liver, kidneys and spleen with gas formation. The uterus was enlarged, soft and congested. Gas was present under the peritoneal coat. The uterus contained soft, haemorrhagic, necrotic material adherent to the inner surface, and small fragments of placenta remained in the upper part of the posterior wall. When Dr Pearson detached the placental tissue, he found a large perforation of the fundus of the uterus towards the left side. He diagnosed the cause of death as acute septic inflammation of the uterus and general peritonitis. Microscopic examination of peritoneal fluid showed profuse gram-positive bacilli resembling *Clostridium welchii*, and other bacteria. In Dr Pearson's opinion, it was quite possible the deceased could have injured herself with an instrument. From his observations he concluded Marguerite had been interfered with, either by herself or by somebody else.

The coroner, acting alone, reiterated the opinion of the pathologist that 'death was due to acute septic inflammation of the uterus and general peritonitis, this condition having been brought about by some unknown person using an instrument and thus procuring abortion.'

While many nurses were employed in public hospitals, these stories confirm the important role of nurses working in their community to provide a wide range of services for women. Although many (if not all) of them were well intentioned, in some cases the nurses' lack of training or slack standards could be disastrous for the women who turned to them for help with miscarriage and abortion.

9. ALL SORTS

Abortion was not the sole preserve of doctors, chemists and nurses – abortionists came from all walks of life. The largest group by far was married women, living ordinary domestic lives and doing abortions on the side to supplement their modest income. Men who performed abortions came from a variety of backgrounds, often not remotely relevant to health care – tobacconists, hairdressers, barbers, masseurs, chemist's assistants, butchers, veterinary surgeons, waterside workers, labourers, jewellers, bootmakers, salesmen, tailors, barmen, hotelkeepers, billiard saloon managers, bus proprietors – even a trick cyclist. Wherever and however abortionists practised, word of mouth discreetly advertised their services, while newspaper reports of court cases or deaths boosted their reputations dramatically. However, not everyone sought out the career abortionist. Because of the need for confidentiality, lovers, friends and family often stepped in to help, sometimes with tragic results. The following cases all resulted in the death of the woman, but there were many more that survived. That we know from many prosecutions in non-fatal cases.

ɞ

Aggie's story is a double tragedy.

Aggie's story[1]
Deceased 7 July 1903, aged 21 years

Agnes Campbell (known in her family as Aggie) lived in Athol Place, Dunedin, with her frail widowed mother and several brothers and sisters. She worked as a tailoress for a waterproofing firm in Princes Street. For three years, she had been keeping company with a quiet young man, John Osmond, 24, a carpenter who lived with his father and brothers in South Dunedin. Aggie and John loved each other and both the Campbells and the Osmonds looked forward to their wedding. Anticipating their future home together, John collected furniture and stored pieces in his room.

On a wintry Dunedin evening, Tuesday 7 July, Aggie sat contentedly doing her embroidery. At 7.30 pm she put her embroidery aside and told her sister Margaret she was going to visit Mrs Henderson, a friendly neighbour. Margaret was the last family member to see her alive. A bread cart driver who knew Aggie well saw her a little while later in a street near her home, with John, who was carrying a brown paper parcel.

Aggie usually let her family know where she went and what time she would be back, so when she failed to return home, her sister Margaret was worried. She went to bed but could not sleep and finally, even though it was late at night, she got up and knocked on Mrs Henderson's door. Mrs Henderson told her Aggie had never visited her. One of Aggie's brothers worked as a baker and had an early start at 3 am, so Margaret made him a cup of tea at 2.40 am. Another brother was also up early. Margaret thought she heard someone turning the back door handle but when her brothers checked nobody was found. That remains a mystery. Was it John?

The next afternoon, around midday, a labourer walking near the University of Otago on the rise known as Tanna Hill spied a hat among some broom bushes beyond the road. Looking closer, he saw the hat covered the face of a young woman lying on her back in a hollow among the broom. He thought she might be sleeping off the effects of drink and continued on his way home for lunch. However, he felt uneasy and returned a short while later with two mates. When they took off the woman's hat they were shocked to discover her dead body, fully dressed and with no signs of violence. Two men waited while the third fetched the police. The headlines next day called it the 'Tanna Hill Mystery'.

Meanwhile, earlier that Wednesday morning at the Jetty Street wharf, another mystery unfolded. A shipping clerk found a small wet handbag, later identified as belonging to John, lying on the wharf. He handed it in to the police for safekeeping. Also that morning, a ten-year-old schoolboy found a hat with the initials 'J. O.' lying next to the piles under the wharf. Floating near the hat was an instrument which would be produced at the inquest and identified as a syringe or enema. The schoolboy brought the hat and syringe home to his mother, who informed the police.

John had not returned home after leaving on Tuesday evening. His father recalled that John had spent some time in his room before going out, saying he was going into town. Initially the police presumed John had committed suicide by drowning. However, a thorough trawling of the harbour failed to recover his body. Armchair sleuths then speculated that the items found may have been deposited there to deflect attention from the escaping culprit. A report of a man hiring a buggy, then discarding it miles away, turned out to be a false lead.

At the coroner's inquest into Aggie's death, some of the mystery was solved. A post-mortem found she was about four months pregnant and there was evidence she had been interfered with, the mouth of the womb being dilated. The doctors concluded she had most likely died of syncope, or heart stoppage, brought on by manipulating the cervix. Another, less likely, possibility was that air had entered her veins and she had died of an air embolism, but this was not confirmed by the autopsy. Post-mortem findings were otherwise unremarkable. Specimens analysed for poisons were negative. The Coroner's Court, with six male jurors, found Agnes 'had met her death through shock caused by improper interference with the genitals but by whom performed there is not sufficient evidence to know.'

John's body was missing for ten weeks and public interest in the mystery dissipated. Then, one morning, two young men spotted a body floating in the harbour. Police recovered a fully clothed decomposing body with the legs tied around the ankles with a blue tie. The only items found on the body were coins (19 shillings and sixpence), two keys and a tobacco pouch. John's two brothers identified his body. The jury of six men at the coroner's inquest into John's death concluded the tying of the legs was self-accomplished, indicating suicide. The verdict stated 'deceased committed suicide by drowning while in a state of temporary insanity.'

One can only imagine how Aggie and John carefully planned their tryst and how devastated John must have felt when his fumbling with the syringe caused her collapse. Would a knowledge of first aid have helped? Both families would have agonised as the double tragedy slowly and publicly unfolded.

Here is another mystery that remained unsolved.

Ethel's story[2]
Deceased 7 February 1911, aged 34 years

Miss Ethel Bradley was employed as a housekeeper for Mr Weston, a Christchurch solicitor, and had just handed in her resignation at the time of her death. For the past nine months, she had been keeping company with Harry Jack, 23, and although not formally engaged, she expected they would marry. His version was less romantic. Harry was employed by Mr Walter Sadler as an assistant in his tobacconist's and hairdressing establishment. Sadler was also known to do a little betting on the side and had a reputation as an abortionist.

On the evening of 7 February, Ethel and Harry went walking along the River Avon. After their walk they returned to Sadler's shop about 9.30 pm and Ethel never came out alive. What happened next became the subject of endless conjecture.

According to one version, Ethel felt ill when she entered the shop. Both men went to the nearby hotel to get her some whisky as a stimulant. When they returned, they found her on the floor, and within minutes she was dead. The two men panicked and fled the scene, going to the hotel for drinks and returning later about 11 pm, when they removed her body from the shop to an adjoining lane. A policeman on duty in the early hours of the morning found her body, and the case became known as the 'Mystery-Lane Tragedy'. The mystery of who was responsible for her death was never solved.

Ethel Bradley.
(NZ Truth, 18 February 1911)

The post-mortem found that Ethel was two-and-a-half months pregnant and her death was caused by poisoning. The coroner concluded 'that the deceased Ethel May Bradley died by prussic acid poisoning. Whether it was administered by

Walter Sadler appeared several times in the *NZ Truth* during his trials. (left to right: 18 February 1911, 18 May 1912, 4 May 1912)

herself or by other persons we cannot say. We are of the opinion that the poison was taken in the presence of Harry Jack.'

Prussic acid (hydrogen cyanide or hydrocyanic acid) is highly toxic: the smallest fatal dose causes death in 30–60 minutes and a larger dose within ten minutes. Symptoms of such poisoning include giddiness, confusion and a staggering gait. Prussic acid is not an abortifacient, but someone suggested it might have been confused with the recognised abortifacient *Hydrastis*, especially if abbreviated names were used on the container. *Hydrastis* is a herb, also known as goldenseal.

Both men made false statements to the police during questioning, trying to conceal their involvement. Was it suicide, murder, an attempted abortion or just an appalling accident?

Trials of Walter Richard Sadler and Harry Jack, 1911

At Sadler's Supreme Court trial, presided over by Justice Denniston, the jury convicted Sadler of manslaughter, but when the case came before the Court of Appeal in July, he was acquitted. The Court of Appeal argued that suspicious circumstances, false statements and discreditable behaviour were not sufficient grounds to convict for murder, and neither should they be for the lesser charge of manslaughter.

At Jack's trial, the prosecution submitted that Jack knew of Ethel's pregnancy, and may have given her the poison in error, thinking it was an abortifacient. He was acquitted on the charge of manslaughter but later pleaded guilty to perjury, for making false

SUICIDE OR HOMICIDE?
CHRISTCHURCH'S LATEST SENSATION.

Ethel May Bradley's Mysterious Ending.

CASHEL STREET, CHRISTCHURCH.
'A' shows Sadler's shop. B is the Zetland Hotel right-of-way where a woman was seen waiting by several witnesses after 8 p.m. on February 7. She was joined by Jack, and one witness stated that Jack went towards the river. C is corner where Constable Cudley met Jack and Sadler at 2 a.m. D is Turnbull and Jones's corner, where Price parted from Sadler, who afterwards went to his shop. Cashel-street bridge and trees overhanging the river Avon are a little over two chains from the shop. According to witnesses, it was the trysting place of Jack and Ethel Bradley. There is no right-of-way between back of Sadler's shop and lane. Body was carried out front of shop, along Cashel-street and into lane.

Top: Headline from *NZ Truth*, 18 February 1911. Centre: Ethel Bradley was found dead in the right-of-way outside Sadler's shop (marked 'A') on Cashel Street, Christchurch (*NZ Truth*, 4 March 1911). Bottom: Walter Sadler (right) leaving the station with Detective Miller (*NZ Truth*, 4 March 1911).

statements under oath at the coroner's inquest. On this charge, he was convicted and sentenced to 12 months' imprisonment with hard labour.

Sadler, 34, then moved to Wellington, where he was employed as a barber in a Wellington hairdressing business, under the name of Walter Richards. He was soon before the courts again.

Trial of Walter Richard Sadler, 1912[3]

Police arrested Sadler on two charges of procuring abortion on Harriet May Keetley (known to her friends as May). The first alleged attempt took place in Kaiapoi on 8 April, and the second in Wellington on 26 April.

May, nearly 19, was learning dressmaking in Christchurch, where she stayed with her sister. For the past three years, she had been friendly with John Wilson, 23, a baker of Kaiapoi, but when she became pregnant, the couple decided against marriage. John contacted Sadler and sent £10 for him to come down to Kaiapoi to carry out an abortion. John's parents were away and the operation took place at his parents' home. However, it was not successful, and arrangements were made for May to go to Wellington. She met Sadler at the top of the cable car and they went into the Botanic Gardens, where he performed the second, successful, operation.

Harriet May Keetley (left) and her lover, John Wilson. (*NZ Truth*, 18 May 1912)

When May sailed for Wellington on the coastal ship *Maori*, she did not inform her parents of her plans, and when they became concerned at her absence they went to the police. As a result of their enquiries, police arrested Sadler. May returned to Lyttelton by ship on the evening of the operation. She made an uneventful recovery and was a witness in the trial against Sadler.

The charges against him were first heard in the Wellington Magistrate's Court, but because most of the witnesses came from the Christchurch area, the case was transferred to the Christchurch Magistrate's Court. After hearing depositions, Sadler stood trial in the Christchurch Supreme Court, presided over by Justice Denniston. Because there was sufficient corroborative evidence, the jury found him guilty and the judge sentenced him to seven years' imprisonment.

ଊ

The following is another sad story, where the death of one young woman mattered less to the justice system than the illness of another.

Olive's story[4]
Deceased 12 June 1920, aged 20 years

Australian-born, Miss Olive Pile lived with her parents at Karitane, near Dunedin. She was recently employed as a wardress at the Seacliff Mental Hospital. About four weeks before her death her father, a fisherman, found out about her pregnancy, accosted the man involved and informed the police. An almighty row ensued and Olive left home without telling her parents where she was going or what she was doing. Her father tried to find her, but eventually had the sad task of identifying her body in the morgue at Dunedin Hospital.

Olive had been keeping company with Charles Burdett, a surfaceman with the Railway Department. They went together to the house of Mrs Helen Glegg, a white-haired 71-year-old, at 15 Phillips Street, South Dunedin, to finalise arrangements for an abortion costing £20, which Charles paid for in notes. Olive was about five or six months pregnant. After the operation on 28 May, she became ill, and she died at Mrs Glegg's place a fortnight later. Mrs Glegg did not seek medical help before Olive's death.

The coroner delayed the inquest into Olive's death pending the result of the post-mortem carried out by Professor Drennan, Professor of Pathology at the University of Otago. He found that Olive died from the effects of a septic infection of the uterus. There was no peritonitis, but infection had spread from the uterus to the lungs, producing an acute pneumonia, and also to the heart, producing an acute endocarditis on top of a chronic heart condition (mitral stenosis from rheumatic fever). A large infected clot was present in the left iliac vein, and there were numerous clots in her other organs.

Further investigations by the police uncovered domestic skewers and other implements in Mrs Glegg's house. During their search, a seriously ill young woman, Rose Williams, was coincidentally found in the house and transferred to hospital. Fortunately, she recovered. Rose came from Clyde, and William McLeod admitted responsibility for her pregnancy. Mrs Glegg had charged £10 for Rose's operation.

Trial of Mrs Helen Glegg, 1920

Mrs Glegg was arrested on 14 June and charged with murdering Olive and performing an illegal operation on Rose. She was committed for trial in the Dunedin Supreme Court, presided over by Justice Sim. She was defended by Mr Hanlon. The jury found her not guilty of the murder of Olive Pile but guilty of procuring the abortion of Rose Williams, with a recommendation for mercy. She was sentenced to 18 months' imprisonment without hard labour. She died four years later, on 3 September 1924.

ɞ

The following story caused a sensation in Blenheim and the district of Marlborough.

Rita's story[5]
Deceased 7 May 1923, aged 18 years

Pretty Miss Rita Nicoll of Blenheim would have been 19 years old on 18 May 1923. For 15 months, she had worked in a private home as a domestic servant for Mr Vincent Dodson, a farmer of Spring Creek. He spoke well of Rita, saying she was the best girl they had ever had. She gave him one week's notice and left on

Saturday 21 April, taking the train to Blenheim. For about nine months she had been keeping company with Thomas Viggars, known to his friends as Tommy, who took her for rides on his motorcycle.

When Rita became pregnant, Tommy arranged for her to see Richard Hollis for an abortion on Monday 23 April. At about 8 pm he took her to the butcher's shop in High Street, Blenheim, owned by Hollis's brother. The three of them went into the shop and then Tommy came out. Hollis told Rita to lie on a table in a back room, where he operated on her. Rita saw something lying in water in an enamel basin, which she took to be the instrument he used.

After the operation, which took about 20 minutes, Hollis told her she must walk around for some time, which she did with Tommy, then he took her home in a car to her aunt, Mrs Bagby. She had told her aunt she was going out to the pictures, and Mrs Bagby was already in bed when she returned about 9.50 pm.

On Tuesday morning when her aunt took her morning tea, she noticed Rita's face was flushed. Her aunt told her she didn't believe she had been to the pictures because she had come home before the pictures were out. Rita then admitted to her aunt she had not been to the pictures but had sat in the Square. After a conversation with her husband, her aunt decided to call in Dr Adams, and he came that afternoon. Rita refused to be examined by him. She remained in bed all day. On Wednesday 25 April, she got up about 8 am and remained up all day until 8.30 pm, but she looked very ill.

About 12.30 pm that night, Mrs Bagby's little daughter, who was sharing a bed with Rita, called her parents. Mrs Bagby went to see Rita and found her crying with pain. Blood had splattered all over the bed and floor. Mrs Bagby immediately rang Dr Adams and he instructed her to send Rita to Holmdale, a private hospital. They could not admit her, and advised Mrs Bagby to take her in a taxi to Wairau Hospital. When her aunt arrived home at nearly 2 am, she went to the bed previously occupied by Rita and found the body of a four-month-old fetus. She telephoned Dr Julian, Medical Superintendent of Wairau Hospital, and he asked her to bring it to him later that morning.

On the day following her admission to hospital, Rita began to show signs of puerperal infection, and doctors operated to remove the remains of the placenta and stop the haemorrhage. Dr Julian telephoned Rita's father, who lived in Christchurch, and he came to Blenheim to be with his daughter. When Rita told her father about the events leading up to her illness, he remonstrated with a very subdued Tommy. Her father was present as a witness on 2 May when Rita made a statement from her hospital bed to Senior Sergeant Clarkson.

Rita developed a severe pneumonia, and on Friday 4 May, when her condition was considered hopeless, Dr Julian informed her of this grave situation and dying depositions were formally taken by Arthur Bent, Clerk of the Court and Registrar of the Blenheim Supreme Court. Rita's state of mind was quite clear and she perfectly understood what was said to her at the time. After the depositions were taken she seemed to rally for a time, but she died about 3.20 am on the morning of 7 May.

Dr Adams conducted the post-mortem. Rita's body showed signs of an extremely virulent type of infection. The primary cause of death was septicaemia caused by injuries to the uterus. Perforations were found which were of the type likely to be used by an unskilled abortionist. The diagnosis of a fatal pneumonia was confirmed by extensive consolidation of lung tissue. Streptococci were found in specimens from both the lungs and uterus.

The coroner, acting alone, found the cause of death was 'septic pneumonia caused by the infection of the blood stream, this infection caused by the septic condition set up owing to an injury to the uterus inflicted by a non-surgical instrument unskillfully used. Apart from the depositions there was no evidence to show by whom the injury was caused.'

Trial of Richard Hollis and Thomas Viggars, 1923

Hollis and Viggars were brought to trial, Hollis charged with unlawfully using an instrument with intent to commit a crime, and Viggars with procuring. Both were charged with the murder of Rita Nicoll on 7 May 1923. Defence counsel raised questions about the admissibility of the depositions and wanted the two men to be tried separately. The judge refused separate trials, and they were both tried in the Blenheim Supreme Court on 5 June, presided over by Sir John Salmond. The grand jury reduced the charge from murder to manslaughter.

After a trial extending over two days, the jury returned a verdict of guilty in the case of both accused, with a recommendation for leniency in the case of Viggars. Hollis, who had a previous conviction for a similar offence, was sentenced to seven years' hard labour, and Viggars was sentenced to 18 months' hard labour.

ଓଃ

Police kept known abortionists under surveillance, but they needed cooperative witnesses in order to bring a case to a successful conclusion. The following case involved Mrs Clark, who was already under suspicion as the accomplice of Mrs Towler in the Dunedin Arcade.

Jessie's story[6]
Deceased 5 December 1927, aged 19 years

Miss Jessie Smart, a strong, healthy young woman, lived with her parents in South Oamaru and worked at the Oamaru Woollen Mills. Her father was a labourer. Mrs Jane Thorpe, a widow, also worked at the Oamaru Woollen Mills. In October Jessie confided in Mrs Thorpe, and asked if she could do anything about her unwanted pregnancy. According to Mrs Thorpe, Jessie did not want to go away and have the baby in a home, and threatened to commit suicide rather than have the baby.

Mrs Thorpe said she knew of a woman, Mrs Clark, in Dunedin who could 'fix her up'. On Tuesday night, 22 November, Mrs Thorpe rang Mrs Clark from the Post Office. She had rung her before and met her on two previous missions for the same purpose, and Mrs Clark had visited Mrs Thorpe in Oamaru in August. Mrs Thorpe said she was bringing someone down on Saturday, and the two women had an understanding about what it was for. Mr Jack Chilcott, a single man who was a confectioner in Oamaru, knew Mrs Thorpe and had given her £24 for Jessie's operation. He had known Jessie for about two months prior to her death and admitted to having had intercourse with Jessie, but said it was no more than twice.

On Saturday 26 November, Jessie left home, saying she was going to Ngapara for the weekend with Mrs Thorpe, and if she was not home on Monday not to worry. Mrs Thorpe accompanied Jessie down to Dunedin on the 1.25 pm express train. On arriving in Dunedin, they booked in at the Leviathan Hotel in their own names. After tea, Mrs Thorpe phoned Mrs Clark and arranged for Jessie to meet her on Sunday 27 November, at 7.30 pm. As arranged, they went to Mrs Clark's residence at 85 MacLaggan Street. Mrs Clark took Jessie into the bedroom, and about ten minutes later came out onto the verandah. Mrs Thorpe asked Jessie how she felt and she said, 'All right'. Mrs Clark said in a lighthearted way, 'She will be all right', but she also said the girl was very hard to do. Mrs Thorpe asked her how much the job would cost and was told '£10 will do.' Mrs Thorpe paid her in notes.

Jessie and Mrs Thorpe returned to the Leviathan Hotel, and early the following morning, Monday 28 November, at 3 am they returned to Oamaru with the rural delivery service van. On the road trip, they had to stop twice because Jessie needed to get out and vomit. Both women went to work that morning. Jessie went home for lunch with Mrs Thorpe, but did not go back to work in the afternoon, as she felt unwell. When Mrs Thorpe came back from work, Jessie was in bed. She stayed at Mrs Thorpe's place for a few days. On Tuesday afternoon, 29 November, when Mrs Thorpe came home from work she asked Jessie how things were and she replied everything had come away and she had destroyed it. Mrs Thorpe understood this to mean she had had a miscarriage and burnt the evidence, as she had been sitting by the fire during the afternoon.

Jessie returned to her parents' home on Thursday 1 December, very ill with a high temperature. Dr Orbell was called in that day, and he came again on Friday and admitted her to hospital. He suspected Jessie had had an abortion, and upon questioning, Jessie admitted she had. Jessie then told her mother about the trip to Dunedin. Her mother went to the hospital on Saturday night, 3 December, and never left her side.

On Friday 2 December, Dr Orbell saw Jessie at the hospital, together with Dr Fitzgerald, who was in charge of the women's surgical ward at Oamaru Public Hospital. On examination, the whole of the abdomen was acutely tender, with all the signs and symptoms of acute peritonitis. Jessie told Dr Fitzgerald what had taken place. She said the lady who had operated on her had had some difficulty finding the opening of the womb, but when she did find it, she pushed an instrument in. She said the instrument was a long black tube about the thickness of a pencil, about a foot long and flexible, and able to be bent up at the end. To keep it in place, a firm pad was placed over her private parts. She was told she could go to work. The instructions were to remove the catheter when bleeding commenced. The bleeding commenced on Monday, and that evening she took out the instrument and burnt it. On Tuesday, something came away and there was some more bleeding. When asked who had done the operation, Jessie said she would rather not tell.

Jessie was seriously ill, and the doctors agreed an operation should be performed that night. On Saturday 3 December, Jessie needed morphine to relieve the pain. In the late afternoon, she became much worse and collapsed. A saline solution was given intravenously and Dr Orbell and Dr Fitzgerald reviewed her treatment at 8 pm. Because her condition had not improved, the doctors decided to operate again, this time opening the abdomen; but the case was a hopeless one. They explained to her she was desperately ill and might not recover, and asked if she would make a statement. She said she would make a statement before the Senior Sergeant of Police, and Dr Fitzgerald telephoned him. Her mind was perfectly clear. She stated she had told her mother the name of the woman who passed the instrument. Her condition worsened the next day, and although she was conscious in the morning, she passed away about 8 pm on 5 December.

A post-mortem confirmed the operative findings of advanced sepsis affecting all organs. No perforation was found. The coroner, acting alone, confirmed the medical evidence that the cause of death was 'acute suppurative peritonitis caused by the illegal use of some instrument to bring about a miscarriage.'

Trial of Mrs Mary Jane Clark, 1928

Police laid charges against Mrs Clark, despite finding no incriminating items when they searched her house. She was accused of committing an unlawful act and thereby causing the death of a young woman on or about 27 November 1927, and charged with using and supplying an instrument for an unlawful purpose. Her defence counsel was Mr Hanlon. Mrs Clark first appeared in the Magistrate's Court in Oamaru, and the court was cleared for the hearing of evidence. She was described as a short, stout, middle-aged woman, neatly dressed.

She was committed for trial in the Oamaru Supreme Court on 6 March, before His Honour Sir William Sim. The defence emphasised the danger of relying on the evidence of accomplices who had been granted immunity, when there was no corroboration of their evidence. The judge pointed out that if she was convicted at all, it should be on the charge of manslaughter, because he doubted there was sufficient evidence to support the other two charges. He then repeated the warning about convicting on the uncorroborated evidence of an accomplice. The jury retired at 3 pm and returned at 3.22 pm with a verdict of not guilty.

Trial of Mrs Mary Jane Clark, 1929[7]

On the morning of 14 February, a healthy newborn baby girl, 16 days old, was found near the gateway of Mrs Clark's home. Police soon traced the mother of the infant: Miss Pearl Hislop, 20, the daughter of highly respected parents. She had recently given birth in the Salvation Army's Redroofs Maternity Hospital. She left one evening at 8.30 pm, saying she was going to visit friends, but after depositing the baby she stayed with an aunt and returned the next day to her home in Balclutha. She was found guilty of abandoning her infant and ordered to be detained in the Salvation Army home for a period of 12 months.

This prompted the police to bring charges in the Magistrate's Court against Mrs Clark, who was again defended by Mr Hanlon. Miss Hislop testified that she and her partner, Sydney Smith, had visited Mrs Clark in September 1928 and paid her £10 to procure a miscarriage, which was obviously not successful.

The other Crown witnesses were Miss Myrtle Duncan, a slightly built young woman, and her widowed mother, Mrs Jane Duncan. They had visited Mrs Clark six or seven months ago to arrange an abortion. However, the daughter was unable to identify the accused as the woman who had a week later visited her home to carry out the alleged offence, and her mother was a hostile witness. The police were criticised for their handling of the cases and their methods of obtaining evidence. Miss Duncan maintained that she had miscarried after falling off the verandah.

The case concerning Miss Duncan was weak and did not proceed to the Supreme Court, but the case concerning Miss Hislop did. In March 1929 in the Dunedin Supreme Court, presided over by Justice Smith, the jury was out for only 20 minutes before returning a not guilty verdict. Spectators in court cheered at the jury's decision and a cry of 'Hurray' disturbed the solemnity of the occasion.

This is the same Mrs Clark who later featured in the 1936 case of Mora MacKenzie, which triggered the Inquiry into Abortion.

The public followed sensational and gruesome cases with great interest.

Gwen's story[8]
Deceased 15 June 1927, aged 20 years

Ellen Gwendoline Isobel Scarff, known as Gwen, was brutally murdered, suffering numerous blows to the head with a spanner and being left to die in the bushes by the roadside at Burwood, Christchurch. She worked as a domestic in the home of Mr and Mrs Wood, Cashmere, Christchurch.

Charles William Boakes, 37, taxi driver, was charged with unlawfully supplying a noxious thing to Gwen on 16 May 1927, and with murdering her in Burwood on or about 15 June 1927.

In the Christchurch Supreme Court trial, presided over by Justice Adams, the Crown called no fewer than 60 witnesses. However, the Crown's case was weak, the defence was robust and it took the jury only 45 minutes to find Boakes not guilty of murder. The lesser charge of unlawfully supplying a noxious thing was abandoned. The mystery of who killed Gwen was never solved.

൞

This loving father would never forget the loss of his daughter.

Millie's story[9]
Deceased 26 July 1929, aged 23 years

Miss Amelia Pipe, known as Millie, enjoyed good health and kept house for her father, a miner in Waihi. On Monday 17 June, she left home for a holiday with her two sisters in Auckland, and her father paid her fare. On the first night, she stayed with her younger single sister, Kathleen, a domestic servant in a private home, and the following day she went to stay with her married sister, Mrs Skinner, at St Heliers.

In June, she wrote to a friend in Auckland, Mrs Doris Jarvis, who had previously lived in Waihi but was now living in Otahuhu with her husband and three children. Millie confided in her about her unplanned pregnancy and asked for her help to get an abortion. Mrs Jarvis contacted Mrs Adeline Pyle, a middle-aged widow who lived at 274 Ponsonby Rd, also known as Castlecliff Flats, and made arrangements for her to see Millie. On the first

THE BURWOOD MURDER.
The accused, Charles William Boakes, arriving at the Christchurch Magistrate's Court to answer a charge of murdering Miss Ellen Gwendoline Scarff on June 15. Detective-Sergeant Young is alongside the accused, and Detective Bickerdike is in the rear.

Top left: Eric Mugford, the 15-year-od boy who discovered Gwen Scarff's body (*NZ Truth*, 23 June 1927). Top right: Ellen Gwendoline Isobel Scarff, murdered 15 June 1927 (*NZ Truth*, 30 June 1927). Bottom left: Charles William Boakes, charged with the murder of Gwen Scarff (*New Zealand Herald*, 1 August 1927).

occasion, she went with Millie to see Mrs Pyle and loaned her £5.

On Wednesday 26 June, Kathleen also went with Millie to the Castlecliff Flats, but did not go in with her. That night they went to the pictures together, and on Friday 28 June, Millie returned home to Waihi. Her father said that on her return she was not well. Dr Short paid a house call on Monday 8 July, and again a week later. Millie was now febrile and vomiting and Dr Short diagnosed gastric influenza. When he visited again on Wednesday 17 July, he arranged for her admission to Waihi Hospital the following day.

Her condition worsened and the possibility of a miscarriage was raised for the first time. She was jaundiced, in pain, had difficulty breathing and was still vomiting. On 24 July, Millie made a statement for the Waihi police and a Justice of the Peace, but she did not disclose who her lover was, nor did she make any accusation against Mrs Pyle. Doctors said she had no hope of recovering, and she closed her statement with the words 'I make the above statement with the fear of death before me and with no hope of recovery.' She died in the early morning on 26 July.

At post-mortem, her whole body was stained a deep yellow due to the jaundice. Her uterus was enlarged and contained some decomposing products of a recent pregnancy of two to three months' duration. Abscesses were present in the pelvis and throughout both lungs. The post-mortem findings themselves gave no definite clue as to the cause of the miscarriage, but according to the pathologist, the clinical course of her illness made it practically certain it was not due to natural causes. The coroner, acting alone, confirmed the medical evidence and found (in a very restrained verdict) that 'death was due to septicaemia the result of a septic miscarriage.'

Crucial evidence from Millie's father led to Auckland police questioning Mrs Pyle and searching her premises. The flat comprised a bedroom and kitchenette. Mrs Pyle at first denied all knowledge of Millie, but police found a letter from Millie in her possession, dated 10 July. Mrs Pyle's reply had been handed by Millie's father to the police in Waihi.

Millie's letter read,

> Dear Mrs Pyle, Just a line to let you know that everything is all right. I was ill nearly all night, and felt listless and tired but everything was successful. I had to have the

doctor in as I was suffering pain, and if he knew about the other he did not mention it. I burnt the article so no-one saw it. Millie Pipe.

The reply read,

> My dear Millie, You must think me a nice one for not answering your letter. I have been very busy on a case. I was very pleased to get your letter, but thank goodness you are all right. All you will have to do now is to look after yourself... Mrs Pyle.

Trial of Mrs Adeline Pyle, 1929[10]

On Monday 29 July, Mrs Pyle was arrested and charged with murder and procuring an abortion. She was committed for trial in the Auckland Supreme Court, presided over by Justice Herdman, and defended by Mr Singer. The case was extensively reported in the press. The judge acknowledged in his summing up that there was a fundamental weakness in the Crown case. After a retirement of ten minutes, the jury returned a verdict of not guilty.

Ten years later, Mrs Pyle was before the courts again.

Trial of Mrs Adeline Pyle, 1939[11]

Police alleged that Mrs Pyle, 56, had unlawfully used an instrument on a 19-year-old woman, Miss A. The offence was alleged to have occurred in Mrs Pyle's bedroom, at a home where she was employed as a housekeeper.

Miss A and a young labourer, Phillip Double, had been lovers for the last four or five months. When Miss A suspected a pregnancy, Double took her to Dr Carew to have the diagnosis confirmed. To arrange an abortion, Double asked a mutual friend, Miss X, if she would act as an intermediary. Miss X, who appeared to be knowledgeable in such matters, went to the Masonic dance hall, because she knew Mrs Pyle usually attended there on a Saturday night.

Following instructions from Mrs Pyle, the two young women went to a chemist shop and, while Miss A waited outside, Miss X went inside and purchased a catheter for three shillings. At an arranged time on Monday 22 May, the two young women went to Mrs Pyle's house and Mrs Pyle used the catheter on Miss A. Double paid Mrs Pyle £3. In a short while, Double met Miss A at the post office and took her home on his motorbike. Mrs Pyle asked Miss X to let her know how her client was next Saturday night at the dance hall. However, on Thursday 25 May, Miss A became ill, and Dr Warnock admitted her to hospital the following day. Her illness led to police enquiries.

Mrs Adeline Pyle (centre) covers her face as she leaves the Auckland Magistrate's Court charged with the manslaughter of Miss Amelia Pipe (*NZ Truth*, 29 August 1929). She was aquitted of this crime, but ten years later she was sentenced to three years' imprisonment with hard labour for another abortion-related death.

In the Magistrate's Court, Mrs Pyle pleaded not guilty and was committed for trial in the Auckland Supreme Court, presided over by Justice Ostler. The jury returned a guilty verdict. In sentencing Mrs Pyle, His Honour reminded her she had been tried on a charge of murder ten years ago, following the death of a young woman from blood poisoning. He said she could not expect leniency and sentenced her to three years' imprisonment with hard labour.

ଓ

In the brutal 1927 murder of Gwen Scarff in Christchurch, the mystery was never solved. Sensationally, in 1931 another brutal murder took place, in Wellington, but on this occasion the murderer hanged.

Phyllis's story[12]
Deceased 26 June 1931, aged 17 years

Phyllis Avis Symons was the fourth of six children, born in Napier on 8 December 1913 to Mary and George Symons. She attended various schools in Napier and Wellington, leaving school at the age of 14 in the fifth standard. She was described as quiet, a slow learner, but otherwise normal and healthy. The family shifted to Wellington in 1923 and lived in Mortimer Terrace, Brooklyn. After leaving school Phyllis stayed at home, unemployed except for a short spell housekeeping. Her brothers gave her a few shillings of pocket money each week and she occasionally asked others for a handout. Her father was a motor body builder. Her married sister, Myrtle, also lived in the family home. Phyllis and her mother did not get on well.

During 1930, relief workers toiled outside the home, and Mrs Symons would sometimes make tea for the men, or they would enter the house to make their own tea. As a result of this interaction, Phyllis met George Coats in August or September 1930. Over the next few months, the friendship became intimate and in February 1931, Phyllis knew she was pregnant. Coats gave her pills to induce an abortion, but the pregnancy continued.

George Errol Coats, 29, nicknamed 'Red Band', was a former ship's steward whose hobbies were mending clocks and watches and operating wireless sets. His wife died on Anzac Day 1930, and their six children were placed in Wellington orphanages. As a widower, he lived in rented rooms and had little contact with the children. Several male friends visited him regularly and played cards of an evening. For the past eight years he had worked for the Wellington City Council as a labourer, but during the Depression, jobs were scarce. He obtained relief work in Hataitai, working at the Ruahine Street tip from 27 April until 8 June, before being

Phyllis Avis Symons.
(*Evening Post*, 9 July 1931)

made redundant. Although no longer employed, he visited the relief works on several occasions during June. He thought of leaving Wellington, but missed out on a job with the Auckland fire brigade.

On 1 March 1931, Phyllis left home after an argument with her mother. She had not told anyone in the family about her pregnancy. Soon after leaving, she wrote to her mother, saying she was staying with friends and doing well. Except on one occasion, when she spoke to a younger sister near the Terrace School, the family had no further communication with her.

Having nowhere else to go, she stayed with Coats in the room he rented in Abel Smith Street, but he was unemployed and had to shift to find cheaper accommodation. They stayed briefly in places in Kent Terrace and Brougham Street, then rented rooms at 140 Adelaide Road, living there from 22 April to 29 June, when Coats was evicted for non-payment of rent. To the friends who visited and to the landladies of the various residences, Phyllis was known as 'Mrs Coats'. From 29 June to 6 July, Coats, now alone, rented a room in another place in Adelaide Road.

When Coats's sister Evie came from Auckland on 14 April to stay in Wellington for three weeks, she was a frequent visitor. During her stay, she found out about the pregnancy and gave her brother some advice about how to get rid of it. She even purchased a glass syringe, also used for washing out ears. She instructed her brother on how to use it, however, this attempt at abortion was as ineffective as the pills. The pregnant Phyllis was last seen alive on 26 June.

When Phyllis disappeared, Coats concocted different stories to explain her absence. After an incriminating letter was found at his residence, police became involved, and on 7 July they published a notice in the *Evening Post* seeking information on the missing girl. She was described as 5ft 2in in height, of pale complexion, with fair hair cut short and a prominent nose. The same day, in the Magistrate's Court, Coats was remanded in custody until 16 July on charges relating to alleged attempts to procure abortion. However, on 12 July, 16 days after she went missing, Phyllis's body was found. The abortion charges were dropped and Coats was charged with her murder.

When the Mount Victoria road tunnel was constructed, truckloads of spoil and rubble were dumped a short distance away on the Kilbirnie Town Belt to fill in a gully and create a new recreation ground. It was here that police, acting on information from witnesses, unearthed Phyllis's body, no mean feat considering the massive effort to shift 2,000 tons of soggy clay in wet, wintry conditions. The body was fully clothed and covered with a sack. Dr Lynch, Wellington Hospital pathologist, inspected the body at the site before police shifted it to the morgue for the inquest into her death. The coroner adjourned the inquest until the conclusion of the court case.

Trial of George Errol Coats, 1931

Over 30 witnesses gave evidence in the preliminary proceedings in the Magistrate's Court from 12 to 17 August, and crowds attended the hearings – likewise at the Supreme Court trial, which commenced on 2 November, before Justice Blair. The Crown's case was that the motive for the crime was to eliminate Phyllis's unwanted pregnancy when attempts at abortion failed. The murder was premeditated. In April, a dog had been run over in Moxham Avenue, Hataitai, and a chemist's son had put the dog in a sack and taken it to the relief works, where he asked one of the workers to bury it. The Crown would produce evidence that linked this event to Coats's alleged actions. Critical evidence to support the Crown's case was elicited from three of Coats's male friends.

Arthur de Maine, waiter and tobacconist's assistant, had known Coats since 1918, and when de Maine returned to Wellington in April 1931 after a prolonged absence, he renewed his acquaintance. He was also very friendly with Coats's sister Evie. He testified about the unwanted pregnancy and an assault on Phyllis, but evaded answering some questions to protect his friend. The Crown regarded him as a hostile witness. De Maine

George Errol Coats (centre front) leaving the Wellington Magistrate's Court charged with the murder of Phyllis Symons. (*Auckland Star*, 17 July 1931)

The Hataitai soil dump where Phyllis's body was found. (*Auckland Star*, 12 November 1931)

was with Coats on 25 June, when Coats said he was going to see a relief workmate about leaving a shovel so he could bury a dog, although he never owned a dog. On the night of 26 June, at 9 pm, Coats visited him alone at the tobacconist's shop in Newtown and told him Phyllis had gone home to her parents.

John Glover, 16, a machinist, was also a frequent visitor, and teased Phyllis about her pregnancy. He testified that Coats wanted to get rid of the pregnancy, and described an occasion one evening when Coats had used an instrument on Phyllis. He also said Coats boasted about wielding a piece of pipe over the back of her neck and knocking her unconscious. He said Coats talked about burying her at the fill, where no one would find her under all the earth. Several days after she went missing, Glover found a letter from Phyllis addressed to her parents. The envelope was tucked under a mattress in the room she had shared with Coats. Glover thought she had gone home, so he was unsure what to do with the letter. Instead of destroying it, he decided to show it to another of Coats's friends, Allan Melville, a taxi driver. Melville read the letter and they discussed the contents. Melville handed the letter back, but decided to go and see Phyllis's father; he then took Mr Symons to meet Glover, and the letter became a significant police exhibit.

The letter, in Phyllis's handwriting, read:

> Dearest Dad, I feel I cannot go on like this. Something has happened to me very dreadful, which makes existence for me a hell. In short, in a very few months' time, I am to be a mother. Many times have I wanted to end all my pain and misery by suicide, but I cannot bring myself to do it. It seems so dreadful. I know what you must think of me, but, Dad, I am innocent. In my hunt for good times, but with the desire to keep decent, I have fallen. I have suffered, am still suffering. Every hour is torture. I have very little to eat. My clothing is in rags, so I am afraid to go outside the door.
>
> I had a job housekeeping for some time, but the people left Wellington, and I was unable to pay my rent of 10/6 weekly and may at any time be put out. The father of my coming child is George Coats, whom Mum so disliked. With your consent we could be married but Mr Coats is out of work, but does his best to keep me in food. You could never imagine how terrible life is. If only I could be back home, receiving the weekly letter from Jack, have the comfortable bed at night and the good food, and have the work to do – how lovely it sounds. But that is not to be.

> Dad, Mum – try to forgive me. Give your consent, so I can marry, and I will never come near you, as I know you could never understand. Maybe, you'd feel sorry for me if you could be a witness to my misery day after day, night after night. I think I shall go mad very soon if things go on much longer as they are at present. I think I shall close now, and please forgive me. I remain, yours sincerely, – Phyllis.

Several workmates from the Hataitai works also gave evidence in the court hearings. One recalled how Coats used a shovel to dig a hole in a bank over four days. The hole was positioned so a load of fill from above would cover it. When asked why he was digging the hole, Coats said, disingenuously, that it was for shelter. Workers recalled a conversation about burying a dog and, at Coats's request, left two shovels under the truck instead of putting them away in the shed. Workers recalled seeing Coats again at the site at about 4.40 pm on 26 June.

On the night of 26 June, Mrs Olive Smith, landlady at 140 Adelaide Road, heard the couple go out at about 8 pm, and heard footsteps returning after 10.30 pm. The next day, Coats told her his 'wife' had gone home. She testified that the vegetable sack used to cover Phyllis was from her shed.

Dr Lynch, for the Crown, supported by Dr Hector, submitted that Phyllis received blows to the temple and the back of the head from a blunt instrument, such as a piece of pipe. Bruising was present on the left arm. Dr Lynch refuted the explanation of the three medical witnesses for the defence that she could have fallen from a height and hit her head on a stone. The immediate cause of death was asphyxia due to stomach contents being inhaled. Her head and face were covered by a scarf tied around her head two or three times. Dr Lynch said the scarf may have been used to stifle the stertorous sounds of breathing as Phyllis lay unconscious. The hunched position of her body indicated she may have been buried while still alive and tried to escape suffocation. Soil had been shovelled over her body to conceal it.

An unusual feature of the Supreme Court trial was the decision of the defence team, led by Mr Treadwell, to put Coats in the witness box. Coats's version of events was that Phyllis had committed suicide and, panic stricken, he had buried her.

On 11 November, after a trial lasting nine days, the jury deliberated for only three hours before returning a guilty verdict. Applause from the women's gallery upstairs was quickly suppressed. Justice Blair, visibly moved, donned the black cap and sentenced Coats to death by hanging. Coats remained calm, as he had been throughout the trial. When asked if he had anything to say, he declared in a firm, clear voice, 'I am innocent and I think the prejudice proved too strong – that's all.' The Court Crier then proclaimed 'Oyez! Oyez! Oyez! All manner of persons are commanded to keep silence while the judgment of death is pronounced by the Court on the prisoner at the Bar on pain of fine or imprisonment.' Silence prevailed.

Coats's defence lawyers had five days to lodge an appeal, and did so on two questions of law regarding the manner in which the police interrogated Coats, and the direction of the judge to the jury. On 4 December, the Court of Appeal, comprising Chief Justice Sir Michael Myers and three learned judges, considered the appeal and unanimously confirmed the conviction. With the assent of the Governor-General, Lord Bledisloe, the execution took place on 17 December, the first to be carried out at Mount Crawford Prison and the first in Wellington since Daniel Richard Cooper was hanged at the old Terrace Gaol in 1923.

The Mount Victoria tunnel was opened on 12 October 1931, and it is a Wellington legend that motorists toot in memory of the murdered teenager.

ಇಾ

Police were unable to assist in the following story.

Gladys's story[13]
Deceased 10 August 1932, aged 30 years

Mrs Gladys Sowman lived with her husband Archibald in Kaikohe. They had four children: eight-year-old twins, a four-year-old and a two-year-old. Mr Sowman was a stock agent for the North Auckland Farmers Co-op. Gladys left home about a fortnight before her death to go to Whangarei, ostensibly to do some shopping. She said she would be staying at the James Hotel.

She ended up staying with Mrs Beryl McGregor, also known as 'Mrs Jones', and needing medical attention. Dr Costello was called to see her at Mrs Jones's house on 26 July. He found her suffering from peritonitis, and suspected interference, although this was strongly denied. He sent her as an urgent admission to the Whangarei Hospital.

Gladys told the doctors that prior to leaving Whangarei, she had given herself an injection of Camfosa disinfectant, but this was not consistent with the medical findings. When her husband visited her in Whangarei Hospital on 6 August, her life was not in danger, but she did not respond to treatment and died a fortnight after admission.

At the inquest into her death, Mr Sowman claimed he knew of his wife's pregnancy but nothing about Mrs Jones or having an abortion. The coroner found, according to the medical evidence, that Gladys had 'died from heart failure resulting from septic abortion.' No charges were laid, but a father was left with four young children to bring up without their mother.

೧೩

Differences between the findings of the Coroner's Court and the criminal court are highlighted in the following case, with accomplices beyond the reach of the law.

Ruth's story[14]
Deceased 1 July 1934, aged 18 years

Ruth Hitchings, 18, an only child, lived in Wellington with her mother. The vivacious office worker was fond of skating at the Glide Skating Rink. She was having an affair with the proprietor of the skating rink, John Tubert, a naturalised British subject of Russian birth, who was married, with two sons.

On 17 May, Ruth's mother found some abortifacient medicine her daughter was taking and put two and two together. She discussed the pregnancy with her daughter. Tubert had provided Ruth with the pills to induce a miscarriage, but they did not work. The day after the discovery of the pills, Tubert came to the house and met Ruth's mother. He made arrangements for Ruth to have an abortion with Mrs Nicholson (also known as 'Mrs Naylor') at her home in Island Bay. He also arranged for another young woman, May Metcalf, to look after Ruth and accompany her to Mrs Nicholson's place. The two young women (who had previously only met casually on the skating rink) made three visits on 8, 10 and 12 June; a catheter was used on Ruth at each visit. Tubert then paid for Ruth to have one week's trained nursing care in Nurse de Burren's home at Lyall Bay. The miscarriage occurred on 16 June and a doctor attended her, also paid for by Tubert. Ruth seemed well on discharge, but when she returned home on

19 June she became ill, and Dr Kemp admitted her to Brougham Street private hospital on 20 June. Initially she improved, but then her condition deteriorated and she died on 1 July.

The post-mortem found generalised peritonitis and sepsis. An injury to the womb caused internal bleeding and the abdominal cavity contained dark, altered blood and pus. In the opinion of Dr Lynch, the pathologist, the penetrating injuries were most likely produced by the unskilful use of a rigid or semi-rigid instrument. At the coroner's inquest the full facts of the case were not revealed and, despite the evidence from the pathologist, the verdict was simply (and rather inadequately) that she 'died from general peritonitis following uterine sepsis.'

However, the police did not let the matter rest there. Further enquiries implicated Mrs Nicholson, 62, a known abortionist who had been under police surveillance for at least ten years. Police arrested her and charged her with manslaughter and performing an illegal act to procure abortion. When police searched her house, they found it in a filthy state. They confiscated catheters, medical books and other articles as criminal evidence. Mrs Nicholson pleaded not guilty in the Magistrate's Court, and was committed to the Wellington Supreme Court for trial.

At the Supreme Court hearing to decide whether this was a true bill, Justice Ostler briefed the grand jury. He said that this was a case of manslaughter. It seemed to His Honour that, as Tubert had seduced the girl, and then paid the money to obtain an abortion, the grand jury should consider whether justice demanded Tubert also be prosecuted. Returning a true bill, the grand jury recommended that Tubert also be charged with being a party to the offence. His Honour said he would see that their recommendation reached the proper

Justice Ostler.
(*NZ Truth*, 7 March 1925)

quarter; however, there was much debate about Tubert's status as an accomplice, and whether he should be granted immunity for assisting the Crown's case against Mrs Nicholson. In the end, Tubert was not charged, and nor was the other accomplice, May Metcalf, whose evidence was critical in establishing the guilt of Mrs Nicholson.

At the Supreme Court trial in November, presided over by Chief Justice Sir Michael Myers, the jury deliberated for 55 minutes and returned a verdict of guilty. Mrs Nicholson was sentenced to five years' imprisonment with hard labour.

ଓ

No-one was held accountable for Mabel's death, but it was a burden two men would have on their conscience for the rest of their lives.

Mabel's story[15]
Deceased 14 January 1937, aged 22 years

Mabel Harding had been married to Lawrence for four years, and they had two young children. Lawrence was a cook by occupation, although work was not constant, and at the time of Mabel's death, he was unemployed. They lived in Timaru. Mabel's parents lived nearby, and Mabel and her mother saw each other practically daily. Mabel was pregnant again and they could not afford another child.

Early in December, Lawrence visited Mr Dewar, jeweller, in his Canon Street shop to ask if he would perform an operation. He said he could and his fee was £5. Lawrence could only give him £3 on account. Dewar gave Lawrence a catheter to take home, with instructions for Mabel to sterilise it. Two or three nights later, he called at the Hardings' home after the children had gone to bed and went into Mabel's bedroom. After a few minutes, he came into the kitchen and Lawrence saw him wash the catheter under the tap. He then returned to the bedroom and this time left the catheter inside Mabel's womb. No miscarriage occurred. Lawrence told Dewar the operation was not a success, and Dewar said he would do it again. He came again at night to the house, about a week after the first attempt. He used the same catheter as before. Mabel had kept it in her top drawer when it had come away. This time Dewar felt sure it was a success, because flooding occurred. Again, the catheter was left in place in Mabel's womb.

No miscarriage occurred. Lawrence went again to Dewar, who was most surprised, saying this had never happened to him before but he would come again. The third operation was performed on New Year's Eve and Lawrence paid Dewar £2. The catheter was left in as before, but it came away of its own accord later that night. Still no miscarriage occurred.

Arrangements were made for a fourth operation on 11 January, but Dewar did not turn up. Nor did he turn up on 12 January, so arrangements were made for him to come again on the night of 13 January. This time, when Dewar turned up, Mabel's parents were visiting and Lawrence had to signal to Dewar that he should not come into the house. By now Mabel was about five months pregnant. The following night, 14 January, Dewar came around and again used the catheter. He came into the kitchen and rinsed the catheter under the tap and then returned to the bedroom. Two minutes later Lawrence heard Mabel groaning and he went as far as the bedroom door. Dewar came out, saying Mabel had fainted. Lawrence went back into the bedroom and found Mabel lying on the bed with her head to one side. The two men tried to revive her with brandy and a cold sponging of the face, but she was already lifeless.

Lawrence went for a doctor, despite protestations from Dewar that this was not necessary. Dewar drank the brandy that had been poured for Mabel's resuscitation. Dr King arrived at 9.05 pm on the evening of 14 January and certified Mabel dead. He also conducted the post-mortem. At the inquest, he informed the coroner about the use of catheters that were sometimes reinforced with a piece of steel wire to provide the rigidity necessary to enter the womb. At the inquest, three pieces of wire were presented as exhibits, as well as two catheters.

The post-mortem showed a five-month-old fetus intact within an unruptured sac. The placenta, however, had been disrupted, and there was bleeding into the uterus and vagina. Air had entered the large veins at the placental site, and all the veins passing from the uterus were blown out with air. Dr Pearson, pathologist at Christchurch Hospital, confirmed the findings of Dr King. In accordance with the medical evidence, the coroner, acting alone, found death 'was due to heart failure due to severe air embolism following an attempt to procure abortion when air was allowed to enter the large uterine veins.' If Mabel had not died of air embolism, she would have surely have developed an infection, such was the ignorance regarding sterility.

Trial of Clement Lyall Dewar, 1937

Police arrested Clement Dewar, 42, jeweller of Timaru, at his shop in February 1937 and charged him with the manslaughter of Mabel Harding and the illegal use of an instrument on several occasions to procure miscarriage. There were five charges in all. When police searched his premises, they found steel wires, used to strengthen the catheter.

Between Dewar's arrest and his appearance in the Magistrate's Court, Lawrence Harding said he had had conversations with Dewar between 2 and 18 February, in which Dewar offered to pay him £50 if he made a statement to the police clearing him of the charge of having performed an illegal operation on Mabel. Dewar said Harding was as guilty as he was. Solicitors were consulted, and Harding signed the statement, but later in court he testified against Dewar.

Dewar was remanded on bail to appear in the Timaru Supreme Court. At the first and second trials, the jury could not agree on all five counts. The Supreme Court registrar received advice from the Solicitor-General to enter a stay in the proceedings. There would be no third trial. With this result the coroner concluded the inquest.

଼

All eleven stories in this chapter are a testament to how women risked their lives in the hands of unqualified operators: Aggie Campbell, dying in the arms of her lover; Ethel Bradley, accidentally poisoned by prussic acid; Olive Pile, dead at the hands of Mrs Glegg; Rita Nicoll, butchered by Hollis; Jessie Smart, fatally operated upon by the notorious Mrs Clark; Gwen Scarff, brutally murdered; Millie Pipe, who left a grieving father; Phyllis Symons, buried alive; Gladys Sowman, mother of four; Ruth Hitchings, who skated on thin ice; and Mabel Harding, killed by an incompetent jeweller.

10. DIY ABORTION

Apart from unusual cases, self-abortion went largely undetected. Women often turned to self-help measures before resorting to other means. The great ingenuity of the methods used reflected both their resolute motivation, and their intense desperation. Self-abortion, an intensely personal matter, was shared with only the most reliable of confidantes. In the public sphere, although self-abortion was (and still is) a crime, it has never been a priority for police, prosecutors or the judiciary. When something untoward happened and a woman died, self-abortion was often one of the possible explanations, but in many cases, it was impossible to tell whether the abortion had been induced by the woman herself or some other person. Women often lied to protect themselves or others.

A woman with an unwanted pregnancy usually started with non-noxious methods, such as excessive or strenuous exercise, jumping up and down, or skipping. Falling from a height was common; any elevated surface around the home would do. Falling down stairs still has an undeserved reputation as a cause of miscarriage. Women often attributed a miscarriage to heavy work, such as carrying heavy tubs of washing. Deep pelvic massage may have been tried. Hot baths and mustard baths were often combined with the taking of gin or Epsom salts. There was no shortage of folk remedies. Half a bottle of gin in a hot bath to drown away the sorrows was a familiar, if unrewarding, instruction.

Home remedies included herbal and plant extracts, such as parsley tea, a source of apiol; tansy, growing wild in many gardens; and cultivated flowering plants, such as the winter rose (*Hellebore*) and Queen Anne's lace (wild carrot). Traditional Māori medicines included concoctions made from mahoe (whitewood) berries, toetoe leaves and flax roots. Some women tried metallic poisons, like mercury, which had the disadvantage that the effective dose was close to the lethal dose. Phosphorus was also commonly used, as it could be found in ordinary household items such as match heads and some rat poisons.

If none of these home remedies worked, chemists had a variety of pills and mixtures on offer.

Laxatives such as castor oil, pennyroyal oil, juniper oil or Beecham's Pills were often tried on the not very credible assumption that activity in the bowel might induce activity in the uterus. Pennyroyal, oil of savin, ergot and quinine were recognised as emmenagogues (an old-fashioned term for drugs used to induce menstruation). These would often be combined in pills or mixtures. Combinations of ergot and apiol were very popular in New Zealand. Recipes often changed. Dr Bonjean's Pills originally contained ergot, ferrous sulphate, aloes and apiol, while in later preparations the apiol was replaced with *Hellebore* and oil of savin. The popular Beecham's Pills kept that name while changing the ingredients over the years. In the 19th century they were advertised widely to regulate menstruation, but in the 20th century they were promoted as a laxative to regulate the bowels.

Chemists were also a source at the next level of intervention. Pills very often failed, and syringes, enemas, catheters and seatangle tents could be used by the woman herself, or administered by another.

Public opinion has generally not supported the harassment or punishment of women suspected of self-abortion, even when they pleaded guilty, as in the following story.

Trial of Miss Florence Williams and Mr Gifford Bowern, 1915[1]

Florence Williams, 23, found herself pregnant to Gifford Bowern, 25, a tally clerk on the wharf. In September 1914, he supplied her with pills, and when these did not work he supplied her with more, which she refused to take, as they made her sick. At the instigation of Bowern, Florence then wrote to a nurse friend, Mrs Mary Reid, explaining the situation and seeking help. Mrs Reid was unable to do anything and advised Bowern to marry Florence. Florence then took court proceedings for pre-maternity costs but Bowern refused to pay. He was bound over not to leave the country.

Unfortunately, another person picked up the letter to Nurse Reid, and when the police arrested the letter bearer for drunken behaviour, they read the letter and acted upon it. Florence was charged in the Auckland Magistrate's Court with having attempted to procure a miscarriage by taking a noxious thing. She was committed to the Auckland Supreme Court for trial. Anticipating a lenient approach by the judge, her lawyer advised her to plead guilty.

At the Supreme Court hearing, Justice Stringer was indeed lenient. He said it seemed to him that the girl before him was more sinned against than sinning, and he did not propose to pass any sentence. He ordered Florence to come up for sentence when called on, and explained to her what the consequences of another appearance would mean. Ordering her release, His Honour added, 'Go and sin no more.'

Bowern, represented by Mr Singer, faced two charges. Regarding the first, he was guilty of ignoring a court order to pay the expenses incurred when, on 5 January, Florence had a miscarriage, a natural event, according to the doctor who attended her. Bowern was sentenced to 14 days' imprisonment, suspended if he paid the pre-maternity costs at £1.5s each week. Regarding the second, he pleaded not guilty to counselling a young woman to take a noxious thing. In the Auckland Supreme Court, presided over by Justice Hosking, the jury could not agree and a retrial was ordered. This time he was found guilty.

However, His Honour said there was no evidence the woman had actually submitted to any treatment, and the question arose as to whether any offence was disclosed. He referred the case to the Court of Appeal, and in July it was considered by the Chief

---

Bowern Bows to the "Beak."

And is not Considering Himself Lucky

The young man, Gifford Bowern, who was some weeks ago committed to stand his trial at the Supreme Court on a charge of causing a young woman to take a noxious thing, to wit, pills, was before Mr. E. Page, S.M., at the Auckland Magistrate's Court on Tuesday to explain why he had ignored an order of the "Coort" to pay the expenses incurred when the girl had a miscarriage.

Mr. Page: Why have you not paid the amount?

Bowern: I have not been in a position to do so. I am out on bail now. An offer of £1 a week was made to Mr. Moody (solicitor for the girl), but he would not listen to it.

MR. MOODY SEEMED DETERMINED

to bring me before the Court again.

Lawyer Hackett (a partner of Moody's): This is a case of suing for birth expenses. Evidently he does not deem himself sufficiently lucky.

Mr. Page: What work do you do?—I am a driver.

What do you earn?—£2 8s a week. I made an offer to pay £1 a week, but this was not accepted.

Mr. Page: I will convict and sentence you to 14 days, but will suspend the warrant so long as you pay £1 5s each week. The first payment to be made this day week.

Bowern: Thank you.

NZ *Truth*, 24 April 1915

Justice Sir Robert Stout and a panel of four learned judges. The Court of Appeal quashed the conviction, stating that no criminal act was proved to have resulted from Bowern having counselled the woman.

ଓ

The jury in the following case could have been more sympathetic.

Trial of Mrs Ellen Johnson, 1908[2]

Ellen Johnson was married to William, coach painter, and they had five children. When William neglected to pay maintenance, Ellen took proceedings against him. On 10 June 1908, the judge sentenced him to one month's imprisonment, the warrant to be suspended so long as he paid off the arrears at 15 shillings per week.

Not long after this, Ellen was charged in the Wellington Magistrate's Court with using an instrument on herself to procure abortion. Dr Fell testified that he attended Ellen for a miscarriage at her house in Vivian Street on 10 May. She had confided to him that she had used a crochet needle, and Dr Fell sent a district nurse to attend her. Mr Wilford, defending Ellen, argued that the doctor had breached patient confidentiality by giving private information to the court. A legal argument then ensued concerning the boundaries of the patient-doctor relationship.

Mr Wilford declared:[3]

> This poor woman, who was living in a state of wretchedness owing to the neglect of her husband who would not give her a penny, had five children, three under ten years of age. She had done a heavy day's work with her body badly nourished and unable to resist trouble, and a miscarriage started. She felt the most fearful pains, and knowing the nature of them, decided to do what she could to get relief. Tents, sold surreptitiously by chemists, at prices which depended on the appearance of the customer, were beyond her reach and she had done what she could with a substitute.

Two district nurses confirmed Ellen's desperate situation, but despite a robust defence, she was committed for trial in the Wellington Supreme Court, presided over by Justice Cooper, on

25 August. The jury, after a short retirement, returned a verdict of guilty, with a strong recommendation of mercy.

His Honour was indeed merciful and referred to a recent precedent where Justice Williams had not sent the woman to prison, nor granted probation. Ellen was convicted and ordered to come up for sentence when called upon. 'Prisoner,' concluded His Honour, 'I release you because your children require a mother's care.'

> **USE OF AN ILLEGAL INSTRUMENT.**
>
> WELLINGTON, June 10.
> At the Magistrates Court to-day, Ellen Johnson, a young married woman, was committed for trial on a charge of using an illegal instrument with intent.

Ashburton Guardian, 11 June 1908

In the following case, we do not know the details, but the gentlemen of two juries could not reach a unanimous verdict.

Trial of Ellen Thompson, 1909[4]

Ellen Thompson, 19, a laundress at Picton Hospital, was charged with self-administering a noxious drug with intent to procure abortion. In the Blenheim Supreme Court, Justice Denniston presided. The jury, after being locked up all day, was unable to agree upon a verdict. His Honour discharged the jury and a new trial took place the next morning. The second jury was also unable to arrive at a verdict, even after being sent back by the judge to deliberate further. At 4 pm the foreman announced that no verdict had been achieved. His Honour discharged the jury and no further trial was held. Justice Denniston concurred with the Crown Prosecutor: 'It is one of those cases about which the least said was soonest mended.'

◊

If an abortion case reached hospital with complications, police were more likely to investigate, much to Alice Platts's chagrin.

Trial of Miss Alice Platts and Anthony Joss, 1923[5]

In the Auckland Magistrate's Court, in September 1923, police charged Alice, 18, with unlawfully using an instrument on herself, and charged Anthony Joss, a well-known artist who conducted a school of sketching, with supplying her with an instrument.

Joseph O'Connor stated he had gone out with Alice over a period of seven weeks. About six weeks after Easter, Alice, accompanied by her father, called at O'Connor's place of business and informed him she was 'in trouble' and he should marry her.

Alice's version of events went as follows:

> I am single and 18 years old. I have been residing in a boarding house at Grafton Rd. About eight to ten weeks ago I found myself pregnant. I had been keeping company with Joseph O'Connor who is employed at Hobdays, New Zealand Insurance Building, Queen St, Auckland. I told O'Connor of my condition as soon as I discovered it and he promised to marry me almost immediately. I obtained my father's consent to be married but O'Connor did not keep his promise. I then decided to try and get a certain instrument and I asked a friend of mine named Anthony Joss who resides with his people in Windmill Rd, Mt Eden, if he could get me a catheter, telling him I wanted it for a girlfriend. Mr Joss gave me an instrument and I used it on myself and two days later a miscarriage took place. The miscarriage took place one Saturday night in the middle of May. I got up the following day but I have been ailing since. I have since been operated on and my appendix removed.

Joss's version of events went as follows:

> I am the principal of the Joss School of Art. I am a married man, living apart from my wife and reside with my parents at No 6 Windmill Rd, Mt Eden. I have known Miss Platts for the past two years. She came to see me in April last at my then place of residence, 466 Queen St. She told me she was going to be married to a man whose Christian name was Joe. I knew she was in trouble and later she told me her intended husband had slipped her up and she was not married. She told me she was about two months pregnant. On May 5 or 12 she rang me up and asked if I had a certain instrument as she knew I had a box of medical instruments at home which I had released from a pawnshop on behalf of a friend in Wellington named Bernard C. Ryder. I met Miss Platts in the city and gave her the instrument. When

I gave it to her she said she wanted it for a cousin, but I knew she was pregnant as she had told me she was. I did not ask her any questions when I gave her the instrument since I had my own suspicions as to why she wanted it. I do not know anything of an illegal operation on Miss Platts. I rang her up one Friday night about three weeks ago and she told me she was not well. I had suggested to her two or three days before she should see a doctor and when I rang I told her I would take her to Dr Endelsberger. I took her to this doctor and after he had examined her she told me he had said she had acute indigestion. She was at my house on Saturday 23 June when she appeared to be in good health.

About two weeks after giving Alice the catheter, Joss was staying at Karaka and received a telegram from Alice saying, 'Everything all right.' When he returned to the city he met Alice, who said the instrument he gave her was too small and she had had to purchase three others from a chemist. She told him her cousin called for her at her boarding house in Grafton Road and drove her in a motor car to her place, where she performed the operation on herself. She remained there for a week.

When Alice became ill and was admitted to hospital, the police became involved. As a result of their enquiries, she ended up in the Auckland Magistrate's Court. Dr Endelsberger, giving evidence, stated Alice consulted him on 8 June suffering from endometritis from an incomplete miscarriage. In his opinion her miscarriage may have been natural, not induced.

SUPREME COURT.
CRIMINAL SESSIONS.

BEFORE MR. JUSTICE STRINGER.

The final session of the year at the Supreme Court was continued to-day before Mr. Justice Stringer.

FOUR BILLS THROWN OUT.

The Grand Jury completed their work yesterday afternoon, finding true bills in every case with the exception of the following, where no bills were returned: Charles Clemm, alleged indecent assault on a female, at Auckland; Alice Platts, alleged unlawful use of an instrument, and Anthony John Joss, alleged supplying of instrument, at Auckland; and Jack Kakanui, alleged unlawful carnal knowledge (two charges), at Pukekohe.

Alice Platts and Anthony Joss's charges are listed alongside indecent assault and unlawful carnal knowledge in the court reports of the *Auckland Star*, 31 October 1923.

Dr Walshe stated he visited Alice at her boarding house on 24 June and found her suffering from peritonitis. The following day he admitted her to hospital, where she underwent surgery for appendicitis. She told Dr Walshe she had miscarried six weeks before. In his opinion, if this were so, the miscarriage would not have been the cause of the infection; he thought venereal disease the more likely cause.

After depositions in the Magistrate's Court, both accused were committed for trial in the Auckland Supreme Court on 31 October 1923, however, the grand jury returned a no bill for both Alice and Joss, and they were discharged. The grand jury may have been sympathetic, or they may have concluded that there was insufficient corroborative evidence.

಄

Falling down has been mentioned in the repertoire of self-abortion techniques, and in Norma Brown's case, it served to divert attention from the real cause.

Norma's story[6]
Deceased 28 October 1937, aged 19 years

Norma Brown and her husband Allen, a milkman, lived in Takapuna, Auckland. They wed on 15 December 1936, when Norma was pregnant, and she gave birth to a stillborn child in March 1937. This was due to a concealed haemorrhage.

When Norma became pregnant again she was not upset, according to her husband. At about three months' gestation she miscarried and blamed this on a fall. Allen said that on 18 October they went for a walk, and as they descended a steep track from the house, Norma slipped and fell sideways onto the bank. After the fall, she complained of pains on her left side. Her mother confirmed the story of falling down the hill. The miscarriage appeared to be a natural event.

On 20 October Norma was unwell, but due to a series of miscommunications the doctor did not arrive until 24 October. When Dr MacKay examined her, he found her seriously ill with septicaemia and admitted her to Auckland Hospital. Norma told the hospital doctor who admitted her that she had had a bad fall down some steps. Despite treatment to control the bleeding, followed by blood transfusion and continuous intravenous infusion, she died on 28 October. She maintained to the end that her miscarriage was due to the fall.

At the post-mortem there was general peritonitis and septicaemia, with marked toxic changes in the liver, spleen and kidneys. The pathologist, Dr Gilmour, found a perforation of the uterus which could not possibly have been caused by a fall. He concluded that some instrument must have been used. The police were unable to obtain sufficient evidence to make a prosecution.

At the inquest, Allen was asked by the police if an abortionist by the name of Mr Brown had visited the home, but he strenuously denied this. The coroner, acting alone and in accordance with the medical evidence, found that the cause of death 'was perforation of the uterus leading to septic abortion and general peritonitis and septicaemia.'

○₹

An accidental injury may well have caused the following miscarriage.

Joyce's story[7]
Deceased 18 June 1926, aged 18 years

Ena Joyce Mansell, known as Joyce, was the only daughter of Jim and Emily Mansell of Auckland. She lived at home and worked as a bookkeeper in the office of her father's grocery business. For the past two and a half years she had been keeping company with Cedric Kayes, 20, of Mount Eden. Cedric said that during the Easter holidays they had intercourse for the first time, but on only two occasions.

Joyce had a history of menstrual troubles and irregularity, sometimes going for seven or eight weeks between periods. Her mother took her to Dr Walton of Mount Eden Road early in May 1926 about this. The doctor diagnosed anaemia and prescribed iron pills. Pregnancy was not even considered. In fact, he made no examination beyond looking at her eyes.

On 12 June, Cedric took Joyce to a dance, and they danced until about 11 pm. As she was about to get into the motorcar, Cedric's dog ran in front of her and she fell in a heap on the footpath and into the gutter alongside the kerbing. She got up and did not appear to have injured herself, but on arrival home ten minutes later, she felt ill and complained of a headache. Cedric called to see her on 15 June at her home, and found her in bed with what was thought to be a touch of influenza.

On Wednesday 16 June, she felt unwell and came home from work. Her usual period had not come on since the visit to the doctor and her mother thought that its arrival was likely to be the problem. About 5 pm her mother told her to go to bed. About 5.30 pm, Joyce called to her mother to come into her bedroom, and asked for a clean diaper. Her mother was shocked at what she saw and exclaimed, 'Oh Joyce, you have had a miscarriage.' Joyce said, 'What is that? It can't be, Mummy.' This was the first time mother or daughter had any inkling she was pregnant. Mrs Mansell immediately told her husband, and they sent for Dr Drier. Her mother thought Joyce did not realise she was pregnant, even though she believed she had prepared her about such matters. Joyce denied doing anything herself or letting anybody else interfere with her. Her father considered Joyce truthful and was certain that she would have told them if there had been any interference. He preferred to think it was the accidental fall which caused a natural miscarriage.

Dr Drier told Mr Mansell he would call as soon as possible, but he was out on another case with Dr Pezaro. The two doctors arrived about 9 pm and found Joyce miscarrying, with a temperature of 100 degrees. The doctors decided to empty the uterus by curetting, and this was done without any particular difficulty. Dr Pezaro administered the anaesthetic and Dr Drier performed the operation.

Dr Drier called next day and found Joyce with a temperature of 104 degrees and in considerable pain. On Friday 18 June, Mr Mansell could not reach Dr Drier by telephone, so he called at the doctor's house about 4.30 am. Joyce was vomiting and the pain was worse. Dr Drier gave instructions and visited about 8 am. Her temperature was normal then, and her pulse was good, but the pain persisted. Dr Drier prescribed a sedative. At about noon, Mr Mansell rang Dr Drier and asked him to come quickly, as Joyce had taken a bad turn. Dr Drier reached the house about five minutes later and found Joyce in a state of collapse. He applied restoratives and sent for Dr Pezaro to come and assist him. They did all they could, but Joyce died at about 1.30 pm. The coroner and the police were notified. Dr Drier saw no evidence that any illegal operation had been performed, and he did not discuss the matter with Joyce.

Dr Murray conducted the post-mortem. On opening the abdomen, he found a quantity of free blood. The lungs, liver, kidneys, spleen and brain were congested and there was blood in the pericardium. The uterus was enlarged, soft and flabby and showed signs of a recent pregnancy of about three months' gestation. There were no signs of perforation of the uterus. Death was due to septicaemia; swabs of the uterine cavity and spleen showed *Streptococcus haemolyticus*.

At the inquest, Cedric said Joyce's death was a complete shock. He was unaware of the pregnancy, and denied any knowledge of an abortion. The coroner, acting alone, found the cause of death was 'septicaemia following on a recent miscarriage.'

The *Auckland Star* of 23 June 1926 reported:

> Joyce's funeral was very largely attended, the deep esteem in which the deceased lady was held being shown in the length of the cortege and in the number of floral tributes. The cortege, comprising upwards of 70 cars, was one of the largest that has ever left the district, and the array of floral emblems, many of which were sent from prominent institutions, reached such proportions that a motor lorry was utilized to convey them to the place of interment at Waikumete, a striking tribute to the popularity of the deceased. Miss Mansell will be remembered by many as an expert exponent of national dancing, for which she held a valuable collection of gold medals, many of which were won at a very early age. The deceased was also an accomplished entertainer and a monologist. To charity she gave freely of her gifts. Miss Mansell's death followed after a few days' illness.

The *New Zealand Herald* of 26 June 1926 reported:

> Mr and Mrs Mansell and Family wish to thank all their kind friends for the wonderful way they showed their sympathy for them in their recent sad bereavement. We wish you to know you have helped us. We cannot thank you individually. Floral emblems, letters, cards and telegrams have been too numerous and words fail us, but may we just say – thank you, one and all.

ಒಳ

Most herbal remedies were relatively safe, but not so instruments used to penetrate the womb. An international symbol for abortion is the wire coat hanger, bent to the shape of a medical curette. More popular with New Zealand women in this era was the knitting needle or crochet hook, made of wood, bone or other

Knitting and crocheting were essential skills for many New Zealand women in the early 20th century, and most homes were likely to have a ready supply of knitting needles and crochet hooks. (*New Zealand Herald*, 17 April 1931)

material. Meat skewers with the ends rounded were also used. A crochet hook allegedly caused the following death.

Jessie's story[8]
Deceased 24 January 1910, aged 32 years

Jessie Chick was married to William, a dentist in Dannevirke. They had two children, a boy and a girl. One Saturday, when Jessie became ill and was in a great deal of pain, Dr Macallan was called in. Jessie confided to the doctor that she thought she was about two or three months pregnant and that on the preceding Thursday she had passed a crochet needle up her insides; the following day, she had had a miscarriage. He diagnosed septic peritonitis, and called in another doctor to assist with the anaesthetic while he emptied the uterus. On Sunday, Jessie was worse and Dr Macallan admitted her to Dannevirke Hospital, where he discussed her case with two other doctors. The doctors decided her only chance of recovery was to open the abdomen and flush out the septic matter. This was done, but she died the following day.

The coroner's inquest, attended by six male jurors, found 'death was due to septic peritonitis.' Her funeral was large, with many floral tributes.

ෙ

A knitting needle was blamed in the following two cases.

Mabel's story[9]
Deceased 17 June 1908, aged 23 years

Mrs Mabel Irwin was married to Jacob (also known as Jack), and they lived in Waihi with their three children. On Tuesday 9 June, Mabel became ill, and that evening took to her bed. The next morning Jack called in Dr Robertson. He found her feverish and suffering abdominal pain, the result of an incomplete abortion. On Thursday, her symptoms worsened, and Mabel told both Jack and the doctor that she had tampered with herself using a knitting needle. Someone in Rotorua had told her how to do it. On Saturday Dr Robertson admitted her to Waihi Hospital, but her condition deteriorated and she died.

At the post-mortem, Dr Craig found peritonitis and pus in one of the Fallopian tubes. The uterus was the size of a two-month pregnancy, with signs of a recent abortion; around the neck of the womb was a wound compatible with her having used a knitting needle. The jury of six men returned a non-committal verdict that 'death was through blood poisoning caused by a miscarriage.'

Alice's story[10]
Deceased 3 October 1930, aged 41 years

Alice McKenzie was single and lived in Dunedin. She was very quiet and reserved, never discussing her personal affairs with others. She had come to New Zealand from Brisbane and for the past four and a half years had worked as a dining-room waitress in the Nurses' Home, Dunedin Hospital. She had been keeping company with Kenneth Bethune, a labourer of Dunedin, who admitted having sexual relations with Alice but denied any knowledge of her pregnancy or abortion.

On Sunday 21 September, Alice told the matron at the Nurses' Home, Sister Valentine, that she felt unwell due to period problems, and she was advised to rest. On Monday morning Sister Valentine found her wiping up something from the floor and noticed she was bleeding. She suggested Alice see a doctor, but Alice adamantly refused. On Tuesday morning Sister Valentine found her washing bloodstained sheets in her room. She called in the hospital superintendent, but Alice refused to be examined. Later that day Sister Valentine allowed her to go and stay with a woman friend, but only on the condition she see a doctor.

Miss Donalena Meed had known Alice for eight years and they went to the same Brethren Church. Alice did not allow her friend to call a doctor, and when finally Donalena did engage Dr Allan, Alice refused point blank to be examined. On Saturday 27 September, Dr Allan insisted on her transfer to the hospital and called an ambulance, but Alice refused to go. The ambulance returned to the hospital empty. Dr Allan visited her the following day, and felt it necessary to ring the South Dunedin police to escort her to the hospital in the ambulance, where she died five days later.

On Monday 29 September, Donalena was sorting through Alice's belongings, and in her attaché case she found a fetus wrapped up in a bloodstained apron. She also found other bloodstained items, and two steel knitting needles about 15 inches long. The police made enquiries as to who may have carried out an illegal operation, but no evidence was forthcoming. Alice most likely had procured her own miscarriage.

The post-mortem, carried out by Dr D'Ath at Dunedin Hospital, found that Alice's death was due to generalised peritonitis and multiple lung abscesses resulting from a septic infection of the uterus, which had recently been delivered of a fetus. There were signs of injury at the entrance to the uterus. Bacteriological examination showed streptococci. The coroner found in accordance with the post-mortem findings.

ଔ

A stick carried an even greater risk than a crochet hook or knitting needle.

May's story[11]
Deceased 20 February 1931, aged 31 years

May Bond was single and worked as a housemaid at the Grosvenor Hotel, New Plymouth, where she got to know the barman there, John McCarty. She left to work in Rotorua and returned to New Plymouth sometime in February. On 12 February, she visited Dr Brown and told him she was about three months pregnant and had been attempting to bring about a miscarriage by passing a stick into her womb on several occasions. The wood had come out again each time except on the last occasion, when it remained inside, and she was worried about the consequences. Dr Brown examined her and gave her a letter of admission to the hospital.

Instead of going straight to the hospital she asked her friend John McCarty if he would help her find somewhere to stay, and on 13 February he took her to Nurse Thompson's. Martha Thompson was a registered maternity nurse and had a nursing home in Fitzroy, but she also took in medical cases and sometimes boarders to help with finances. On 15 February, May felt unwell and told Nurse Thompson that she had used an instrument on herself. Sensibly, Nurse Thompson accompanied May to the hospital in a taxi. That afternoon May was examined under an anaesthetic, and pus was found coming from the uterus. The following day she was still profoundly ill and doctors operated on her. A foreign body was found inside the abdomen, consistent with her history. She did not respond to treatment, and died on 20 February.

The coroner found that 'death was due to toxaemia from peritonitis caused by the passage (by herself) of an instrument from the vagina into the abdominal cavity'. She refused to give any information to the detective who interviewed her in the hospital, and took her secrets to the grave. She never identified her lover, and John McCarty said they were just friends.

ଔ

Sometimes, as mentioned previously, it was impossible to tell whether a miscarriage was self-induced or carried out by another.

Janet's story[12]
Deceased 10 August 1930, aged 24 years

Janet Morley was happily married for six years to Vincent Morley, a dairy farmer of Waiuku, south of Auckland. They had four children: Vincent, the eldest, was five years old, Jean was nearly four, and Margaret and Stella, the twins, were three years old. About a fortnight before her death, Janet told her husband she thought she was pregnant, as her courses had stopped. She mentioned more than once she thought four children were enough. She said she did not wish to see their local doctor because she owed him an account. Instead, she opted to take the bus and see a doctor in Auckland. The doctor confirmed the pregnancy, but Janet did not say anything else about the consultation.

She remained in good health until Tuesday 5 August, when she started vomiting and remained in bed all day. On Wednesday and Thursday, she managed to care for the children and the farm helper, who had his meals in the house. On Friday, she was drinking but not eating. On Saturday, she remained in bed, but the vomiting had returned, along with diarrhoea. She looked ill, but declined Vincent's offer to call the doctor. On Sunday, she awoke about 3 am and said she thought she should go to the hospital. Vincent called a taxi to take her to the Waiuku Memorial Hospital, while he stayed at home to mind the children and milk the cows. By 8 am, Janet was dead.

Between one and two years earlier, she had had another miscarriage and had ended up in Waiuku Hospital. Vincent thought on that occasion it may have been brought on by overwork. There were no poisons in the house apart from a bottle of Jeyes' Fluid. When the police searched the house, they found bloodstained clothing, a pencil and a syringe.

A post-mortem disclosed a ragged wound in the uterus and signs of acute septicaemia. The coroner, acting alone, found the cause of death was 'acute septicaemia due to perforation of the uterus by an instrument introduced through the vagina.' There was insufficient evidence to allow any judgement as to whether it had been carried out by someone in Auckland the day she visited, or whether it had been self-induced.

ଓଃ

All chemists purveyed syringes, enemas and douche cans, and women could adapt these appliances to squirt fluid into the vagina, through the cervix and into the womb.

Myra's story[13]
Deceased 5 August 1938, aged 27 years

Miss Myra Wall left her home town of Hastings in October 1937 to live and work in Wellington at the Anglo-Russian Fur Company, a factory in Cuba Street. She boarded in Mrs Bartlett's boarding house in Wallace Street, sharing a bedroom with Mrs Bartlett's 16-year-old daughter. On the morning of 3 August Myra felt unwell and did not go to work, but went instead to see a doctor. That evening she was restless and in pain, and vomited throughout the night.

The next morning, Mrs Bartlett was so concerned she telephoned Dr Cotton, but about 11.30 am Myra decided she would sooner go to hospital, and Dr Cotton was contacted to arrange her admission. Myra went to the hospital about 1 pm, and Mrs Bartlett sent a telegram to Myra's parents in Hastings and also contacted the police in Hastings to make sure they got the message.

Myra was having rigors (shivering) and was cyanosed (blue from lack of oxygen) and breathless. She had generalised abdominal pain and a headache. She told the admitting doctor that she had taken quinine tablets ten days ago and had used a syringe on five occasions. She also said that on the night of 2 August she had inserted a piece of rubber tubing. Bleeding from the uterus commenced on 3 August. The doctors diagnosed peritonitis and septicaemia. Treatment was of no avail and she died at 1 am on 5 August, about 12 hours after admission.

Dr Lynch, Wellington Hospital pathologist, conducted the post-mortem. The uterus was enlarged but it was impossible to assess the duration of the pregnancy, as the uterine wall was swollen and thickened from the presence of gas gangrene. There was a large amount of pus in the abdomen and the organs were distended with gas.

In searching Myra's room, the police found a vaginal whirling syringe, a piece of rubber tube, a vulcanite manicure instrument, a bottle of olive oil, a bottle partly filled with gin, a cake of soap and a bottle of cascara sagrada tablets. The enema, rubber tubing, and manicure instrument were contained in a cardboard box. In the bathroom was a bottle of Jeyes' Fluid. The enema was still wet with white fluid. In Myra's handbag were detailed handwritten instructions for procuring an abortion by douching with Sunlight soap, hot water, salad oil and Jeyes' Fluid – and the rather lighthearted instruction to take a large gin or two as well.

The coroner, acting alone, found in accordance with the medical evidence that Myra died 'from septic abortion. The evidence in this case indicates that the abortion was self-inflicted.'

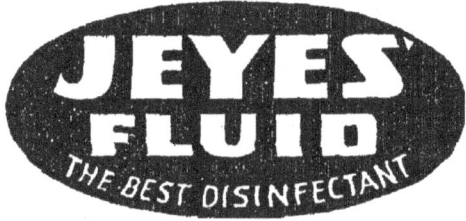

HYGIENIC NECESSITIES
For Women.

"Surety" Whirling Syringe.
17/6 —— Post Free —— 17/6
Sent under plain label, any address.
Write Madame "X,"
c/o UTILITY RUBBER COY.
Box 1209 • Wellington.

Newspaper advertisements for some of the items used by Myra Wall to abort her pregnancy – Sunlight soap (*Grey River Argus*, 10 September 1916), Jeyes' Fluid (*Press*, 4 March 1938) and a whirling syringe (*NZ Truth*, 20 October 1923).

ଔ

Various substances used for douching also occasionally proved fatal.

Myrtle's story[14]
Deceased 5 October 1938, aged about 39 years

Myrtle Ward was married to Cecil, who worked on rotational employment through the Labour Department. They lived in Linwood, Christchurch, with their five children aged from nine to nineteen years. In 1929 Myrtle had a mastectomy for breast cancer, from which she recovered.

Early in July, Myrtle informed Cecil she had missed her period and suspected a pregnancy. On Saturday 1 October, Cecil arrived home to find Myrtle unwell. She told him she had syringed herself. As the evening wore on and she did not improve, Cecil called for Dr Duncan, who visited and prescribed aspirin. He called again on the following two days, and because of her deteriorating condition, admitted Myrtle to hospital.

Myrtle told the hospital doctors she had used a piece of wire and a syringe. On the morning of 5 October, she underwent an operation, but died soon after. Dr Thomson, pathologist at Christchurch Hospital, conducted the post-mortem. The injury to the uterus was consistent with some strong irritant chemical having been used in the syringe.

Detectives searched Myrtle's home for evidence of any equipment used for procuring abortion. They found no strong irritant chemical among her possessions, although there was a bottle of permanganate of potash in the kitchen. They found a Higginson syringe and a catheter, but no wire.

The coroner found, in accordance with the medical evidence, that death 'was due to peritonitis and broncho-pneumonia arising from an infection of the uterus brought about by the action of some strong chemical irritant.'

ଔ

Catheters were sold by chemists for home use, for example, they were commonly used to empty the bladder in men with an enlarged prostate that obstructed urine flow. Anyone working in a hospital would have ready access to a catheter.

Maria's story[15]
Deceased 20 January 1934, aged 25 years

Miss Maria Te Motunga Amohau had worked at the King George V Hospital, Rotorua, for eight years and had many friends, male and female. She lived at the Ohinemutu Pa, but often stayed with her cousin Catherine at Ohinemutu. When she became pregnant, her boyfriend John Murphy provided her with pills and she took about 20 of them. On 9 January she had a miscarriage, which she induced herself using a soft catheter. She continued to work at the hospital until 15 January, when she took sick leave. When her aunt and uncle heard Maria was ill, they took her to stay with them on Taupo Road. Her aunt had once loaned her a syringe, which was found in Maria's possession.

On 19 January, when Maria was very unwell with a fever, her aunt and uncle sent for the native district nurse. The nurse wanted her to go to hospital, but at first Maria refused, saying that she was too well known there. The following morning, 20 January, the nurse took her to the hospital in her car, but she died soon after admission. The post-mortem revealed peritonitis, with patches of gas gangrene and no evidence of perforation. The coroner certified the cause of death as 'septicaemia following a miscarriage'.

ଔ

Abortifacient pills were commonly ingested, and were often combined with other methods if they did not appear to work. The commonly purveyed abortifacients from chemists were relatively safe in healthy women, but may have contributed to a fatal outcome in the following two stories.

Mary's story[16]
Deceased 19 May 1902, age not recorded (but described as a young girl)

Mary Stevens was single, in good health and employed as a servant in a boarding house in Ashburton. When she found she was pregnant, she took medicine from 16 to 24 April to bring about a miscarriage, then on 25 April she took another two 'female pills'. She refused to name the man from whom she had obtained the medicines. She had a miscarriage, then, feeling unwell, she went to stay with her married sister, Emily.

On 4 May the doctor was called, and because of the seriousness of Mary's symptoms he brought in another doctor for a second opinion. Because her symptoms resembled diphtheria, the doctors admitted her to the Fever Ward at Ashburton Hospital. Her illness lasted a fortnight and she died without making dying depositions. The post-mortem showed peritonitis but no signs of instrumental injury to the uterus. In the Coroner's Court, the jury found 'the cause of death was peritonitis brought on by miscarriage caused by medicine given by a person name unknown.'

Ellen's story[17]
Deceased 12 October 1910, aged 26 years

Miss Ellen McGuire worked as a domestic servant in a private home in Grafton Road, Auckland. On 1 October she stayed at the home of her friend Kate Reilly, telling Kate she thought she had the flu. Her illness turned out to be more than influenza, and she never returned to work. On 7 October her condition worsened, and Dr Kinder was sent for. She then divulged that she had miscarried on 30 September, after taking pills and salts. She denied seeing anyone else, being interfered with, or doing anything to herself.

The following day, 8 October, Dr Kinder admitted Ellen to Auckland Hospital, where she died four days later. Because of the suspicious nature of her death, the police made enquiries, but as often happened in such cases, they did not discover any wrongdoing. The post-mortem, carried out by Dr Kinder, was inconclusive, showing a recent pregnancy of about ten weeks' gestation and extensive signs of septicaemia, but no definite signs of interference.

The coroner and jury of six men found the cause of death was 'acute blood poisoning as a direct result of a miscarriage but there was no evidence to enable them to determine the cause of the miscarriage.' Hundreds of other women in similar circumstances would have had an abortion without mishap, and Ellen's case was only brought to the attention of the police through her unfortunate death.

ଔ

One type of abortifacient that could be fatal if taken in excess was ergot.

Jean's story[18]
Deceased 28 October 1939, aged 16 years

Jean Brosnan was the illegitimate daughter of Mrs Mary Brosnan, who lived apart from her husband. Jean and her mother had a close relationship and lived with her biological father in Auckland. Jean was employed as a typist at MK Manufacturers Ltd, a firm in Great South Road, Auckland, which also employed her mother. Sometime before Christmas 1938, Jean started a friendship with Murray Cameron, 20, a film inspector, who lived with his parents in Remuera, Auckland. When she was about four months pregnant, Jean's mother noted changes in her daughter and asked her if she was pregnant. She replied that she was, and that Murray was responsible. Murray was a regular visitor to their house and came to tea every Sunday. When they discussed what should be done, Murray said he would marry Jean, and Mrs Brosnan then visited his parents' home and discussed the situation with Murray's mother. Despite what both families thought was best, Jean did not wish to get married and leave her mother.

Jean continued at work until the evening of Thursday 26 October, when she had a bad cold and a nosebleed. On Friday morning her mother suggested she remain in bed, and she did so. As a result of a telephone message received at 4 pm that day, Mrs Brosnan returned home to find Jean vomiting. By 8 pm she was not only vomiting but vomiting blood, and she also had excessive diarrhoea. Mrs Brosnan tried to get a doctor and eventually got in touch with Dr Brockway. Dr Brockway arrived at about midnight and stayed with Jean while she gave birth to a dead fetus at about 2 am, followed about half an hour later by the placenta. Dr Brockway diagnosed ergot poisoning – which caused vomiting, diarrhoea, cyanosis (blueness) of the face, pain on swallowing, and thirst – and Jean admitted she had drunk some 'black stuff', then thrown the bottle away. At 7 am Jean was much worse, and Dr Brockway was sent for again. Her pulse was weak and her temperature elevated. He sent her to Auckland Public Hospital, where she died 12 hours after admission.

She told the house-surgeon she had been taking some dark-coloured medicine from a bottle for the past fortnight, four times daily; by Thursday, two days before her admission, she had swallowed half the contents of the bottle. The government analyst found no ergot in the tissues sent for examination, but the pathologist, Dr Walter Gilmour, said this did not exclude the diagnosis of ergot poisoning. The post-mortem findings revealed no sepsis. Taken in conjunction with Jean's history and clinical symptoms, the conclusion was that death was due to ergot poisoning. The coroner, acting alone, found accordingly.

ଓ

Women resorted to poisoning less often than other methods, but hazardous substances found in most households, such as match heads, rat poison, Lysol (a common household disinfectant) and kerosene, were occasionally used to self-abort.

Geraldine's story[19]
Deceased 29 March 1900, aged 19 years

Miss Geraldine Harrop worked as a saleswoman, and lived at home with her parents in Auckland. Her mother became aware of Geraldine's pregnancy when she was about six or seven months pregnant, and to avoid gossip, was planning to send her away to the country for her confinement. Geraldine told her mother who had fathered the child and that she had twice written to him but he had not replied. Even though her mother was supportive, Geraldine had her own plan, and on Friday 23 March she swallowed the heads from three packets of household wax matches; such was the despair, disgrace and shame that she felt. The match heads contained phosphorus and were known as an abortifacient.

Geraldine became unwell and on Monday 26 March her mother called in Dr Reid, who saw her several times over the next few days. On Tuesday Geraldine told Dr Reid she had had a fall, and that night she miscarried. Geraldine began to behave strangely and suffered severe pain. Dr Reid was unaware that she had swallowed the matches and gave her medicine to relieve her pain. The following day she was much worse, and was bleeding from the gums and the back of the throat, a symptom of phosphorus poisoning.

On Thursday morning Dr Reid recommended her transfer to hospital, but her mother thought Geraldine would fret too much. That evening her condition worsened, but the family could not reach Dr Reid and called in another doctor, Dr Sharman, who arrived at 10 pm. He telephoned Dr Reid later to say he had arrived too late and Geraldine was already dead. Mrs Harrop knew her daughter had swallowed the match heads but was unaware of the severity of phosphorus poisoning and thought Geraldine's excessive vomiting would have got rid of the poison.

The inquest was held at the Eden Vine Hotel on Saturday morning by the city coroner and a jury. After a few minutes' deliberation the jury returned a verdict that Geraldine 'did take a large quantity of a certain deadly poison called phosphorus dissolved in water, being at the time not of sound mind but temporarily insane by reason of mental trouble and did die of the sickness thereof.'

Sarah's story[20]
Deceased 8 June 1908, aged 33 years

In the eyes of her friends, Mrs Sarah Armstrong was happily married to Albert. She and Albert lived with their children in Waihi. Sarah was about two months pregnant and had been feeling unwell for three or four weeks, but put this down to the fact she always suffered when pregnant. She attended Dr Robertson about a fortnight before her death, complaining that she felt weak and depressed, but she was certainly not suicidal.

Her symptoms of pain and vomiting increased, and Albert thought they were much worse than her usual pregnancy sickness, so much so that on 8 June, he finally called in Dr Robertson. Sarah was livid in colour, complained of a very severe headache and writhed with abdominal pain. Dr Robertson immediately arranged for her admission to Waihi Hospital, where she collapsed and died later that evening.

At the post-mortem carried out by Dr Craig, there was evidence that Sarah had recently taken an irritant poison, and on chemical analysis, a large amount of phosphorus was found in her stomach and liver. In the uterus, there was evidence of a recent incomplete abortion at about three months' gestation.

When Albert was questioned about the source of the poison, he said that about four years ago he had bought 'Rough on Rats' to rid the house of rats, and the only other source of phosphorus would have been matches. In the opinion of the doctors, Sarah had ingested a large quantity of phosphorus. The jury of six men found that Sarah 'met her death by phosphorus poisoning, taken by misadventure.'

Mercury poisoning could also be fatal.

Ina's story[21]
Deceased 9 November 1933, aged 14 years

Ina Blake, 14, a schoolgirl from Belfast, Christchurch, did some domestic work for a neighbour, Mrs Mundy. The Mundy family comprised Mr and Mrs Mundy and their two sons – Colin, 17, and Trevor, 19. The boys worked as farm labourers on their father's farm. If it was late, the boys would often accompany Ina home, but both denied engaging in sexual relations with her.

On 28 October, after a day out in Christchurch with her 17-year-old sister, Ina came home late after the pictures and her mother heard a bump as she fell to the floor. Over the next two or three days she became unwell and complained of a sore throat. On 1 November, Dr Thomas made a house call but was not too concerned. After the doctor had left, Ina told her mother that Colin had interfered with her two or three times over the past four or five weeks, and he had given her a 'blue pill', which she had placed in her vagina. On 3 November, she was seriously ill and Dr Thomas admitted her to hospital by ambulance, where she died six days later. Both young men denied giving her any pills.

There was no chemist in Belfast, but Detective Thomas made enquiries of chemists elsewhere regarding the availability of 'blue pills'. They contained mercuric chloride and were sometimes used as an unsafe method to procure abortion. All chemists stocked them, but they were not usually recorded as poison entries. They were provided to doctors, nurses and veterinarians, and some chemists required a prescription. Diluted, they were sometimes used as a disinfectant, and before the advent of antibiotics, they were used for the treatment of syphilis. They were available in tablets of two grains and eight grains. The government analyst stated that the pills containing two grains were dangerous if taken, and the pills containing eight grains would be fatal.

In Ina's case, the coroner found she died 'of haemorrhage and acute nephritis due to mercurial poisoning', and added a rider that the attention of the authorities be drawn to the ease with which such pills were obtained from chemists. No charges were laid.

The Director-General of Health responded to the accusation that the pills were too easy to obtain, pointing out that the coroner should be advised that corrosive sublimate is already covered by the Poisons Act: 'It must not be sold except by a registered vendor of poisons and the purchaser must be known to the vendor; entry of the sale is to be made in the poison book and other formalities complied with under the Poisons Act 1908.'

ଔ

Sometimes the poisoning was an act of suicide.

Mamie's story[22]
Deceased 13 April 1912, aged 29 years

Miss Mary Ellen Carroll, known as Mamie, lived with her parents and siblings in Auckland. She was employed as a domestic in a private family home. She consulted Dr Kinder and when he informed her that she was pregnant, she was so upset that she went home and swallowed Lysol from her brother's room. She was found dead in her bedroom, where she had taken the poison, a glass lying by her side. The post-mortem confirmed the pregnancy. The jury found 'the cause of her death was syncope resulting from Lysol poisoning, self administered, and that the said Mary Ellen Carroll, whilst temporarily insane, did kill herself.'

ଔ

Air embolism was a particularly dangerous risk for women who carried out a self-abortion using a syringe, just as it was in cases when the syringe was manipulated by another. It was fatal for Isabella, Gladys and Edith.

Isabella's story[23]
Deceased 17 November 1924, aged 24 years

Isabella Paterson was a single woman who cared for her four-year-old son and worked as a housekeeper for Mr James Anderson, farmer of Waipahi, Otago. She had been with Mr Anderson for two and a half years, and received 20 shillings a week plus board. Mr Anderson spoke well of Isabella, but denied any knowledge of or responsibility for her pregnancy. When asked who might have been responsible, he said he was not aware she had been keeping company with any man. From April to November he had employed a young fellow about 19 years of age, who lived

Above: Lysol poisoning was considered dangerous enough to be the topic of the front page cartoon in the *Observer* on 7 December 1912, with the caption: "LYSOLITIS – WHY IS THE SALE NOT RESTRICTED? Death Lysol, the Tempter: Come, here's an easy road out of your sorrow. I'm right at your elbow day and night." Right: Mercuric chloride, or corrosive sublimate, was far too easy to obtain from chemists, according to the coroner investigating Ina Blake's death (*New Zealand Herald*, 3 February 1934).

DEATH OF GIRL

COMMENT BY CORONER

DRUG EASILY PROCURED

"AN EXTRAORDINARY THING"

[BY TELEGRAPH—OWN CORRESPONDENT]
CHRISTCHURCH, Friday

A rider drawing the attention of the authorities to the ease with which pills composed of corrosive sublimate can be procured from chemists was added by Mr. E. D. Mosley, S.M., coroner, to the verdict which he gave at an inquest to-day concerning the death of Ina Adelaide Blake, aged 14, of Belfast.

alongside the house in a hut. Otherwise, the nearest house was about a mile and a half or two miles away. Isabella had not left the farm since last Christmas.

Mr Anderson last saw Isabella alive at 2 pm on 17 November, when he noticed nothing unusual. When he returned from working on the farm about 6 pm, Isabella's little boy was sitting on the doorstep crying. He said, 'Mummy's not dead, come and have a look.' When Mr Anderson went into Isabella's bedroom, he found her lying dead on the floor. He telephoned for the doctor and notified her parents, who lived in Oamaru.

The last person to see Isabella alive was William Budd, a drapery traveller from Dunedin. That afternoon he passed Mr Anderson working on the farm, spoke to him, and then went on up to the house. Isabella came out and made a few purchases. He had called at the house three or four times before. Isabella seemed to him to be in good health and as bright as usual. He gave the time when he left her as about 4 pm. He did not see anyone about the house except Isabella and her young son.

Dr Brown received the call from Mr Anderson at 6.30 pm and arrived at the homestead at 8.30 pm, with Constable Dart. Isabella was sprawled on her back, fully dressed, on the floor of her bedroom. There were no marks of violence about her body, but her undergarments were stained with fresh blood. Examination showed that she was six months pregnant, and there was evidence of interference with the pregnancy.

In her room, on the washstand, Dr Brown and Constable Dart found a crude self-made instrument, shaped like a stilette, made of wood and soaking in Jeyes' Fluid. They also found a broken enema syringe soaking in Jeyes' Fluid. In Dr Brown's opinion, the probable cause of death was asphyxia due to a pulmonary air embolism, caused by interference most likely carried out by Isabella herself. The coroner, acting alone, simply stated Isabella 'died as the result of an attempt made to procure her miscarriage.'

Gladys's story[24]
Deceased 15 February 1932, aged 32 years

Miss Gladys Milligan kept in good health, apart from contracting influenza in the epidemic of 1918. She lived with her parents in Sydenham, Christchurch. Her father was a retired foreman and linesman with the Post and Telegraph Department. Her mother,

67, did not keep good health and was largely confined to bed. Gladys's parents had known about her pregnancy since the latter part of 1931, but abortion was never discussed. She was about six months pregnant.

On the morning of 15 February, Gladys got up as usual for breakfast and then helped with the housework. At 11 am her mother heard groaning sounds, and both her parents and her brother were quickly on the scene to find Gladys apparently dead. She lay on her back on her bed with her right leg over the edge, fully clothed except for bloomers and shoes. Dr Marks and the police were called immediately. A Higginson syringe lay alongside the body and her mother removed it before the doctor arrived. Police searched and found the syringe.

Dr Pearson, pathologist at Christchurch Hospital, carried out the post-mortem and found the placental veins had been torn, allowing air to enter the circulatory system and travel to the heart. In accordance with the medical evidence, the coroner, acting alone, found that Gladys's death was caused by 'heart failure due to air embolism associated with air in the womb resulting from self-attempted abortion.'

Edith's story[25]
Deceased 9 April 1934, aged 'early 30s'

Edith Weir lived in Kent Terrace, Wellington. She had recently separated from her husband Robert, a locomotive driver with the New Zealand Railways. They had married in 1922 and had two children – Dora, aged eleven, and Gerald, aged nine. The separation was amicable and Robert visited the family, bringing his washing, which Edith obligingly did. Robert blamed the breakup on another man paying too much attention to his wife.

The day before her death, Edith wrote a letter to her lover, anxious about having an abortion. This was familiar territory, as four or five years before she had needed hospital treatment for a septic abortion. On Monday morning, 9 April, the children went to school as usual. When they came home at lunch time, they could not open the door, and went to see Mr Partridge, a neighbourly grocer not far away in Ellice Street. He came back with the children and found the back door barred from the inside with a chair. He broke the door in and went inside. Downstairs, everything else was in order. Upstairs, he found Edith dead, lying on the bed in her bedroom, practically naked. He called

Dr Henry, who who confirmed that Edith had died. The police also attended, in company with Dr Lynch, Wellington Hospital pathologist.

On the floor were two small basins, one empty and one containing a harmless alkaline fluid. Near Edith's hand lay a Higginson's syringe. Wrapped around the nozzle of the syringe was a cuff of cloth that looked like a handkerchief. This appeared to have been used to prevent the escape of injected fluid.

At the inquest, Dr Lynch explained that if the deceased injected fluid into the vagina with the syringe and then continued to squeeze the bulb, a quantity of air would be injected with every squeeze. With the opening of the vagina plugged with the cloth cuff, air could very readily gain entrance to the cavity of the uterus. The large vessels in the pregnant uterus would provide an easy channel of entry to the general circulation, assisted by the sucking action of the blood in the large veins of the abdomen. At the post-mortem, on opening the body, all the vessels, large and small, arteries and veins, presented a remarkable appearance due to numerous air bubbles. Even in the small vessels in the skin and superficial tissues, the blood which exuded had a frothy appearance from admixed air. The great veins, especially the inferior vena cava, were almost completely filled with air, and air distended the right side of the heart.

The enlarged womb contained a fetus of about five months' gestation. Air was present within and between the membranes, and also between the membranes and the wall of the womb. The coroner, acting alone, found in accordance with the medical evidence that death was due to 'air embolism which occurred while deceased was attempting to abort herself by means of an enema syringe.'

ଓ

While these three women died in dramatic circumstances at home, most of the other women described in this chapter died in hospital suffering serious complications from the dangerous methods that they were forced to resort to, largely due to the secrecy, stigma and ignorance surrounding birth control and abortion. Imagine the dilemma for single women faced with the shame and hardship of an unwanted pregnancy, so extreme for Mamie Carroll that she took her own life. We do not know how many other women committed suicide. Imagine the desperation of married women such as Ellen Johnson, already burdened with five young children and in wretched circumstances. Imagine the deep sadness of Mr and Mrs Mansell, unable to reveal the truth behind their beloved daughter's death. The reality of self abortion is indeed sobering.

11. SOME OBSERVATIONS

> The past is a foreign country: they do things differently there.
>
> – L. P. Hartley, *The Go-Between*

With the advantage of hindsight, here are some observations on times past.

On young women

Young Māori women have not featured in this narrative, except for the high-profile murder of Mary Raymond and the self-abortion of hospital employee Maria Amohau, as they were usually supported by their whānau. Young European women found society less accommodating: premarital relations were strongly disapproved of and chastity revered; knowledge of sexual matters was left to chance and contraception remained out of bounds; and the stigma of bearing a child out of wedlock brought shame not only on the young woman but also on her family. Emancipation brought many changes in young women's lives, but not access to birth control or safe abortion.

Parents often forced daughters to marry (in so-called 'shotgun marriages') to avoid an illegitimate pregnancy. Going solo was frowned upon and, for most young women, impractical. For those who decided to keep a child, family support was essential. Seeking maintenance from the father was a humiliating ordeal, as Sarah Boulton found out, and the sum (if granted) was meagre. The term 'illegitimate child' was a persistent reminder of transgression against society's accepted standards.

Little wonder young women resorted to abortion – first trying to self-abort, and if that failed, seeking a solution elsewhere. We may laugh derisively at some of the old wives' tales that people believed back then, but they still persist in modern folklore: in the 2006 television series *Desperate Housewives,* Gabrielle falls down the stairs and has a miscarriage; in the 2010 television series *Downton Abbey,* Lady Grantham has a miscarriage after slipping on the bath soap.

Abortionists existed in every community, but finding out about them was not easy. In those stories where a good relationship existed, the young man made enquiries or purchased abortifacients from a chemist for his girlfriend. In other cases, it was regarded as the woman's problem, and she sought advice from other women. Because abortion was illegal (unless doctors considered it necessary to save a woman's life), such information was clandestinely obtained by word of mouth.

Adoption was an option, either informally or according to the Adoption of Children Act 1895, but carrying a child to term and giving it up for adoption has never been an easy choice for the mother. Attitudes to the rights of the birth mother and the adopting parents have since changed, with adoptions becoming more open. Current adoption laws dating back to 1955 were recently reviewed to give greater recognition to the rights of children.

Late abortions (after 12 weeks) occurred more often in times past. Pregnancy tests did not exist to aid early diagnosis, and many women missed two periods before realising they were pregnant. Waiting for the next period was a female preoccupation, exploited by chemists with numerous products to regulate the menses. A positive outcome of this preoccupation was that women regarded early abortions as restoring normal physiology, devoid of any ethical dilemma. Concern about early zygotes or embryos is a modern preoccupation, mainly for those opposed to abortion.

The earlier an unplanned pregnancy is diagnosed, the safer it is to have an abortion. Early diagnosis also gives more time to explore all the options. In this sense, modern pregnancy tests are a boon: available over the counter from a pharmacy or supermarket, and very reliable as soon as the first period is late, they are simple to use and can be employed in the privacy of one's home. Schools for teen parents now enable education to continue after pregnancy, which was undreamt of in the early 20th century.

The biggest change for young women is that abortion is now a lawful (albeit complicated) procedure, and a girl under 16 years can make the decision to either continue her pregnancy or seek abortion.

On young men

Education in sexual matters was just as haphazard for young men as it was for young women. The double standard meant that young men were encouraged to 'sow their wild oats', while respectable young women remained chaste if they valued their reputation. Condoms were not popular, as their quality could not be assured and it was embarrassing for young men to purchase them. Withdrawal or 'being careful', while admirable in intention, was not a reliable method of contraception. Supplying the young woman with an abortifacient was seen as a convenient solution to the problem of an unplanned pregnancy. In the early 20th century there were many examples of loutish and appalling behaviour by young men, but in modern times, drugs, alcohol and gangs have increased the potential for harm to women.

On married women

Once a woman was married, society expected her to care for her husband and raise a family. Marie Stopes's *Married Love* in 1918 contributed to the gradual emancipation of women, but opinion leaders like Dr Doris Gordon resisted these changes. Most women found it difficult to obtain birth control, and although the risks associated with childbirth decreased between 1900 and 1939, maternal mortality was still a concern. Abortion was also risky. How risky? We do not know, but most women felt it was a risk worth taking when compared to the risks and consequences of continuing the pregnancy.

In 1935, the annual number of abortions was estimated to be about 6,000, and the number of deaths that year from reported septic abortion alone was 23 (17 married women and 6 single women). That gives a risk of about 4 deaths per 1,000 abortions, but not all septic abortion deaths were reported, and there were other causes of abortion mortality. Therefore an estimate of 4 per 1,000 can be regarded as too low. On the other hand, if 6,000 is a conservative estimate for the number of abortions, then an estimate of 4 per 1,000 may be too high. In the same year, the total number of childbirth-related deaths was 86, with a rate of about 4 deaths per 1,000 births. What we can say is that abortion and childbirth were both more risky then than they are today.

In 2013, the total maternal mortality (from both direct and indirect causes) in New Zealand was 0.2 per 1,000 births.[1] There has not been a single death directly attributable to abortion since accurate statistics became available in 1980. From 1980 to 2015, the total number of abortions was 475,189.[2] Abortion deaths under good medical conditions in developed countries vary with age and length of gestation. An overall figure is 0.2–2 deaths per 100,000 abortions, or as low as 1 death per 500,000 abortions. In New Zealand, abortion is now a very safe procedure.

A study in the United States, published in 2012, found the risk of death for women who delivered live babies was 8.8 per 100,000, and the risk of death for women who had legal induced abortions was 0.6 per 100,000, which makes the risk of childbirth about 14 times higher than the risk of abortion.[3] Deaths, however, are the bottom line; there are other risks associated with abortion, including chronic pelvic pain and reduced fertility, possibly even sterility. Of course, there are also many risks associated with giving birth: prolapsed uterus, haemorrhage, pelvic floor problems and post-natal depression, to name a few.

Married women resorted to abortion more often than single women. Giving birth and caring for young children without home help was demanding even in the good times, and particularly challenging during the war years and the Depression years. Couples faced the prospect of one more mouth to feed, and one more child to raise, with apprehension. There is a notable absence of well-to-do women in these stories, which is not surprising. In the history of abortion worldwide, the wealthy have always been able to buy the services they need.

On husbands

Society expected a husband to be the breadwinner and protector of his wife and family, and in return, conjugal rights were taken for granted. The pressure to conform was all-pervasive, and when times were tough, a man's self-esteem was likely to suffer. Extramarital relations were not condoned. Divorce was difficult and publicly shameful, so separation and desertion became more practical options.

Divorce laws changed throughout the era, but adultery and desertion were the commonest grounds for divorce. Finding fault and punishing wrongdoers were the underlying principles behind divorce laws, the aim of which was to preserve the sanctity of marriage. *NZ Truth*, a weekly newspaper launched in Wellington in June 1905, published divorce proceedings as a regular feature, scandal being a reliable generator of sales. Contrast this with today, where there is much less stigma surrounding divorce. Now the sole grounds for divorce or dissolution are irreconcilable breakdown of the marriage (or civil union) and living apart for two years.

Society expected men, but not women, to perform civic duties. Until the system changed in 1908, men were called upon to serve as jurors in the Coroner's Court. Dealing with suspected abortion deaths was unfamiliar territory for most men, and they would have had little insight into the woman's plight. A woman's point of view was also excluded in cases dealt with in the Magistrate's Court and the Supreme Court by all-male juries.

In the stories recounted here, the male partners involved ranged from uncaring bastards to loving husbands who totally supported their wives. As with young men, it was often the husband who made enquiries on the woman's behalf and obtained the necessary equipment for an abortion. It was often he who had the task of seeking medical help when things went wrong, and he who was left with the devastating consequences if his wife died, leaving him with young children to care for. The children, in most cases, would be the ones most affected by the loss of their mother.

On doctors

The medical establishment disapproved of abortion. Most doctors did not provide this service themselves, nor did they suggest that the woman see a local abortionist. When Dr Jacobsen was accused of this, the Medical Council took action. If there was a serious risk to the health of the woman, a therapeutic abortion could be carried out in a hospital, usually requiring the approval of more than one doctor. The law was vague as to what constituted a lawful abortion, and doctors developed their own guidelines for handling these cases.

Those doctors who did provide abortion services carried out their work discreetly, and unless something unfortunate occurred, they practised under the radar. Despite lapses by unscrupulous members of the profession, such as Dr Temple, doctors were generally held in high regard. In contrast to the 19th century, few doctors were prosecuted for providing abortion services, Dr Hennessy being a notable exception.

More is known of those doctors who campaigned against abortion. One of the most prominent anti-abortion doctors, Dr Doris Gordon, died on 9 July 1956, and in June 1961 the two organisations who had been most involved in her various campaigns, the Obstetrical and Gynaecological (O&G) Society and the National Council of Women (NCW), jointly established the Doris Gordon Memorial Trust and Fund for 'the purpose of commemorating and furthering the works of the late Dr Doris Gordon' and 'to promote, undertake, sponsor, cooperate in or otherwise further the study and/or the teaching and/or the practice of gynaecology and obstetrics in all their respective branches.' Reforms of the 1990s resulted in a transference of maternity care from general practitioners to midwives, and the O&G Society became inactive and was deregistered. The Doris Gordon Memorial Trust also became inactive, but the Trust Fund remained.

In July 2015, the Royal Australian and New Zealand College of Obstetricians and Gynaecologists (RANZCOG) and NCW jointly formed a new Doris Gordon Memorial Trust, in order to access the funds for an annual Doris Gordon Memorial Lecture, alternating between meetings of the New Zealand section of RANZCOG and NCW. The lecturer receives a Doris Gordon medal (actually a substantial bronze medallion) and an honorarium, to be used for furthering the health and wellbeing of women in New Zealand. As mentioned in the introduction, the inaugural lecture, a eulogy to Doris, was delivered by Honorary Professor Ron Jones at the RANZCOG Scientific Meeting held in Wellington on 2 October 2015.[4]

Yes, Doris did a great deal for the advancement of maternity services in New Zealand, and she must be remembered for that, but her legacy is flawed.[5] While it is unreasonable to expect anyone to be faultless, and it is unfair to judge Doris for holding views that were predominant in her time, nevertheless, in bestowing an honour and a medal, a higher than usual standard of critical appraisal is warranted.

Her opposition to birth control held back advances available to women in England, Europe and America. She publicly and vehemently opposed abortion, but in later years, she was known to help women who, in her opinion, were deserving cases. She considered the emancipation of women as the leading cause of the increased number of abortions. In *Gentlemen of the Jury* she wrote, 'There is only one calling in which Modern Woman has failed – a calling in which poor despised grandmother succeeded – the task of keeping the cradles reasonably full.'[6] It has already been noted that her reluctant co-author, Dr Francis Bennett, distanced himself from the views expressed in the book.[7]

This intelligent, energetic and capable woman, while advancing professional interests in one sphere – maternity – not only failed to understand the needs of ordinary women in a changing world, but opposed the very things that would have made their lives better – contraception and safe legal abortion. By eulogising Doris, RANZCOG and NCW are inviting acceptance and tolerance of her contributions, dismissing as negligible her shortcomings, and perpetuating the stigma surrounding abortion, in particular.

The Obstetrical Society was responsible for funding the first professorial chair in obstetrics at the University of Otago, and later the O&G Society funded travel scholarships to enable New Zealand doctors to train overseas in obstetrics and gynaecology. In 1998, when RANZCOG was established, training could be undertaken in New Zealand and changes to eligibility were made. A valuable University of Otago Postgraduate Scholarship in Obstetrics and Gynaecology is now available for medical graduates, and this is a fitting memorial to all those who donated to the O&G Society.

On chemists and nurses

In the early 20th century, chemists and nurses were an approachable source of information, and since then their status has only increased due to improved training and the maintenance of professional standards. Since 2002, trained pharmacists can dispense the emergency contraceptive pill over the counter without a doctor's prescription. In 2016 the Ministry of Health approved over-the-counter supply of the contraceptive pill by trained pharmacists, provided the woman has seen a doctor in the last three years. Nurses with special training can now prescribe all methods of contraception, including the pill, and can insert and remove intrauterine devices and implants. There is no reason why nurses could not be trained to provide early outpatient abortion services.

On coroners

Coroners had an unenviable role, initially acting with a jury of men, then acting alone. Deaths referred to the coroner through police or medical channels were not necessarily typical of abortion deaths. Single, working-class women are over-represented in coroners' cases. Of the 160 case reports located, 60 per cent were single women, whereas in the maternal mortality statistics for the years 1930–1935, only 22 per cent were single women. Married women and women of higher socio-economic status were more likely to have their death certified by a doctor.

The verdicts of the coroners are carefully worded, often coming across as detached from the emotional impact of the loss they are examining. In most cases the verdict relies heavily on the evidence of the doctors. Sometimes, coroners were criticised for their actions. They also contributed to the public debate by expressing their opinions from time to time, and Mr Bartholomew's frustration, in the case of Mora MacKenzie, was one of the factors that led to the setting up of the Inquiry into Abortion in 1936. Sadly, although they were in a privileged position to comment on abortion cases, they did little to initiate discussion on the prevention of such deaths.

On the legal profession

During the period 1900–1939, three Chief Justices held office (Rt Hon Sir Robert Stout, 1899–1926; Hon Sir Charles Skerrett, 1926–1929; and Rt Hon Sir Michael Myers, 1929–1946), but none of them provided leadership on the management of abortion cases.

Many factors influenced sentencing, such as the nature of the crime, whether or not the offender was a first time or repeat offender, and whether the sentencing judge believed, as did Justice Denniston, that the punishment should act as a deterrent. No judge of that era employed the maximum sentence available to them – life imprisonment. The harshest sentence in this period was that of Justice Stringer, when he sentenced Mrs O'Shaughnessy to ten years' imprisonment in 1926, after repeated abortion offences. The second most severe sentence was that of Justice Denniston for another repeat offender, Mrs Bridget Chalk. She received eight years' imprisonment in 1912, following the death by air embolism of a woman she had assisted with an abortion.[8]

The following Supreme Court judges handed down sentences of seven years for abortion-related offences: Chapman, Denniston and Stringer (three times each), Sim and Smith (twice each), and Edwards, Herdman, Martin, Reed, Salmond, Stout and Williams (once each).

Judges' homilies on the criminality of abortion made little impact. The law was unable to deter abortionists, and defence lawyers found ample ways to demolish the case for prosecution. The evidence of accomplices was routinely challenged. Dying declarations were mostly ineffective. Juries frequently failed to convict, and decisions in many cases relied more on luck than reason.

We have not learned much from this experience. Abortion remains in the Crimes Act, despite overwhelming evidence that this is an inappropriate and ineffective response to what is best regarded as a personal health issue. Women were rarely charged for self-abortion, and from 1900 to 1939, none received a prison sentence, although statute law decreed a penalty of up to seven years' imprisonment, and this remained in the Crimes Act until 1977. Since then, the penalty for self-abortion has been reduced to a fine of $200 in the Contraception, Sterilisation and Abortion Act, but, as in the 20th century, this archaic crime is largely ignored.

On abortionists

Women risked their lives to end their pregnancies, and abortionists risked their freedom. Most doctors did not openly get involved, because to do so was a risk to their careers and their reputation, although a compassionate doctor might want to help women in distress, and many no doubt found a way to do so without being prosecuted. Clandestine operations were possible because doctors had legitimate access to the instruments used in an abortion – a speculum to open the vagina and view the cervix, a tenaculum to grasp the cervix, a metal sound to determine the size and position of the uterus, a series of dilators to open the cervix and a curette to scrape away the lining of the uterus. Since the 1970s, curettage has been replaced by the much safer technique of suction. Doctors had the training to recognise gynaecological abnormalities and, given the publicity about maternal sepsis in childbirth, were well aware of the importance of sterile technique. They could always claim they were investigating a gynaecological problem, as in the case of Dr Carew. A procedure purporting to be investigative in nature, and referred to as a diagnostic D&C (dilatation and curettage), may well have concealed an intended abortion. Doctors knew that if help was not provided, the woman might well resort to an unsafe procedure, and this fact had to be balanced against the risk of being exposed. Some abortionists acted out of compassion, but for those who made it a part-time career, the strongest motivation was the fees they could charge vulnerable women and their male partners.

The methods used by non-medical abortionists varied. Most started by recommending abortifacients readily available from chemists. Deep pelvic massage did not emerge as a common method in New Zealand at this time, although the pathologist described probable signs in the post-mortem of Freda Clark. The commonest method, as used by Jimmy Hayne and Mrs O'Shaughnessy, was a rubber catheter sold by chemists and either inserted repeatedly through the cervix, or left in place for 24 hours. Others, like Mrs Annie Aves, preferred to use a tent, which gradually dilated the cervix. Strict attention to antiseptic principles reduced the risk of infection, but rogue abortionists who did not understand or employ safety precautions were a menace.

Modern techniques for early outpatient abortions are much safer. As already mentioned, emptying the uterus by suctioning the contents with a flexible cannula has replaced sharp curettage. Since 2001 mifepristone (the abortion pill) has been available in New Zealand, so women now have a choice between having a medical or a surgical abortion.[9]

Based on intelligence from hospital admissions, police had some knowledge of illegal activities in the community and kept suspicious operators under surveillance, waiting to act if and when corroborative evidence made prosecution worthwhile. Since 1977 a legal pathway has been established for abortion, so the fear of being arrested for illegal activities is no longer a problem. However the stigma attached to abortion remains, and this adversely affects recruitment, training and research in this important area of women's health.

On politicians

Politicians only became involved in abortion law reluctantly, when under public pressure. The government responded in 1936 by setting up a Committee of Inquiry, but disappointingly, this did not lead to significant changes. The law remained as it was, and the greatest improvement for women was just over the horizon with the development of antibiotics.

Things have not changed on the political front. Politicians still regard abortion as a divisive issue, best avoided. The grounds for abortion are still relegated to the Crimes Act and make no sense when 98 per cent of abortions are carried out on the spurious grounds of mental health. Abortion should be regarded as a health and human rights issue. Equality for women will not be achieved until women have control over their fertility, and this will not happen until politicians accept that it is women who are best able to decide whether to continue an unplanned pregnancy or seek a safe abortion.

One way of divesting politicians of their unwanted and unwarranted interference is for medical advances to make their role superfluous. I have a dream: in the best possible future, researchers will develop something safe, simple, reliable, cheap and effective that women of all ages can take, once a month, in the privacy of their own home, without medical intervention, or whenever their period is late and they do not wish to be pregnant.

NOTES

1. Setting the Scene

1. *The Press*, 26 March 1900. Taking inflation into account, the Reserve Bank estimates that £1,000 in 1910 would be equivalent to approximately $163,000 in today's currency, in 1920 it would be equivalent to $89,000, and in 1930, $95,000; see http://www.rbnz.govt.nz/monetary-policy/inflation-calculator.
2. Doris Gordon and Francis Bennett, *Gentlemen of the Jury* (New Plymouth: Avery & Sons Ltd, 1937).
3. *New Zealand Parliamentary Debates (NZPD)*, 9 September–29 October 1937, Vol. 248.
4. Damien Fenton, *New Zealand and the First World War 1914–1919* (Auckland: Penguin Books in association with the Ministry for Culture and Heritage, 2013).
5. Jane Tolerton, *Ettie: A Life of Ettie Rout* (Auckland: Penguin Books, 1992); *Ettie Rout: New Zealand's Safer Sex Pioneer* (Auckland: Penguin Books, 2015).
6. Dick Scott, *Seven Lives on Salt River* (Auckland: Hodder & Stoughton, 1987); Fiona Kidman, *The Trouble with Fire* (Auckland: Random House, 2011), pp. 263–280.
7. Report of the Committee of Inquiry into the Various Aspects of the Problem of Abortion in New Zealand, *Appendix to the Journal of the House of Representatives (AJHR)*, 1937, H-31A.
8. Coroner's Report 1915/869; *Sun*, 30, 31 July 1915.
9. *The Press*, 13 February, 15 May 1917; *NZ Truth*, 20 January, 19 May 1917.
10. *Auckland Star*, 7 December 1914.
11. *Dominion*, 22 February 1918; *Auckland Star*, 10, 18 December 1917, 1, 19, 20, 21 February 1918; *New Zealand Herald*, 19, 20, 22 February 1918; *NZ Truth*, 9 February, 2 March 1918.
12. *Otago Daily Times*, 9, 16 January, 7, 14 February 1917; *NZ Truth*, 20 January, 24 February 1917.
13. *Otago Daily Times*, 14 February 1917; *NZ Truth*, 24 February 1917; *Dominion*, 14 February 1917.
14. *Colonist*, 14 August 1918; *Evening Post*, 31 August 1918, 5 December 1921; *New Zealand Herald*, 5 December 1921.

15 *Auckland Star*, 2, 14 February, 9, 14 May 1924; *The Press*, 14 February, 18 March, 10, 13, 15, 18 May 1924; *Otago Daily Times*, 11 March 1924; *Dominion*, 10 March 1924; *NZ Truth*, 29 March, 24 May 1924.
16 Jamie Mackay, 'Cooper, Daniel Richard and Cooper, Martha Elizabeth', *Dictionary of New Zealand Biography*, Te Ara – the Encyclopedia of New Zealand, http://www.TeAra.govt.nz/en/biographies/4c33/cooper-daniel-richard; *The Press*, 16, 17, 18, 19, 21, 22, 23 May 1923; *NZ Truth*, 12, 19 May 1923, 29 September 1964; *Dominion*, 13 October 1984; *Dominion Post*, 16 June 2012, 6 March 2015; *Wellingtonian*, 17 January 2013.
17 Mary Findlay, *Tooth and Nail: The Story of a Daughter of the Depression* (Wellington: A. H. & A. W. Reed, 1974), pp. 168–183.
18 Coroner's Report 1930/1014; *The Press*, 3, 23 July 1930; *Evening Post*, 3 July 1930.
19 Coroner's Report 1939/1519; *New Zealand Herald*, 2, 7 November 1939.

2. The McMillan Report

1 Report of the Committee of Inquiry into the Various Aspects of the Problem of Abortion in New Zealand, *AJHR*, 1937, H-31A.
2 Coroner's Report 1934/752.
3 Coroner's Report 1904/392; *The Press*, 28 April 1904.
4 Coroner's Report 1936/614; BMA Report, 'Death Due to Illegal Operation', *New Zealand Medical Journal*, 1936: 239–241; *Otago Daily Times*, 27 April, 2 June 1936; *Evening Post*, 24 April, 30 May 1936; *Dominion*, 30 May, 2, 10, June 1936; *NZ Truth*, 29 April, 3 June 1936.
5 This is a direct quotation from Sydney Smith, *Forensic Medicine: A Text Book for Students and Practitioners*, 3rd edition (London: J. & A. Churchill, 1931), p. 362.
6 Coroner's Report 1927/972; *The Press*, 12 July, 10 September 1927; *NZ Truth*, 15 September 1927.
7 *Dominion*, 12 April 1937.
8 *The Press*, 12 April 1937.
9 H. A., 'The report on abortion' [letter], *Tomorrow*, 26 May 1937, pp. 479–480.
10 C. J. O'Neill, 'Fertility: Past, Present, and Future', in R. J. Neville and C. G. O'Neill (eds) *The Population of New Zealand: Interdisciplinary Perspectives* (Auckland: Longman Paul, 1979).
11 Doris Gordon and Francis Bennett, *Gentlemen of the Jury* (New Plymouth: Thomas Avery & Sons, 1937).
12 Francis Bennett, *A Canterbury Tale: The Autobiography of Dr Francis Bennett* (Wellington: Oxford University Press, 1980), p. 167.
13 Doris Gordon, 'Modern Problems in Maternal Welfare in New Zealand, Part II: The Abortion Evil', *New Zealand Nursing Journal*, 15 January 1937.
14 *The Press*, 21, 24, 27, October 1937; *NZ Truth*, 27 October, 3 November 1937.
15 Barbara Brookes, 'The Committee of Inquiry into Abortion in New Zealand 1936–37', long essay for BA, University of Otago, September 1976.

16 Report of Committee of Inquiry into Maternity Services, *AJHR*, 1938, Session I, H-31A.

3. Medical Matters: Mainly Sepsis

1   'Charles White and The Arrest of Puerperal Fever', *Archives of Internal Medicine (Chicago)*, 1924, 34(5): 735, http://jamanetwork.com/journals/jamainternalmedicine/article-abstract/534646.
2   Peter M. Dunn, 'Dr Alexander Gordon (1752–99) and contagious puerperal fever', *Archives of Disease in Childhood (Fetal and Neonatal Edition)*, May 1998, http://dx.doi.org/10.1136/fn.78.3.F232.
3   P. M. Dunn, 'Oliver Wendell Holmes (1809–1894) and his essay on puerperal fever', *Archives of Disease in Childhood (Fetal and Neonatal Edition)*, July 2007, 92(4): F325–F327, http://doi.org/10.1136/adc.2005.077578.
4   M. Best and D. Neuhauser, 'Ignaz Semmelweis and the birth of infection control', *Quality and Safety in Health Care*, 2004, 13: 233–234, http://dx.doi.org/10.1136/qshc.2004.010918.
5   Imre Zoltan, 'Ignaz Semmelweis', *Encyclopaedia Brittanica*, https://www.britannica.com/biography/Ignaz-Semmelweis.
6   D. Pitt and J.-M. Aubin, 'Joseph Lister: father of modern surgery', *Canadian Journal of Surgery*, 2012, 55(5): E8–E9, doi:10.1503/cjs.007112.
7   Joseph Lister, 'On the Antiseptic Principle of the Practice of Surgery', *British Medical Journal*, 21 September 1867.
8   'Louis Pasteur', Chemical Heritage Foundation website, https://www.chemheritage.org/historical-profile/louis-pasteur.
9   Steve M. Blevins and Michael S. Bronze, 'Robert Koch and the "golden age" of bacteriology', *International Journal of Infectious Diseases*, September 2010, 14(9): e744–e751, https://doi.org/10.1016/j.ijid.2009.12.003.
10 Derek A. Dow, 'Mason, James Malcolm', *Dictionary of New Zealand Biography*. Te Ara – the Encyclopedia of New Zealand, http://www.TeAra.govt.nz/en/biographies/3m46/mason-james-malcolm.
11 Report of Commission, 'St Helens Maternal Hospital, Auckland', *AJHR* 1913, Session I, H-31B.
12 'Maternal Mortality in New Zealand. Report of Special Committee and a Criticism of the Report of the Special Committee', *New Zealand Medical Journal*, 1921: 353–360.
13 Philippa Mein Smith, *Maternity in Dispute: New Zealand 1920–1939* (Wellington: Government Printer, 1986), pp. 7–22.
14 Report of Commission, 'Kelvin Maternity Hospital', *AJHR*, 1924, Session I, H-31a; *New Zealand Herald*, 25 January, 16, 18, 27, 28, 29 February, 4, 5, 6 March, 24, 28 May, 25 June 1924; *NZ Truth*, 1, 8 March, 31 May, 28 June, 12 July 1924.
15 Coroner's Report 1930/1388; *Auckland Star*, 5 November 1930; *New Zealand Herald*, 5, 13 November 1930.
16 Coroner's Report 1904/392; *New Zealand Herald*, 23, 24, 25 August 1904.
17 Coroner's Report 1934/1004.
18 Coroner's Report 1903/248; *The Press*, 16 February 1903.
19 Coroner's Report 1908/356; *New Zealand Herald*, 20 March 1908.

20 Coroner's Report 1914/1339; *Evening Post*, 21 November 1914; *Dominion*, 23 November 1914.
21 Coroner's Report 1924/172; *The Press*, 28 January 1924; *Auckland Star*, 30 January 1924.
22 Coroner's Report 1935/441; *The Press*, 19, 29, 30 March, 10 April, 15 May 1935; *Evening Post*, 29 March, 10 April 1935; *New Zealand Herald*, 18 May 1935; *NZ Truth*, 22 May, 3, 17 April 1935.
23 Coroner's Report 1936/1307.
24 Coroner's Report 1935/360 (not found); *Auckland Star*, 9 May 1935; *New Zealand Herald*, 16 February, 10, 30 May 1935; *NZ Truth*, 3 April, 15 May 5 June 1935; Charles Belton, *Outside the Law in New Zealand* (Gisborne: Gisborne Publishing Co. Ltd, 1939), pp. 180–182. Detective Charles Belton investigated this case.
25 *New Zealand Herald*, 10 May 1935; *NZ Truth*, 15 May 1935.
26 Coroner's Report 1926/488; *The Press*, 19 April 1926.
27 Coroner's Report 1912/393; *New Zealand Herald*, 26 February 1912; *NZ Truth*, 13 April 1912.
28 Coroner's Report 1922/1244; *Evening Post*, 5, 6, 20 October 1922; *NZ Truth*, 7, 21 October 1922.
29 Kevin Brown, 'Sir Alexander Fleming', *Encyclopaedia Britannica*, https://www.britannica.com/biography/Alexander-Fleming.
30 'Gerhard Domagk', *Encyclopaedia Britannica*, https://www.britannica.com/biography/Gerhard-Domagk.
31 *Evening Post*, 14 July 1936, 30 January 1937; *New Zealand Herald*, 20 June 1938.
32 Coroner's Report 1937/920; *Auckland Star*, 15 May, 5 June 1937; *New Zealand Herald*, 17 May, 5 June, 17 July 1937; *Evening Post*, 16 July 1937; *NZ Truth*, 2 June, 21 July 1937.
33 Coroner's Report 1938/1997; *New Zealand Herald*, 23 December 1938; *NZ Truth*, 22 February 1939.
34 Coroner's Report 1939/537; *New Zealand Herald*, 28 April 1939.

4. Contraception: Mainly Barriers

1 Gordon Tait, *The Bartlett Syndrome: Censorship in New Zealand* (Christchurch: Freedom to Read, 1979); C. E. Beeby, *Books You Couldn't Buy: Censorship in New Zealand* (Wellington: Price Milburn, 1981).
2 *NZ Truth*, 3 May 1924.
3 Marie Stopes, *Married Love* (London: Fifield, 1918); Advertisement, *The Press*, 8 October 1919; *Northern Advocate*, 6 June 1923.
4 Ettie Rout, *Safe Marriage: A Return to Sanity* (London: Heinemann Medical Books, 1922); *Northern Advocate*, 10 October 1922.
5 *The Press*, 10, 11 October 1922.
6 *The Press*, 8, 10 January 1923.
7 *Maoriland Worker*, 16 May 1923.
8 *Evening Post*, 27 July, 2 August 1929; *Auckland Star*, 3 August 1929; *NZ Truth*, 29 August 1929.
9 Coroner's Report 1904/167; *Otago Daily Times*, 15 February 1904.
10 *New Zealand Parliamentary Debates (NZPD)*, 1906, Vol. 137, pp. 406–413.
11 *New Zealand Medical Journal*, December 1922, 21(106): 341–342.

12   Editorial on Contraception, *New Zealand Medical Journal*, 1932: 223–225.
13   H. E. A. Washbourn, 'The Ethics of Birth Control', *New Zealand Medical Journal*, 1932: 417–420.
14   *Wanganui Herald*, 13 February 1903.
15   *Auckland Star*, 14 January 1904.
16   *Oamaru Mail*, 22 June 1906; *North Otago Times*, 14 May 1909.
17   *Otago Daily Times*, 3, 6, 12 March 1923; *NZ Truth*, 17 March 1923.
18   *NZ Truth*, 6 January 1923.
19   *Otautau Standard and Wallace County Chronicle*, 13 May 1930.
20   *Auckland Star*, 12 June 1935.
21   *New Zealand Herald*, 17 July 1935.
22   *Evening Post*, 22 February, 2 March 1926; *NZ Truth*, 4, 11 March 1926.
23   *Evening Post*, 31 May 1926; *The Press*, 1 June 1926; *NZ Truth*, 1 April, 10 June 1926; Advertisements, *NZ Truth*, 23 February, 1 March 1924.
24   Jean H. Baker, *Margaret Sanger: A Life of Passion* (New York: Hill and Wang, 2011); Peter Bagge, *Woman Rebel: The Margaret Sanger Story* (Canada and USA: Drawn & Quarterly, 2013); Newsletters of Margaret Sanger Papers Project, New York University, 2011–2015.
25   Margaret Sanger, *Motherhood in Bondage* (New York: Brentano's, 1928), pp. 221–237.
26   Jonathan Eig, *The Birth of the Pill: How Four Crusaders Reinvented Sex and Launched a Revolution* (New York: Norton, 2014).
27   Aylmer Maude, *The Authorised Life of Marie C. Stopes* (London: Williams & Norgate, 1924); Ruth Hall (ed.), *Dear Dr Stopes: Sex in the 1920s* (London: André Deutsch, 1978); June Rose, *Marie Stopes and the Sexual Revolution* (London: Faber and Faber, 1992); William Garrett, *Marie Stopes: Feminist, Eroticist, Eugenicist* (San Francisco: Kenon Books, 2007).
28   Jane Tolerton, *Ettie: A Life of Ettie Rout* (Auckland: Penguin Books, 1992), p. 216.
29   Jane Tolerton, *Ettie: A Life of Ettie Rout* (Auckland: Penguin Books, 1992); Jane Tolerton, 'Rout, Ettie Annie', *Dictionary of New Zealand Biography*, Te Ara – the Encyclopedia of New Zealand, http://www.TeAra.govt.nz/en/biographies/3r31/rout-ettie-annie); Jane Tolerton, *Ettie Rout: New Zealand's Safer Sex Pioneer* (Auckland: Penguin Random House, 2015).
30   Ettie Rout, *Safe Marriage: A Return to Sanity* (London: Heinemann, 1922), revised and reissued under her married name as Ettie A. Hornibrook, *Practical Birth Control* (1927); Ettie Rout, *Sex and Exercise: A Study of the Sex Function in Women and Its Relation to Exercise* (London: Heinemann, 1925), republished in an abbreviated edition under her married name as Ettie A. Hornibrook, *Exercises for Women* (1927); Ettie Rout, *Native Diet: With Numerous Practical Recipes* (London: Heinemann, 1926); Ettie Rout, *Maori Symbolism: Being an Account of the Origin, Migration, and Culture of the New Zealand Maori as Recorded in Certain Sacred Legends* (London: Kegan Paul, Trench, Trubner, 1926).
31   *Evening Post*, 19 September 1936.
32   H. G. Wells, *You Can't Be Too Careful: A Sample of Life 1901–1951* (London: Secker & Warburg, 1947), p. 116.

33 Coroner's Report 1915/768; *Ellesmere Guardian*, 30 June 1915.
34 Marie Stopes, *Contraception: Theory, History and Practice*, 4th ed. (London: Putnam, 1934), p.108.
35 Coroner's Report 1935/896; *Auckland Star*, 9, 11, 15, 16 May, 3, 4, 5, 6, 7, 8, 10, 11, 13, 14, 19 June, 11, 12, 15, 16, 17 July, 29 November 1935; *New Zealand Herald*, 5, 6, 7, 8, 10, 11, 13, 15, 17, 18 June, 6, 9, 16, 17 July, 30 November 1935; *NZ Truth*, 5, 12, 19, 26 June, 3, 17, 24 July, 4 December 1935; *Weekly News*, 5, 12, 19 June 1935.
36 'Kyusaku Ogino and the calculation of the (in)fertile days in the female cycle: A brief biography', Museum of Contraception and Abortion, http://en.muvs.org/topic/kyusaku-ogino/.
37 Marie Stopes, *Contraception: Theory, History and Practice*, 4th ed. (London: Putnam, 1934).
38 Ibid.
39 Ibid.
40 *NZ Truth*, 6 September 1924.
41 *Hastings Standard*, 5 August 1910; *Poverty Bay Herald*, 4, 5 March 1914.
42 Percy Skuy, *Tales of Contraception* (History of Contraception Museum, 1995).
43 Marie Stopes, *Contraception: Theory, History and Practice*, 4th ed. (London: Putnam, 1934).
44 Coroner's Report 1928/1400; *Auckland Star*, 12, 23, 26 November 1928.
45 'Ernst Graefenberg (1881–1957)', Museum of Contraception and Abortion, http://en.muvs.org/topic/ernst-graefenberg-1881-1957-en/.
46 Margaret Sparrow and Lesley Bond, *Vasectomy: Practical Information and Advice* (Wellington: GP Publications, 1999), pp. 5–13.
47 *Auckland Star*, 14 April, 8 August 1928; 16 November 1932; 6 March 1935; *Otago Daily Times*, 6 July 1928; *Evening Post*, 26 September 1928; *The Press*, 4 November 1933, 20 April 1934, 12 September 1935.
48 *NZ Truth*, 2 May 1934.

5. A Flawed Law

1 Offences Against the Person Act 1866 (30 Vict No 19); *Nelson Examiner and New Zealand Chronicle*, 27 November 1866; *Wellington Independent*, 25 July 1867.
2 Coroner's Report 1903/399; *New Zealand Herald*, 1, 2 April 1903.
3 Coroner's Report 1931/822; *Auckland Star*, 23 March, 16 April 1931; *The Press*, 24 March, 17 April 1931; *NZ Truth*, 23 April 1931.
4 Coroner's Report 1932/567; *New Zealand Herald*, 5, 6 April, 6 May 1932; *Auckland Star*, 5 April, 6 May 1932.
5 *R. v Bourne* (1939) 1 KB 687; *Auckland Star*, 19 July 1938; *Evening Post*, 19, 20 July 1938; *New Zealand Herald*, 20 July 1938; *Women Today*, 1 November 1938.
6 A. C. Hanlon, *Random Recollections: Notes on a Lifetime at the Bar* (Dunedin: Otago Daily Times, 1939); Ken Catran, *Hanlon: A Casebook* (Auckland: BCNZ, 1985); Geoffrey G. Hall, 'Hanlon, Alfred Charles', *Dictionary of New Zealand Biography*, Te Ara – the Encyclopedia of New Zealand, http://www.TeAra.govt.nz/en/biographies/2h11/hanlon-alfred-charles.

7   NZ Truth, 5, 19 August 1922, 21 November 1925, 9 October 1930, 14, 21 July 1937; Auckland Star, 18 October 1929, 31 October 1934, 10, 12, 15, 21 July, 7, 26 August 1937, 2 September 1941, 16, 23 December 1944, 26 March 1961; New Zealand Herald, 10, 12, 20 July, 9, 27, 26, 27 October 1937, 16 December 1944, 15 March 1961; Evening Post, 6 July 1945; Niel Wright, Poetry Notes, Quarterly Newsletter of PANZA, Summer 2013, 3(4): 6–9.
8   Richard Arnold Singer, 24 Notable Trials, Richard Singer's Crime Broadcasts (Auckland: Oswald-Sealy, 1944).
9   Grey River Argus, 4, 9, 10, 11, 13, 15 March 1905, 28 March, 4, 11, 19, 27 April, 2, 12 May, 13, 18, 21, 26 September, 2, 6, 8, 10 October, 13, 15 November 1906; Otago Witness, 15 March 1905, 10 October 1906; West Coast Times, 3, 11, 13, 14 March 1905, 12, 21, 22, 24 September, 3, 6, 9 October 1906; Evening Post, 22 September, 8 October 1906; NZ Truth, 29 September, 17 November 1906.
10 Coroner's Report 1914/368; The Press, 20 March 1914; NZ Truth, 28 March 1914.
11 Coroner's Report 1919/300; Nelson Evening Mail, 18, 19, 20 June 1919; Grey River Argus, 18, 19, 20 June, 26 September 1919; Colonist, 18, 19, 20, 21, 28 June, 16, 21, 23, 25 July, 24, 26 September, 13, 15 October, 22 December 1919; NZ Truth, 28 June, 19 July, 4 October 1919; Otago Witness, 30 September 1919.
12 Grey River Argus, 21 February 1917; Nelson Evening Mail, 5, 6, 13, 14, 15, 24 March 1917; NZ Truth, 24 March 1917.
13 The Press, 20, 22 March, 15 April, 13 May 1915; Evening Post, 20, 26 March, 14 April 1915; NZ Truth, 20, 27 March, 17 April, 1, 22, 29 May, 11 December 1915.
14 Coroner's Report 1923/118; Gisborne Times, 20 February 1923; The Press, 20 February 1923; NZ Truth, 10 February, 3, 24 March 1923.
15 NZ Truth, 10 February, 3, 24 March 1923; Gisborne Times, 20 February 1923.
16 NZ Truth, 24 March 1923.
17 Taranaki Daily News, 14, 17, 20 September, 15, 19 October 1904; Taranaki Herald, 10, 13, 19, 20, 26 September, 1, 5, 6, 7, 10, 14, 17, 19, 20, 21, 27 October 1904; Grey River Argus, 19 October 1904; Observer, 1, 8, 22 October 1904; Hawera & Normanby Star, 12, 26 September, 15 October 1904; Evening Post, 1, 5 October 1904.
18 Coroner's Report 1915/1228; Otago Daily Times, 7 October, 13 November 1915; NZ Truth, 30 October, 13, 20 November 1915, 19 February 1916.
19 Star, 2, 6 September, 16 November 1904; The Press, 7 September, 14, 15, 16, 17 November 1904, 29 March, 10 April, 17 May 1905; Hawera & Normanby Star, 16 November 1904, 16 May 1905; Evening Post, 16 November 1904, 16 May, 8 April 1905.
20 The Press, 17 May 1905.
21 New Zealand Herald, 10, 13, 14 December 1918; NZ Truth, 21 December 1918.
22 NZ Truth, 21 December 1918.
23 Coroner's Report 1912/394; New Zealand Herald, 30 March 1912; NZ Truth, 6, 27 April, 8 June 1912.
24 NZ Truth, 8 June 1912.

25 *Hawera Star*, 2, 7 February 1934; *Otago Daily Times*, 3 February 1934; *Taranaki Herald*, 3, 7, 12, 13 February 1934; *NZ Truth*, 24 January, 14, 21 February 1934; *Auckland Star*, 3, 17 January 1934.
26 *Hawera & Normanby Star*, 6 February, 1 April 1905; *Evening Post*, 23 September, 21 October 1904, 4, 6 February, 31 March, 1 April 1905; *West Coast Times*, 3 April 1905; *Grey River Argus*, 8 April 1905; *Gazette Law Reports*, Vol. 7, 14 June 1905.
27 *Auckland Star*, 4 July, 22 August, 11 September, 29, 30 October, 4, 5, 9 November 1929; *New Zealand Herald*, 12 July, 13, 21 September 1929; *NZ Truth*, 19 September, 3 October, 7, 14 November 1929; *The Press*, 21 September 1929.
28 Coroner's Report 1926/54; *The Press*, 9 November 1925, 6, 11,12 February 1926; *Auckland Star*, 9, 16 November 1925, 11 February 1926; *Evening Post*, 11 February 1926; *New Zealand Herald*, 10 November 1925; *NZ Truth*, 14, 28 November 1925, 18 February 1926.
29 Coroner's Report 1906/1043; *Taranaki Herald*, 7 November 1906; *Feilding Star*, 7, 22 November 1906; *Grey River Argus*, 2 October, 8 November 1906, 6 March 1907; *Evening Post*, 7, 22, 23 November 1906; *Hawera & Normanby Star*, 23 November 1906, 5 March 1907; *Manawatu Times*, 8, 14, 22, 23 November 1906; *Manawatu Standard*, 8, 20, 21, 22, 29 November, 5, 6 March 1907; *Wairarapa Age*, 8, 23 November 1906; *Wairarapa Daily Times*, 8, 14 November 1906, 6 March 1907; *Mataura Ensign*, 13 November 1906; *Wanganui Herald*, 13 November, 4 March 1907.
30 Coroner's Report 1914/295; *Manawatu Daily Times*, 23 February 1914.

6. Doctors

1 *Nelson Evening Mail*, 20 July, 12, 13, 14, 17, 18, 19, 21 December 1900, 17 January, 4, 5, 6, 7 March 1901, 3, 6 January 1902; *Colonist*, 21 July, 11, 13, 14, 15, 17, 18, 19, 22 December 1900, 22 January, 6, 7, 19 March 1901, 3, 4, 6, 7 January 1902; *Evening Post*, 7 November 1990, 22 January, 6 March 1901; *The Press*, 22 January 1901; *Hawera & Normanby Star*, 6 March 1901.
2 *Southland Times*, 30 January 1903; *Otago Witness*, 4 February, 11 March 1903; *Otago Daily Times*, 9 February, 4, 9 March 1903; *Evening Post*, 13 February 1903; *Southland Times*, 6, 9 March 1903.
3 *The Press*, 22 December 1937; *Otago Daily Times*, 1 November 1975; Diane Williams, personal communication, April 2016.
4 Diane Williams, personal communication, April 2016.
5 Coroner's Report 1906/475; *Otago Daily Times*, 11, 19 May, 2 June 1906; *Otago Witness*, 16 May 1906.
6 *Otago Daily Times*, 2 June 1906.
7 Linda Bryder, *A Voice for Mothers: the Plunket Society and Infant Welfare, 1907–2000* (Auckland: Auckland University Press, 2003).
8 F. Truby King, 'A Plea for Stringent Legislation in the Matter of Corrupt and Immoral Publications', *New Zealand Medical Journal*, October 1890, 4: 18.
9 Coroner's Report 1907/852; *Otago Daily Times*, 16 September 1907.
10 *Evening Post*, 31 August 1908; *The Press*, 14, 22 August, 14 September

1908; *NZ Truth*, 1, 29 August, 5 September 1908; *Grey River Argus*, 22 August 1908.
11 Margaret Sparrow, *Rough on Women: Abortion in 19th-Century New Zealand* (Wellington: Victoria University Press, 2014), pp. 130–134.
12 Coroner's Report 1921/1209; *The Press*, 12, 22, 24, 28 October 1921; *NZ Truth*, 29 October, 5 November 1921.
13 *Evening Post*, 22, 28 July, 25, 27, 28 August, 1, 9, 10, 16 September 6, 7, 8, 9, 11 December 1926; *Auckland Star*, 28 July, 5, 23, 27 August, 2, 9, 10, 16 September 1926; *New Zealand Herald*, 4 September 1926; *NZ Truth*, 5 August, 9, 16, 23 September, 2, 9, 16 December 1926, 14 April 1927; *The Press*, 4 September, 9 December 1926.
14 *NZ Truth*, 8 December 1927, 28 July 1928.
15 *NZ Truth*, 5, 12, 26 April, 10, 17 May, 23 August 1928; *Evening Post*, 9 May 1928; *Auckland Star*, 9 May 1928; *The Press*, 10 May 1928.
16 Coroner's Report 1928/1039; *NZ Truth*, 6 September 1928; *New Zealand Herald*, 5 September 1928; *The Press*, 5 September 1928.
17 *NZ Truth*, 10 October, 7 November 1929, 20 March, 29 May 1930.
18 Coroner's Report 1931/241; *New Zealand Herald*, 10, 11, 26 February 1931; *Auckland Star*, 11, 25, 26 February 1931.
19 Coroner's Report 1938/1848; *NZ Truth*, 7 December 1938.
20 *NZ Truth*, 17 December 1952, 7 January, 25 February 1953.
21 Linda Bryder, *The Rise and Fall of National Women's Hospital: A History* (Auckland: Auckland University Press, 2014), pp. 9–45.
22 Doris Gordon and Francis Bennett, *Gentlemen of the Jury* (New Plymouth: Avery & Sons Ltd, 1937), p. 39.
23 Ibid, pp. 17–18.
24 Ibid, pp. 100–105.
25 F. A. Bennett, *A Canterbury Tale: The Autobiography of Dr Francis Bennett* (Wellington: Oxford University Press, 1980), p. 167.
26 Margaret Sparrow, *Abortion Then and Now* (Wellington: Victoria University Press, 2010), pp. 17–18; P. P. Lynch, *No Remedy for Death* (London: John Long, 1970), pp. 91–98; *Auckland Star*, 26, 27 June, 3, 17, 24, 25 July, 3, 4, 5, 6 August, 19, 21, 19, 21, 22 October 1936, 3, 5, 6, 17 February, 9 March 1937; *New Zealand Herald*, 11 August 1936, 20 February 1937; *Evening Post*, 17 February 1937; *Dominion*, 4, 5, 11 October 1938; *NZ Truth*, 24 February 1937; Barbara Brookes, 'Aves, Isabel Annie 1887–1938', *Dictionary of New Zealand Biography*, Te Ara – the Encyclopedia of New Zealand, http://www.TeAra.govt.nz/en/biographies/4a25/aves-isabel-annie.
27 *Auckland Star*, 3, 5, 10, 26, 27, 30, 31 October, 1, 24, 27 November 1938; *New Zealand Herald*, 2 November 1938; *Evening Post*, 28 April 1939.
28 Margaret Sparrow, 'Dr Doris Gordon: a flawed legacy', letter to the editor, *O&G Magazine*, Summer 2016, 19(4): 71–72.

7. Chemists

1 *The Press*, 22 April, 20 May 1910; *Manawatu Standard*, 6 August 1910; *King Country Chronicle*, 5 October 1910, 24 March 1915; *Taranaki Daily News*, 6 October 1910; *Bush Advocate*, 16 January 1911; *Feilding*

Star, 2 May 1912; *Rodney and Otamatea Times, Waitemata and Kaipara Gazette*, 1 April 1914; *Evening Post*, 3 April 1915.
2   *Otago Daily Times*, 6 January 1900; *Otago Witness*, 24 May 1900, 23 April 1902.
3   *Thames Star*, 22 January 1900.
4   *Evening Post*, 20 January 1900; *Otago Witness*, 24 May 1900; *Wairarapa Daily Times*, 10 December 1900; *Oamaru Mail*, 15 March 1901.
5   *Free Lance*, 4 May 1901; *Evening Post*, 7 October 1901; *Wairarapa Daily Times*, 9 October 1901.
6   *Thames Star*, 25 August 1904; *Ohinemuri Gazette*, 14 November 1904.
7   *Auckland Star*, 13 June 1911.
8   *North Otago Times*, 14 December 1912.
9   *Otago Witness*, 4 January 1905; *Observer*, 25 December 1920.
10 *Akaroa Mail and Banks Peninsula Advertiser*, 21 April 1925.
11 *NZ Truth*, 5 August 1926–28 July 1927.
12 Coroner's Report 1930/1379; *Auckland Star*, 10 November 1930.
13 Coroner's Report 1902/48; *Wanganui Herald*, 6, 7, 8, 9 January 1902; *Wanganui Chronicle*, 7 January 1902; *West Coast Times*, 7 January 1902.
14 *Southern News*, 2 October 1906; *Wanganui Chronicle*, 2, 10 October 1906, 14 March, 29 April, 3, 6 May 1907; *Wanganui Herald*, 18 October 1906, 8, 11, 13 March, 16, 19, 26 April, 1 June 1907; *Mataura Ensign*, 14 March 1907; *Gazette Law Reports*, Vol. 9, 14 June 1907; *Wairarapa Daily Times*, 29 November 1907.
15 Coroner's Report 1902/897; *Auckland Star*, 31 October, 10 December 1902, 13 February 1903; *Evening Post*, 1, 28 November 1902, 11, 13, 17 February 1903; *Manawatu Standard*, 3 November 1902; *Otago Daily Times*, 13 November 1902; *Southland Times*, 25 November 1902; *Feilding Star*, 14 February 1903; *Timaru Herald*, 16 February 1903; *New Zealand Herald*, 18 February, 14 February 1903; *The Press*, 20 February, 13 May 1903.
16 *Feilding Star*, 14 February 1903.
17 *Feilding Star*, 13 May 1903.
18 *NZ Truth*, 13 July, 31 August, 7 December 1907; *Wanganui Herald*, 26 August 1907; *Wairarapa Daily Times*, 29 November 1907.
19 Coroner's Report 1911/586; *New Zealand Herald*, 8 June 1911.
20 Coroner's Report 1923/389; *Northern Advocate*, 13 February 1923; *The Press*, 15 February 1923; *New Zealand Herald*, 2 March 1923.
21 Coroner's Report 1906/878; *Otago Daily Times*, 24, 25, 29 September 1906; *Otago Witness*, 25 September, 3, 10 October, 28 November 1906; *Evening Post*, 24 November 1906.
22 Coroner's Report 1913/1160; *Otago Daily Times*, 6, 11, 18 October 1913; *Dominion*, 18 October 1913; *Evening Post*, 18 October 1913; *NZ Truth*, 11, 18, 25 October 1913.
23 *NZ Truth*, 25 October 1913.
24 *NZ Truth*, 11, 18, 25 October, 20 December 1919, 7 February, 20 May, 14 August 1920; *Dominion*, 19 November 1919; *New Zealand Times*, 20 May, 10, 11 August 1920.
25 Coroner's Report 1921/1330; *The Press*, 18, 28 February, 13, 22 May, 11 August 1923; *NZ Truth*, 27 May 1922, 18 August 1923.
26 *The Press*, 11 August 1923; *NZ Truth*, 14 July, 11, 18 August 1923.
27 *The Press*, 11 August 1923.

28 *NZ Truth*, 25 July 1925; *New Zealand Herald*, 2 September 1925.
29 Coroner's Report 1929/697; *NZ Truth*, 13 June, 15 August, 7 November 1929; *Evening Post*, 7 June 1929; *Auckland Star*, 7 June 1929.
30 Coroner's Report 1933/392; *Auckland Star*, 29, 30 December 1932; *New Zealand Herald*, 30 December 1932.
31 Coroner's Report 1935/837; *Auckland Star*, 3, 29 May, 17, 25 June 1935; *New Zealand Herald*, 3 May, 18, 26 June 1935; *NZ Truth*, 26 June, 3 July 1935.
32 *NZ Truth*, 13 May 1936.
33 *NZ Truth*, 29 January, 13 May 1936, 8 December 1954, 16 February, 2 March 1955.
34 *New Zealand Herald*, 27 July 1937; *NZ Truth*, 4, 23 August 1937; Margaret Sparrow, *Abortion Then and Now* (Wellington: Victoria University Press, 2010) p 47.

8. Nurses

1   Margaret Tennant, 'Neill, Elizabeth Grace', *Dictionary of New Zealand Biography*, Te Ara – the Encyclopedia of New Zealand, http://www.TeAra.govt.nz/en/biographies/2n5/neill-elizabeth-grace.
2   Patricia A. Sargison, 'Maclean, Hester', *Dictionary of New Zealand Biography*. Te Ara – the Encyclopedia of New Zealand, http://www.TeAra.govt.nz/en/biographies/3m25/maclean-hester.
3   Beryl Hughes, 'Bicknell, Jessie', *Dictionary of New Zealand Biography*, Te Ara – the Encyclopedia of New Zealand, http://www.TeAra.govt.nz/en/biographies/3b32/bicknell-jessie.
4   Report of British Medical Association Council Meeting, *New Zealand Medical Journal*, 1923: 117.
5   Jan Rodgers, 'Lambie, Mary Isabel', *Dictionary of New Zealand Biography*. Te Ara – the Encyclopedia of New Zealand, http://www.TeAra.govt.nz/en/biographies/4l2/lambie-mary-isabel
6   *NZ Truth*, 15 January, 26 February 1910; *New Zealand Herald*, 8 January, 1, 7 February 1910; *Auckland Star*, 7 January, 21 February 1910; *Evening Post*, 22 February 1910.
7   *Auckland Star*, 22, 24 November 1909, 7 January, 21 February 1910; *New Zealand Herald*, 25 November 1909, 8 January, 1, 7 February 1910; *NZ Truth*, 15 January, 26 February 1910; *Evening Post*, 23, 25 February 1910.
8   Coroner's Report 1911/903A; *New Zealand Herald*, 5, 6 July 1911; *NZ Truth*, 8, 15, 22, 29 July, 5, 12, 19, 26 August, 9, 16 September, 7, 14 October, 2, 9, 16 December 1911; *Evening Post*, 3 May 1912; *Gazette Law Reports*, 12 July 1912, Vol. 14; Owen J. Cherrett, *Without Fear or Favour: 150 Years Policing Auckland 1840–1990* (Auckland: New Zealand Police and L. Patrick Hunter, 1989).
9   Coroner's Report 1922/1051; *Auckland Star*, 18 August, 4, 29 September, 2, 12 October 1922; *Weekly News*, 24 August 1922; *New Zealand Herald*, 19 August, 5 September, 2, 13, 28 October 1922; *NZ Truth*, 9 September, 21 October 1922.
10 *Northern Advocate*, 22 January 1925; *Auckland Star*, 3, 16 February, 19 November, 18 December 1925, 2 February 1926; *New Zealand Herald*, 19 December 1925, 2, 7, 8, 14, 15 January, 11 February 1926; *NZ Truth*, 21 January, 11 February 1926; *The Press*, 6 February 1926.

11 *The Press*, 6 February 1926.
12 Coroner's Report 1900/1552; *New Zealand Mail*, 13, 20 September, 29 November, 6 December 1900; *The Press*, 10, 18 September, 28, 29 November, 5, 8, 10 December 1900; *Evening Post*, 8, 17, 18, 19 September, 26, 28, 29 November, 4, 5, 7, 8 December 1900; *Hawera & Normanby Star*, 6 December 1900; *Otago Witness*, 12 December 1900.
13 *Free Lance*, 15 September 1900.
14 *NZ Truth*, 18 May 1912.
15 *The Press*, 5, 11 February 1925; *Auckland Star*, 10 February 1925; *NZ Truth*, 14, 21 February 1925.
16 Coroner's Report 1913/1362; *New Zealand Herald*, 21, 28 February 1913; *Auckland Star*, 27, 28 February 1913; *Auckland Weekly News*, 29 May 1913; *Evening Post*, 1, 26 May, 17 July, 25 August 1913; *NZ Truth*, 22 February, 8 March, 31 May 1913; *Dominion*, 19 July 1913; *Gazette Law Reports*, 19 September 1913, Vol. 15, pp. 671–674.
17 Coroner's Report 1917/1362; *Auckland Star*, 6, 9, 29 November 1917, 19, 20, 21 February 1918; *Dominion*, 6, 12 November 1917, 20, 21 February 1918; *NZ Truth*, 17 November, 15 December 1917, 2 March 1918; *New Zealand Herald*, 22 February 1918.
18 *NZ Truth*, 17 November 1917.
19 *Auckland Star*, 23 April, 5, 6 May 1927; *New Zealand Herald*, 1 April, 6 May 1927; *NZ Truth*, 7 April, 12 May 1927.
20 *NZ Truth*, 12 May 1927.
21 Coroner's Report 1930/1246; *New Zealand Herald*, 23, 24 January, 5 February 1930; *NZ Truth*, 16, 30 January, 6, 13 February 1930; *The Press*, 11 February 1930.
22 Coroner's Report 1936/646; *The Press*, 28 March 1936; *NZ Truth*, 13, 20, 27 May 1936.
23 *New Zealand Times*, 18 May 1920; *New Zealand Herald*, 27 May, 17, 26 June, 24 August 1920; *NZ Truth*, 28 August 1920.
24 Coroner's Report 1929/819; *Auckland Star*, 27 November 1928; *NZ Truth*, 8, 29 November, 6 December 1928, 11, 18 July 1929.
25 *Evening Post*, 29 September, 12, 13, 14, 17, 25, 26, 27, 28 October 1938, 27 March, 5 April, 3 May 1939; *NZ Truth*, 2 November 1938; *Dominion*, 6 April 1939.
26 Coroner's Report 1910/430; *Otago Daily Times*, 2, 7, 19 April 1910; *NZ Truth*, 9, 16 April 1910; *New Zealand Herald*, 24 May 1910.
27 Coroner's Report 1914/71; *Auckland Star*, 2, 3, 10 February 1914; *New Zealand Herald*, 4, 11 February 1914.
28 Coroner's Report 1929/309; *New Zealand Herald*, 19 February 1929; *Auckland Star*, 19 February 1929; *Evening Post*, 19 February 1929; *NZ Truth*, 28 February 1929.

9. All Sorts

1 Coroner's Report 1903/637; *Otago Daily Times*, 9, 10, 11, 14, 15, 16, 17, 27 July, 15, 16 September 1903; *The Press*, 9, 11, 15, 17 July 1903; *Otago Witness*, 15, 16, 22 July 1903.
2 Coroner's Report 1911/226; *NZ Truth*, 4, 20, 27 May, 8, 15, July, 26 August, 2, 9 September 1911; *Grey River Argus*, 25 February, 7 July 1911;

Evening Post, 2, 18 May 1911.
3   NZ Truth, 4, 11, 18 May 1912; Evening Post, 30 April 1912; The Press, 9, 14, 15, 16, 17 May 1912.
4   Coroner's Report 1920/774; Grey River Argus, 14 June 1920; NZ Truth, 19, 26 June, 10 July, 14 August 1920; Otago Daily Times, 2 July 1920.
5   Coroner's Report 1923/501; The Press, 14 May, 7 June 1923; Nelson Evening Standard, 16 May 1923; Nelson Evening Mail, 16 May, 7 June 1923; NZ Truth, 19, 26 May, 16 June 1923; New Zealand Herald, 16 May 1923.
6   Coroner's Report 1928/102; Otago Witness, 15 December 1927, 4, 31 January, 13 March 1928; NZ Truth, 19 January, 2 February, 15 March 1928.
7   NZ Truth, 14, 21, 28 March, 9 May 1929.
8   The Press, 17, 18, 20, 21, 24, 27 June, 5, 9, 28 July, 5, 13, 27, 31 August, 1, 2 September, 9, 16, 22, 23, 24, 26 November 1927; NZ Truth, 4, 11 August, 1, 8 September, 17, 24 November, 1 December 1927.
9   Coroner's Report 1929/1019; New Zealand Herald, 23 August, 6 November 1929; Auckland Star, 29, 30 July, 8, 22 August, 29 October 1929; NZ Truth, 1, 29 August, 14 November 1929.
10 New Zealand Herald, 23 August, 6 November 1929; NZ Truth, 29 August, 14 November 1929.
11 Auckland Star, 29 May, 22, 26 July 1939; New Zealand Herald, 30 May, 22, 27 July 1939; NZ Truth, 14 June, 26 July, 2 August 1939.
12 P. P. Lynch, No Remedy for Death (London: John Long, 1970), pp. 83–90; NZ Truth, 16, 23 July, 20 August, 5, 12, 19 November, 17, 24 December 1931; Evening Post, 7, 8, 9, 10, 11, 13, 15, 22, 23, 30 July, 6, 11, 12, 13, 14, 15, 17 August, 21, 27 October, 2, 3, 4, 5, 6, 7, 9, 10, 11, 12, 13, 14 November, 3, 4, 5, 11, 17, 23 December 1931; New Zealand Herald, 17 July 1931; Dominion Post, 29 October 2012, 16 April, 4 September 2015.
13 Coroner's Report 1932/975; Auckland Star, 11 August 1932; New Zealand Herald, 20 August, 12 October 1932.
14 Coroner's Report 1934/875; Evening Post, 6 July, 30, 31 October, 2 November 1934; NZ Truth, 15 August, 31 October, 7 November 1934.
15 Coroner's Report 1937/740; NZ Truth, 10, 24 February, 12 May, 23 June 1937; Otago Daily Times, 7 May 1937; Evening Post, 7 May 1937; New Zealand Herald, 7 May 1937.

10. DIY Abortion

1   Auckland Star, 5, 9, 12 March 1915; NZ Truth, 24 April, 13, 20 March 1915; Dominion, 3, 16 July 1915.
2   NZ Truth, 13 June 1908; Evening Post, 10 June, 25 August 1908.
3   NZ Truth, 13 June 1908.
4   Marlborough Express, 27 November, 2, 4 December 1909; Nelson Evening Mail, 1 December 1909; Evening Post, 2 December 1909; Star, 2 December 1909.
5   NZ Truth, 15, 22 September, 10 November 1923; New Zealand Herald, 26 October 1923; Auckland Star, 31 October 1923.
6   Coroner's Report 1937/1587; New Zealand Herald, 29 October 1937; Auckland Star, 29 October 1937; The Press, 2 December 1937.

7   Coroner's Report 1926/826; *Auckland Star*, 19, 23 June 1926; *New Zealand Herald*, 26 June 1926.
8   Coroner's Report 1910/130; *Bush Advocate*, 24, 25, 26, 28 January 1910.
9   Coroner's Report 1908/568; *Auckland Star*, 18 June 1908; *New Zealand Herald*, 19 June 1908.
10 Coroner's Report 1930/1460; *The Press*, 6 October 1930.
11 Coroner's Report 1931/496; *Evening Post*, 23 February 1931; *NZ Truth*, 23 April 1931.
12 Coroner's Report 1930/969; *Auckland Star*, 11, 15 August 1930; *New Zealand Herald*, 12, 16 August 1930.
13 Coroner's Report 1938/1524.
14 Coroner's Report 1938/1834.
15 Coroner's Report 1934/206.
16 Coroner's Report 1902/445; *Hawera & Normanby Star*, 21 May 1902; *Otago Witness*, 28 May 1902.
17 Coroner's Report 1910/1119; *New Zealand Herald*, 14, 15, 26 October 1910; *Auckland Star*, 25 October 1910.
18 Coroner's Report 1940/231.
19 Coroner's Report 1900/262; *Auckland Star*, 30 March 1900; *New Zealand Herald*, 2 April 1900.
20 Coroner's Report 1908/554; *New Zealand Herald*, 10, 13 June 1908.
21 Coroner's Report 1934/119; *NZ Truth*, 7 February 1934; *The Press*, 10 November 1933, 2 February 1934; *New Zealand Herald*, 3 February 1934.
22 Coroner's Report 1912/384; *Star*, 15 April 1912; *Auckland Star*, 15 April 1912; *New Zealand Herald*, 16 April 1912; *NZ Truth*, 20 April 1912.
23 Coroner's Report 1924/1358; *Evening Post*, 18 November 1924; *The Press*, 19 November 1924.
24 Coroner's Report 1932/402; *The Press*, 16 February, 15 March 1932.
25 Coroner's Report 1934/388.

11. Some Observations

1   Perinatal and Maternal Mortality Review Committee, *Ninth Annual Report of the Perinatal and Maternal Mortality Review Committee: Reporting Mortality 2013* (Wellington: Health Quality & Safety Commission, June 2015).
2   Abortion Supervisory Committee, *Annual Reports*, 1980–2016 (Presented to the House of Representatives pursuant to Section 39 of the Contraception, Sterilisation, and Abortion Act 1977).
3   E. G. Raymond and D. A. Grimes, 'The comparative safety of legal induced abortion and childbirth in the United States', *Obstetrics and Gynecology*, February 2012, 119: 215–219.
4   Ronald W Jones, 'Honouring Doris Gordon: the foundation of a legacy', *O&G Magazine*, Spring 2016, 18(3): 69–72.
5   Margaret Sparrow, 'Dr Doris Gordon: a flawed legacy', letter to the editor, *O&G Magazine*, Summer 2016, 18(4): 71–72.
6   Doris C. Gordon and Francis Bennett, *Gentlemen of the Jury* (New South Wales: Thomas Avery, 1937), p. 40.

7   F. A. Bennett, *A Canterbury Tale: The Autobiography of Dr Francis Bennett* (Wellington: Oxford University Press, 1980), p. 167.
8   Margaret Sparrow, *Rough on Women: Abortion in 19th-Century New Zealand* (Wellington: Victoria University Press, 2014), pp. 130–134.
9   Margaret Sparrow, 'Introducing mifepristone into New Zealand', *O&G Magazine*, May 2004; 6(2): 145–146.

FURTHER READING

Brookes, Barbara, 'The Committee of Inquiry into Abortion New Zealand 1936–37', BA Hons Thesis, University of Otago, 1976.
Brookes, Barbara, 'Housewives Depression: The Debate Over Abortion and Birth Control in the 1930s', *New Zealand Journal of History*, 15(2), October 1981.
Brookes, Barbara, 'Reproductive Rights: The debate over abortion and birth control in the 1930s', in Barbara Brookes, Charlotte Macdonald and Margaret Tennant (eds), *Women in History: Essays on European Women in New Zealand* (Wellington: Allen & Unwin/Port Nicholson Press, 1986).
Brookes, Barbara, *Abortion in England 1900–1967* (London, New York, Sydney: Croom Helm, 1988).
Brookes, Barbara, 'The Crime of Abortion in New Zealand 1900–1939', *Women's Studies Association Conference Papers*, 1988.
Coney, Sandra, *Standing in the Sunshine: A history of New Zealand Women Since They Won the Vote* (Auckland: Penguin Books, 1993), pp. 70–79.
Findlay, Mary, *Tooth and Nail: The story of a daughter of the Depression* (Wellington: A. H. & A. W. Reed, 1974).
Gordon, Doris and Bennett, Francis, *Gentlemen of the Jury* (New Plymouth: Avery & Sons Ltd, 1937).
Gordon, Doris, *Back-Blocks Baby-Doctor* (London: Faber, 1955).
Gordon, Doris, *Doctor Down Under* (London: Faber, 1957).
Lévesque, Andrée, 'Grandmother took ergot: an historical perspective on abortion in New Zealand 1897–1937, Part 1: The abortionists', *Broadsheet*, Vol. 43, October 1976, pp. 18–22.
Lévesque, Andrée, 'Grandmother took ergot: an historical perspective on abortion in New Zealand 1897–1937, Part 2: The women', *Broadsheet*, Vol. 44, November 1976, pp. 26–31.

McCulloch, Alison, *Fighting to Choose: The Abortion Rights Struggle in New Zealand* (Wellington: Victoria University Press, 2013).
Mein Smith, Philippa, *Maternity in Dispute: New Zealand 1920–1939* (Wellington: Government Printer, 1986).
Mein Smith, Philippa, 'Mortality in childbirth in the 1920s and 1930s', in Barbara Brookes, Charlotte Macdonald and Margaret Tennant (eds), *Women in History: Essays on European Women in New Zealand* (Wellington: Allen & Unwin/Port Nicholson Press, 1986).
Richdale, Joanne, 'The "problem" of abortion in 1930s Aotearoa New Zealand: a study of social attitudes in selected print media, 1936–1938', Research Essay, University of Auckland, 2005.
Richdale, Joanne, 'Lifting the Veil of Silence: Personal Abortion Narratives in New Zealand 1919–1937', PhD Thesis, University of Auckland, 2010.
Smith, Lesley, 'The Problem of Abortion in New Zealand in the Nineteen-Thirties', MA Thesis Research Essay, University of Auckland, 1972.
Sparrow, Margaret, *Abortion Then and Now: New Zealand Abortion Stories from 1940 to 1980* (Wellington: Victoria University Press, 2010).
Sparrow, Margaret, *Rough on Women: Abortion in 19th-Century New Zealand* (Wellington: Victoria University Press, 2014).

INDEX

Numbers in italics indicate illustrations

24 *Notable Crimes*, 138

A Letter to Working Mothers, 108
A New Gospel, 105
'A Plea for Stringent Legislation in the Matter of Corrupt and Immoral Publications', 179–180
A Treatise on the Epidemic Puerperal Fever of Aberdeen, 61
Abbot, Dr, 248
abortifacients, 89, *122*, 147, 202–203, 215, 281, 328–334, 342, 349
Abortion Law Reform Association, 133
Abortion Then and Now: New Zealand Abortion Stories from 1940 to 1980, 9
abortionists, doctors as, 171–173, 348
abortionists, motivations of, 349
abstinence, 114. *see also* periodic abstinence
Adams, Dr, 286–287
Adams, Justice, *161*, 166, 228, 292
adoption, 341
Adoption of Children Act (1895), 341
advertisements
    for abortion, 203–206, *204*, *206*
    for contraception, 89, 91, 94–96, *118*, 119, *120*, *122*
air embolism, 70, 72–75, 184, 208, 279, 307, 334, 336–338, 347
Aitken's Book Arcade, 86
Aldred, Guy, 100–101, 107

Alexander, Dr, 66
All Blacks, 15–16
Allan, Dr, 322
Allan, Robert, 29
Allen, Dr, 200
Allen, James, 93, 111
American Birth Control League (ABCL), 100–102
American Medical Association, 102
American Medicine, 101
Amohau, Maria Te Motunga, 328, 340
Ancell, Lottie, 211–213
Anderson, James, 336
Andrews, Kate, 113–114
Andrews, Leonard, 113–114
Anson, Dr, 253
Anstice, Mrs, 145
antibiotics, 79–81, 127, 350
anti-Semitism, 136
Arcade (Dunedin), 28, 30, 95–96, 152, 288
Ardagh, Dr, 215
Armstrong, Albert, 332
Armstrong, Jessie, 138
Armstrong, Sarah, 332
Arnott, Margaret, 138
Arrow Detective Agency, 265
Ashcroft, Mr, 254–256
Aston, Charles, 25
Aston, Ellen, 25
Atkins, Charles, 226
Atkins, Violet, 218, 226–228
Austin, George, 274

Index • 369

Austin, Hugh, 161–162
autologous infection, 42–43
Aves, Charles, 200
Aves, Isabel Annie, 133, 198–201, 349

Backblocks Baby Doctor, 176
Bagby, Mrs, 286
Baker, Don, 165–166
Baker, Mrs R.D., 53
Baker, Vera, 260–262
Balfour, Lady Frances, *16*
Barber, Dr, 259
Barraclough, Dr Herbert, 93
Barson, Eliza, 185–186
Bartholomew, J.R., 47–49, *48*, 347
Bartlett, Mrs, 325
Batchelor, Dr Ferdinand, 176, 184
Batchelor, Gladys, 218, 223–226, *224*
Bates, Dr, 186
Bates, Margaret, 173
Baume, Rosetta, 22
Baynes, Florence, 71–72
Baynes, Harold, 71
Beadle, Beatrice, 32, 34
Beagles, Edith, 138
Beecham's Pills, 74, *204*, 208, 310
Bell, Sir Francis Henry Dillon, 23
Bennett, Alfred, 129
Bennett, Dr Francis, 55, 198, 265, 346
Bennett, Edward Henry Dudley, 115–116
Bennett, Sarah, 129
Bent, Arthur, 287
Bernard, Herbert, 65–66
Bernard, Violet, 65–66
Bernardi, Dr, 158
Besant, Annie, 106
Bethune, Kenneth, 322
Bett's Improved Female Pills, *204*
Beuth, Louisa, 138
Bickerdike, Detective, *293*
Bickerton, Prof. A.W., 109
Bicknell, Jessie, 238–239
Biessel, Christina, 219
Bilman, Ivy, 267
birth control. *see* contraception
Birth Control Clinical Research Bureau (BCCRB), 100–102

Birth Control Council of America, 102
Birth Control Federation of America, 102
Birth Control Review, 100
birth rate, declining, 93
Births and Deaths Registration Act, 49–50
Black, Dr Tim, 109
Black, Jean, 109
blackmail, 146–147
Blair, Justice, *161*, 199, 299, 303
Blair, Kenneth Patrick, 236–237
Blake, Ina Adelaide, 333–334, *335*
Blake, John, 28–29, 136
Blake, Violet, 28–29
Blanchfield, Wilfred (Fred), 81
Blaud's Pills, 214
Bledisloe, Lord, 303
blood poisoning. *see* septicaemia
Bluett, Mr, 265
Boakes, Charles William, 292, *293*
Bobbett, William, 163–164
Boer War, 11, 15, 21
Bond, May, 323–324
Boniface, Herbert, 78–79
Boniface, Myrtle, 78
Booker, Julia, 156–157
booksellers (and censorship), 86, 88, 89
Borrie, Dr, 46–47
bougies, 206
Boulton, Sarah, 14, 340
Bourne, Dr Aleck, 133
Bowerbank, Dr, 78–79
Bowern, Gifford, 138, 310–312
Bowie, Dr, 152
Bradbury, Charlotte, 136
Bradlaugh, Charles, 106
Bradley, Adeline May, 72–73
Bradley, Ethel May, 280–283, *280*, 308
Bradney, Betty, 123–125
Bradney, Elizabeth, 123–125
Bradney, Fred, 123
breastfeeding, 117
British Medical Association, 49
  New Zealand Branch, 51, 238–239
British Royal Society, 103
Brockway, Dr W., 67, 243, *245*, 330

370 • Risking Their Lives

Brosnan, Jean, 330–331
Brosnan, Mary, 330
Brown, Allen, 316–317
Brown, Dr, 83, 323, 336
Brown, Dr Bevan, 165
Brown, George, 145
Brown, Miss, 187–188, 250–252
Brown, Norma, 316–317
Brown, Norman, 89
Brown, Thomas, 151–152
Brown, William, 176–178
Brownlee, Dr, 25
bubonic plague pandemic (1900), 63
Budd, William, 336
Bull, Dr Stanley, 158, 215, *245*, 273
Bunn, Bertram, 146–147
Burdett, Charles, 284
Burdis, Jean (née Munn), 263–264
Burdis, John, 263
Burley, Queenie, 130–131
Burnham Industrial School, 126
Burns, Agnes, 56–58
Bush, Minotaur, 258–259
Butler, Mary Ann, 245
Butterfield, Pansy, 153
Buxton, Dr, 103
Byrne, Ethel, 100

Caldicott, Dr, 273
Callan, Justice, 237
Cameron, Murray, 330
Campbell, Agnes (Aggie), 277–279, 308
Campbell, Charlotte (Lottie), 244–246, 247
Campbell, Margaret, 278
Campbell, Mary, 138
Campbell, Robert, 138
Campbell, William, 173
Carew, Dr Walter Granville, 192–196, 295, 349
Carlyle, Mrs. *see* Forgeson, Norah ('Mrs Carlyle')
Carolan, Dr, 241
Carpenter, Edward, 109
Carr, Thomas, 271–272
Carroll, Mary Ellen (Mamie), 334, 338
Casey, Dr. *see* Kelly, George Arthur
Casey, Kenneth, 266–267

Casti connubii, 113
catheters, 206–207, 232, 327, 349
Catholic Church, 108, 117
causes of abortion, 52–53, 85
censorship, 86–89
cervical caps, 108, 119, 120
Chalk, Bridget, 184, 347
Chamberlain, Laura, 64
Champness, Ellen, 236
Champness, Ivy, 236
Chapman, Dr Sylvia, 42, 59
Chapman, Justice Frederick Revans, 14, 34, 145–146, *145*, 168, 211, 228, 244–246, 348
chemists, 202–237, 333
    equipment supplied by, 206–207, 310, 325
    mail order, 96, 97, 119, *120*, *122*, 202, 233, 236
    present-day roles, 346
Chick, Jessie, 321
Chick, William, 321
Chilcott, Jack, 288
childbirth fever. *see* puerperal sepsis
Chinosol, 112, 119
Christey, Charles, 138, 156–158
Christmas, Mrs, 123–125
Church, Dr, 177–179
Clark, Elizabeth, 74
Clark, Freda, 267–270, 349
Clark, Mary Jane, 47, 95–96, 136, 288–291, 308
Clark, Mr, 269
Clarkson, Joseph Frederick David, 72–73, 75
Clarkson, Senior Sergeant, 287
Clay, Dr, 191
Cleopatra, 120
Clifford, Charles, 273
Clostridium perfringens, 67–68
coal-tar dyes, 80
Coates, Gordon, 23
Coats, Evie, 298–299
Coats, George Errol, 297–303, *300*
coitus interruptus, 117
Cole, Susan, 167–168
Collins, Dr, 149
Colnett, George, 268–270
Colnett, Georgina, 138, 253, 267–270, *269*

Committee to Inquire into the Various Aspects of the Problem of Abortion in New Zealand (1936). *see* McMillan Report
community networks, 208
Comstock Act (1873), 99, 100
condoms, 117–119, *118*
confidentiality, doctor-patient, 132, 160–161, 179, 312
Connolly, Dr, 209
Connolly, Justice, 172
contempt of court, 146
contraception, 52–54, 85–127, 338, 340, 342. *see also* Rout, Ettie; Sanger, Margaret; Stopes, Dr Marie
  advertisements, 89, 91, 94–95, 96, *118*, 119, *120*, *122*
  devices, 99, 102, 108
  Doris Gordon's view of, 127, 197, 201, 345–346
  methods, 113, 116–123, 126–127, 180, 342
  socio-economic reasons for, 94
  Truby King's view of, 87, 112, 181
Contraception, Its Theory, History and Practice, 108
Contraception, Sterilisation and Abortion Act, 348
Cook, Agnes ('Mrs West'), 185–187
Cook, Dr, 84
Cook, Mary, 89–91, 92
Cook, Robert, 89
Cook Islands Christian Church (Avarua), 113
Cooke, Aileen, 22
Coombes, Fanny, 151
Cooper, Daniel Richard, 32–34, *33*, 303
Cooper, Justice, 27, 64, *64*, 140, 153, *154*, 155–156, 259, 261, 312–313
Cooper, Martha Elizabeth (née Stewart), 32–34, *33*
Corkill, Dr T.F., 42, 59
coroners, role of, 347
Coroner's Court, conduct of, 128–129
corroborative evidence, 134, 151–152
Costello, Dr, 303

Cotter, Dr, 35
Cotton, Dr, 325
court findings, differences between, 304–306
Court of Appeal, role of, 133
Craig, Dr, 321–322, 332
Craike, Mrs. *see* Aves, Isabel Annie
Crane, Robert, 209
Crawshaw, 37
Crichton, George, 77
Crimes Act, 348, 350
Crimes Act (1908 amendment), 128
Criminal Code Act (1905 amendment), 128
Cruickshank, Margaret, 175
Cruickshank, Mr, *245*
Cruickshank, Mrs, *245*
Cullen, Iris ('Mrs Hennessy'), 192
cultural changes, 18–19
Cusack, Ivy, 25–26
Customs Act (1913), 86–88
Customs Department, 87–88

Dalton, Hannah Matilda, 138, 252, 259–263
Dannefeard, Doris, 268–269
Dart, Constable, 336
D'Ath, Dr, 47, 323
Davidson, Dr, 275
Davidson, Josephine, 274–275
Davis, Mrs, 187–188
Davison, Emily, 16
Dawson, Prof. Joseph Bernard, 58, 59, 196–198
de Burren, Nurse, 304
De La Mare, Dr Sophia Ruth, 59, 197
De Lautour, Dr, 229
de Maine, Arthur, 299, 301
Dean, Minnie, 31, 134
death certificates, issuing of, 48–50
death penalty, 34, 303
Declaration of the Rights of the Child, 17
Dennis, Beatrice, 161
Denniston, Justice Sir John, 140, 147, 153, 155, 162, 184, 281, 284, 313, 347–348
Department of Health. *see* Health, Department of

Destitute Persons Act (1910), 17
Dewar, Clement Lyall, 306–308
Dewar, Peter McFarlane, 26–28, 27
diaphragms, 99, 108, 120
dilators, 206–207
divorce, attitudes toward, 343–344
Doctor Down Under, 176
doctor-patient confidentiality, 132, 160–161, 179, 312
doctors, abortion by, 171–173, 348
doctors, shortage of, 24
Dodson, Vincent, 285
Domagk, Gerhard, 80
Dominion newspaper, 53
Donkin, Sir Bryan, 88
Donnelly, Margaret, 218, 220–221
Doris Gordon Memorial Lecture, 345
Doris Gordon Memorial Trust, 345
Double, Phillip, 295–296
douching, 121, 206
Dowdle, Clive, 160
Dowdle, John James, 160–161
Dowdle, Josephine, 160
Downes, Joseph, 274
Downes, Marguerite, 274–275
Dr Bonjean's Pills, 208, 310
Dreams in Exile, 136
Drennan, Prof., 285
Drier, Dr, 260, 318
Drysdale, George, 180
Duncan, Dr, 327
Duncan, Jane, 291
Duncan, Myrtle, 291
Dunedin Hospital, abortion admission figures for, 59
Dunedin Medical School, 59
Dunedin Shakespeare Society, 134
Durston, Annie, 271–272
Dushol, 121, 125, 233
dying depositions, 164–170, 348

Eadie, Ethel, 28, 136
earthquakes, 11, 239
Ebers Papyrus, 120
Eccles, Mr, 215
eclampsia, 41
Edmonds, Richard Pahoro, 30–31
Edwards, Justice, 12, 140, 172, 213, 224, 226, 241, 242, 348
Egypt, Ettie Rout's work in, 110

Elements of Social Science, 180
Ellis, Elizabeth, 185
Ellis, Havelock, 99, 109
Elmslie, Dr, 91, 92
emancipation of women, 19, 54, 56, 197, 340, 342, 346. *see also* women's suffrage
emergency war regulations, 111
emmenagogues, 205, 310
employment for women, 11
Endelsberger, Dr, 315
endometritis, 41
Enduring Passion, 89, 108
enema equipment, 206
Enovid, 102
Epsom salts, 34, 121, 125, 309
Ergoapiol, 76–77, 203, 207, 216–217
erysipelas, 80
eugenics movement, 103, 108, 126
Evans, Dr, 90, 219
Ewart, Dr, 254

Fair, Justice, 235, 271
family allowance, 19, 23
Family Limitation, 99, 100–101, 107
Family Planning Association, 108
Family Planning Association (New Zealand), 119–120
Fawcett, Mrs Henry, 16
Feeding and Care of Baby, 182
Fell, Dr, 312
Fenwick, Dr, 141
Fergus, Eileen, 83–84
Ferguson, Doody, 212
fertility, 54, 59, 117, 343, 350
Fighting to Choose: The Abortion Rights Struggle in New Zealand, 9
Findlay, John (Attorney-General), 86
Findlay, Mary (née Wilkinson), 34–35
Finlay, Jemima, 72
Fisher, Daniel, 266–267
Fitzgerald, Dr, 229, 289–290
Flannery, Hazel, 130
Fleming, Dr, 221
Fleming, Prof. Alexander, 79–80
Fletcher, Emma Caroline, 141, 143–144
Foley, Dr, 44
folk remedies, 91, 119–120, 309–310, 341

Food and Drug Administration (FDA), 102
Forbes, George, 23
Forgeson, Norah ('Mrs Carlyle'), 208
Fraider, Elsie, 240, 246, 248–249
Fraider, Lornel, 246, 248
Francis, Bonython (Bon), 234–235
Francis, Eunice, 234–235
Fraser, F.V., 245
Fraser, Janet, 42, 59
Fraser, Peter, 42
Free Lance, 254–255
Frew, Rosie, 78–79
Fullarton, Dr James Alexander, 173

gas gangrene, 67–68
Gates, Reginald Ruggles, 104
Gaylor, Emma, 267
Geange, Arthur, 68
Geange, Doris, 68
Gentlemen of the Jury, 55–56, 197–198, 265, 346
George Street School (Dunedin), 173
Gerraty, Edith May, 253, 266–267
Gilby, Charles, 109
Gilby, Horace, 109
Gilmour, Dr Walter, 36, 125, 195, 317, 331
Glegg, Helen, 134, 136, 284–285, 308
Glenn, Maud Amy, 165–166
Glover, John, 301
Godfrey, Mrs, 76
Godley, Major-General Sir Alexander, 17
Gordon, Dorothy, 216
Gordon, Dr Alexander, 61
Gordon, Dr Bill, 41
Gordon, Dr Doris Clifton, 10, 41, 55–56, 55, 65, 94, 127, 176, 196–198, 201, 237, 265, 342, 345–346. *see also* Doris Gordon Memorial Lecture; Doris Gordon Memorial Trust
Goudie, Alexander, 218
government, leadership changes in, 19–24
Gräfenberg, Dr Ernst, 126
grand jury system, 132
Grant, Dr, 192–193

Gray, Dr T.G., 126
Gray, Lena, 165–166
Great Depression, 18–19, 23, 34, 59, 239, 297
Green, Alma, 144–146
Green, Mrs, 249
Griffin, Arthur, 186
Grigg, Raymond, 138
Grimmer, Harold, 36–40
Griswold, Estelle, 103
Griswold v. Connecticut, 103
grounds for abortion, 350
Guthrie, Dr, 25

haemorrhage, 70–72
Hall-Jones, Sir William, 21
Hammersley, Dr Percy, 245
Hammond, Richard, 251–252
Hamon, Mona, 148–149
Hanafin, James George, 97
Hanlon, Alfred Charles, 28, 29, 134, 135, 136, 147, 149, 232, 233, 285, 290–291
   Hayne defence, 218, 220–221, 224, 228
Hanlon, Doris, 251
Hanlon, Jack, 134
Hanlon, Polly, 134
Hansen, Mrs, 194
Hardie Boys, Mr, 57
Harding, Lawrence, 306–308
Harding, Mabel, 306–308
Harker, Dick, 130
Harland, Mr and Mrs, 136
Harper, Reverend Canon, 12
Harris, Albert Ernest, 136, 148–150
Harris, Dr, 79
Harrop, Geraldine, 331–332
Hart, Alice, 215
Hartley, Jane, 243, 247
Haselden, Mr, 241–242
Haslett, Mary. *see* Rush, Mary ('Mary Haslett')
Hassall, Mary, 241, 244–246, 247
Hawkins, Louisa, 203
Hay, James Urquart, 83–84
Hayne, Elisabeth, 217
Hayne, James Reynolds (Jimmy), 136, 217–231, 222, 225, 230, 233, 349
Healey, Rosina, 70–71

Health, Department of, 41–42, 65, 132, 185, 196
Health Act (1920), 50, 238
Hector, Dr, 302
Hegarty, Catherine, 141
Hegarty, Mary Ann, 141–142
Henderson, Martha, 184
Henderson, Mary, 252–254, 256–257, *256*
Henderson, Mrs. *see* Waddell, Mrs, 278
Hennessy, Dr Joseph Patrick, 138, 188–192, *189*, 345
Henry, Dr, 338
Henry, Percy Norman, 260–261
Herbert, Maud, 138, 252, 263–264
Hercock, Colin Herbert, 200–201
Herdman, Justice Sir Alexander, *159*, *161*, 163–164, 224, 264–265, 295, 348
Heron, Ada, 232–233
Hewer, 'Dr' George, 115–116, 138
Hewlett, Cecil, 169–170
Hill, Catterina, 265–266
Hill, Edward, 265–266
Hilton, Fred, 226–227
Hislop, Pearl, 291
Hitchings, Ruth, 304–306, 308
Hogan, Rose, 194–196
Hogg, Dr, 71
Holdsworth, Bernard, 82–83
Holdsworth, Jean, 82–83
Holford, Alice, *175*
Holland, Elsie, 240, 242–246
Holland, Harold George, 144–146
Hollis, Hugh Richard, 29–30
Hollis, Richard, 286–288, 308
Hollis, Ruth, 30
Holmes, Dr Oliver Wendell, 61
Hopkins, Sadie, 182–183
Hornibrook, Fred, 109, 112
Hornsby, John, 91
Horton, Dr, 81–82, 268
Hosking, Justice, 30, 143, 261, 311
hospitals, private, 46–47, 65–66, 149, 185–187, 242, 263, 265, 272–274, 276, 305. *see also* nursing homes, private
Hospitals and Charitable Institutions Act (1926), 185

Houston, James, 153
Hughes, Hinemoa, 162
Hughes, Jane, 28
Hughes, Mr and Mrs, 115
Hughes, Victoria, 28
Hulley, George, 214
Hunt, Frederick Knight, 195–196, *195*, 263–264, 269–270
Hutchinson, Amy, 59
Hutchison, Dr, 74
Hutton, Dell, 192

illegitimate children, 12, 340
immorality concerns, 11–14, 93–94
immunity (from prosecution), 139, 143
Imrie, David, 138, 248
Imrie, Jean. *see* O'Shaughnessy, Martha Jane
Imrie, Kathleen (Kitty), 240, 246, 248–249
indecent publications, 85–89, 91, 96–97, 180
Indecent Publications Act (1910), 85–87, 89, 180, 203
infant mortality, 182
infection, autologous, 42–43
infection control, 41, 42, 61–65, 126, 306–307, 349
influenza pandemic (1918), 11, 18, 238
Inglis, Elizabeth Simpson, 136, 217–218, 221, *222*, 223–224, 227–230, *230*, 232
inquests, conduct of, 128–129
instrumental abortion, equipment for, 206–207, 210, 319–321, *326*, 348
International Planned Parenthood Federation (IPPF), 102–103
intrauterine devices (IUDs), 126
Irwin, Jacob (Jack), 321
Irwin, Mabel, 321–322
Irwin, Stanley, 176
Isaacs, Hyman, *95*, 96, 136

Jack, Harry, 280–283
Jackson, Louisa, 144–145
Jackson, Thomas, 144
Jacobsen, Dr George Oscar, 187–188, 344

Jamieson, Dr, 143
Japan, Dr Stopes visit to, 103–104
Jarvis, Doris, 292
Jellett, Dr Henry, 65
Jenner, Nurse, 145
Jerrard, Eileen, 236
Jervois, Charlotte, 216–217
Johnson, Ellen, 338–339
Johnson, William, 312
Johnston, Ellen, 312–313
Johnston, Justice, 73
Johnston, Mrs. *see* Waddell, Mrs
Jones, Honorary Prof. Ron, 345
Jones, Mr and Mrs, 209
Joss, Anthony, 314–316
judges, powers of, 128
Julian, Dr, 286–287
juries, attitudes of, 138–139, 150, 157, 199–201, 231, 237, 246, 348
Juries Act (1908), 128
jury system, 57–58, 198, 344
justice, attempting to obstruct, pervert or defeat, 162, 163–164
Justices of the Peace Act, 166

Kahlenberg, Dr, 83
Kai Tiaki (nursing journal), 203, 238
Karitane Hospitals, 182
Kaye, Mrs, 194–196
Kayes, Cedric, 317–319
Kean, John, 28–29
Keen, Andrew, 73–75
Keetley, Harriet May (May), 283–284, *283*
Keith, Dr, 242
Keller, Dr Florence, 260
Keller, Dr Martin, 260
Kelly, George Arthur, 30–31
Kelvin Private Maternity Hospital (Remuera), sepsis deaths at, 65
Kemp, Dr, 305
Kendrick, Margaret (Maggie), 218–220
Kendrick, Thomas, 218
Kenrick, Dr, 234
Kent-Johnson, Agnes, 59
Key, Ellen, 109
Keynes, John Maynard, 101
Kinder, Dr, 329, 334
King, Dr, 307

King, Sir Frederick Truby, 65, 87, 112, 175, 176, 179–183, *181*, 206
King's evidence, 151–152
Kingsland Nursing Home, *240*
Kitchen, Dr, 44
Knaus, Hermann, 116
Koch, Robert, 62

labour movement, 109–110
Lactational Amenorrhea Method (LAM), 117
Lambeth Conference (Anglican Church), 105, 113
Lambie, Mary, 238–239
Landsberry, Minnie, 182–184
Lane, Sir William Arbuthnot, 87, 105
late abortions, 341
law, ineffectiveness of, 133–134
Lawrence, Thomas, 153
Lawson, Joan, 130
laxatives, 310
League of Nations, 17
legal profession, attitudes of, 347–348
Leggatt, Dr Alfred John, 171–173
Legge, Ada, 35, 67
Legge, Athol, 35
Leviathan Hotel (Dunedin), 177, 183, 226, 288, 289
Liggins, Dr, 267
Lilburne, John, 218–219
Lilly, Melva, 235
Lindop, Arthur, 214–215
Lister, Joseph, 62
Lister, Lily, 34
Llewellyn, Charlotte, 272–274
London Missionary Society Church (Avarua), 113
Longville, Edward, 233–234
Louisson, Dr, 76
Lucas, Dr, 143
Luke, Mary Alice Winifred (Winnie), 253–257
Luke, Mrs, 253–256
Lusk, Dr, 36
Lynch, Dr Philip Patrick, 44, 68, 74, *191*, 192, 299, 302, 305, 325–326, 338
Lyon, Lydia, 65–66, 138

Lysol, 121, 125, 136, 186, 331, 334, 335

Macallan, Dr, 321
Macdiarmid, Dr, 215
Macdonald, Dr, 90
MacKay, Dr, 316
Mackay, Thomas, 258–259
MacKenzie, Clare, 46–47
MacKenzie, Mora May, 46–48, 60, 96, 291, 347
Mackenzie, Thomas, 22
Mackie, Leslie Ward, 82
Mackie, Yvonne Helen, 82
Maclean, Hester, 238
Macnaghten, Justice, 133
Macpherson, Dr, 221
Magee, Mrs, 72
Magistrates Court, conduct of, 132
Maher, Frank, 187
mail order chemists, 96, 97, 119, *120*, *122*, 202, 233, 236
male sexuality, 180
Malleson, Dr Joan, 133
Malthusian League, 180
Mander, A.E., 54
Mansell, Emily, 317–319, 339
Mansell, Ena Joyce (Joyce), 317–319, 339
Mansell, Jim, 317–319, 339
Māori healers, 63
Māori medicines, 309–310
Maori Symbolism, 112
Māori women, whanau support for, 340
Maoriland Worker, 88–89, 110
Marie Stopes Clinic, 119
Marie Stopes International, 108, 109
Marks, Dr, 337
Married Love, 18, 86–87, 89, 104–105, *106*, 180, 342
Married Women's Questionnaire, 119–120, 126
Marsack, Richard, 232, 241, *245*
Martin, Justice, 348
Martin, Mr and Mrs, 147
Martin's Pills, *206*
Mason, Dr James Malcolm, 63, *63*, 93
Massey, William, 22, 112

masturbation, 91, 126, 180
maternal mortality, 23–24, 41, 42, 62, 64–65, 342–343
Maternal Mortality report, 64–65
Maternity Benefit scheme, 59
Matthewson, Annie, 176, 177
Matthewson, Kathleen, 176–179
Maude, Aylmer, 104
Maxwell, John, 239
Maxwell, Martha Jane. *see* O'Shaughnessy, Martha Jane
Mays, Selwyn, *245*
Mazengarb, O.C., 190
McBrearty, Dr, 51
McCarty, John, 323–324
McColl, Dugald, 271–272
McColl, Janet (Jennie), 271–272
McCombs, Elizabeth, 23
McCormick, Katharine, 102
McCormick, Mary, 139–140
McCulloch, Alison, 9
McDougall, Dr, 194, 260
McDowell, Edith, *245*
McFarland, Elsie, 26–27
McFie, Rosina Sarah, 136, 231–232, *231*
McGill, Catherine, 158–159
McGill, John, 158–159
McGirr, George, 50
McGlinchy, Ellen, 75–77
McGlinchy. John, 76
McGowan, James, 151–152
McGregor, Beryl ('Mrs Jones'), 303–304
McGregor, Justice, 161, *161*
McGuire, Dr, 158
McGuire, Ellen, 329
McInnes, Dr, 232
McKenzie, Alice, 322–323
McKenzie, Mabel, 192–193
McKinnon, Alexander, 46
McKinnon, James, 175
McLeod, Detective, 149
McLeod, Mary, 34
McLeod, William, 285
McLiver, Isabella, 69–70
McMaster, Dr, 77
McMenamin, Mr, 266
McMillan, Dr David Girvan, 42, *43*, 59

McMillan Report, 9, 23–24, 41–60, 85, 102, 119–120, 126, 127, 197, 237, 291, 347, 349–350
McPherson, Charles, 139–140
Meale, Gwendoline, 81–82
Medaille de la Reconnaissance francaise, 112
Medical Council of New Zealand, 187, 344
medical practitioners. *see* doctors
Medical School (University of Otago), 174, 196–197
medico-legal aspects, 53
Meed, Donalena, 322
Melville, Allan, 301
Melville, Ellen, 22
Melville, John, 183–184
Melville, Martin Joseph, 136, 232–233
menstrual cycle, 121, 123
menstruation, drugs used to induce, 205, 310
Mental Defectives Act (1911, 1928, 1935), 126
mercuric chloride, 243, 333–334, 335
Metcalf, May, 304, 306
Midwives' Registration Act (1904), 238
mifepristone (abortion pill), 349
Miller, Detective, 282
Miller, Dr, 263
Milligan, Gladys, 336–337
Mills, Ernest, 208
Mills, Mary Ann, 211–213
Milsom, Dr Edward, *245*
Mincham, Harriet Garaway, 159
Mitchell, Mrs, 45
modern abortion techniques, 349
Moir, Dr, 129
Moody, Dr, 46–49
Moore, Dr, 51, 131, 148, 263
Moore, Thomas, 211–213
Morkane, Dr, 186
Morley, Janet, 324–325
Morley, Vincent, 324
Morris, Jessie, 138, 162–164
Morris, Mrs, 259
mortality, maternal. *see* maternal mortality

Moselen, Ivy, 162–164
Moselen, Roy, 163–164
Mosley, Mr, 130
Motherhood in Bondage, 102
Mothers Clinic (London), 108
motivations of abortionists, 349
Moughan, Agnes (née Dawson, alias 'Smith'), 166–168
Moughan, John, 166–168
Mugford, Eric, *293*
Mundy, Colin, 333
Mundy, Trevor, 333
Mundy Mr and Mrs, 333
Murchison earthquake, 11
Murphy, Dr, 66–67
Murphy, John, 328
Murray, Dr, 125, 269, 318–319
Myers, Rt Hon Sir Michael, 199–201, *199*, 271, 303, 306, 347
'Mystery-Lane Tragedy,' 280–283

Nalder, A.S., 74
Napier earthquake, 11, 239
Natea, Nellie, 78
National Birth Control Council, 108
National Council of Women (NCW), 59, 127, 175, 239, 345–346
Neill, Grace, 238
Nelson Clinical Society, 94
Nevill, Mrs. *see* Wylie, Mrs ('Mrs Nevill')
New Zealand Army Nursing Service, 238
New Zealand Child Welfare Act (1925), 19
New Zealand Drug Co., 203
New Zealand Expeditionary Force (NZEF), 17, 110–111
New Zealand Family Planning Association, 103
New Zealand Federation of Labour, 110
New Zealand Law Society, 136
New Zealand Medical Corps, 110
New Zealand Medical Journal, 49, 93–94, 179
New Zealand Medical Soldiers Club, 110, 112
New Zealand Nursing Journal, 56

New Zealand Obstetrical and Gynaecological Society (O&G Society), 41–42, 49, 65, 196, 345–346
New Zealand Obstetrical Society. *see* New Zealand Obstetrical and Gynaecological Society (O&G Society)
New Zealand Returned Soldiers' Association, 113
New Zealand Shearers' Union, 110
New Zealand Society for the Protection of Women and Children. *see* Plunket Society
New Zealand Times, 110
New Zealand Trained Nurses Association, 238
New Zealand Volunteer Sisterhood, 110
New Zealand Wars, 11
Newland baby farm murders, 31–34
Newman, Edwin, 176–177
Newport, Emily, 142, 143
Neylon, Norman, 218, 223–226, 225
Nicholson Mrs ('Mrs Naylor'), 304–306
Nicoll, Rita, 285–288, 308
Noakes, Dr, 36
Norman, Mrs, 178
Northcroft, Justice, 57–58, 266
Nosworthy, James, 209–211, 215
Noxious Weeds Act, 202–203
nurses, present-day roles of, 346
Nurses and Midwives Registration Act (1925), 239
Nurses' Registration Act (1901), 238
nursing homes, private, 41, 141, 145, 167, 185–187, 189, 193, 194, 217–218, 238–239, 240, 274, 276, 323. *see also* hospitals, private
nursing regulations, 272
NZ Truth, 12–14, 77–78, 86, 141–142, 344

O&G Society. *see* New Zealand Obstetrical and Gynaecological Society (O&G Society)
O'Brien, Dorothy, 251
O'Brien, Dr, 167
occupational backgrounds of abortionists, 277
O'Connor, Joseph, 314
O'Donnell, Eliza, 146–147
O'Donoghue, Eileen, 147–148
Offences Against the Person Act (1866), 128
Offensive Publications Act (1892), 86, 203
Ogino, Kyusaku, 116
Ongley, Mr, 270–271
oral contraceptive pill, development of, 102
Orbell, Dr, 289–290
Orchard, Dr, 72
O'Shaughnessy, James Edward, 239, 243, 246, 247
O'Shaughnessy, Martha Jane, 138, 239–252, 240, 245, 250, 347, 349
Osmond, John, 278–279
Ostler, Justice, 161, 271, 296, 305
Otago Girls' High School
Otto, May, 273–274

Page, E., 89
Paget, Dr T.L., 42, 59
Pairman, Dr, 25
Paris, Ettie Rout's work in, 112
Parkes, Dr, 77, 249
Parr, Dr, 71–72
Partridge, Mr, 337–338
Pascoe, John, 139–140
Pasteur, Prof. Louis, 62
patent medicines, 91, 93, 94–95
paternity, 140–141
Paterson, Isabella, 336
Pearson, Dr Arthur B., 73, 76–77, 130, 216, 217, 275, 307, 337
Pearson, 'Dr' John, 184
'pencils', 207
penicillin, 80
Penicillium notatum, 80
pensions, 11, 22–23
periodic abstinence, 116–117
peritonitis (description), 41
Perry, William, 15–16
pessaries, 119–120, 126
Peterson, Mary, 36, 37

Pezaro, Dr, 318
Pharmacy Act (1880), 211
Pickering, Marjorie, 253, 270–271
Pile, Olive, 284–285, 308
Pincus, Dr Gregory, 102
Pipe, Amelia (Millie), 292, 294–295, 308
Pipe, Kathleen, 292, 294
Pitt, Dr, 223
Planned Parenthood Federation of America, 100, 102
Platt, Alice, 313–316
Plunket, Lady Victoria, 182
Plunket, Lord William, 182
Plunket nurses, 182, 239
Plunket Society, 175, 179, 182
poisoning, 70, 75, 136, 157, 202–203, 243, 246, 280–281, 308, 310, 330–334
Poisons Act (1908), 333–334
police, obligation to inform, 49–50
politicians, attitudes of, 349–350
Pope Pius XI, 113, 117
Pople, Albert, 66–67
Pople, Maud, 66–67
population statistics, 17
Porter, Adelaide ('Mrs Thornton'), 138
Post Office Act (1883, 1900, 1906), 89, 91, 203
Potter, Jean, 189
Potter, Marjorie, 131–132
Potter, Ralph, 131
pregnancy tests (modern), 341
Pritchard, David Kennedy, 96–97
private hospitals. *see* hospitals, private
prohibition, 18
prontosil, 80
prophylactic kit (Ettie Rout's), 110–111
proprietary medicines, 119, 202–206, *207*, 233, 236, 310
prosecution, immunity from, 139
Prout, Daisy, 160
Prout, Gladys Harriet, 160–161
Prussing, Katherine, 172
Public Health Act (1900), 63, 202
public health regulations, 272

puerperal sepsis, 41, 42, 61–62, 64–65, 80
Pyle, Adeline, 138, 292, 294–297, *296*

Quackery and Other Frauds Prevention Bill (proposed), 91, 93
Quackery Prevention Act (1908), 63, 89, 93, 203
Quedley, Leonard, 36–40
Queen Charlotte's Hospital (London), 80
Queen Victoria, 15
Quilliam, Justice, 270–271
Quin, Dr, 75
quinine, 75
Quinn, Frances, 147–149

racist concerns, 14, 53, 197
Radiant Motherhood, 108
Ralph's Reliable Remedies, 233
Rarotonga, 112–113
Raven, Edward Arthur, 151–152
Ray, Frederic James, 203
Raymond, Mary, 114–116, 340
Reader, Martha, 209–210
Reader, Mr and Mrs, 267–268
Redroofs Maternity Hospital, 291
Reed, Justice, 31, 75, 149–150, *150*, 161, 187–188, 189–190, 249, 270, 348
Reid, Dr, 124, 331
Reid, Lena, 214
Reid, Mary, 310–311
Reid, Mrs, 214
Reid, Sir Archdall, 88
Reilly, Kate, 329
Rendell's pessaries, 119
Rhind, Dr, 191
Rice-Wray, Dr Edris, 102
Richard, Jack, 142, 143
Richards, John, 136
Richards, Walter. *see* Sadler, Walter Richard
Richardson, Hilda, 138
Richter, Dr Richard, 126
risk comparisons, 342–343
Roberts, Dr, 152–153, 179, 184, 219
Roberts, Jessie, 50–51

Robertson, Dr, 74, 215, 321, 332
Rock, Dr John, 102
Rockerfeller, John D. (Jr), 100
Roe, Humphrey Verdon, 104, 107, 108
Roman Catholic Methods of Birth Control, 108
Ross, Dr, 211–213
Rough on Women: Abortion in 19th-Century New Zealand, 9
Rout, Ettie, 17–18, 22, 87–89, 93, 97–101, 105–107, 109–113, *111*, 126, 180
Royal Australian and New Zealand College of Obstetricians and Gynaecologists (RANZCOG), 345–346
Royal College of Physicians, 53
Royal Commission (1977), 9
Royal Commission into the Burnham Industrial School, 126
rugby, 15–16
Rush, Mary ('Mary Haslett'), 26–28
Russell, Bertrand, 101
Russell, Dora, 101

Sadler, Walter Richard ('Walter Richards'), 280–284, *281*, *282*
Safe Marriage: A Return to Sanity, 87–89, 97, 101, 106, 112, 180
Sale of Preventives Prohibition Bill, 19
Salmond, Justice Sir John, 287, 348
salpingitis, 41
Salvation Army, 160, 291
Sandel, Friede, 142–143
Sanft, Alfred, 138, 233, 235–236
Sanft, Ralph Walter Frank, 138, 233–236
Sanger, Margaret, 97–103, *98*, 104, 107, 197
Sanger, William, 99
Savage, Michael Joseph, 23–24, *24*
Scarff, Ellen Gwendoline Isobel (Gwen), 292, *293*, 297, 308
School of Obstetrics and Gynaecology (University of Auckland), 197
Scott, Dr, 253–254
Scott, Phillipa, 25–26, 27

Scott, Prof. J.H., 174
Scurr, Mr, 29
Seacliff Mental Asylum, 179, 182–184
Seddon, Richard, *16*, 19–21, *20*
Semmelweis, Dr Ignaz, 62
sepsis, 41–43, 61–84
septicaemia, description of, 41
Sex and Exercise, 112
Sex Hygiene and Birth Regulation Society. *see* Family Planning Association (New Zealand)
sexual immorality, public concerns about, 11–14
'sexual toilet outfit' (Ettie Rout's), 112
sexually transmitted diseases. *see* venereal diseases
Sharland & Co. Ltd, 203
Sharman, Dr, 331
Shaw, Henry, 216–217
Sheerin, Andrew, 147
Shirley, Reubena, 252–253, 265–266
Short, Dr, 294
Siedeberg McKinnon, Dr Emily Hancock, *20*, 127, 173–176, *174*, *175*, 178–179
Sigley, Billie, 236
Sim, Justice, 28–29, 159, *159*, 161, 228, 230–231, 232, 258, 285, 290, 348
Simpson, Dr, 141
Simpson, Isabella, 45
Sims, Joan, 36–40
Sindlen, Elizabeth, 244, *244*
Singer, Dorothy, 136
Singer, Dr, 83, 148
Singer, Richard Arnold, 66, 134, 136, *137*, 138
  Bowern defence, 311
  Christey defence, 157
  Clark inquest, 268, 270
  Dalton defence, 261–262
  Hennessy defence, *189*, 190
  Hewer defence, 116
  Morris defence, 162–163
  O'Shaughnessy defence, 241, 243, *245*, 248–251
  Pyle defence, 295
  Sanft defence, 235–236

Skellon, Sarah Eliza, 252, 258–259, 259
Skerrett, Hon Sir Charles, *161*, 347
Skinner, Mrs, 292
Slee, James Noah H., 100
Smart, Jessie, 95, 288–290, 308
Smith, Dr Hardwick, 190
Smith, Justice, 271, 291, 348
Smith, Mr, 208
Smith, Mrs, 90
Smith, Olive, 302
Smith, Sydney, 291
Snell, Amelia, 27
Snow, Charles, 210
Snowden, Mrs, 196
Snowden, Reuben, 172
Social Security Act (1938), 59
social stigma, 40, 79, 114, 119, 338, 340, 343–344, 346, 349
Solomon, Mr, 219–220
Sowerby, Percy, 268–270
Sowman, Archibald, 303–304
Sowman, Gladys, 303–304, 308
Spence, Mr, 235
'Spencer, Miss,' 172
spermicidal pessaries, 119–120
sponges, 120
St Helens Hospital (Auckland), 64
St Helens Hospital (Dunedin), *20*, 175
St Helens Hospital (Wellington), 239
St Helens maternity hospitals, *20*, 21, 52, 238
Stafford, Dorothy, 200–201
Stand up and Slim Down, 101
Stanley, Catherine (Katie), 152–153
Stanley, Percival, 152–153
statistics
  abortion, 52, 54, 59, 342–343, 347
  fertility, 54
  maternal mortality, 41, 42, 62, 343, 347
  population, 17
  World War I, 17
Steed's Chemist, 185–186
stem pessaries, 126
sterilisation, 85, 126–127, 197
Stevens, Mary, 328–329
Stewart, Charlie, 229

Stopes, Dr Marie, 18, 86–87, 89, 97–99, 102–109, *107*, 114, 117–121, 126, 180, 197, 342
Stopes-Roe, Harry, 108
Stouppe, Adrienne, 190–192
Stout, Lady, 112
Stout, Rt Hon Sir Robert, 155, 172, 213, 246, 257, 311–312, 347, 348
Stowe, Dr, 167
Strickland, Howard, 194–196
Stringer, Dr, 275
Stringer, Justice, 27–28, 144, 157–158, *159*, *161*, 251–252, 262–263, 267, 311, 347–348
sulfonamides (sulfa drugs), 80–81
Supreme Court, conduct of, 132–133
Sutcliffe, William Henry, 153
Sutherland, Dr Halliday, 108
Syme, Dr, 45
Symes, Dr William Henry, 126
Symons, George, 297, 301
Symons, Mary, 297
Symons, Phyllis Avis, 297–303, *298*, 308
syncope, 76–77, 279, 334

Taylor, Gertrude Grace, 56–58
Taylor, Mary Ellen, 241–242
Teape, Mr, 194
techniques in modern abortions, 349
Tel El Kebir Soldiers' Club, 110
Telfer, Alma, 75
Telfer, Archibald, 75
Temple, Dr Adolph, 185–187, 345
'tents' (sea-tangle and sponge), 207, 210, 214
The Expectant Mother and Baby's First Months, 182
The Fruits of Philosophy or the Private Companion of Young Married People, 106
The Human Body, Sex and the Young, 108
The Lancet, 80
The Management of Pregnant and Lying-in Women, 61
The Press (Christchurch), 53–54
The Truth About Venereal Disease, 105
The Woman Rebel, 99

The Years Go Round, 136
therapeutic termination, 82–83, 171–172, 344
Thomas, Detective, 333
Thomas, Dr, 333
Thompkins, Gwendoline, 75, 77–78
Thompson, Ellen, 313
Thompson, Martha, 323
Thomson, Dr, 35, 327
Thomson, James, 165
Thomson, Lucy, 165
Thomson, Mr (S.M.), 167
Thomson, Myrtle Veronica, 165–166
Thornton, Mrs. *see* Porter, Adelaide ('Mrs Thornton')
Thorpe, Jane, 288–289
Thorpe, Myrtle. *see* Thomson, Myrtle Veronica
Timms, Ada, 69
Tizard, Dr, 183
To Alarm New Zealand (pamphlet), 54
Tohunga Suppression Act (1907), 63
Tomorrow (feminist magazine), 54
Toohey, Martha, 50–51
Towler, Edith, 95, 136
Towler, Elizabeth, 28, 95, *95*, 152–153, *207*, 288
Towler, Walter, 152–153
Towle's Pills, *204*
toxaemia, 41, 42, 51
Treadwell, Mr, 302
Trillo, Charles, 130
Trott, E., *175*
Tubert, John, 304–306
Turner, Maud, 152–153
typhoid fever, 69–70

ulcerative endocarditis, 84
University of Manchester, 103
University of Otago, 174, 346

vaginal barriers, 120
vaginal discharge, 121
Valentine, Sister, 322
Valintine, Dr T., 89
venereal disease, 17–18, 22, 68–69, 87, 105, 110–112, 117–118, 121, 180, 206, 333

Viggers, Thomas (Tommy), 286–288
Villers Brettoneux, Ettie Rout's work in, 112
Vincent, Kate, 172
Volckman, Dr, 114
von Zglinicki, Dagmar, 116

Wackrow, Eva, 168–170
Wackrow, Wilfred, 168–169
Waddell, Mrs ('Mrs Johnston', 'Mrs Henderson'), 89–91
Wall, Myra, 325–326
Walshe, Dr, 316
Walton, Dr, 317
Ward, Cecil, 327
Ward, Myrtle, 327
Ward, Sir Joseph, 21–22
Warner, Emmil, 138
Warner, James, 243
Warnock, Dr, 296
Washbourn, Dr H.E.A., 94, 197
Watson, Margery. *see* Watts, Eileen
Watt, Dr, 42, 89
Watts, Eileen ('Margery Watson'), 73–75
wealth and abortion, 343
Wear, Ralph, 190
Webb, Mrs, 194
Weir, Edith, 337–338
Weir, Robert, 337
Wells, H.G., 99, 100, 113
Welsh, William, 34
Weston, Mr, 280
What Every Girl Should Know, 99
What Every Mother Should Know, 99
White, Dr Charles, 61
White, George, 14
Whiteman, Thomas, 136
Whittington, Minnie, 244, 246
Wilford, Mr, 145–146, 224, 257, 312
Wilkinson, William Michael, 30–31
Williams, Albert Herbert (Bert), *245*, 246
Williams, Dr, 152
Williams, Florence, 310–312
Williams, Gladys, 233–234
Williams, Justice Sir Joshua, 173, 258, 313, 348
Williams, Rose, 285

Williamson, Helen, 130
Williamson, Mr, 209
Wilson, Allan, 43–45
Wilson, Dr, 167–168
Wilson, Grace, 226–227
Wilson, John, *283*
Wilson, Mrs, 115
Wilson, Myrtle, 43–45
Wilson, Susan, 252, 257–258
Wise Parenthood, 105
Witcop, Rose, 100–101, 107
Withers, Dr, 114
Women's Christian Temperance Union, 110–111
Women's Parliamentary Rights Extension Bill, 22
women's suffrage, 11, *16*. *see also* emancipation of women
Women's Sunday, 16
Woodley, Alfred, 138
World Population Conference (Geneva), 101
World War I, 11, 17–18, 29, 30, 238
World War II, 11, 35, 80
Wylie, Mrs ('Mrs Nevill'), 187–188

Young, Detective-Sergeant, *293*
Yvonne, Madame, 112 Dame

About the Author

Margaret Sparrow has had a long career in general and reproductive health. She is Honorary Vice President of New Zealand Family Planning, past President of the Abortion Law Reform Association of New Zealand and a Director of Istar Ltd, a not-for-profit company that imports the abortion pill mifepristone. She was awarded an MBE in 1987, the New Zealand Suffrage Centennial Medal in 1993, and the DCNZM for services to medicine and the community in 2002, which in 2009 became a DNZM.